ESSAYS ON JEWS AND CHRISTIANS IN LATE
ANTIQUITY IN HONOUR OF ODED IRSHAI

CULTURAL ENCOUNTERS IN LATE ANTIQUITY
AND THE MIDDLE AGES

VOLUME 40

General Editor
Yitzhak Hen, *The Hebrew University of Jerusalem*

Editorial Board
Barbara Bombi, *University of Kent*
Paul M. Cobb, *University of Pennsylvania*
Adam S. Cohen, *University of Toronto*
Kate Cooper, *Royal Holloway, University of London*
Maria Mavroudi, *University of California*
Judith Olszowy-Schlanger, *University of Oxford and*
École Pratique des Hautes Études, Paris
Carine van Rhijn, *Universiteit Utrecht*
Peter Sarris, *University of Cambridge*
Daniel Lord Smail, *Harvard University*

Previously published volumes in this series
are listed at the back of the book.

Essays on Jews and Christians in Late Antiquity in Honour of Oded Irshai

Edited by

BROURIA BITTON-ASHKELONY *and*
MARTIN GOODMAN

BREPOLS

British Library Cataloguing in Publication Data
A catalogue record for this book is available from the British Library

© 2023, Brepols Publishers n.v., Turnhout, Belgium.

All rights reserved. No part of this publication may be reproduced,
stored in a retrieval system, or transmitted, in any form or by
any means, electronic, mechanical, photocopying, recording,
or otherwise without the prior permission of the publisher.

ISBN: 978-2-503-60245-5
e-ISBN: 978-2-503-60246-2
DOI 10.1484/M.CELAMA-EB.5.131626
ISSN: 1378-8779
e-ISSN: 2294-8511

Printed in the EU on acid-free paper.

D/2023/0095/20

Table of Contents

List of Illustrations	7
Ode to Oded Paula FREDRIKSEN, with Osnat RANCE	9
Introduction Martin GOODMAN	15

Part I
Religion and the Visual

The Emperor's New Clothes: The 'Jewish Helios' Enigma in its Christian Imperial Context Yonatan MOSS	21
Between Heaven and Earth: The Hand of God in Ancient Jewish Visuality Noa YUVAL-HACHAM	55
Shaping Religious Space: Pagans, Jews, and Christians in Ancient Sepphoris Zeev WEISS	75

Part II
Christian Perspectives

Cyril's New Jerusalem and His Omission of Local Church History Yonatan LIVNEH	95
Eudocia, Pulcheria, and Juvenal: Competition in the Field of Religion and the Built Environment of Jerusalem in the Fifth Century CE Jacob ASHKENAZI	119

6 TABLE OF CONTENTS

'Although Their Names Escaped Me': Local Patriotism
and Saints Commemoration in Late Antique Syria
Osnat E. Rance   141

Rethinking the Eschatological Ingathering
of Israel in Early Christianity
Aryeh Kofsky and Serge Ruzer   159

Divina Vestigia: Tracking the Early History of Jesus's
Footprints at the Mount of Olives
Ora Limor   183

Reinach and Stephanus, Philo and Josephus: A Note on
the *Testimonium Flavianum*
Daniel R. Schwartz   205

Part III
Jewish Perspectives

When in Rome
Joshua Levinson   221

Where Were the Two Huts of Remus and Romulus
in Rome?
Eyal Ben-Eliyahu   241

Part IV
Influence and Competition

The Hebrew *Book of Elijah* and Commodian's *Carmen de
duobus populis*
Hillel I. Newman   253

And the Rest is History: Sabbath Versus Sunday
Israel Jacob Yuval   271

List of Contributors   295

Index   299

List of Illustrations

Fig. 2.1.   The Exodus, wall painting, Dura Europos synagogue, Syria, 244/5 CE.   58

Fig. 2.2.   Divine hand holding a bundle of lightning bolts, carved altar, the Temple of the Standards in Palmyra, Syria, 214 CE   59

Fig. 2.3.   Divine hand holding sheaves of grain, carved stone slab from Palmyra, Syria, 228 CE   60

Fig. 2.4.   The Exodus, carved wooden door, the church of Santa Sabina, Rome, fifth century   69

Fig. 3.1.   Suggested reconstruction of Roman Sepphoris, with the temple located in the *insula* south-east of the main intersection in lower Sepphoris   78

Fig. 3.2.   General view of the synagogue uncovered at the north-eastern end of lower Sepphoris, looking north-west   81

Fig. 3.3.   Mosaic medallion with a Greek inscription incorporated into the eastern pavement of the *cardo*   84

Fig. 3.4.   Reconstruction of late antique Sepphoris   85

Fig. 5.1.   Eudocia's building initiatives in Jerusalem   121

PAULA FREDRIKSEN, WITH OSNAT RANCE

Ode to Oded

Summarizing Oded Irshai's contributions to the social and religious history of Roman antiquity is not easy. His control over a broad range of various multiform and polyglot ancient corpora — archaeological data; rabbinic legal, liturgical and aggadic texts; Christian para-canonical and patristic works in Latin, Greek, and Syriac; late Roman and Byzantine historiographers, from Eusebius to Malalas and beyond; 'interfaith' esoterica dating the always-approaching End of Days — defies easy generalization. He approaches all his sources with empathetic imagination and interpretive finesse, sharpened by the hermeneutics of suspicion. And the various contesting communities represented by these sources transmute, through the alchemy of Oded's scholarship, from contentious traditions into solid and vibrant social worlds, thickly peopled by ancient agents whose aspirations, interactions, strategies, and successes — and failures — Oded so skillfully reconstructs.

What accounts for such intellectual versatility? In part, the confluence of happy accidents that shape one's life. Blessed with a prodigious memory, Oded further trained his powers of recall with seven years of yeshiva. In effect, his mind houses a database of rabbinic sources, instantaneously accessible. Later, at the Hebrew University, his academic work in Talmud and in Jewish History was further honed and broadened by studying with senior scholars whose expertise bridged Christian studies and other Greek sources as well. And along the way, Oded handled the hard currency of antiquity: the material remains of archaeological data.

But a major inflection point in this rich curriculum vitae was Oded's postgraduate year in Cambridge, England. Giants then bestrode the earth: Henry Chadwick and Christopher Stead together conducted an advanced patristics seminar at the Old Divinity School under the steady gaze of a huge oil portrait of the nineteenth century's Bishop Lightfoot. Oded additionally did an independent study of church fathers with the luminous Caroline Bammel.

> **Paula Fredriksen**, a fellow of the American Academy of Arts and Sciences, is Aurelio Professor of Scripture emerita at Boston University.
>
> **Osnat Emily Rance** has a PhD from the Hebrew University of Jerusalem in 2022. She is a post doctorate fellow at the Centre for Advanced Studies "Beyond Canon" at Universität Regensburg. Her dissertation, on representations of religious violence between Christians and Jews in late antiquity was supervised by Professor Oded Irshai.

Essays on Jews and Christians in Late Antiquity in Honour of Oded Irshai, ed. by Brouria Bitton-Ashkelony and Martin Goodman, CELAMA 40 (Turnhout: Brepols, 2023), pp. 9–14
BREPOLS ❧ PUBLISHERS   10.1484/M.CELAMA-EB.5.132523

And — a special dispensation of fortune — he entered into the warm and energizing personal acquaintance of one of the fathers of the modern study of Mediterranean antiquity, Arnaldo Momigliano. Who knows how many coffees and conversations with this great man fostered further thoughts as formal textual training proceeded? Whether by serendipity or by design, then, Oded embarked on his scholarly career empowered by remarkable binocular vision, his scope encompassing Jewish and Christian corpora both.

Oded brings these rich materials into fruitful interaction over a number of favoured topics, of which we identify, in particular, three: 1) violence, verbal and otherwise; 2) eschatology; and 3) local real estate and power politics.

Sacred Violence

Pagan anti-Christian violence; Christian anti-Jewish violence; Jewish anti-gentile violence: Oded has investigated it all. (After three years of graduate seminars, seriatim, on 'The Fall of Jerusalem in Jewish and Christian Imagination', 'The Fall of Rome in Jewish and Christian Imagination', and 'Sacred Violence: Pagan, Jewish and Christian', Oded remarked cheerfully to me, 'Well, we have killed off just about everybody. Let's do something else next year'.)

Such work invariably requires gauging the gap between rhetoric and reality. When does vicious language translate into or reflect actual violence? And if no hard violence seems ever to have ensued, then what was the point of the representation? What social and political goals do reports or accusations of violence seek to meet? In his 1996 essay, 'Jewish Violence in the Fourth Century CE – Fantasy and Reality'[1] Oded looked closely at the 'profusion of discursive images' in the period after Constantine retailed by various Christian writers putatively describing two periods of violent actions by Jews. The first, the 'Gallus revolt' of 351/52 in Palestine, shrinks in his examination to small local incidents of unrest inflated by patristic authors overstimulated by apocalyptic expectations and celestial phenomena (p. 408). But what about Ambrose's lurid descriptions of Jews, supposedly emboldened by the pagan sympathies of the emperor Julian (361–63), burning numerous Christian basilicas? Two in Damascus, several in Gaza, Ascalon, Beirut, in 'nearly all the towns in that region', and in Alexandria, Ambrose claims (*Ep.* 74). The charge is not borne out by Christian historiographers (p. 413), the evidence of unrest entangled in other incidents involving pagans as well (p. 414). Whence, then, these descriptions of 'Jewish violence'? They are pieces on the rhetorical chessboard of later Theodosian ecclesiastical politics and community identity-formation, Oded concludes (pp. 415–16).

---

1 Irshai, *Jewish Identities in Antiquity: Studies in Memory of Menahem Stern*, ed. by Lee I. Levine and Daniel R. Schwartz (Tübingen: Mohr Siebeck, 1996), pp. 391–416.

ODE TO ODED

Does a similar gap yawn between fact and its representation when we turn to fifth-century Alexandria?[2] The question lands us in the early years of Cyril of Alexandria's episcopacy (414/15), and in the report later tendered by Socrates Scholasticus in his *Historia Ecclesiastica* (c. 439). The rhetorical Jews of Socrates' account find themselves in the theatre rather than in shul one Sabbath morning. In the presence of the (Christian) Roman governor Orestes, who is attempting to curb theatre performances — they could often lead to urban unquiet — these Jews accuse a local Christian firebrand, Hierax, of exciting sedition. Things rapidly go from bad to worse. Jews supposedly ambush Alexandrian Christians; Cyril appropriates synagogues and drives Jews from the city; both the governor and the bishop — united in deep mutual dislike — file complaints with the emperor (the beleaguered Theodosius II); marauding monks, dog-whistled by Cyril, lynch the pagan philosopher Hypatia. At the end of the day, Cyril emerges the victor over Orestes — and cosmopolitan Alexandria — in the contest of urban power politics.

What happened? Oded sorts this story out by gazing west, toward a seemingly unrelated incident in North Africa, when Christians in Calama occasioned a violent confrontation with local pagans (408 CE). No Jews were involved. The North African bishops secured an imperial ruling in their favour (*Sirmondian Constitution* 12): pagan anti-Christian activities were not to be tolerated. Cyril, it would seem, appropriating to himself the governor's prerogatives, acted against proximate others both Jewish and pagan, thereby winning the local power sweepstakes.

But this is not the end of the story. Socrates' description of Cyril encrypts a covert attack on the Alexandrian bishop. Cyril comes out the poorer leader when compared with Atticus of Constantinople. Atticus was mild and prudent; Cyril was conniving and thuggish. Atticus won converts; Cyril drove potential converts away. This history, ostensibly about Jewish/Christian urban violence, in short, masks an intra-Christian critique of inter-urban episcopal political styles. When dealing with ecclesiastical histories, there is more there than meets the eye — if one's vision can penetrate surfaces while scanning the periphery.

So many more instances of people behaving badly! Pagan anxieties about Christians alienating heaven, leading to repressive measures and, eventually, to Christian anti-Christian persecutions; evolving Christian rhetorical and theological traditions *adversus Iudaeos* leading eventually to Jewish legal and social disabilities; internal Jewish political positioning between patriarchs, sages, and priests in Tiberias eventuating in anti-Christian violence in far-away Yemen.[3] By patiently excavating all of these layers of traditions, Oded gives

---

2 Irshai, 'Christian Historiographers' Reflections on Jewish-Christian Violence in Fifth-Century Alexandria', in *Jews, Christians and the Roman Empire. The Poetics of Power in Late Antiquity*, ed. by Natalie B. Dohrmann and Annette Yoshiko Reed (Philadelphia: University of Pennsylvania Press, 2013), pp. 137–53 and 306–15 (notes).

3 On pagan anti-Christian persecution, see Irshai, 'Christian anti-Judaism: Polemics and Policies,

us a vivid appreciation of the complexities of power (and of powerlessness), both intra- and inter-communal.

Eschatology

How many times can the world End? The answer you get depends on how you count, where you look, and whom you ask. On this issue, Oded wields an incredible amount of expertise. He decodes apocalyptic chronographical calculations (the 'scientific' approach to estimating the Endtime). He detects subtle hints of messianic enthusiasms stimulated by local events whether terrestrial (earthquake, hostile legislation, war) or celestial (like brilliant crosses illumining the daytime sky over Jerusalem). And he traces the ripple-effects of catastrophes (like the falls of Jerusalem, and of Rome) on the apocalyptic *imaginaire*.[4]

Cyril of Jerusalem's shining cross in the sky was a multi-purpose miracle, serving for the bishop several important purposes. It gave him the opportunity to ingratiate himself with Constantius II over against the current imperial pretender, Magnentius. But it also buffed Jerusalem's status as prime eschatological real estate, ground zero for the return of Christ. It also stimulated his rhetorical burnishing of himself as an agent of local pagan and, later, of Jewish conversion. And it provided Cyril with a certain flexibility when discerning the identity of the Antichrist whether as a pagan (stimulated by the much-maligned Julian) or as a Jew.[5] A lot of mileage out of one miracle — almost as much as that afforded Cyril's fifth-century successor, John, by the later discovery of St Stephen's bones.[6] Stephen's relics enhanced John's and Jerusalem's prestige (vis-à-vis other bishops) as they travelled the Mediterranean spreading curative miracles and, on Minorca, social chaos between Jews and Christians. Meanwhile, as attested by *piyyutim*, assorted commentaries, earthquakes, and the fall(s) of Rome, Jews also cultivated similar hopes for the approach of messianic

---

First through Seventh Centuries', with Paula Fredriksen, *CHJ*, IV (2006), 977–1035; Irshai, 'The Jews of Tiberias and their Leadership in the Byzantine Period', *Idan*, 9 (1988), 57–64 (in Hebrew).

4 E.g., Irshai, 'Dating the Eschaton: Jewish and Christian Apocalyptic Calculations in Late Antiquity', in *Apocalyptic Time*, ed. by A. I. Baumgarten (Leiden: Brill, 2000), pp. 113–53; Irshai, 'The Jerusalem Bishopric and the Jews in the Fourth Century: History and Eschatology', in *Jerusalem: Its Sanctity and Centrality to Judaism, Christianity and Islam*, ed. by Lee I. Levine (New York: Continuum, 1999), pp. 204–20.

5 Irshai, 'Cyril of Jerusalem: The Apparition of the Cross and the Jews', in *Contra Iudaeos*, ed. by Ora Limor and Guy G. Stroumsa (Tübingen: Mohr Siebeck, 1996), pp. 85–104; Irshai, 'The Jerusalem Bishopric' (see note 4 above).

6 Irshai, 'St Stephen's Bones Between East and West: A Chapter in the History of Judeo-Christian Confrontation in the early Fifth Century CE', in *Ut Videant et Contingent: Essays on Pilgrimage and Sacred Space in Honor of Ora Limor*, ed. by Y. Hen and I. Shagrir (Ra'anana: Open University Press, 2011), pp. 49–69 (Hebrew).

ODE TO ODED   13

redemption — never deterred, just like their Christian counterparts, as the religiously roiled centuries came and went.[7]

Local Real Estate and Power Politics

Caesarea had been the Roman administrative capital of Judea since shortly after the death of Herod. Under the great Origen, it flourished as a centre of high Christian learning, attesting to fascinating interplay between Christians and Jews on how to read shared sacred texts. (Rabbi Abbahu encouraged his co-religionists to brush up on their Tanach for precisely this reason.[8]) Caesarea's early fourth-century bishop, Eusebius, tirelessly ingratiated himself with the newly Christian empire while elevating his see's status as a charismatic and blood-soaked site of local (or more-or-less 'local') martyrdoms. Eusebius's *Martyrs of Palestine* was more than a tale of perfected piety. It also had precise political goals: to swing the balance of prestige and thus, episcopal power away from the former Aelia — now (once again) Jerusalem — back to Caesarea, where (in his view) it belonged.[9]

Power see-sawed locally not only between competitive Christian bishops, but also between Christians and Jews — especially, via Christian pilgrimage and imperial architectural projects, over the invention of the Christian 'holy land'. Big works of public architecture had always been part of the imperial repertoire of power, and Constantine — aided by bookish pilgrims revisioning the local landscape through the lens of New Testament texts and retrospectively Christian understandings of the Old — lavished new projects on 'ancient' sites with numinous reputations (many identified as such for exactly this purpose: to stimulate Christian traffic).[10] Pilgrims were the foot soldiers in this war of cultural conquest.

The internal politics of Galilean Jewish communities were no less highly charged, as sages, rabbis, 'davidide' patriarchs, priests, *batei midrash* and synagogues all contested for authority if not for 'hard' power (though the Patriarchate, while it existed, certainly enjoyed that, too). The office seems to have been created for the convenience of imperial dealings with the Roman

---

7   As unpacked by Oded in his new introduction to 1954's *Midrashei Geula: Chapters of Jewish Apocalyptic Literatures*, ed. by Y. Even-Shmuel (2017; orig. pub. 1954), i–li (in Hebrew).

8   For a glimpse of this fascinating figure's acquaintance with intra-Christian controversies, see Irshai, 'Rabbi Abbahu said: "If a man tells you he is God, he is a liar"', *Zion*, 47 (1982), 173–77 (in Hebrew).

9   Irshai, 'Holy Cartography Engraved with Blood: A Historical Appraisal of Eusebius of Caesarea's *Martyrs of Palestine*', with Osnat Rance, forthcoming from Mohr-Siebeck, 2022.

10   Irshai, 'The Christian Appropriation of Jerusalem in the Fourth Century: The Case of the Bordeaux Pilgrim', *Jewish Quarterly Review*, 99 (2009), 465–86, commenting elegiacally, that the Christian city 'configured […] a new and eternal spiritual edifice over the remains and ruins of the local Jewish past', p. 486.

Jewish population, while its holders — to the irritation of ecclesiastics — claimed descent from David's line. Power abhors a vacuum. Once Gamaliel VI over-reached, and the office became defunct, local rabbis and priests (sometime rabbis were priests) vied for community loyalties, while the Babylonian exilarch weighed in on the fray. In a wide-ranging and comprehensive treatment of this kinetic intra-Jewish positioning (with sideways glances at Christian interests both ecclesiastical and imperial), Oded unravels all these snarled sources — archaeological as well as textual — to see who emerged as the human victors (the priests, who had a lot to say about a liturgy increasingly focused on the Good Old Days of the Temple) and also as the institutional ones (synagogues more than *batei midrash*).[11] And while so doing, Oded keeps his eye on traditions about the ever-approaching End (pp. 61–64).

***

This appreciation of Oded's *oeuvres* scarcely touches the surface of his multiple contributions to our field. What we really want to address, however, is our tremendous appreciation of Oded himself, his character and his warm collegiality. Oded's intellectual generosity — sharing bibliography, homing in with sharp observations, always asking the Big Questions — is as legendary as his footnotes. These meaty footnotes, indeed, again give the measure of his intellectual generosity, his prodigious memory, and his astounding breadth of knowledge: they enable other scholars to benefit from the fruit of his own research. Collaborative work with colleagues and selfless dedication to administering important academic programmes (Center for the Study of Christianity; Jewish Studies; chairing his department; heading the Yad Ben Tzvi) stand in further evidence. There is a reason why his dance card at conferences both at home and especially abroad is always full: Oded by his very presence inspires and enables people to work together and to think harder together. Where he finds solitude, he creates synergy.

Dear, dear Oded: thank you for your work. And thank you for being you.

---

11 Irshai 'Confronting a Christian Empire: Jewish Life and Culture in the World of Early Byzantium', in *Jews in Byzantium: Dialectics of Minority and Majority Cultures*, ed. by Robert Bonfil, Oded Irshai, Guy G. Stroumsa, and Rina Talgam (Leiden: Brill, 2012), pp. 17–64.

MARTIN GOODMAN ————————————

Introduction

The writings of Cyril of Jerusalem may have seemed like a surprising choice of topic for a doctoral dissertation by a scholar embarked on a career devoted to understanding the history of the Jews in the Roman world of Late Antiquity, but the groundbreaking study of this episcopal politician by Oded Irshai exemplified the broad approach to writing Jewish history within a wider context in which Oded has led the way. The studies here presented in his honour by colleagues, friends, and students who have all learned from his example and scholarship reflect that approach: examination of the patristic, archaeological, legal and rabbinic sources combine to illuminate vividly the complex religious landscape of late antique Palestine and its environs.

The world of Late Antiquity can only be understood properly through judicious investigation of a wide range of such sources. The first task for scholarship is always accurate exposition of the evidence itself — a process which can itself be fraught with difficulty as a result of traditions of misinterpretation entrenched over centuries, sometimes, as Daniel Schwartz's sobering contribution to this volume lays bare, based in the first place on errors in translation on which may be based a multitude of ingenious but ultimately wholly misleading theories. But even when the sources have all been correctly interpreted, reconstruction of ancient societies simply by presentation of these materials produces at best incomplete comprehension, since each source provides only a partial perspective. The Roman legal texts which document measures to control the activities of Jews within the empire provide no insights into the nature of Jewish religious communities beyond the existence of synagogues and communal officials, leaving opaque the relationship, if any, between the Jewish patriarchs of the late fourth and early fifth century to whom they refer and the *nesi'im* found in rabbinic texts. Similarly, study of the archaeology of religious buildings in the Roman Near East provides a good idea of the spread of architectural styles and iconography across religious divides but cannot in itself aid understanding of the significance of similarities and differences — a not inconsiderable drawback in light of the evidence from more recent religious history of the importance to contemporaries of differences which may seem of minuscule significance to later generations and unsympathetic contemporaries from other traditions. Even the solidity of epigraphic evidence on stone, plaster, mosaic, and coins is misleadingly reassuring, since the inscribed texts can

Martin Goodman is Professor emeritus of Jewish Studies and Fellow of Wolfson College at the University of Oxford.

only reveal the intended self-representation of the person who produced or commissioned the inscription for a specific context or audience. And the patristic sources which delve deep into the complexities of church politics and theological controversy often leave unspoken the political realities which both constrained and encouraged Christian leaders under volatile imperial rulers and make no attempt to come to terms with the complexities of other religious traditions, whether pagan or Jewish.

Above all, although anyone who writes about the history of the Jews in this period must be acutely aware that only close familiarity with halakhic and midrashic sources can enable insight into the rabbinic society of Palestine in this period, these rabbinic sources provide only hints about the lives of non-rabbinic Jews and only faint reflections of the preoccupations of contemporary Christians and pagans or the impact of imperial Roman rule, including the burgeoning influence of Christianity on the Roman state and the impact of this transformation of the state on Jews under Roman rule. If we only had rabbinic sources, it is doubtful that we would be able to deduce the Christianization of the Roman empire from the fourth century, let alone the development of Palestine as a Christian holy land. Rabbinic sources can be slotted only with qualification into the search for continuities and general themes which have characterized study of Late Antiquity over the past half century.

But much can still be achieved provided these limitations are borne in mind as the varied studies in this volume demonstrate. The rabbis may tell us little that is new or reliable about non-Jewish society, but the insights into rabbinic mentality provided by rabbinic texts are themselves of historical import, as is shown in the two contributions which examine traditions about the city of Rome. Eyal Ben-Eliyahu discusses the rabbinic traditions which seem to show awareness of Roman identification of two ancient buildings in the city with the huts of Romulus and Remus, and Joshua Levinson illuminates the Palestinian rabbinic perspective on the Jewish community of Rome in Late Antiquity through a detailed and sophisticated analysis of a narrative in the Talmud Yerushalmi of a contest between rabbis who, having travelled from Palestine to Rome, overcame there a local witch who threatened Jewish continuity in the city.

It is hard to know how much awareness of the real city of Rome is revealed in such stories, and some of the references to place in the Christian texts discussed in the volume, such as the highly varied motifs concerning the eschatological ingathering of Israel in early Christianity analysed by Aryeh Kofsky and Serge Ruzer, are similarly speculative. But others are more concrete: Ora Limor traces the fascinating early traditions about the traces of Jesus's footprints allegedly observed on the Mount of Olives and Osnat Rance examines the relations of saint commemoration in Palestine to local patriotism. Yonatan Livneh identifies political reasons for the omission of local church history by Cyril of Jerusalem in his promotion of the city where he was bishop. Jacob Ashkenazi brings together the evidence for the religious as well as political capital gained by Eudocia, Pulcheria, and Juvenal in their building programmes in Jerusalem and Constantinople.

These ecclesiastical politicians had the Christian state on their side and could afford to pay little attention to minority groups such as the Jews, but, as Zeev Weiss shows graphically, Christians shared urban space in cities like Sepphoris not only with distinctively Jewish buildings but with the remnants of the pagan past which remained architecturally visible. Yonatan Moss's study of the significance of the Helios image in Jewish religious contexts confronts directly the significance of such shared imagery in a world where pagan images had been adapted for Christian use, and Noa Yuval-Hacham delves into the depiction of the hand of God in Jewish as in Christian art.

Unless the evidence is explicit, identifying borrowing or competition between different traditions in any of this evidence is always difficult, but Hillel Newman makes a strong case that the similarities in the eschatological speculation in Commodian and the much later Hebrew *Book of Elijah* reflect a common tradition which should warn readers against too simplistic readings of apocalypses as reflections of contemporary crises, and Israel Yuval argues that the Christian replacement of the Jewish Sabbath with Sunday is reflected not just in Christian polemic but also in corresponding apologetic passages within Jewish liturgy.

Between them, these variegated studies paint an integrated picture of a complex religious landscape. The volume demonstrates the vitality and diversity of contemporary scholarship on the history of this period as a tribute to the remarkable scholar to whom it is dedicated.

PART I

Religion and the Visual

YONATAN MOSS

The Emperor's New Clothes

*The 'Jewish Helios' Enigma in its
Christian Imperial Context*

Introduction

The complex of late ancient Palestinian synagogue mosaic pavements portraying Helios and the zodiac has drawn much attention in scholarship. Archaeologists, art historians, philologists, historians, and religious studies scholars have struggled to understand why the late ancient Jewish congregations of fourth-century Hammat Tiberias, fifth-century Sepphoris, and sixth-century Naʿaran, Bet Alpha, and Ḥuseifa, chose to place depictions of the Greco-Roman sun god and the zodiac cycle in the centre of their places of worship.[1] A recent study has called this motif and the historical enigma surrounding it 'arguably *the* most intriguing aspect of Jewish art in late antiquity'.[2]

---

1 I mention here only the five unequivocal and somewhat intact cases. Some scholars include in this category also the synagogue mosaics of Susiya, ʿEn Gedi, Yafia, Khirbet Wadi el-Hammam, and Huqoq, even if they do not present clear, complete, unequivocal representations of Helios and the zodiac. For the complications posed by the borderline cases, see Ness, 'The Stars in their Courses Fought against Sisera', pp. 157–59. For the more recent discoveries of the Khirbet Wadi el-Hammam mosaic, see Leibner, 'Khirbet Wadi Hammam' (in Hebrew), and, for the Huqoq mosaic, see Magness and others, 'The Huqoq Excavation Project', pp. 106–11. See, further, Bonnie, 'The Helios-and-Zodiac Motif in Late Antique Synagogues', p. 300. Naturally, different scholars, including both those mentioned in the footnotes below, and the many others who could not be mentioned within the limited confines of this essay, cut the cake differently, some counting fewer, some more, cases within the category. I thank Prof. Rina Talgam, Prof. Brouria Bitton-Ashkelony, Dr Shraga Bick, Rebecca Eisenstadt, and Roey Porat for reading this essay, and offering several very valuable comments. I also thank Rebecca Eisenstadt for her research assistance in the early stages of preparation, and Roey Porat for his work on the final stages. Work on this essay was supported in part by the Azrieli Foundation and by ISF Grant No. 771/19.

2 Bonnie, 'The Helios-and-Zodiac Motif', p. 299.

> **Yonatan Moss** (PhD from Yale University in 2013), is Leeds Senior Lecturer in Comparative Religion at the Hebrew University of Jerusalem.

Essays on Jews and Christians in Late Antiquity in Honour of Oded Irshai, ed. by Brouria Bitton-Ashkelony and Martin Goodman, CELAMA 40 (Turnhout: Brepols, 2023), pp. 21–54
BREPOLS ❧ PUBLISHERS   10.1484/M.CELAMA-EB.5.132482

This is not the place to rehearse the rich and varied scholarship on the question (including treatments by this Festschrift's honoree[3]), which has been systematically reviewed multiple times.[4] Explanations range from the decorative to the symbolic, to the ritual, to the calendrical. Do Helios and/or the zodiac represent the sun and the constellations, God, the calendar, the messiah, various biblical or other figures from Jewish history, or certain angels? That is just a partial list of interpretations that have been proposed over the years, alongside two key questions that often come up in this context: should Helios and the zodiac be interpreted separately, or as one unit, and should the phenomenon as a whole be connected to the Palestinian rabbinic culture known to us from contemporary literary sources?[5]

In what follows I offer yet another interpretation, yet another attempt to solve the enigma. My interpretation is at variance with certain assumptions found in scholarship, not only on the specific question of this iconographic motif, but also more generally within the study of Judaism in Late Antiquity. There are likely weaknesses in my proposal that I, as someone who works primarily on written Christian sources in Late Antiquity, am blind to, and that scholars of late ancient Jewish art will kindly point out to me. Nevertheless, I think the idea is worth proposing, both in its own right, and because of the more general questions it raises.

My choice to proceed, despite the risks, has been inspired by Oded Irshai — in two ways. On the one, more concrete, level, I am encouraged by words that Irshai has written on this very topic:[6]

---

3 See Irshai, 'The Priesthood in Jewish Society of Late Antiquity', p. 91; Irshai, 'Confronting a Christian Empire', pp. 17–18 and 52–53. Irshai, 'Confronting a Christian Empire', p. 17 opens with a wonderful, whimsical scene imagining a fictional fourth-century Palestinian rabbi's reaction to the Helios mosaic at Hammat Tiberias. The titles of subchapters 2–4 below are homages to Irshai's evocative scene.

4 To cite only some of the relatively recent studies, see, e.g., Hachlili, *Ancient Mosaic Pavements*, pp. 35–56; Weiss, 'Between Rome and Byzantium'; Levine, *Visual Judaism in Late Antiquity*, pp. 244–59 and 317–36; Talgam, 'The Zodiac and Helios in the Synagogue' (in Hebrew); Talgam, *Mosaics of Faith*, pp. 270–81; Fine, 'The Jewish Helios'; Werlin, *Ancient Synagogues of Southern Palestine, 300–800 CE*; Stewart, 'The Bet Alpha Synagogue Mosaic in Late Antique Provincialism'; Deines, 'God's Revelation through Torah, Creation and History'; Hezser, '"For the Lord God is a Sun and a Shield" (Ps. 84:12)'; Bonnie, 'The Helios-and-Zodiac Motif'; Laderman, *Jewish Art in Late Antiquity*, pp. 44–51.

5 Virtually every study of the issue raises the question of the relationship to rabbinic culture. For two articles focused squarely on this question, with opposite conclusions, see Miller, '"Epigraphical Rabbis", Helios and Psalm 19' (a harmonizing approach), vs. Friedheim, 'Sol Invictus in the Severus Synagogue at Hammath Tiberias, the Rabbis, and Jewish Society' (an oppositional approach).

6 Irshai, 'The Priesthood in Jewish Society', p. 91 n. 65 (my translation). See further Talgam, 'The Zodiac and Helios', p. 63; Talgam, *Mosaics of Faith*, p. 271; Magness, *The Archaeology of the Holy Land*, p. 315; and Hezser, '"For the Lord God"', pp. 213–14, who make the point that already in their original, late ancient, context, these images would have borne multiple meanings. On the other hand, see also Levine, *Visual Judaism*, p. 329 n. 60.

Indeed, much ink has been spilled in the attempts up-to-date to explain the appearance of this attribute [= Helios] in the synagogues [...] yet the gates of interpretation have not been shut, and there is still room to add another element to the already extant interpretations.

On another, more abstract, level, I am inspired by Oded Irshai's interdisciplinary, holistic approach to the study of Late Antiquity. His expertise in Jewish history has not limited his perspective to the confines of late ancient Judaism. On the contrary. He has always studied questions of Jewish history within their larger contexts and has even made valuable contributions to the study of Christianity that are not immediately related to the Jewish angle.[7] Irshai's success in this regard has inspired me to attempt to bring a fresh perspective to the Helios enigma, one that is, it must be admitted, also different from his own.

In my reconsideration of the question, I would like first of all to emphasize the historical context of all instances of the phenomenon. All these Helios-and-zodiac mosaics were produced in Byzantine Palestine, within a surrounding population, culture, and imperial government that was becoming increasingly Christianized. This point has often been missed in the past[8] since the earliest specimen of our phenomenon, the Hammat Tiberias synagogue, to which I will return in a moment, originally had been dated by its excavator, Moshe Dothan, to the decades right before the dawn of the Byzantine period.[9] Since, however, several subsequent scholars have convincingly argued for a later date for the Hammat mosaic, namely the second half of the fourth century,[10] the phenomenon as a whole must be viewed squarely within a Christian Byzantine context.[11] If then, as I suggest, the historical context is significant, and the Helios-and-zodiac motif owes its emergence and

---

7   Two important, interrelated, examples are Irshai, 'The Dark Side of the Moon' (in Hebrew); Irshai, 'Fourth Century Christian Palestinian Politics'.

8   There are, however, also important exceptions, to be discussed more below. See Talgam, 'The Zodiac and Helios', p. *65 and pp. *76–*77; Talgam, *Mosaics of Faith*, pp. 277–79; Levine, *Visual Judaism*, pp. 251–59. Talgam and Levine adopt perspectives different from mine, but they both take seriously the *later* fourth-century context of the Hammat mosaic.

9   Dothan, *Hammath Tiberias*, p. 42: the 'last quarter of the third, or the first third of the fourth century CE'; see also Dothan, *Hammath Tiberias*, p. 66: '*c.* 300 CE'; Dothan, *Hammath Tiberias*, p. 68: 'the early fourth century'.

10 Talgam, 'Mosaic Floors in Tiberias', p. 125 (in Hebrew); Goodman, 'The Roman State and the Jewish Patriarch in the Third Century', p. 130 n. 11; Talgam, 'Similarities and Differences between Synagogues and Church Mosaics in Palestine during the Byzantine and Umayyad Periods', p. 100 n. 51; Magness, 'Heaven on Earth', pp. 8–13. See Bonnie, 'The Helios-and-Mosaic Motif', p. 300; and Bonnie, 'The Helios-and-Mosaic Motif', p. 300 n. 3 for more literature.

11 One possible exception could be the Wadi Hammam mosaic, if we accept its excavator's dating to the 'late third or early fourth century'. See Leibner, 'Khirbet Wadi Hammam', p. 34 and pp. 39–40. Nevertheless, the degree to which Helios and the zodiac are in fact represented in this mosaic is, as noted in n. 1 above, unclear. Furthermore, Magness and others, 'Huqoq Excavation Project', pp. 117–18, postpone the date of the Wadi Hammam mosaic to the fifth century, due to its striking similarities to the Huqoq mosaic which they date to that later time. I thank Prof. Rina Talgam for bringing this issue to my attention.

endurance precisely to its Christian Byzantine setting, the question is what was it about post-Constantinian Christianity that made this development possible, let alone reasonable?

My answer lies at Hammat Tiberias, but it will take some explaining to get to it. The explanation travels through earlier scholarship on that mosaic, then through the world of Constantine and his successors, and finally through the version of that world advertised by the imperial propagandists, primarily Constantine's most famous episcopal advocate, Eusebius of Caesarea.

Following Dothan, and others after him, I treat the Hammat mosaic as the 'prototype' for the other members in the group.[12] Although there are naturally important differences among the various members of the group, they display a remarkable series of commonalities across the centuries and over a wide swath of geographical locales within Byzantine Palestine.[13] It stands to reason that all later instances owe their origin to the initial prototype that is, arguably, not only the most naturalistic and most impressive member of the group, but also would have benefited from its location in the leading city of Jewish Byzantine Palestine, Tiberias, the seat of the Patriarchate, at the height of its power, and home of the main rabbinic academy.[14] Nevertheless, it must be stated at the outset, that although I think my argument may be extended beyond Hammat Tiberias to the other specimens of the phenomenon, it can also stand on its own. It can also be taken, more minimally, to provide a key only to the Hammat mosaic, rather than to the phenomenon as a whole.

Moshe Dothan at Hammat Tiberias

The Hammat Helios, as noted by Dothan and many others, is a clear, unmistakable representation of the Roman imperial Sol Invictus type, that had been especially popular in the late third and fourth centuries.[15] Dothan correctly

---

12 Dothan, *Hammath Tiberias*, p. 48, with reference to the later synagogue mosaic representations of Helios writes: 'though crude and inaccurate, [they] still seem to reflect a specific prototype of which Hammath Tiberias presents the earliest and best example'. A much fuller development of this intuition, both on the iconographical and social-historical levels, can be found in Levine, *Visual Judaism*, pp. 329–35. For an opposite approach, that views Hammat Tiberias as fundamentally different from the later cases, see Talgam, 'The Zodiac and Helios', pp. *65–*66 and *76.

13 Levine, *Visual Judaism*, pp. 321–31.

14 Levine, *Visual Judaism*, pp. 329–32. See, however, Bonnie, 'The Helios-and-Zodiac Motif', pp. 308–09, for some challenges to this theory.

15 Dothan, 'The Image of Sol Invictus in the Mosaic at Hammath Tiberias' (in Hebrew); Dothan, 'The Representation of Helios in the Mosaic of Hammath-Tiberias'; Dothan, *Hammath Tiberias*, pp. 41–43. The link between the Hammat solar figure and Sol Invictus is accepted in most subsequent studies. For an early example, see Baumgarten, 'Art in the Synagogue – Some Talmudic Views', p. 197. For more recent examples, see, e.g., Belayche, *Iudaea-Palaestina*, pp. 46, 92, and 157 (I thank Prof. Brouria Bitton-Ashkelony for bringing my attention to the discussion of Helios in this study); Talgam, 'The Zodiac and Helios',

notes that the process of wholly or partially identifying the Emperor with the sun conceived as a victorious universal ruler received a strong impetus in the time of Aurelian, and was adopted by Constantius Chlorus who, in retrospect, can be said to have founded a 'Solar dynasty' of Roman emperors, who continued to employ Sol Invictus symbolism into the second half of the fourth century.[16] The Hammat Helios provided a textbook case of the imperial Sol Invictus type, documented in a variety of media in that period, as it ticks off all the boxes associated with the type: he drives a quadriga; has an elevated right hand; an orb and a whip in the left hand; an imperial paludamentum cloaking his shoulders; and a crown and radiating nimbus framing his head.[17]

Thus far I think Dothan was spot on. But, as noted above, when it came to the crucial issue of dating, he erred. More importantly for our purposes, his slightly earlier dating led to consequential complications in the way he and many others interpreted the significance of the mosaic in its Jewish context. These complications continue, I believe, to impact scholarship on the mosaic, even though the erroneous date has since been corrected. Dothan, as mentioned, dated the stratum of the synagogue containing the Helios mosaic to the turn of the third and fourth centuries. That date created a serious problem of interpretation for him and for others. The problem is that it means that the 'prototypical' example of the Helios-and-zodiac motif was created in a historical context in which the imperial cult was at its height. Emperor worship was one thing that all Jews — and not just the rabbis — would have been strongly opposed to.[18] Limiting the question to the specifically rabbinic context, as Dothan did, the problem was even more acute. In rabbinic sources, the Roman Emperor, as well as the sun itself, are considered the very epitomes of pagan worship. The Mishnah provides specific definitions of prohibited idolatrous representations that closely hew to the very image depicted in the Hammat Tiberias mosaic.[19] How could the

---

pp. *76–*77; Talgam, *Mosaics of Faith*, p. 278; Levine, *Visual Judaism*, pp. 251–59; Stern, 'Images in Late Antique Palestine', pp. 115–16. Interestingly, the more recent publications noted above (note 4) do not mention this link.

16 See Dothan, *Hammath Tiberias*, p. 41, for evidence from the reign of Constantius II down to 361. See further, Berrens, *Sonnenkult und Kaisertum von den Severern bis zu Constantin I (197–337 n. Chr.)*, pp. 229–34. Despite the book's title, the pages in question deal with the Christian emperors from Constantius II to the end of the fourth century. Berrens shows the continuation of solar imperial imagery for this period.

17 The quadriga and horses were almost completely destroyed by later walls, but part of the mane of one of the horses survives, as well as the tips of five hooves. Dothan, *Hammath Tiberias*, p. 40, reasonably conjectures that there were four horses harnessed to the chariot.

18 For a review of the evidence (including, alongside much evidence against Jewish participation in the cult, also some very rare, borderline cases demonstrating sporadic, minimal Jewish participation), see Noy, '"A Sight Unfit to See": Jewish Reactions to the Roman Imperial Cult'.

19 Mishnah Avoda Zara 3.1, famously prohibiting the use of images that hold in their hand 'a staff, or a bird, or as sphere'. See Urbach, 'The Rabbinical Laws of Idolatry in the Second and Third Centuries', pp. 229–45. Although Urbach argues that there developed a more lenient

central mosaic of a synagogue located in the heart of rabbinic leadership, at the height of rabbinic influence, add insult to injury by portraying the sun in a manner that made him look like a Roman Emperor in the guise by which he was the focus of cultic worship?[20]

Dothan presented the question point blank. His answer conceded its premise: indeed, the Roman Emperor could *not* be *symbolically* represented as Sol Invictus in a late ancient synagogue. That would be an unthinkable expression of emperor worship. The very same image that a contemporary non-Jewish Roman would view as a symbolic representation of the emperor was in Jewish eyes a decorative, anthropological representation of the sun, admittedly inspired by the contemporary imperial iconographic idiom, but not meant to be an actual reference to the Roman emperor, and thus not meant to be worshipped.[21] Dothan finds support for this interpretation in the fact that although the imagery is imperial, it does not depict a *specific* emperor. He writes:[22]

> Although the imperial insignia of the crown and the globe appear at Hammath Tiberias, the explanation for the fact that the central image of the mosaic was allowed seems to be that an image of Helios as Sol Invictus — with no inscription and rendered stereotypically as a young man — could not be identified with a *specific* Emperor and therefore could not be worshipped.

---

approach to figural representation beginning in the late second century, he insists that this did not extend to the imperial context. See Urbach, 'The Rabbinical Laws of Idolatry in the Second and Third Centuries', pp. 238–39: 'Nowhere in our sources is there the slightest suggestion of indulgence where the cult of emperor-worship was concerned [...] Everything connected with this cult was absolutely forbidden'. Urbach, 'The Rabbinical Laws of Idolatry in the Second and Third Centuries', p. 239: 'the equanimity with which the rabbis could regard other forms of "idolatry" did not apply to emperor-worship; it was more tempting to Jews, and statues of the emperor could not be desecrated in the way that other idols could'. See further Talgam, 'The Zodiac and Helios', p. *76; Talgam, *Mosaics of Faith*, p. 278, with discussion of Ze'ev Weiss's earlier work on this question.

20 For a more recent rearticulation of this position, see Friedheim, 'Sol Invictus'.

21 See Dothan, 'The Image of Sol', p. 134 (my translation): 'What did this image [of Sol in the Hammath Tiberias mosaic] express? In answering this question, I think we need to distinguish between two kinds of people, for each of whom this picture was understood completely differently. The architects, the planners, and maybe also the non-Jewish workers, who made the mosaic, saw in the image of Sol Invictus an expression of an artistic fashion, which fit the demands of royal propaganda. Indeed, according to their understanding the image of the emperor was identical to the image of the empire's supreme god. It fit the propaganda pattern that prominently, and consistently, presented itself before the eyes of every person, from every coin, statue, and painting, and embodied the identity of political power and religious cult. To the Jew, however, it was clear that the image of Sol, as long as it was not accompanied by inscriptions explicitly identifying it as a god or an emperor, is just a neutral character. The people who did not accept the identity of the characters of the emperor and of god saw in Sol's image nothing more than a personification of the sun, standing, nevertheless, in the center of the universe'. For another formulation of this argument, see Dothan, 'The Synagogues at Hammath-Tiberias', p. 121 (in Hebrew). For a more recent recapitulation of this argument, see England, 'Mosaics as Midrash', pp. 189–214, and n. 55.

22 Dothan, *Hammath Tiberias*, p. 68.

If the reader detects an apologetic tone in this passage, it is for good reason. Dothan was responding to early critiques of his 'imperial interpretation' on the theological-sociological grounds presented above: how could contemporary Jews, connected to the Jewish patriarchate (as the surviving synagogue inscriptions make clear) display in the very heart of their house of worship the prime image of the imperial cult?[23] The already familiar Na'aran and Beit Alpha mosaics, which had been discovered decades before the Hammat Tiberias synagogue, had accustomed scholars to the interpretation of the central image in line with the traditional, centuries-old, pre-imperial Helios iconography.[24] Both their later date, subsequent to the heyday of the popularity of Sol Invictus, and their more schematic, less detailed and less naturalistic, iconography allowed such an interpretation. When excavated, Hammat Tiberias presented a different picture — of the imperial Sol Invictus, not just the 'traditional' Greco-Roman Helios — which some found difficult to see.

Dothan's approach to the problem was to meet it halfway. His answer was essentially to insist that what looks like a duck, swims like a duck, and quacks like a duck, is *not* in fact a duck.[25] Yes, it seems *just* like any other image of the imperial Sol Invictus, worshipped throughout the empire, but the synagogue worshippers saw it as no more than a decorative image of the astronomical sun,[26] which — as the sun, not as the emperor — was important to them for religious calendrical purposes.

Despite the tenuous, incomplete nature of Dothan's attempt to neutralize the challenge, most subsequent scholarship has accepted his basic framework of interpretation. It is at the same time both widely agreed that the central image of the Hammat synagogue mosaic corresponds to late Roman imperial iconography, and it is equally agreed that despite the surrounding practices associated with such iconography, contemporary Jews would not have understood the image as a reference to the emperor, but to something else, each scholar offering a different 'something else', according to her or his theory.[27] The further question of why it was that precisely then, and only

---

23 Lifshitz, 'L'ancienne synagogue de Tibériade, sa mosaïque et ses inscriptions'.

24 Sukenik, *The Ancient Synagogue of Beth Alpha*, p. 35: 'This motif, the Sun in the act of rising, is based on the traditional pictures of Helios in Greek art [...] At Beth Alpha the whole picture [...] remains the selfsame conception which hovered before the Greek artist a thousand years before'.

25 See Dothan, *Hammath Tiberias*, p. 70: 'In Tiberias, the spiritual capital of Judaism [...] in a synagogue closely affiliated with the House of the Patriarchs, there was little likelihood that the motifs of Helios as Sol Invictus, the Zodiac, and the Seasons would have been used had they transgressed the limits of the law against idolatry as it was understood in that period [...] However close their [i.e. the planners of the synagogue] choice of motifs may have come to violating the prohibition, they managed not to cross the line'. Dothan does not explain how it was possible to come so close to violating the prohibition and yet manage not to.

26 See note 21 above, and further, Dothan, *Hammath Tiberias*, pp. 69–70, 87–88, and n. 530.

27 See, e.g., Belayche, *Iudaea-Palaestina*, p. 92; Goodman, 'The Jewish Image of God in Late Antiquity', p. 142; Magness, 'Heaven on Earth', p. 31; Hachlili, *Ancient Synagogues – Archaeology and Art*, p. 368; p. 370; Talgam, 'The Zodiac and Helios', p. *76; and Talgam,

then, namely in the fourth century and not before, that Jews would have felt comfortable enough to present the sun with iconography borrowed from the imperial cult, does not get asked.

Nevertheless, as already indicated, the whole premise for the big challenge with which Dothan had to deal is simply wrong. If the Hammat mosaic is the product of the late fourth century, and *not*, as he thought, a product of the decades around the turn of the fourth century, it becomes removed from the historical context of emperor worship as it was known in the late third-early fourth centuries. The more we proceed into the fourth century, the more the change in imperial context from a polytheistic[28] to a Christian one would seem to make a critical difference. The challenge that Dothan faced, and that subsequent scholarship inherited, falls away. Dothan was forced to say that the imperial image was not thought of as such because he could not accept the presence of an imperial image in a synagogue within a surrounding historical context that literally worshipped the emperor with sacrifices and other offerings. If, however, this image was produced at a time when the emperor was Christian and had, on theological grounds, curbed that imperial cult,[29] concerns about surrounding emperor worship turn out to be anachronistic.

Constantine, and Successors, at Hammat Tiberias

Regardless of Jewish-Christian debates about the messiahship and divinity of Jesus and other matters, late ancient Christians were no less opposed to emperor worship than their Jewish contemporaries.[30] Christian opposition to the imperial cult was, after all, the heart of the large-scale imperial persecutions at the turn of the third and fourth centuries that only came to an end with Constantine's policy change. Although there is much debate about Constantine's personal attitude to the question of imperial worship in the early years of his reign, it is clear that by the 320s he was actively legislating, and taking other actions, to restrain it, especially when it came to animal sacrifice.[31] Even if ritualized expressions of loyalty to the emperor did indeed continue, and in that sense the imperial cult did not die overnight, it was, nevertheless, beginning to lose many of the traditional practices which for centuries had been at its core, such as sacrifices and gladiatorial contests. Some scholars have referred

---

Mosaics of Faith, p. 277, conceptualizes the Jewish adoption of this imperial symbolism as 'appropriation as a means of neutralization'.

28 Aware of the complications, I use this term, rather than 'pagan', faute de mieux. See Salzman, 'Pagans and Christians'. For an argument in favour of retaining the term 'pagan' in scholarly discourse, see Alan Cameron, *The Last Pagans of Rome*', pp. 14–32.

29 The question of the precise degree to which Constantine and his successors imposed restrictions on the imperial cult will be touched on immediately below.

30 See Noy, 'A Sight Unfit to See', pp. 81–82.

31 See Curran, 'Constantine and the Ancient Cults of Rome: The Legal Evidence', pp. 76–77; Lee, 'Traditional Religions', pp. 170–76.

to this development as a Christian 'de-sacralization' or 'quasi-secularization' of the imperial cult.[32] There is evidence of the polytheistic internalization of this new reality. To use Noel Lenski's apt phrasing, Constantine's polytheistic subjects 'had sensed the shifts in the religious winds and trimmed their sails accordingly'.[33] Jews must also have taken note of these dramatic changes happening all around them.

As with the question of the imperial cult, also with regard to Constantine's original intentions in his active adoption of, and association with, solar imagery there is an ongoing debate in Constantinian scholarship.[34] There are also indications that Constantine's own understanding of his relationship to the sun was something that evolved over time.[35] The fact remains, however, that thanks to widely distributed coins, imposing statuary, and the language used by imperial panegyrists, in the minds of contemporary subjects of the empire Constantine's imperial image, as well as that of his successors, would have been closely linked to the sun.

The important question then becomes how contemporaries would have interpreted this link. Scholarship on the solar imagery of the Constantinian dynasty has reached the conclusion that its meaning varied depending on the beholder.[36] Polytheists would have viewed it within the context of the trend towards solar monotheism that had been steadily growing in the empire in the generations preceding Constantine.[37] They would have seen the emperor as an embodiment of the sun, both thus worthy of their worship, in a manner that dated back to Aurelian, and, to some degree, even as far back as Nero. Some

---

32 This is a matter of longstanding debate in scholarship. See, on the one side, Doerries, *Constantine the Great*, pp. 182–83; Salzman, *On Roman Time*, pp. 141–46; Salway, 'Constantine Augoustos (not Sebastos)'; Cameron, *The Last Pagans of Rome*, pp. 59, 67, and 170–72; Barnes, *Constantine: Dynasty, Religion and Power*, pp. 22–23; Lenski, *Constantine and the Cities*, pp. 114–30, 141–44, 202–03, 212–13, and 220. On the other side, see Bowersock, 'The Imperial Cult: Perceptions and Persistence', pp. 176–77; Cameron, 'Herrscherkult III. Altkirche ab Konstantin'. This point will be returned to below.

33 Lenski, *Constantine and the Cities*, p. 220.

34 See Bardill, *Constantine, Divine Emperor of the Christian Golden Age*, pp. 326–37; Wallraff, 'Constantine's Death'.

35 See Lenski, *Constantine and the Cities*, pp. 38 and 48–52.

36 For some representatives, see Liebeschuetz, *Continuity and Change in Roman Religion*, pp. 277–91; Frakes, 'The Dynasty of Constantine down to 363', pp. 104–05; Lenski, *Constantine and the Cities*, pp. 51–52, and, more generally, pp. 72–75 and 281; Wallraff, 'Constantine's Death'. For an interesting presentation of the contradictions and ambiguities both in Constantine's personality and in his heritage, including his reception in scholarship, see Lenski, 'Introduction'. For a dissenting view, see Bowersock, 'The Imperial Cult', pp. 178–79.

37 For the trend towards solar monotheism, see Fauth, *Helios Megistos*. On the problematics and dilemmas involved in using the term 'monotheism' in 'pagan' (or 'polytheistic'!) contexts, see Van Nuffelen, 'Pagan Monotheism as a Religious Phenomenon', pp. 16–33. For a demonstration that the term 'one God' (*heis theos*) itself, did *not* have, at least in ritual contexts, a monotheistic meaning, see Belayche, '"Deus deum… summorum maximus" (Apuleius)'. For further complications surrounding the terms 'monotheism' within the study of antiquity more generally, see note 39 below.

might have viewed Constantine's unique focus on the sun as an intentional reversal of the immediately preceding ideology of the Tetrarchy that had associated the different *augusti* and *caesares* with different other deities.[38] Fourth-century Christians, by contrast, could not have accepted the sun as an object of worship. Instead, they would have viewed the sun as a non-divine, created being, that, in its universal reach and blessed life-giving bounty, is a natural symbol of imperial sovereignty and beneficence. That, at least, is the line of interpretation we find articulated by Constantine's chief Christian propagandist, Eusebius of Caesarea, to which we will return below.

Given these two divergent interpretations of early Byzantine imperial solar iconography, we may ask what contemporary Jews thought. Did they see things like their polytheistic neighbours, or their Christian ones? Unfortunately, the Jewish sources are silent on the matter (this silence, after all, is the reason for our Helios enigma). To me it seems that contemporary Jews would have welcomed the Christian perspective. Would it not have been experienced as a monotheistic breath of fresh air?[39] Would Jews not prefer an emperor who (even if his language towards them was at times polemical)[40] discouraged solar and imperial worship over all the preceding emperors who had encouraged it?

This major difference alone, it would seem, can go a long way to explain why the zodiac had not been depicted in the Temple,[41] while it figured prominently in the synagogues of Byzantine Palestine. It must be remembered that in this early period of Byzantine rule, religiously motivated anti-Jewish legislation, let alone persecution, was minimal; such developments only began to be felt in the fifth century, and even then they were gradual.[42] When it came to the position of the Jews as a religious organization and the power of their elites to exercise authority over members of the group, the situation in the late fourth century considerably improved, rather than deteriorated.[43] The patriarchal leadership, in whose milieu the Hammat synagogue and mosaic

---

38 See Leeb, *Konstantin und Christus*, p. 9; Lenski, *Constantine and the Cities*, p. 33.

39 Fully aware that the term 'monotheism' is a modern coinage, I use it as an etic, second-degree category to describe a theological position that neither Jews nor Christians called by that name in Late Antiquity. For a history of this category, and some problems inherent in it, see Chayes, 'Blavatsky and Monotheism', pp. 250–55.

40 Linder, *The Jews in Roman Imperial Legislation*, pp. 58 and 60. Constantine's rhetoric is counter-balanced by his policies, which in some ways improved the situation of the Jews. See below.

41 Josephus, *Jewish War* 5.214 (quoted by Levine, *Visual Judaism*, p. 322 n. 20).

42 Cohen, 'Roman Imperial Policy toward the Jews from Constantine until the End of the Palestinian Patriarchate'; Linder, *The Jews in Roman Imperial Legislation*, pp. 55–67; Schwartz, *Imperialism and Jewish Society*, pp. 182–84; Goodman, 'The Roman State'; Ulrich, *Euseb von Caesarea und die Juden*, pp. 252–54. Compare the more recent studies of Nemo-Pekelman, *Rome et ses citoyens juifs*, and Kraemer, *The Mediterranean Diaspora in Late Antiquity*, pp. 75–158, who offer a more pessimistic outlook on the matter, but concede that legislation concerning the Jews in the fourth century was not focused on Christianizing them.

43 Levine, 'The Status of the Patriarch in the Third and Fourth Centuries', pp. 30–32; Goodman, 'The Roman State', pp. 138–39; Schwartz, *Imperialism*, pp. 191–99.

were produced, would have had reasons to be favourably inclined towards the Christian emperors of the fourth century.[44]

Nevertheless, scholarship has generally tended to assume that Jews would have preferred the polytheistic perspective on the role of the emperor to the Christian one. This is evident, for example, in the work of Lee Levine. Although Levine, unlike many others, reckons seriously with the late fourth-century re-dating of the Hammat mosaic, he still seeks to pinpoint its origin to the very short period of emperor Julian's reign (361–63), rather than to connect it to the decades of Christian rule before and after Julian.[45] Practically, if we are speaking about the second half of the fourth century, that means either the reign of Constantine's son, Constantius II (337–61), or of one of the three emperors from the Valentinian line who ruled the eastern part of the empire in the last third of the century, namely Valens (364–378), Theodosius I (379–95) or Arcadius (395–408). It is true that Julian's governmental policy was in some ways 'pro-Jewish' (although more precisely 'anti-Christian'), but he actively reinstituted worship of the sun as well as the imperial cult after these had been without official sanction in the years before his rise (and after his demise).[46]

If fourth-century Jews begin for the first time in history (as far as we know) to depict solar and zodiacal figurations in their worship spaces would it not make more sense for them to have done so precisely during the, far longer, period in which these symbols were *not* aggressively promoted as part of the imperial cult, rather than during the very short period in which they were?[47] Despite evidence that Julian actually sought to limit the autonomy of the Patriarch,[48] Levine goes to great lengths to explain why the Patriarch would have had a special relationship with emperor Julian, and thus would have created the Hammat mosaic as a 'statement of affiliation' with him and his dedication to the sun. But would it not make much more sense for the Patriarch to support a Christian ruler, who both granted him more power over his people and did not worship the sun as Julian and the pre-Constantinian emperors had done? Furthermore, at least some of the Christian emperors who ruled in this period displayed active favouritism towards the Jewish

---

44 See Kraemer, *The Mediterranean Diaspora*, p. 80: 'While not minimizing either the short-term or the long-term consequences of Christian hostility to Jews, I am wary of constructing a teleological narrative, in which what happened in the fourth and fifth centuries had to lead inevitably to its subsequent horrific history. In those centuries, life may have looked very different'. My argument here is that life, at least in the fourth century, *did* indeed look very different from how it is often read back from the perspective of later developments.

45 Levine, *Visual Judaism*, pp. 249–58.

46 Smith, *Julian's Gods*, pp. 114–78 (referred to by Levine, *Visual Judaism*, p. 249 n. 33).

47 For Julian and the imperial cult of Sol Invictus, including the aggressive promotion of animal sacrifices, see Smith, *Julian's Gods*, pp. 164–66; p. 169. For more on Julian's theological conception of the sun and its relation to his own rule, see Elm, *Sons of Hellenism*, pp. 286–99.

48 Levine, *Visual Judaism*, p. 252, citing a letter that Julian wrote to Patriarch Hillel II, admonishing him for oppressing his people with heavy taxation.

community.[49] That would be another reason to display publicly adherence to the emperor.

It should be noted that Levine does finally concede that '[e]ven if the floor had been laid sometime after Julian's death, following the return to power of Christian rulers, such a statement of affiliation might not necessarily have been deemed politically inappropriate, as the Patriarchate and Judaism generally continued to be regarded with respect and honor by subsequent Christian emperors until the fifth century'.[50] Thus, Levine entertains the possibility that an imperial Christian context could somehow make sense, but his operating assumption is that a polytheistic context is more natural. It is precisely this assumption that I seek to challenge. Perhaps the policies of the early Christian emperors, and, consequently, Jewish impressions of those emperors, were in fact more positive than what we are led to believe by the literary sources written mostly by anti-Jewish Christian authors, who were eager to draw a sharp distinction between Jews and Christians.[51]

Eusebius, and Pacatus Drepanius, at Hammat Tiberias

To better appreciate how imperial solar symbolism was understood in a monotheistic context, we may call on the help of Eusebius. While we might not have literary evidence of how Byzantine Palestinian Jews understood imperial solar symbolism, we can gain a very clear idea of how their Christian neighbour, the bishop of Caesarea, wished to present this matter to the outside world, including, possibly, to them. An analysis of Eusebius's understanding of the link between Constantine and the sun can give a decent idea of what it meant within the early Byzantine context to associate solar imagery with the Christian emperor.[52]

---

49 See Lenski, *Failure of Empire*, p. 238, with reference to the pro-Jewish legislation and attitudes of Valens (364–378) in the East and his brother Valentinian I (364–375) in the West. See Kraemer, *The Mediterranean Diaspora*, pp. 114–20, with reference to the legislation regarding Jews of Valens, Valentinian, and Gratian (Western emperor, 367–383). Kraemer, *The Mediterranean Diaspora*, p. 118, describes Gratian's legislation regarding Jews as 'mild, and not only by comparison'.

50 Levine, *Visual Judaism*, pp. 257–58.

51 The literary sources usually quoted in histories of Jewish-Christian relations in the fourth century are John Chrysostom's *Homilies against the Jews* and Epiphanius of Salamis's *Panarion* (especially his description of the case of Joseph of Tiberias, a Jewish convert to Christianity). It is far from clear, as many scholars have pointed out, to what degree these, and similar, sources are reflective of facts on the ground or are wishful rhetorical constructions. On the episcopal fashioning of Constantine's anti-Jewish image, contrary to the evidence of the historiographical sources, see Irshai, 'Constantine and the Jews'. For evidence of Jewish appreciation of Constantine in fourth-century Palestine, see Stepansky, 'Archeological Discoveries in Mughar', detailing the discovery and reconstruction of an inscription in praise of Constantine that probably belonged in a Jewish context. See further on this, Talgam, 'Between Christians and Jews', p. *37 (in Hebrew).

52 Regardless of what we think about the historicity and degree of Constantine's Christianness, Eusebius himself definitely sought to project a righteous Christian image of him.

Eusebius touches upon the connection between Constantine and the sun in several places in his writings,[53] but his most concentrated development of the theme can be found in one of his very last works, the panegyric he delivered in 336 CE in Constantinople in celebration of thirty years of Constantine's rule.[54] It is important to note that Eusebius's panegyric was meant to reflect the official imperial outlook. The emperor himself selected Eusebius to deliver the keynote oration at this landmark political occasion.[55] Thus, although Eusebius sees things from his own episcopal perspective, given the public, official nature of this speech, we can be reasonably confident that it would have needed to align with Constantine's perspective. Eusebius fleshes out a sustained comparison between the emperor and the sun in the following terms:[56]

> As the light of the sun shines upon settlers in the most remote lands by the rays sent off from itself into the distance, so too does he assign, like beacons and lamps of the brilliance emanating from himself, this son here to us who inhabit the East [i.e. Constantius II], an offspring worthy of himself; and another of his sons to the other division of mankind, and yet another elsewhere [i.e. Constantine II, in Gaul; and Constans in Italy, Africa and Pannonia]. Thus, having yoked the four valiant Caesars like colts beneath the single yoke of the Imperial chariot, he controls them with the reins of holy harmony and concord. Holding the reins high above them, he rides along, traversing all lands alike that the sun gazes upon, himself present everywhere and watching over everything.

In language that at times almost feels like an ekphrastic description of the imperial Helios of Hammat Tiberias, Eusebius takes pains to cast the connection between Constantine and Sol Invictus as symbolic, rather than literal. With his recurrent usage of the preposition *like* (ὡς) in his linkage of the two, his language ensures that the comparison remain completely in the range of the simile. The emperor is *like* the sun; his brilliance is *like* its rays; his four sons are *like* the four horses of the sun's imagined quadriga; the governing attributes of harmony and concord are *like* the reins he uses to drive it; and, finally, the breadth of Constantine's surveillance throughout his reign is compared to the reach of the sun's rays.[57]

Eusebius goes on to extol the virtues of the monarchic political system in contrast to models of shared rule. The exclusive rule of the Roman emperor

---

53 See Tantillo, 'Attributi solari'.
54 On the historical setting of this work, see Barnes, *Constantine and Eusebius*, pp. 253–55. See also Levine, *Visual Judaism*, p. 249, who cites a passage from this work of Eusebius, but according to the translation found in Browning, *The Emperor Julian*, p. 22.
55 See Lenski, *Constantine and the Cities*, p. 44, with n. 105.
56 Eusebius, *In Praise of Constantine*, 3.4 (trans. p. 87).
57 By contrast, see *In Praise of Later Roman Emperors*, pp. 286–87 n. 61, for an interesting note (on *Panegyrici Latini*, 5.14) on the problematic usage, within a polytheistic panegyrical context, of the word *quasi* if it is interpreted to denote the relationship between the emperor and Apollo-Sol.

is an earthly imitation of God's own sole presence and authority as Ruler of all.[58] Imperialism recapitulates monotheism.

> Thus outfitted in the likeness of the kingdom of heaven, he pilots affairs below with an upward gaze, to steer by the archetypal form. He grows strong in his model of monarchic rule, which the Ruler of All has given to the race of man alone of those on earth. For this is the law of royal authority, the law which decrees one rule over everybody. Monarchy excels all other kinds of constitution and government. For rather do anarchy and civil war result from the alternative, a polyarchy based on equality. For which reason there is one God, not two or three or even more. For strictly speaking, belief in many gods is godless.

Towards the very end of the panegyric Eusebius returns to the sun. He emphasizes its created, non-divine status, God's uniqueness as the only non-created being, and the sun's subordination to him.[59] It is in fact, precisely because of Constantine's rule, according to Eusebius's telling, that the divinization of the sun and other heavenly bodies is becoming a thing of the past:[60]

> And so, all who are being converted to the Higher Power now spit on the faces of the dead idols, trample under the rightless rites of the demons, and ridicule the dated delusions of their forefathers. Everywhere men have organized for the study of Holy Writ and are edified by the saving doctrines, so as no longer to be frightened by any creature visible to the eyes of the flesh nor to look with awe upon the sun or moon or stars and attribute miracles to these, but rather to acknowledge the One above these, the invisible and imperceptible Universal Creator, having learned to worship Him alone [...] what was not before shines forth to all in rays of piety.[61]

---

58 Contrast this with the polytheistic panegyric of Constantius Chlorus, *Panegyrici Latini*, 8.4 (ed., p. 545; trans., p. 114): 'But neither the Sun itself nor all the stars watch over human affairs with such unremitting light as you, who illuminate the world with scarcely any discrimination of night and day and provide for the well-being of nations not only with these eyes which animate your immortal countenances, but much more with those eyes of your divine minds, and bless with your healing light not only the provinces where the day rises, passes by and disappears from view, but also those in the northern belt. Thus, Caesar, the benefactions which you distribute over the world are almost more numerous than those of the gods'. Not only is Constantius not subordinated to the gods; he is said to be greater than them.

59 See also Eusebius, *In Praise of Constantine*, 1.5 (trans. p. 85): 'Even the all-shining sun, which ranges far through all eternity, recognizes Him (i.e., "the One and only God") alone as Lord and, obedient to His nod, never dares to cross beyond its bounds'. See Tantillo, 'Attributi solari', p. 47, who rightly stresses the word 'even' (καί) at the beginning of this sentence. Eusebius finds it necessary to stress the sun's, more than other natural elements', subordination to God.

60 Eusebius, *In Praise of Constantine*, 10.2–3 (trans. p. 102).

61 The subject of this final clause is not entirely clear. What 'was not before' and now 'shines forth'? Blessings? Virtues? See Eusebius, *In Praise of Constantine* (trans. p. 172 n. 3). I would say, in line with the imperial solar imagery found elsewhere in the text, that it refers again to Constantine himself, or to the overall character of his reign.

This was a theological message, but not a specifically Christian one. Eusebius clearly did not view his oration in celebration of the emperor as a platform for pontificating on the virtues of Christianity. The words 'Jesus', 'Christ', 'Christian', and 'Christianity' are not to be found throughout the text. There are only oblique references to the 'royal Logos', and 'the Only-Begotten Logos of God', as well as to the 'great and wonderful sign, through which all that was evil no longer exists'.[62] On the other hand, the panegyric is shot through with a clear insistence on a monotheistic interpretation of imperial solar symbolism, and it does not mince words about the errors of paganism, and the blessings of its defeat.[63] If a polytheist had been tasked with composing Constantine's tricennial oration, it would have been a very different text.[64]

This combination of an imperial ideology that is, on the one hand in line with biblical monotheism, but on the other hand, not specifically Christian, would seem to be ideally suited to the contemporary Jewish ear. It is almost as if Eusebius had his Jewish Palestinian neighbours in the back of his mind when he wrote this text.[65] The result is a form of imperial propaganda that Jews, perhaps for the first time since the Judean wars, could get behind.[66]

Eusebius wrote his panegyric at the end of the first third of the fourth century. I have used him as a guide to the emerging Christian interpretation of imperial solar imagery because he provides the clearest example of what I am arguing became a new ideological paradigm within an increasingly Christianized empire. Given that our mosaic dates to the second half of the century, it is necessary to show that this paradigm did indeed strike roots and that it continued to be the common frame-of-reference at the end of the century. To prove that is somewhat more challenging. This is because the emperors who ruled in the first decades after the death of Constantine were judged insufficiently orthodox by the standards of the pro-Nicene,

---

62 E.g., Eusebius, *In Praise of Constantine*, 10.3 (trans. p. 102). These were terms that any Jew who subscribed to some form of Logos, or Wisdom theology, would not necessarily find offensive.

63 See, e.g., Eusebius, *In Praise of Constantine*, 6.21–9.8 (trans. pp. 94–99).

64 Compare, by contrast, the polytheistic panegyric to Maximian and Constantine (on the occasion of the latter's marriage to the former's daughter, Fausta), as it apostrophizes the recently deceased Constantius Chlorus in *Panegyrici Latini* 7.14 (ed., p. 571; trans., p. 209): 'Divine Constantius […] you whom Sol himself (*Sol ipse*) took up on a chariot almost visible, to carry you to heaven when, in setting, he was seeking once more his sunrise nearby'. The phrase 'his sunrise nearby' refers to Constantine, who is assimilated with Sol. See further, Turcan, 'Images solaires dans le *Panégyrique* VI', pp. 697–706.

65 For a study of the role of Jews in Eusebius's theology, see Ulrich, *Euseb von Caesarea und die Juden*. A more socially oriented study is a desideratum.

66 Jews are not mentioned in the text. The closest thing to this is a positive description of Constantine's Christian building projects in Palestine, at Eusebius, *In Praise of Constantine*, 9.16–17 (trans. p. 101): 'In the Palestinian nation, in the heart of the Hebrew kingdom, on the very site of the evidence for salvation, he outfitted with many and abundant distinctions an enormous house of prayer and temple sacred to the Saving Sign'.

36   YONATAN MOSS

'anti-Arian' authors, whose writings comprise the bulk of what survives to us from this period.[67]

Thus, the Christian perspectives we find on imperial rule during much of the period until Theodosius I is oppositional, and far from panegyrical.[68] But when it comes to the latter emperor's period, we are in different territory. Here we may call on the evidence provided by the Latin panegyrist Pacatus Drepanius, whose speech in honour of Theodosius was delivered in Rome in 389.[69] It is admittedly a matter of scholarly debate whether Pacatus was himself a Christian.[70] Yet, even if he was not, his rhetoric demonstrates an internalization of the Christian perspective, perhaps deemed especially appropriate due to the expressly Christian character of the object of his praise. Twice in his oration, Pacatus compares Theodosius to the sun. The first comparison is brief:[71]

> Just as tireless revolution makes the sky go round, just as the seas are stirred up by the waves, and the sun does not know how to keep still, so you, Emperor, are constantly kept engaged in ceaseless activity which recurs as if in a cycle.

Like Eusebius two generations before him, and in contradistinction to the polytheistic panegyrical tradition, Pacatus underlines the symbolic, non-literal, nature of the comparison of the emperor to the sun. But he touches on an element not found in Eusebius. If the latter dealt with Constantine's ubiquitous presence and surveillance, Pacatus stresses Theodosius's incessant activity. Later in the panegyric, Pacatus raises yet another element not found in Eusebius:[72]

> But how different the custom of other Emperors [...] who considered their royal majesty diminished and cheapened unless they were shut up within some remote part of the palace, as if in some sanctuary of Vesta, to be consulted with reverence and in secret, and unless a carefully arranged solitude and widely imposed silence protected them like a rampart as they lay buried in the shade of their abode [...] But our Emperor offers himself to the gaze of all, and one can see him as often as one can the daylight

---

67 See Ross, 'The Constantians' Return to the West: Julian's Depiction of Constantius II in *Oration 1*', p. 183.

68 See, e.g., Humphries, 'Savage Humour: Christian Anti-panegyric in Hilary of Poitiers' *Against Constantius*'.

69 Another example from this period is Ambrose of Milan's funeral lament for the Western emperor Valentinian II, delivered in 392. Despite the youthful emperor's initial 'Arian' sympathies, he became increasingly pro-Nicene towards the end of his short life, and thus earned Ambrose's praise. For solar imagery in the lament, see Ambrose, *On the Death of Valentinian*, 64 (*De Obitu Valentiniani*, ed. by Faller, pp. 359–360; *On the Death of Valentinian*, trans. by Deferrari, p. 292).

70 See *In Praise of Later Roman Emperors*, pp. 439, 450 n. 7, 470 n. 62; Lippold, 'The Ideal Ruler and the Attachment to Tradition in Pacatus' Panegyric', pp. 378–86.

71 *Panegyrici Latini* 2.10 (ed., p. 652; trans., p. 460).

72 *Panegyrici Latini* 2.21 (ed., p. 659; trans., p. 472).

and sun. Furthermore, although when things are permitted one, disdain is never far away, admiring eyes never have their full of him. People seek him more and more, and — a novel thing to relate — he is longed for even when he is present.

If Eusebius's focus was on the sun and the emperor always 'gazing upon, and watching everything', Pacatus highlights the reverse perspective: how the emperor offers himself, like the sun, and as often as it, to 'the gaze of all'. Despite this variation in detail, the newly Christianized paradigm of solar imperial imagery had become ensconced in Byzantine imagination and would remain so for centuries. Thus, in 565 CE the late Roman poet Corippus could praise the elevation of emperor Justin II in the following terms:[73]

> The brave prince stood on that shield, looking like the sun; A second light shone out from the city. One and the same propitious day marveled at the rising of twin suns.

This and other passages in Corippus's poem offer yet another, although later, example of the analogy between the emperor and the sun, a theme which was, as Averil Cameron put it, 'fundamental to Byzantine thought and [...] expressed equally in art'.[74]

In sum, regardless of the precise nature of Constantine and his successors' personal beliefs about their connection to the sun, the official understanding of imperial solar symbolism developed by Eusebius and reflected at the century's end in the panegyric of Pacatus, had transformed the sun from its former status as the very epitome of Greco-Roman paganism into a symbol of imperial sovereignty that is subsumed to the oneness of God. One almost wonders how fourth-century Jews, rabbinic and otherwise, could *not* have been glad about this transformation. Here was an opportunity for the traditional ideal of respect and prayer for the 'peace of the kingship' not to veer dangerously close to acceptance of the idolatrous context of emperor worship. The religio-political transformation embodied in the new, Christian monotheistic, understanding of the traditional image of Sol Invictus, and of the emperor more generally, might just have opened up new possibilities for the Jews of the Roman empire.[75]

---

73 Corippus, *In Laudem Iustini Augusti Minoris*, 2.149 (trans., p. 97).

74 Cameron, 'Corippus' Poem on Justin II: A Terminus of Antique Art?', p. 148.

75 The situation may be compared with contemporary Babylonia, where Jews, as reflected in the Bavli, developed a highly patriotic stance towards the Sassanian rulers, deliberately ignoring, and even denying, the religious, Zoroastrian, aspects of the kings. Religious persecution in the Bavli is always associated with the Magi; never with the crown. See Herman, '"In Honor of the House of Caesar"', pp. 114–15.

Minimalist and Maximalist Interpretations

How specifically does this impact our interpretation of the Hammat Tiberias mosaic, or indeed, of all the other mosaics in the cluster (if we view the former as the latter's prototype)? I see two possible interpretations, one that may be called minimalist, the other maximalist. The minimalist interpretation, by virtue of its more conservative nature, seems more secure, and thus easier to defend. The maximalist interpretation, by contrast, will require readers to stretch their historical imaginations in a manner that some may feel also stretches their credulity. Nevertheless, I think it is worth presenting, for others may refine or buttress it — or refute it — with further evidence.

The minimalist option casts the Christian transformation in the understanding of imperial solar symbolism as an enabler. The new Christian imperial framework had enabled a 'de-sacralization' of imperial imagery and art that until the fourth century had been generally understood by everyone — polytheists, Christians, Jews, etc. — within a polytheistic religious context. The Christian emperors, or their Christian spokesmen, now stamped this imagery with a new, somewhat 'de-sacralized' interpretation, which had now become generally accepted by all. Another phenomenon that may be viewed within this pattern is the extensive use of spolia, including many ancient cult statues, that characterized the Constantinian period. That has also been described as a form of 'de-sacralization'. The act of relocating objects of polytheistic devotion into other spaces, whether they be Christian or urban (primarily the newly founded Constantinople) transmuted them from religious objects into aesthetic ones.[76]

According to this logic, the distinction between 'religious' and 'decorative' types of art, which historians had previously assumed to have developed in the second or third century 'naturally', or perhaps even due to some general Christian influence, now receives a later, and more specifically logical, and thus more understandable, historical context.[77] According to the minimalist option, Eusebius is a guide for us to the route by which the Jews of Palestine could have first embraced iconography that had previously been polytheistically religious, thanks to a process which may be defined as a form of Christian

---

76 See Elsner, 'Perspectives in Art', p. 265.

77 Urbach, 'The Rabbinical Laws of Idolatry', p. 245, famously wrote that 'the influence of Christianity also served to mitigate the attitude of Halakhah to painting and the plastic arts at the end of the second and throughout the third century'. While this may be true, the suggestion here is that the more significant change happened in the fourth century, only when Christianity gained political power. That is the proper context for synagogue art in late ancient Palestine. See Levine, 'Why did Jewish Art Flourish in Late Antiquity', esp. at pp. 64–65 and 71. See Stern, 'Images in Late Antique Palestine', pp. 120–29, who offers a different perspective on the question, founded on the Roman legal distinction between consecrated and profane statutes. The weakness with this suggestion, as Stern acknowledges, is that the distinction is almost exclusively limited to Latin sources in the Roman West, and barely found in Greek, in the Roman East. In addition, the references seem to be limited to statuary.

'de-sacralization', or even 'quasi-secularization'.[78] How then do we interpret the specific meaning of Helios and the zodiac? Here we must revert to the myriad other interpretations that have already been offered in scholarship. What the minimalist option offers is not so much an interpretation of Helios and the zodiac in the synagogue, as an explanation as to why it is that this phenomenon only first appears in a Byzantine context. It is thus concerned with the timing of a historical change, not with its substance, or precise character.

The maximalist option, by contrast, offers an interpretation not just of the 'why *then*' question, but also of the 'what' question. The depiction of Helios in the synagogue associated with the patriarch, according to this reading, was meant as a declaration of allegiance to the emperor in his guise as Sol Invictus. Echoing the imperial propaganda that presented the emperor's power as similar, in its breadth and depth, to the unconquerable sun, Sol Invictus at Hammat Tiberias was meant to represent none other than the Roman emperor himself. Concerns about emperor worship had become irrelevant in the Christian setting of the late fourth century. There is no need to argue, as Dothan did, that 'the fact that the central image of the mosaic was allowed' was because the lack of an inscription rendered the image unidentifiable with 'a specific Emperor, and therefore [it] could not be worshipped'.[79]

Unlike the situation a century earlier (and during the brief reign of Julian in the early 360s) when the emperor had encouraged, and sometimes demanded, a cult surrounding his identification with the sun, the Christian emperor not only did not demand such cult, but actively discouraged it. Thus, on the one hand, we know, thanks to the *Tabula Peutingeriana* and other sources, that there was a large statue in Constantinople that represented Constantine in the guise of Helios, but on the other hand, we also know that Constantine banished his likeness from polytheistic shrines and temples erected in his honour.[80] Jews would have viewed such a policy as a game changer. They could now openly declare their allegiance to the emperor using the emperor's own iconography, without fear of it being interpreted — by themselves or by others — as emperor worship. It is presumably precisely for this reason that Helios in Hammat Tiberias is not identifiable, as Dothan pointed out, with 'a specific emperor'. Such an identification would have contravened the emperor's own desires (or at least the image of those desires that was mediated through the likes of Eusebius). Furthermore, from a Jewish perspective solar iconography would have been a far more convenient means for declaring

---

78 I am aware of the anachronistic connotations of this term. This is a question I will return to towards the end of this essay.

79 Dothan, *Hammath Tiberias*, p. 68 (see the discussion above). To be sure, I am not claiming that the Sol Invictus of Hammat was meant to represent Constantine specifically; rather it was meant to represent the notion of imperial power through a 'generic' image of the emperor, any emperor, as the unvanquished sun.

80 See Irshai, 'Constantine and the Jews', p. 171; Edwards, 'The Beginnings of Christianization', p. 154 (but see Barnes, *Constantine: Dynasty, Religion and Power*, pp. 23–25, for a different perspective on the statue); Lenski, *Constantine and the Cities*, pp. 215–18.

allegiance to the emperor than explicitly Christian iconography, involving symbols such as the cross.[81] The general climate of the fourth century was one in which the sun, now a symbol of the power of the state, was ceasing, just as the cross was beginning, to signify a god.[82]

The original connection of the prototype of our motif to the Patriarch's milieu makes good sense, as Levine has argued, given the consolidation of power enjoyed by the patriarchal elite under the Christian emperors of the late fourth century. But it would also make sense for this prototype to have been imitated in other synagogues also outside of the patriarchal context, and even once the patriarch's position waned. Helios became, according to this explanation, the standard symbol in Byzantine Jewish Palestine to declare allegiance to the imperial government. It could have continued in this function even as the emperors of the fifth and sixth centuries introduced increasingly anti-Jewish policies.[83] If in the fourth century allegiance to the early Christian emperors was something the Jews of Palestine, especially in the patriarch's milieu, would have embraced with enthusiasm, similar expressions of allegiance would still be a sage — although less exciting — stance for Jews to adopt in subsequent centuries. Presumably, even the more Christianized emperors of the fifth and sixth centuries would be more likely to vouchsafe the rights of their Jewish subjects if the latter publicly demonstrated their fealty to the imperial government.

What then about the zodiac? Sol Invictus is a clear symbol of imperial rule, but how, according to the maximalist option, might the zodiac have been a part of this iconographical scheme? Here again, we may call on the help of Eusebius. But this time Eusebius needs to be supplemented by a degree of historical reconstruction, which, I admit, is less likely than the arguments I have been making thus far. If Eusebius's *In Praise of Constantine* was our main source for understanding the official Christian interpretation of imperial solar symbolism, the latter's *Life of Constantine*, written soon after the emperor's death,[84] provides a possible key to understanding the zodiacal symbolism.

The *Life of Constantine* fittingly concludes with a description of its subject matter's final days, death, and burial. In that context Eusebius reports on the construction of the so-called 'Church of the Apostles', which the emperor had himself designed as the mausoleum that would be his final resting place in the new imperial capital that he had recently founded in his own name. The building, situated on the crest of the hill between the Sea of Marmara and the Golden Horn, is inaccessible to archaeological investigation since it

---

81 Besides which, many of the earliest iconographical appearances of the cross show up in contexts of private devotion, not as symbols of imperial propaganda. Thus, besides the religious reasons, there were also political reasons for preferring the sun over the cross as a demonstration of loyalty to the empire. See Jensen, *The Cross*, pp. 71–73.

82 See Alföldi, *The Conversion of Constantine and Pagan Rome*, p. 58: 'The sun is no longer a god, but simply the glorious fame of the State'.

83 See note 42 above.

84 See Barnes, *Constantine and Eusebius*, pp. 265–71.

sits under the prominent Fatih Mosque, the first monumental construction in the Ottoman imperial architectural tradition. Thus, we must rely on literary sources, primarily Eusebius, to reconstruct the shape and programme of Constantine's last major building project.[85]

Eusebius states that Constantine had 'twelve tombs (θῆκαι) set up, like sacred pillars (στῆλαι ἱεραί), in honor and memory of the chorus (χορός) of the apostles, and put his own coffin (λάρναξ) in the middle with those of the Apostles ranged six on either side'.[86] There has been much debate about the precise meaning of these words — what the set-up looked like and what it was supposed to signify. It has been argued that the entire structure was round, based on the evidence of the mausoleum of Constantine's daughter, Constantina, that survives in Rome and is thought to have been modelled on Constantine's own mausoleum. Within the middle of that round structure it stands to reason that Constantine's coffin was located in the centre of a circle composed of two semicircles of six apostolic tombs on either side, that together formed a 'chorus' around him.[87]

Much has been written about the intention behind the layout of Constantine's mausoleum.[88] Did he wish to present himself as 'equal to the apostles' (ἰσαπόστολος), as the later Byzantine tradition would have it, or perhaps, in surrounding himself with the twelve apostles, he sought to cast himself as equal to Christ (ἰσόχριστος)? It is impossible to say.[89] What does seem likely, however, is that just as with his adherence to solar symbolism, also here Constantine chose an arrangement that was sufficiently multivalent to speak to more than one crowd.[90] Christians entering the mausoleum would naturally have seen, together with Eusebius, the twelve monuments surrounding the dead emperor as representations of the twelve apostles. They would then have to ask themselves the question we just mentioned, namely, whether Constantine was to be seen as a thirteenth apostle, or as equal to Christ.

Polytheists entering the mausoleum, on the other hand, might have seen something very different. It would appear to them as a manifestation of a motif they had become accustomed to during the reign of the Tetrarchs, wherein the emperor was portrayed as a supreme god, sometimes in the guise of Sol Invictus, surrounded by the traditional twelve gods of the Greco-Roman pantheon.[91] More specifically, when the role of the central figure was occupied by Sol,

---

85 For various proposals as to the precise location, see Asutay-Effenberger and Effenberger, *Die Porphyrsarkophage der oströmischen Kaiser*, pp. 134–45.

86 Eusebius, *Life of Constantine*, 4.60 (trans. p. 176; with several critical adaptations).

87 See Asutay-Effenberger and Effenberger, *Die Porphyrsarkophage*, pp. 52–59; Wallraff, 'Constantine's Death', pp. 124–25.

88 See Rebenich, 'Vom dreizehnten Gott zum dreizehnten Apostel'; Wallraff, 'Constantine's Death', p. 123 n. 5.

89 For a strong argument in favour of the *isochristos* theory, see Rebenich, 'Vom dreizehnten Gott', pp. 316–17.

90 See Leeb, *Konstantin und Christus*, p. 117; Wallraff, 'Constantine's Death', pp. 125–26.

91 Long, *Twelve Gods of Greece and Rome*, p. 316.

the surrounding twelve figures would sometimes be cast as the *zodia*. Martin Wallraff, in his discussion of the 'idiosyncratic configuration' of Constantine's mausoleum, summarizes the idea succinctly. He interprets the set-up as 'a reflection of the particular role of *Sol* in Constantine's religious world [...] A non-Christian visitor would not have seen Christ and the apostles, but the sun and the twelve *zodia* (months)'.[92]

If this theory of an intentionally multivalent arrangement is correct, what, we may ask, would Jewish spectators see when entering Constantine's mausoleum? Would they view things more along Christian lines or polytheistic ones? I think the picture that would make most sense for Jews to adopt in this situation would be a 'quasi-secularized' version of the polytheistic one. The Christian perspective, with its twelve apostles, is not one that Jews could identify with. The polytheistic version, if taken literally, would obviously have been no better. But if the polytheist spectator could see the twelve tombs surrounding the one coffin as representations of the sun and the zodiac, so could the Jewish spectator. The fact that his or her polytheistic neighbour understood these as images of divine beings, while the Jew understood them as images of imperial power, would not have bothered the Jew the way it would have done a generation or two earlier, before panegyrists close to the imperial court, and perhaps also the emperor himself,[93] had made a point of 'de-sacralizing' those heavenly bodies.

Thus, Eusebius and the scholarship on the mausoleum of Constantine jointly show a way for the maximalist interpretation of the mosaics of Jewish Byzantine Palestine to account not just for Helios, but also for the zodiac. According to this interpretation, the 'quasi-secularization' of Greco-Roman religious art triggered by the Constantinian shift did not just make representations of the sun and the zodiac possible in the synagogue; it also explains why it was that precisely those images were chosen. They were chosen due to their associations with the new line of Christian emperors that had begun with Constantine. Until now I have argued that these images were chosen as an expression of loyalty to the regime. If we wish to take the argument yet one step further than that, we may even speculate that these images were chosen as a token of identification with the new regime's monotheistic leanings and as a sign of gratitude for the new cultural possibilities it had opened, such as those embodied in the very mosaics themselves.

On the other hand, there is, as noted above, also a more conservative interpretive option, which asks less of our imaginations. We can view the Christian imperial context as no more than an enabler. It is not what gave the mosaics their positive content, their specific semiotic significance. It is what opened the possibility for the very usage of images of the sun and the

---

92 Wallraff, 'Constantine's Death', p. 126. See also Bardill, *Constantine, Divine Emperor*, p. 376.

93 See the 'monotheistic' prayer Eusebius, *Life of Constantine* 3.18–20, claims that Constantine taught his non-Christian soldiers to say on Sundays, with discussion in Lenski, *Constantine and the Cities*, p. 74.

zodiac within a Jewish ritual context, however their meaning may have been understood. The Christian imperial context did this by disassociating Helios, Sol Invictus and the *zodia* from their automatically polytheistic connotations. We can either apply this minimalist option to the entire cluster of synagogue mosaics, or we can further limit it to the earliest case of Hammat Tiberias.

Conclusion: Premises and Ramifications

Acceptance of the argument here presented — whether in its minimalist or maximalist forms — has ramifications on larger issues in our understanding of the study of Judaism in Late Antiquity. This is because the argument is predicated on two premises, neither of which is self-evident in current scholarship. Acceptance of the argument hinges on an acceptance of these premises, which, in turn, has ramifications on one's picture of Jewish life in Byzantine Palestine. The first premise is of a social-psychological nature; the second relates to theoretical-historical matters of classification and terminology. The confines of this essay do not allow me to go into either of these premises, and ensuing ramifications, in much detail. I offer just a thumbnail sketch of each.

The social-psychological premise of the argument presented here is that some late antique Jews could have had a positive outlook on some aspects of the Constantinian shift, which would have made them feel in some ways closer to the imperial regime and to surrounding society than they had been in the period of the High Empire. Only if we accept this possibility can we argue that it was the Christian interpretation of imperial iconography, hitherto off-limits due to its unambiguous associations with the imperial cult, that enabled Jews to bring that iconography into their synagogues.

Such an assumption goes against the grain of scholarly models that understand the Christianization of the Roman empire as a development that distanced Jews from their non-Jewish surroundings and put them more at variance with those surroundings than they had been before Christianization. Whether it was through persecution, de-legitimization, and marginalization that Jews were passively subjected to,[94] or through the more active strategies of polemics and appropriation that Jews are thought to have engaged in vis-à-vis their Christian neighbours and rulers,[95] one common scholarly picture paints

---

94 For examples of the persecution and discrimination models, see Fine, 'The Menorah and the Cross'; Kraemer, *The Mediterranean Diaspora*; for an example of the marginalization model, see Schwartz, 'Some Types of Jewish-Christian Interaction in Late Antiquity', pp. 209–10.

95 See Schwartz, 'Some Types', pp. 197–202, as well as many other recent studies. For an example of this line of interpretation within the context of our mosaics, see Talgam, 'The Zodiac and Helios'; Talgam, *Mosaics of Faith*, pp. 276–79. See further Milson, *Art and Architecture of the Synagogue in Late Antique Palestine*, p. 242, which explicitly casts 'the impact of Christian art and architecture on synagogues in Byzantine Palestine', documented throughout the book, as reflecting 'the underlying rivalry and competition between Jews and Christians' and as stemming from 'underlying antagonism'.

the Constantinian shift as a process that increasingly separated Jews from their social surroundings, and that, to put it quite simply, Jews were not happy about, even if they reformulated and consolidated their own identity in the process.[96] Unlike the second and third centuries when the Jews of the empire had been much more embedded within the ambient polytheistic society, the Constantinian shift, according to this model, ushered in a period of growing disengagement that isolated the Jews, that 'Judaized' them. Seth Schwartz succinctly summarized that understanding of the impact Christianization had on the Jews of Late Antiquity, as follows:[97] 'Partial compromise with paganism was the mark of a successful accommodationist; partial compromise with Christianity was the mark of a heretic'.

The argument presented here does not deny the validity of such models for the fifth and sixth centuries, but it is predicated on a reverse premise when it comes to the fourth century: the Constantinian shift opened new possibilities for Jews that they embraced, at least initially, with alacrity, and not as a means of resistance, appropriation, or defence. Thus, the Helios-and-zodiac mosaics — rather than being seen as a sign of 'Jewish resilience under Byzantine Christianity',[98] or as a cultural expression developed 'under Byzantium, both in the face of hostile Christianity and, perhaps ironically, stimulated by Christian artistic models'[99] — are seen as a sign of 'Jewish creativity and innovation',[100] facilitated, quite *un*-ironically, by Byzantine Christianity.

One possible ramification of this alternative view is that it would require us to nuance our chronological understanding of the effects of Christianization on the Jews.[101] Perhaps Jewish attitudes to Christianization shifted as the character of Christianization changed over time. Even if, as argued here, Jews accepted some of Constantine's new policies with excitement, as the policies changed under his fifth-century successors that excitement must have given way to resentment.

The second premise that is necessary for the argument of this essay has to do with a theoretical-historical matter of classification and terminology. The argument here is founded on the notion that Constantine and Eusebius

---

96 See, e.g., Boyarin, *Border Lines*, pp. 202–25, and especially p. 219 (following Jacob Neusner): 'rabbinic Judaism provided a winning set of responses to the Christian questions'.

97 Schwartz, 'Some Types', p. 210.

98 Levine, *Visual Judaism*, p. 336, in specific discussion of the Hammat mosaic.

99 Levine, *Visual Judaism*, p. 221, speaking of the Jewish art of the Byzantine-Christian period more generally.

100 Levine, *Visual Judaism*, p. 220.

101 The confines of this essay do not allow a discussion of whether its claim extends to rabbinic Jews. At the moment, I leave open the question of whether a shift can be determined in rabbinic attitudes to the empire, and indeed to Christianity, between the third, fourth, and fifth centuries. For a discussion of that question, see Schremer, 'The Christianization of the Roman Empire and Rabbinic Literature'. The question is complicated by the fact that, unless we date the redaction of the Palestinian Talmud to the final decades of the fourth century, at the very earliest (a disputed question in its own right [see Gray, *A Talmud in Exile*, p. 2]), most of our Palestinian rabbinic sources are either from the third, or from the fifth and sixth centuries. The key period in our discussion is rabbinically underrepresented.

had to some degree 'secularized' or 'de-sacralized' the imperial iconography of the sun. While the distinction between the realms of the 'secular' and the 'religious' is often accepted by art historians and historians of late antique Judaism,[102] many anthropologists and religious studies scholars have challenged the historical appropriateness of such distinctions in the late ancient context.[103] In their understanding, the very invention of 'the secular', and thus also its functional opposite, 'religion', are developments of the modern period. Such scholars would view any historical explanation that is founded on notions of 'secularization', or even 'quasi-secularization', as completely anachronistic.

On the other hand, there are those who relocate the very invention of 'the secular', and its corollary 'religion', away from the modern period, and re-situate it precisely in our period, as a Christian development that rabbinic Jews resisted.[104] According to this argument, it was fourth- and fifth-century Christian bishops, beginning as early as none other than Eusebius, who invented 'religion' as a domain that is separate from other areas of life and serves as a mode of self-definition that is independent of other aspects of cultural identity, such as kinship, language, and land.[105] This Christian invention of the category of 'religion', allowed, in turn, for there to be multiple members in it: Christianity, Judaism, Hellenism. This classification was adopted by non-Christians, but, so the argument goes, just by Hellenists, such as Julian the Emperor, and *not* by the Jews, who resisted the category of 'religion', and thus also self-identification with the Christian word used to refer to their 'religion', namely 'Judaism'. Jews would only come to accept these as terms relevant to their own self-understanding in the modern period.[106]

Inasmuch as this essay is concerned with an interpretation of visual artefacts, not verbal texts, it does not intervene directly in the question of terminology and linguistic self-definition. Yet, insofar as it relies on the premise that the key to interpreting those visual artefacts is a postulated Jewish reception of

---

102 For an art historical example of the secular-religious distinction applied to the Helios-and-zodiac motif, see Stewart, 'The Bet Alpha Synagogue', p. 79. See also, by comparison, Belayche, *Iudaea-Palaestina*, pp. 308–09 (with reference to the public clock in Gaza in the early sixth century): 'It perpetuated Hellenism, which Christianity had adopted by separating it from its religious component, in the guise of the two victorious/*invicti* pagan gods, Sol-Helios and Hercules'. For an example from the study of Jewish history, see Goodman, 'The Roman State', pp. 138–39. The distinction, discussed above, between 'decorative' and 'religious' art is parallel to the 'secular-religious' distinction.

103 The literature is rich. See, e.g., Asad, *Formations of the Secular*; Nongbri, *Before Religion*. For a recent challenge of this dichotomy in the specifically Christian context of Late Antiquity, see Elm, 'Julian the Emperor on Statues (of Himself)', pp. 132–34 and 148. On the other hand, see Stern, 'Images in Late Antique Palestine', pp. 120–29, which shows that polytheistic Romans made a clear distinction between sacred and profane, consecrated and decorative, images.

104 Elm, 'Orthodoxy and the True Philosophical Life: Julian and Gregory of Nazianzus', pp. 69–85; Boyarin, *Border Lines*, pp. 202–20; Boyarin, 'Nominalist "Judaism" and the Invention of Religion'.

105 Boyarin, 'Nominalist "Judaism"', pp. 28–29.

106 Boyarin, 'Nominalist "Judaism"', pp. 25–26.

the new Christian isolation of a 'de-sacralized' realm, it accepts the possibility that at some level certain Jews participated in the opportunities that this new Christian discourse had created. In contradistinction to their polytheistic predecessors, Constantine and his immediate successors sought to project a form of public imperial ideology that different religious groups in the empire could endorse, even if they did not share the emperor's personal religious ideology. The prototypical mosaic of Hammat Tiberias, and possibly even its later imitations, can be viewed as expressions of allegiance to this new accommodating public ideology.

Like the child in the Hans Christian Andersen tale, I have tried to point out something that others have seen differently. Unless the Hammat mosaic happened to have been laid during the short nineteen months that Julian was in power, its context is an imperial Christian one. That is the historical setting that has guided my analysis. Outwardly, the Christian emperor wears the same solar guise of Sol Invictus that his polytheistic predecessors wore, but it is really a new set of clothes, as it is denuded of blatant cultic significance. Seeing the fourth-century emperor's new clothes for what they make him — an emperor who is *compared to* the sun, but *not worshipped as* the sun — paves the way to solving the Helios enigma in the synagogues of Byzantine Palestine.

Unlike the usual models in the study of Jewish-Christian relations in Late Antiquity, the suggestion made here does not view the Christian impact on Judaism (in this case) as a matter of direct influence, appropriation, or polemical response. Rather, what we have here is an indirect effect. Imperially backed Christianity's reconfiguration of its own attitude to the state and the latter's iconographical manifestations created a new space — one that Jews began to feel comfortable in — that had not existed before: a 'quasi-secular' sphere of public governance and culture[107] not inextricably tied to religious identity. Subsequent developments in Byzantine culture would eventually erode that initial reconfiguration. The more Christianized the empire became, the more the 'quasi-secular' sphere was diminished, until it shrank into oblivion.[108] But the prototypical Hammat Tiberias mosaic offers us a vista onto the new reality initially created by the Constantinian shift. And the subsequent synagogue mosaics that followed suit possibly give us a glimpse of the wishful attempts to hold on to that reality even as it was rapidly disappearing.[109]

---

107 The degree to which we can speak of a 'secular' realm of culture in the fourth century is a matter of debate among scholars of Christian Late Antiquity. See, on the one side, Markus, *The End of Ancient Christianity*, pp. 16–17 and 107–21, and Salzman, *On Roman Time*, pp. 56–60 and 196–99, and, on the other side, Elm, *Sons of Hellenism*, p. 464; p. 486.

108 Nevertheless, Jews continued to express their loyalty to Christian rulers throughout the Middle Ages, both in the eastern and western Mediterranean. See Decter, *Dominion Built of Praise*, pp. 243–76.

109 For one interesting study of the disappearance of the distinction between the 'civil' and 'clerical' realms in sixth-century Byzantine imperial symbolism, see Irshai, 'Uniformity and Diversity in the Early Church'.

Bibliography

Primary Sources

Ambrose, *De Obitu Valentiniani*, ed. by Otto Faller, Corpus Scriptorum Ecclesiasticorum Latinorum, 73: Sancti Ambrosii opera 7 (Vienna: Hoelder-Pilcher-Tempsky, 1955), pp. 327–67

——, *On the Death of Valentinian*, trans. by Roy J. Deferrari, in *Funeral Orations by Saint Gregory of Nazianzen and Saint Ambrose*, trans. by Leo P. McCauley and others (New York: Fathers of the Church, 1953), pp. 263–99

Corippus, Flavius Cresconius, *In Laudem Iustini Augusti Minoris, Libri IV*, ed. and trans. by Averil Cameron (London: Athlone, 1976)

Eusebius, *Eusebius: Life of Constantine: Introduction, Translation, and Commentary*, trans. by Averil Cameron and Stuart G. Hall, Clarendon Ancient History Series (Oxford: Clarendon Press, 1999)

——, *Oratio de Laudibus Constantini*, ed. by Ivar A. Heikel, Die griechischen christlichen Schriftsteller, 7, Eusebius 1 (Leipzig: J. C. Hinrichs, 1902), pp. 223–59

——, *In Praise of Constantine: A Historical Study and New Translation of Eusebius' Tricennial Orations*, trans. by H. A. Drake (Berkeley: University of California Press, 1976), pp. 83–127

——, *Über das Leben des Kaisers Konstantins*, ed. by Friedhelm Winkelmann, Die griechischen christlichen Schriftsteller, 7, Eusebius 1, rev. edn (Berlin: de Gruyter, 1991)

In Praise of Later Roman Emperors: The 'Panegyrici Latini': Introduction, Translation and Historical Commentary, ed. by R. A. B. Mynors, C. E. V. Nixon and B. Saylor Rodgers (Berkeley: University of California Press, 1994)

Secondary Studies

Alföldi, Andrew, *The Conversion of Constantine and Pagan Rome*, trans. by Harold Mattingly (Oxford: Clarendon Press, 1948)

Asad, Talal, *Formations of the Secular: Christianity, Islam, Modernity*, Cultural Memory in the Present (Stanford: Stanford University Press, 2003)

Asutay-Effenberger, Neslihan, and Arne Effenberger, *Die Porphyrsarkophage der oströmischen Kaiser*, Spätantike, frühes Christentum, Byzanz. Reihe B, Studien und Perspektiven, 15 (Wiesbaden: Reichert, 2006)

Bardill, Jonathan, *Constantine, Divine Emperor of the Christian Golden Age* (Cambridge: Cambridge University Press, 2012)

Barnes, Timothy D., *Constantine and Eusebius* (Cambridge, MA: Harvard University Press, 1981)

——, *Constantine: Dynasty, Religion and Power in the Later Roman Empire* (Chichester: Wiley, 2011)

Baumgarten, Joseph M., 'Art in the Synagogue – Some Talmudic Views', *Judaism*, 19 (1970), 196–206

Belayche, Nicole, '"Deus deum … summorum maximus" (Apuleius): Ritual Expressions of Distinction in the Divine World in the Imperial Period', in *One God: Pagan Monotheism in the Roman Empire*, ed. by S. Mitchell and P. Van Nuffelen (Cambridge: Cambridge University Press, 2010), pp. 141–66

——, *Iudaea-Palaestina: The Pagan Cults in Roman Palestine (Second to Fourth Century)*, Religion der römischen Provinzen, 1 (Tübingen: Mohr Siebeck, 2001)

Berrens, Stephan, *Sonnenkult und Kaisertum von den Severern bis zu Constantin I (197–337 n. Chr.)*, Historia – Einzelschriften, 185 (Stuttgart: Franz Steiner, 2014)

Bonnie, Rick, 'The Helios-and-Zodiac Motif in Late Antique Synagogues', in *Magic in the Ancient Eastern Mediterranean*, ed. by N. Nikki and K. Valkama, Mundus Orientis: Studies in Near Eastern Cultures, 3 (Göttingen: Vandenhoeck & Ruprecht, 2021), pp. 299–311

Bowersock, G. W., 'The Imperial Cult: Perceptions and Persistence', in *Jewish and Christian Self-Definition: Volume III*, ed. by B. F. Meyer and E. P. Sanders (Philadelphia: Fortress, 1982), pp. 171–82

Boyarin, Daniel, *Border Lines: The Partition of Judaeo-Christianity*, Divinations: Rereading Late Ancient Religion (Philadelphia: University of Pennsylvania Press, 2006)

——, 'Nominalist "Judaism" and the Invention of Religion', in *Religion, Theory, Critique: Classic and Contemporary Approaches and Methodologies*, ed. by R. King (New York: Columbia University Press, 2017), pp. 23–39

Browning, Robert, *The Emperor Julian* (Berkeley: University of California Press, 1976)

Cameron, Averil, 'Corippus' Poem on Justin II: A Terminus of Antique Art?', *Annali della Scuola Superiore di Pisa. Classe di Lettere e Filosofia*, Serie III, 5 (1975), 129–65

——, 'Herrscherkult III. Alkirche ab Konstantin', *Theologische Realenzyklopädie*, 15 (1986), 253–55

——, *The Last Pagans of Rome* (Oxford: Oxford University Press, 2010)

Chayes, Julie, 'Blavatsky and Monotheism: Towards the Historicisation of a Critical Category', *Journal of Religion in Europe*, 9 (2016), 247–55

Cohen, Jeremy, 'Roman Imperial Policy toward the Jews from Constantine until the End of the Palestinian Patriarchate', *Byzantine Studies*, 3 (1976), 1–29

Curran, John, 'Constantine and the Ancient Cults of Rome: The Legal Evidence', *Greece and Rome*, 43 (1996), 68–80

Decter, Jonathan, *Dominion Built of Praise: Panegyric and Legitimacy among Jews in the Medieval Mediterranean*, Jewish Culture and Contexts (Philadelphia: University of Pennsylvania Press, 2018)

Deines, Roland, 'God's Revelation through Torah, Creation and History: Interpreting the Zodiac Mosaics in Synagogues', in *Jewish Art in its Late Antique Context*, ed. by U. Leibner and C. Hezser, Texts and Studies in Ancient Judaism, 163 (Tübingen: Mohr Siebeck, 2016), pp. 155–86

Doerries, Hermann, *Constantine the Great*, trans. by Roland H. Bainton (New York: Harper Torchbooks, 1972)

Dothan, Moshe, *Hammath Tiberias* (Jerusalem: Israel Exploration Society, 1983)

——, 'The Image of Sol Invictus in the Mosaic at Hammath Tiberias', in *All the Land of Naphtali*, ed. by H. Z. Hirschberg and Y. Aviram (Jerusalem: Israel Exploration Society, 1968), pp. 130–34 (In Hebrew)

——, 'The Representation of Helios in the Mosaic of Hammath-Tiberias', in *Atti del convegno internazionale sul tema: Tardo antico e alto medioevo – La forma artistica nel passaggio dall'antichità al medioevo* (Rome: Accademia nazionale dei Lincei, 1968), pp. 99–104

——, 'The Synagogues at Hammath-Tiberias', *Qadmoniot*, 1 (1968), 116–23 (in Hebrew)

Edwards, Mark, 'The Beginnings of Christianization', in *The Cambridge Companion to the Age of Constantine*, ed. by N. Lenski (Cambridge: Cambridge University Press, 2006), pp. 137–58

Elm, Susanna, 'Julian the Emperor on Statues (of Himself)', in *Classical Philology and Theology: Entanglement, Disavowal, and the Godlike Scholar*, ed. by Catherine Conybeare and Simon Goldhill (Cambridge: Cambridge University Press, 2020), pp. 126–48

——, 'Orthodoxy and the True Philosophical Life: Julian and Gregory of Nazianzus', *Studia Patristica*, 37 (2001), 69–85

——, *Sons of Hellenism, Fathers of the Church: Emperor Julian, Gregory of Nazianzus, and the Vision of Rome*, Transformations of the Classical Heritage, 49 (Berkeley: University of California Press, 2012)

Elsner, Jaś, 'Perspectives in Art', in *The Cambridge Companion to the Age of Constantine*, ed. by N. Lenski (Cambridge: Cambridge University Press, 2006), pp. 255–77

Englard, Yaffa, 'Mosaics as Midrash: The Zodiacs of the Ancient Synagogues and the Conflict between Judaism and Christianity', *Review of Rabbinic Judaism*, 6 (2004), 189–214

Fauth, Wolfgang, *Helios Megistos: Zur synkretistischen Theologie Theologie der Spätantike*, Religions in the Graeco-Roman World, 125 (Leiden: Brill, 1995)

Fine, Steven, 'The Jewish Helios: A Modest Proposal Regarding the Sun God and the Zodiac on Late Antique Synagogue Mosaics', in *Art, History and the Historiography of Judaism in Roman Antiquity*, ed. by S. Fine (Leiden: Brill, 2014), pp. 161–80

——, 'The Menorah and the Cross: Historiographic Reflections on a Recent Discovery from Laodicea on the Lycus', in *Art, History and the Historiography of Judaism in Roman Antiquity*, ed. by S. Fine (Leiden: Brill, 2014) pp. 195–214

Frakes, Robert M., 'The Dynasty of Constantine down to 363', in *The Cambridge Companion to the Age of Constantine*, ed. by N. Lenski (Cambridge: Cambridge University Press, 2006), pp. 91–107

Friedheim, Emmanuel, 'Sol Invictus in the Severus Synagogue at Hammath Tiberias, the Rabbis, and Jewish Society: A Different Approach', *Review of Rabbinic Judaism*, 12 (2009), 89–128

Goodman, Martin, 'The Jewish Image of God in Late Antiquity', in *Jewish Culture and Society under the Christian Roman Empire*, ed. by R. Kalmin and S. Schwartz (Leuven: Peeters, 2003), pp. 133–45

——, 'The Roman State and the Jewish Patriarch in the Third Century', in *The Galilee in Late Antiquity*, ed. by L. I. Levine (New York: Jewish Theological Seminary of America, 1992), pp. 127–39

Gray, Alyssa M., *A Talmud in Exile: The Influence of Yerushalmi Avodah Zarah on the Formation of the Bavli* (Providence: Brown Judaic Studies, 2020)

Hachlili, Rachel, *Ancient Mosaic Pavements: Themes, Issues, and Trends* (Leiden: Brill, 2009)

——, *Ancient Synagogues - Archaeology and Art: New Discoveries and Current Research*, Handbook of Oriental Studies, The Near and Middle East, 105 (Leiden: Brill, 2013)

Herman, Geoffrey, '"In Honor of the House of Caesar": Attitudes to the Kingdom in the Aggada of the Babylonian Talmud and Other Sassanian Sources', in *The Aggada of the Bavli and its Cultural World*, ed. by G. Herman and J. L. Rubenstein (Providence: Brown Judaic Studies, 2018), pp. 103–24

Hezser, Catherine, '"For the Lord God is a Sun and a Shield" (Ps. 84:12): Sun Symbolism in Hellenistic Jewish Literature and in Amoraic Midrashim', in *Jewish Art in its Late Antique Context*, ed. by U. Leibner and C. Hezser, Texts and Studies in Ancient Judaism, 163 (Tübingen: Mohr Siebeck, 2016), pp. 213–36

Humphries, Mark, 'Savage Humour: Christian Anti-panegyric in Hilary of Poitiers' *Against Constantius*', in *The Propaganda of Power: The Role of Panegyric in Late Antiquity*, ed. by M. Whitby, Mnemosyne Supplements, 183 (Leiden: Brill, 1998), pp. 199–223

Irshai, Oded, 'Confronting a Christian Empire', in *The Jews of Byzantium: Dialectics of Minority and Majority Cultures*, ed. by R. Bonfil, O. Irshai, G. G. Stroumsa, and R. Talgam (Leiden: Brill, 2011), pp. 17–64

——, 'Constantine and the Jews: The Prohibition against Entering Jerusalem – Historiography and Hagiography', *Zion*, 60 (1995), 129–78 (in Hebrew)

——, 'The Dark Side of the Moon: The Political History and Image of Eusebius of Caesarea', *Cathedra*, 122 (2007), 63–97 (in Hebrew)

——, 'Fourth Century Christian Palestinian Politics: A Glimpse at Eusebius of Caesarea's Local Political Career and its *Nachleben* in Christian Memory', in *Reconsidering Eusebius: Collected Papers on Literary, Historical, and Theological Issues*, ed. by S. Inowlocki and C. Zamagni, Vigiliae Christianae Supplements, 107 (Leiden: Brill, 2011), pp. 25–38

——, 'The Priesthood in Jewish Society of Late Antiquity', in *Continuity and Renewal: Jews and Judaism in Byzantine-Christian Palestine*, ed. by Lee I. Levine (Jerusalem: Yad Ben-Zvi, 2004), pp. 67–106 (in Hebrew)

——, 'Uniformity and Diversity in the Early Church – The Date of Easter, the Jews, and Imperial Symbolism in the Sixth Century and Beyond', in *Between Personal and Institutional Religion: Self, Doctrine, and Practice in Late Antique Eastern Christianity*, ed. by B. Bitton-Ashkelony and L. Perrone (Turnhout: Brepols, 2013), pp. 295–309

Jensen, Robin M., *The Cross: History, Art, and Controversy* (Cambridge, MA: Harvard University Press, 2017)

Kraemer, Ross Shepard, *The Mediterranean Diaspora in Late Antiquity: What Christianity Cost the Jews* (Oxford: Oxford University Press, 2020)

Laderman, Shulamit, *Jewish Art in Late Antiquity: The State of Research in Ancient Jewish Art*, Religion and the Arts (Leiden: Brill, 2022)

Lee, A. D., 'Traditional Religions', in *The Cambridge Companion to the Age of Constantine*, ed. by N. Lenski (Cambridge: Cambridge University Press, 2006), pp. 159–79

Leeb, Rudolf, *Konstantin und Christus. Die Verchristlichung der imperialen Repräsentation unter Konstantin dem Grossen als Spiegel seiner Kirchenpolitik und seines Selbstverständnisses als christlicher Kaiser* (Berlin: de Gruyter, 1992)

Leibner, Uzi, 'Khirbet Wadi Hammam: A Village and Synagogue from the Roman Period in Galilee', *Qadmoniyot*, 139 (2010), 30–40 (in Hebrew)

Lenski, Noel, *Constantine and the Cities* (Philadelphia: University of Pennsylvania Press, 2016)

——, *Failure of Empire: Valens and the Roman State in the Fourth Century A.D.* (Berkeley: University of California Press, 2002)

——, 'Introduction', in *The Cambridge Companion to the Age of Constantine*, ed. by N. Lenski (Cambridge: Cambridge University Press, 2006), pp. 1–13

Levine, Lee I., 'The Status of the Patriarch in the Third and Fourth Centuries', *Journal of Jewish Studies*, 47 (1996), 1–32

——, *Visual Judaism in Late Antiquity: Historical Contexts of Jewish Art* (New Haven: Yale University Press, 2012)

——, 'Why did Jewish Art Flourish in Late Antiquity', in *Jewish Art in its Late Antique Context*, ed. by U. Leibner and C. Hezser (Tübingen: Mohr Siebeck, 2016), pp. 49–74

Liebeschuetz, J. H. W. G., *Continuity and Change in Roman Religion* (Oxford: Clarendon Press, 1979)

Lifshitz, B., 'L'ancienne synagogue de Tibériade, sa mosaïque et ses inscriptions', *Journal for the Study of Judaism*, 4 (1973), 43–55

Linder, Amnon, *The Jews in Roman Imperial Legislation* (Jerusalem: Israel Academy of Sciences and Humanities, 1987)

Lippold, Adolf, 'The Ideal Ruler and the Attachment to Tradition in Pacatus' Panegyric', in *Latin Panegyrics*, ed. by R. Rees, Oxford Readings in Classical Studies (Oxford: Oxford University Press, 2012), pp. 360–86

Long, Charlotte R., *Twelve Gods of Greece and Rome*, Études préliminaires aux religions orientales dans l'Empire romain, 107 (Leiden: Brill, 1987)

Magness, Jodi, *The Archaeology of the Holy Land: From the Destruction of Solomon's Temple to the Muslim Conquest* (Cambridge: Cambridge University Press, 2012)

——, 'Heaven on Earth: Helios and the Zodiac Cycle in Ancient Palestinian Synagogues', *Dumbarton Oaks Papers*, 59 (2005), 1–52

Magness, Jodi, Shua Kisilevitz, Matthew Grey, Dennis Mizzi, Daniel Schindler, Martin Wells, Karen Britt, Ra'anan Boustan, Shana O'Connell, Emily Hubbard, Jessie George, Jennifer Ramsay, Elisabetta Boaretto, and Michael Chazan, 'The Huqoq Excavation Project: 2014–2017 Interim Report', *Bulletin of the American Schools of Oriental Research*, 380 (2018), 61–131

Markus, Robert, *The End of Ancient Christianity* (Cambridge: Cambridge University Press, 1990)

Miller, Stuart S., '"Epigraphical Rabbis", Helios and Psalm 19: Were the Synagogues of Archaeology and the Synagogues of the Sages One and the Same?' *Jewish Quarterly Review*, 94 (2004), 27–76

Milson, David W., *Art and Architecture of the Synagogue in Late Antique Palestine: In the Shadow of the Church*, Ancient Judaism and Early Christianity, 65 (Leiden: Brill, 2007)

Mynors, R. A. B., C. E. V. Nixon, and Barbara Saylor Rodgers, *In Praise of Later Roman Emperors: The Panegyrici Latini: Introduction, Translation and Historical Commentary*, The Transformations of the Classical Heritage, 21 (Berkeley: University of California Press, 1994)

Nemo-Pekelman, Capucine, *Rome et ses citoyens juifs (IVᵉ–Vᵉ siècles)*, Bibliothèque d'études juives, 39 (Paris: Honoré Champion, 2010)

Ness, Lester, 'The Stars in their Courses Fought against Sisera: Astrology and Jewish Society in the Later Roman Empire', in *The Light of Discovery: Studies in Honor of Edwin M. Yamauchi*, ed. by J. D. Wineland (Eugene: Pickwick, 2007), pp. 149–66

Nongbri, Brent, *Before Religion: A History of a Modern Concept* (New Haven: Yale University Press, 2013)

Noy, David, '"A Sight Unfit to See": Jewish Reactions to the Roman Imperial Cult', *Classics Ireland*, 8 (2001), 68–83

Rebenich, Stefan, 'Vom dreizehnten Gott zum dreizehnten Apostel? Der tote Kaiser in der Spätantike', *Zeitschrift für antikes Christentum*, 4 (2000), 300–24

Ross, Alan J., 'The Constantinians' Return to the West: Julian's Depiction of Constantius II in *Oration 1*', in *Imagining Emperors in the Later Roman Empire*, ed. by D. P. W. Burgersdijk and A. J. Ross (Leiden: Brill, 2018), pp. 183–203

Salway, B., 'Constantine Augoustos (not Sebastos)', in *Wolf Liebeschuetz Reflected: Essays Presented by Colleagues, Friends and Pupils*, ed. by J. F. Drinkwater and B. Salway (London: Institute of Classical Studies, 2007), pp. 37–50

Salzman, Michelle Renee, *On Roman Time: The Codex-Calendar of 354 and the Rhythms of Urban Life in Late Antiquity*, Transformations of the Classical Heritage, 17 (Berkeley: University of California Press, 1991)

——, 'Pagans and Christians', in *The Oxford Handbook of Early Christian Studies*, ed. by S. A. Harvey and D. G. Hunter (Oxford: Oxford University Press, 2008), pp. 186–98

Schremer, Adiel, 'The Christianization of the Roman Empire and Rabbinic Literature', in *Jewish Identities in Antiquity: Studies in Memory of Menahem Stern*, ed. by L. I. Levine and D. R. Schwartz (Tübingen: Mohr Siebeck, 2009), pp. 349–66

Schwartz, Seth, *Imperialism and Jewish Society, 200 BCE to 640 CE* (Princeton: Princeton University Press, 2001)

——, 'Some Types of Jewish-Christian Interaction in Late Antiquity', in *Jewish Culture and Society under the Christian Roman Empire*, ed. by R. Kalmin and S. Schwartz, Interdisciplinary Studies in Ancient Culture and Religion, 3 (Leuven: Peeters, 2003), pp. 197–210

Smith, Rowland, *Julian's Gods: Religion and Philosophy in the Thought and Action of Julian the Apostate* (London: Routledge, 1995)

Stepansky, Yosef, 'Archeological Discoveries in Mughar', *Cathedra*, 97 (2000), 169–71 (in Hebrew)

Stewart, Peter, 'The Bet Alpha Synagogue Mosaic in Late Antique Provincialism', in *Jewish Art in its Late Antique Context*, ed. by U. Leibner and C. Hezser, Texts and Studies in Ancient Judaism, 163 (Tübingen: Mohr Siebeck, 2016), pp. 75–95

Stern, Sacha, 'Images in Late Antique Palestine: Jewish and Graeco-Roman Views', in *The Image and its Prohibition in Jewish Antiquity*, ed. by Sarah Pearce (Oxford: Journal of Jewish Studies, 2013), pp. 110–29

Sukenik, Eleazar Lipa, *The Ancient Synagogue of Beth Alpha: An Account of the Excavations Conducted on Behalf of the Hebrew University, Jerusalem*, trans. by E. L. Sukenik (Jerusalem: Oxford University Press, 1932)

Talgam, Rina, 'Between Christians and Jews: The Penetration of Christianity into Eastern Galilee in Late Antiquity', in *Between Sea and Desert: On Kings, Nomads, Cities and Monks; Essays in Honor of Joseph Patrich*, ed. by O. Peleg-Barkat, J. Ashkenazi, U. Leibner, M. Aviam and R. Talgam (Tzemah: Kinneret College, 2019), pp. *31–*41 (in Hebrew)

——, *Mosaics of Faith: Floors of Pagans, Jews, Samaritans, Christians, and Muslims in the Holy Land* (Jerusalem: Yad Ben Zvi, 2014)

——, 'Mosaic Floors in Tiberias', in *Tiberias from its Foundation to the Muslim Conquest*, ed. by Y. Hirschfeld (Jerusalem: Ben Zvi, 1988), pp. 123–32 (in Hebrew)

——, 'Similarities and Differences between Synagogues and Church Mosaics in Palestine during the Byzantine and Umayyad Periods', in *From Dura to Sepphoris: Studies in Jewish Art and Society in Late Antiquity*, ed. by L. I. Levine and Z. Weiss (New York: The Jewish Museum, 2000), pp. 93–110

——, 'The Zodiac and Helios in the Synagogue: Between Paganism and Christianity', in *'Follow the Wise': Studies in Jewish History and Culture in Honor of Lee I. Levine*, ed. by Z. Weiss, O. Irshai, J. Magness, and S. Schwartz (Winona Lake: Eisenbrauns, 2010), pp. *63–*80 (in Hebrew)

Tantillo, Ignazio, 'Attributi solari della figura imperiale in Eusebio di Cesarea', *Mediterraneo Antico*, 6 (2003), 41–59

Turcan, Robert, 'Images solaires dans le *Panégyrique* VI', in *Hommages à Jean Bayet*, ed. by M. Renard and R. Schilling (Bruxelles-Berchem: Latomus, Revue d'études latines, 1964), pp. 697–706

Ulrich, Jörg, *Euseb von Caesarea und die Juden*, Patristische Texte und Studien, 49 (Berlin: de Gruyter, 1999)

Urbach, E. E., 'The Rabbinical Laws of Idolatry in the Second and Third Centuries in the Light of Archaeological and Historical Facts', *Israel Exploration Journal*, 9 (1959), 229–45

van Nuffelen, Peter, 'Pagan Monotheism as a Religious Phenomenon', in *One God. Pagan Monotheism in the Roman Empire*, ed. by S. Mitchell and P. van Nuffelen (Cambridge: Cambridge University Press, 2010), pp. 16–33

Wallraff, Martin, 'Constantine's Death. Solar and Christian Elements of Imperial Propaganda', in *Costantino il Grande: Alle radici dell'Europa*, ed. by E. dal Covolo and G. S. Gasparro (Vatican City: Libreria Editrice Vaticana, 2014), pp. 121–38

Weiss, Ze'ev, 'Between Rome and Byzantium: Pagan Motifs in Synagogue Art and their Place in the Judaeo-Christian Controversy', in *Jewish Identities in Antiquity: Studies in Memory of Menahem Stern*, ed. by L. I. Levine and D. R. Schwartz (Tübingen: Mohr Siebeck, 2009), pp. 367–90

Werlin, Steven H., *Ancient Synagogues of Southern Palestine, 300–800 CE: Living on the Edge*, Brill Reference Library of Judaism, 47 (Leiden: Brill, 2015)

NOA YUVAL-HACHAM

Between Heaven and Earth

The Hand of God in Ancient Jewish Visuality

Numerous biblical verses describe God as having a human body and human qualities: of all the bodily organs referenced, the hand of God is most prevalent. The third-century CE wall paintings that adorned the ancient synagogue at Dura Europos in eastern Syria include several depictions of an independent hand stretching out from the Heavens, usually downwards towards Earth. The synagogue paintings that encompass all four walls of the synagogue, cover an impressive range of biblical themes. Five of them — the sacrifice of Isaac, the Exodus, Moses and the burning bush, Elijah reviving the son of the widow, and Ezekiel's vision of the dry bones — incorporate a hand that functions as an independent entity.[1] A similar hand recurs only once in ancient Jewish art: in the mosaic carpet decorating the prayer hall of the sixth-century synagogue at Beit Alpha. In the depiction of the sacrifice of Isaac that adorns the carpet's northern panel, a hand emerges from a dark circle that emits seven rays of light and extends towards Abraham who is holding the knife. These visual depictions and the biblical metaphor of the hand of God are widely regarded as being closely intertwined.[2]

In this essay I would like to re-examine the image of the hand of God in ancient Jewish art,[3] while shining a spotlight on the Exodus panel in the

---

1 Four of the five depictions are located on the synagogue's western wall facing Jerusalem, a location that attests the importance and centrality of these panels in the decorative programme of the synagogue. The depiction of the sacrifice of Isaac adorns the upper section of the Torah niche at the centre of the western wall, and the depictions of Moses and the burning bush, the Exodus and Elijah are scattered across the wall. The long panel representing the vision of the dry bones is located in the lower section of the northern wall and includes no fewer than five Divine hands engaged in fascinating conversation with the prophet. See Kraeling, *The Synagogue*, pl. 51, 76, 63, 69–71, 52–53.
2 Kraeling, *The Synagogue*, p. 83; Sukenik, *Ancient Synagogue of Beth Alpha*, pp. 40–42, fig. 19.
3 For previous and significant discussions on this issue see Hachlili, *Ancient Jewish Art*, pp. 144–46; Revel-Neher, 'Seeing the Voice', pp. 8–16; Lander, 'Revealing and Concealing God'.

> **Noa Yuval-Hacham**, PhD from the Hebrew University of Jerusalem in 2011, is Dean of the Schechter Institute of Jewish Studies, where she is a lecturer in the Jerusalem and Land of Israel studies and Judaism and the Arts tracks.

Essays on Jews and Christians in Late Antiquity in Honour of Oded Irshai, ed. by Brouria Bitton-Ashkelony and Martin Goodman, CELAMA 40 (Turnhout: Brepols, 2023), pp. 55–74
BREPOLS ❧ PUBLISHERS   10.1484/M.CELAMA-EB.5.132483

synagogue of Dura Europos, which contains an extraordinary and thought-provoking portrayal of the hand(s) of God (Fig. 2.1). I will attempt to trace the roots and sources of this image within its physical and cultural breeding ground, and discern its general meaning and significance in Jewish art and in the panel specifically. In addition, the affinity between the Dura Europos panel and other late antique Exodus depictions, in Jewish and Christian art, particularly in the Syria-Palestine region, will be examined. The conspicuity of the hand of God at Dura Europos, and its contrasting absence from Byzantine synagogues — the singular case of Beit Alpha notwithstanding — shroud this image with a measure of ambiguity, an issue that will also be examined below. The discussion will alternate between two perspectives: broad analysis of the overall image and more focused scrutiny of the Exodus panel — two complementary and mutually enhancing viewpoints.

The Hand of God in Roman Art in the Area of Syria-Palestine

The appearance of the hand of God in the third-century synagogue of Dura Europos points to Roman art in Syria in the first centuries as a possible matrix and source of inspiration. Full-body anthropomorphic representations of local deities in paintings, reliefs, and three-dimensional sculpture were plethoric in the art of this region throughout this period. At the same time, carved stone items containing depictions of a human hand grasping some sort of element — understood as abstract representations of a Divine power or entity — were discovered at several sites including Dura Europos, some of which will be described.[4] A fragment of a carved stone slab, upon which a right hand is depicted facing downwards from above was discovered in a residential house in Dura Europos. The hand is closed, and its fingers grasp a bundle of lightning crowned by what appears to be flames. The lightning depiction leads to the interpretation of this image as Hadad, the Semitic storm god whose identifying attribute is lightning, while the hand articulates the deity's power and presence. Susan Downey assumes that this slab was mounted on the house's walls as a defensive element that protected the house and its inhabitants from the evil eye.[5] A limestone altar was uncovered at the

---

4 This might be echoed in *Mishnah Avodah Zarah* 3, 2: 'In the case of one who finds unidentifiable fragments of statues, these are permitted, i.e., one may derive benefit from them. If one found an object in the figure of a hand or in the figure of a foot, these are forbidden, as objects like those are worshipped'. The Mishnah permits deriving benefit from fragments of statues, however, 'in the figure of a hand or in the figure of a foot' (תבנית יד או תבנית רגל) i.e., independent images of hands or feet are prohibited since these usually serve as cultic objects. The Mishnah uses the word 'figure' (תבנית) that is generally interpreted as a three-dimensional object, yet it is not unimaginable that the reliefs that will be discussed below, of equally pagan nature, might also be included in the category of a 'figure of a hand'.
5 Downey, *Stone and Plaster*, pp. 146–47; Moon, 'Nudity and Narrative', p. 648.

Temple of the Standards in the city of Palmyra: a right arm that includes a hand and part of a forearm encased in a sleeve is carved on its façade. The arm emerges from the right and holds a bundle of lightning. Inscribed on the carved cornice at the top of the altar is a dedicatory inscription to an anonymous god who delivered his people in the year 214 (Fig. 2.2).[6] A stone slab from Palmyra depicts a similar divine arm that includes part of a forearm encased in a lavish garment: here, however, the hand clutches three sheaves of grain. The dedicatory inscription at the top of the slab notes its dedication to Baalshamin — the city's supreme god — in the year 228 (Fig. 2.3).

Henry Seyrig asserts that the depiction of the sheaves of grain expresses the bounty and blessing that the god bestows on his adherents.[7] The image of the hand bearing three sheaves of grain is also known from a series of coins minted by Herod Philip, Agrippa I, and Agrippa II in the city of Paneas during the first century CE. The hand depicted on these coins represents bounty and fertility, which are specifically associated with the water-rich area of Paneas.[8] The visual images depicted in the two Palmyrene works — an anonymous hand holding a symbolic image that functions as a divine attribute — are almost identical. Their significance is seemingly the same: an articulation of the god's power and providence in the world. The dedicatory inscriptions greatly enhance our ability to refine the precise meaning of the visual depictions and facilitate the dating of the findings to the first decades of the third century — just slightly earlier than the synagogue frescoes. This modest group of findings posits a different visual paradigm for depicting the Divine, that diverges from the anthropomorphic depictions of the gods that were widespread in Roman culture. The iconographic and conceptual novelty of these depictions inheres in the retreat from extensive, detail-laden anthropomorphic imagery and its minimalization to one limb that encapsulates the significance and symbolism of the entire image.[9] Seyrig, who published a major portion of these findings,

---

6 <https://virtual-museum-syria.org/palmyra/altar-with-dedication-text-from-taimar%e1%b9%a3u-and-shalmallat/> [accessed 22 November 2022]

7 Seyrig, 'Antiquités syriennes', pp. 33–34, pl. I.6.

8 A coin from the thirty-fourth year of the reign of Herod Philip (30/31 CE) bears a portrait of Livia, the mother of the emperor Tiberius on the obverse side, while its reverse side displays a hand holding three sheaves accompanied by the inscription ΚΑΡΠΟΦΟΡΟΣ — 'fruit-bearing' — a designation for the fertile and water-rich region of the city of Paneas. Philip minted an identical coin in the thirty-seventh year of his reign. According to Anthony Giambrone, the coin's iconography sets up an affinity between the image of Livia and the cult of Demeter through the hand holding sheaves: the coin portrays the Emperor's mother as a queen-mother who bestows blessings and prosperity to the Empire. This image recurs on a coin minted by Agrippa I in 38 CE, the second year of his reign, which bears a portrait of his wife Cypros on its obverse side, and on a coin of Agrippa II in 67 CE. It thus corresponds with the specific characteristics of the city of Paneas on the one hand, and with the supreme source of prosperity — Demeter, the goddess of grain — on the other hand. See Meshorer, *A Treasury of Jewish Coins*, pp. 82, 85, 96; Giambrone, 'The Coins', pp. 210–211, 218.

9 A similar phenomenon occurs in several Zodiac depictions painted on the ceilings of Eastern European synagogues of the seventeenth and eighteenth centuries, which include a hand or

FIGURE 2.1. The Exodus, wall painting, Dura Europos synagogue, Syria, 244/5 CE. Courtesy of the Center for Jewish Art, Hebrew University of Jerusalem.

discerns the chasm between the notably resplendent and lavish full-blown anthropomorphic depictions and these minimalist representations. He rejects the possibility that these depictions reflect a religious disavowal of anthropomorphic Divine representations — his position regarding the depictions of the hand of God at the Dura Europos synagogue — or inferior artistic capabilities. He contends, rather, that these unusual and singular findings echo aesthetic concepts and abstract trends — pre-existent for centuries in the Syrian-Mesopotamian area — that sought to depict the gods in a focused and concise manner in opposition to the Greco-Roman tradition.[10]

Is there a dialogue between these carvings and the depictions of the hand of God on the Dura Europos synagogue? Seemingly, the works are connected by a common idea: the disembodied hand acts as an independent, autonomous entity and its appearance emphasizes and exposits the connection between heaven and earth, between metaphysical divinity and the physical, human world. Further scrutiny, however, exposes essential differences between the works: first, whereas the Syrian reliefs represent the god's beneficent involvement in the world as a general and eternal theme, unbound by time or place, the hand at Dura Europos represents concrete Divine revelation that occurred at a defined time and place.

Second, the hands in the Syrian reliefs grasp an element that discloses the deity's identity: this ability to grasp is also possibly the reason that a hand was chosen. In the synagogue, by contrast, the hand is outstretched and holds nothing — a depiction drawn from the monotheistic belief of God's unity that obviates the need for specific identifiers. An additional difference that warrants consideration is the direction of the Divine hand. In the Syrian reliefs the hand's direction varies: it emerges from the side, from below, and in one case from above. These variations might reflect a polytheistic view that assigns

---

a pair of hands that replace the entire human form. Thus, for example, Gemini is portrayed through two hands that appear from two opposite sides, each holding a different motif (flowers, chalice, scythe). Sagittarius is depicted by a hand or pair of hands holding a bow and Virgo through a hand carrying a bouquet of flowers. See Davidovitch, *Wall-Paintings*, p. 32, figs 9, 16; Fishof, 'The Many Faces of the Zodiac'.

10 Seyrig, 'Antiquités', pp. 193–94; Schröer, 'Zur Deutung der Hand', pp. 193–99.

FIGURE 2.2. Divine hand holding a bundle of lightning bolts, carved altar, the Temple of the Standards in Palmyra, Syria, 214 CE. Courtesy of Dr Aleksandra Kubiak-Schneider.

diverse roles and spheres of operation to the various gods in the heavens and on earth. By contrast, the synagogue frescoes (aside from the depiction of the sacrifice of Isaac[11]) present a unified conception in which the hand emerges from above, from the heavens, and is directed downwards towards the earth. These depictions align with the prevailing biblical conception that views the heavens as the Divine abode.[12] Joining these differences, is Seyrig's distinction between abstract trends in pagan art that are mainly stylistic and those in Jewish art that are fundamentally religious and motivated by opposition to anthropomorphic depiction of the Divine.

This notwithstanding, and despite the obvious differences, I perceive an essential similarity between the pagan reliefs and the synagogue paintings deriving from their common selection of an identical image — the hand — to express the same idea: Divine intervention in the human world. The concomitant appearance of these images — in themselves rare in both Jewish and Roman art — among two different yet neighbouring religious groups raises the inevitable question of the affinity between them. The fact that the pagan reliefs preceded those at the synagogue and were more widely dispersed posits them as the latter's possible and probable source of inspiration and visual model. The pagan model was adapted and redesigned to fit the needs and worldview of the Jewish community in a process that resulted in a new visual image that comported with monotheistic faith. The focus will now turn to the Exodus panel at the Dura Europos synagogue and to its exposition of the hand of God.

---

11 The panel above the Torah niche (in which the depiction of the sacrifice of Isaac is located) predates the other panels that include the hand of God, and its depiction diverges from theirs. The hand is not exposed but rather bursts out of a white element — a cloud or a sleeve. Moreover, the hand does not reach down from above but rather appears to hover in the air, turning to the left towards the depiction of the Temple. See Kraeling, *The Synagogue*, p. 40.
12 See for example: Deut. 26:15; i Kgs 8:39, 43, 49; Isa. 33:16; Isa. 66:1; Ps. 2:4; Ps. 115:16; Ps. 123:1. See also in the Jewish Hellenistic Literature: ii Macc. 3:39; iii Macc. 2:15.

FIGURE 2.3. Divine hand holding sheaves of grain, carved stone slab from Palmyra, Syria, 228 CE. After: Henri Seyrig, 'Antiquités syriennes', *Syria*, 26 (1949), pl. I.6.

The Exodus Panel at Dura Europos

The panel that portrays the story of the Israelites' Exodus from Egypt and their deliverance at the Red Sea is located in the upper register on the western wall and is read from right to left: it begins in the land of Egypt and concludes with the Israelites' emergence from the Red Sea.[13] The depiction opens with a jagged wall at the front of which are two stylized columns, that some scholars identify as the pillars of cloud and fire that accompanied the Israelites on their wanderings through the wilderness.[14] To the left of the pillars is a doorway in the wall beneath a sealed arch, its two doors wide open. This concise depiction portrays the physical and narrative starting point of the story: the land of Egypt, whose open gates represent the Israelites' Exodus. To the

---

13 Kraeling views this panel as exceptional among the other panels in respect to its style and the special attention to detail that is not evident in the other panels. It is not, in his opinion, the work of a different artist: rather, it was the first panel painted on the synagogue walls and after its completion the patrons changed their approach and issued different instructions to the artists. See Kraeling, *The Synagogue*, p. 381.
14 Kraeling, *The Synagogue*, p. 76; Weitzmann and Kessler, *The Frescoes*, pp. 41–42.

left of the wall the Israelites are depicted as leaving Egypt in four horizontal rows: the upper row and the third row depict warriors armed with shields and the second and lower rows depict unarmed figures. All the Israelites face left — the direction in which the narrative develops.

At the left, leading the group, is the monumental figure of Moses dressed in a tunic and pallium, striding towards the Red Sea, his right hand raising his staff aloft. The Red Sea is depicted to the left of Moses. It fills the entire height of the panel and contains numerous images of drowning Egyptians, depicted naked, as well as several fish.[15] Moses is depicted again, smaller than in the previous appearance but still monumental, on the other side of the sea. He stands in a frontal position, and his right hand holds his staff which he extends above the sea. To the left, Moses is depicted for a third time: his right hand holds his staff which is directed downwards to the narrow strip of water out of which fish are jumping. In the background, behind the last two figures of Moses, the Red Sea is depicted as dried up: it is divided by black lines widthwise into narrow strips. Above the narrow strip of sea to the left of Moses, the Israelites are depicted exiting the Red Sea in two horizontal rows: the lower row is crowded with warriors armed with shields; above them is a row of figures in Roman garments. Each of them carries a long staff topped by a square panel resembling the standards of the Roman Legion.

Finally, a pair of hands bursts out of the upper frame in the left third of the panel. The depiction includes the hand itself and the forearm — of both the right and left hands. The hands are pointed in opposite directions, towards the two main events in the panel: the right hand is directed downwards and to the right, towards the Egyptians drowning in the sea, and the left hand is directed downwards and to the left towards the Israelites who are crossing the Red Sea.[16] The depiction of the hands is significantly anthropomorphic: they are designed as human hands in every way — the skin tone is akin to that of the figures in the panel, and they present as a pair, right and left. That said, the fact that they emerge, disembodied, from the heavens and are recognizably larger than the human hands in the panel, implies that they are

---

15 Several explanations have been proffered for the uncommon depiction of the Egyptians' drowning in the nude: Kraeling found a reverberation of this in *Midrash Esther Rabbah* 3:14: 'Rabbi Nathan said: But Egyptians in their descent into the sea they were not judged except naked. How do we know this? "At the blast of Your nostrils the waters piled up"' (Exod. 15:8). According to Moon, the nudity indicates the non-Jewishness of the drowning, and Smith proposes that the nudity is an allusion to death — the anticipated death of the Egyptians. See Kraeling, *The Synagogue*, p. 83 n. 248; Moon, 'Nudity and Narrative', p. 597; Smith, *Map is Not Territory*, p. 5 n. 16. Gutmann notes a later analogy to the rare, nude depiction of the drowning: a miniature in the eleventh-century Ripoll Bible from Spain, that also includes a depiction of the hand of God extended downwards from Heaven. See Gutmann, 'The Dura Europos Synagogue Paintings', pp. 26–28.

16 Kraeling, *The Synagogue*, p. 83, pl. 52–53. To create space for the outspread hand, the artist lowered the fourth flag from the right in the upper row of flags, hence the conclusion that the hands were painted before the flags. This conclusion reinforces the importance of the Divine hands in the work.

not human. The hands' proportions reflect a stylistic phenomenon that recurs in the synagogue's paintings, according to which the physical size of the figure (or its part) expresses and reflects its importance. This hierarchy is visually blatant in the comparison between the (large) heavenly hands, the (midsize) hands of Moses, and the (small) hands of the Israelites and the Egyptians in the panel. The enormous size of the hands, their autonomy, their heavenly source, and their downward direction towards earth therefore attest a distinct, non-human entity that transpires as the hand of God.

The Hand of God: Between Literary and Visual Image

The initial appearance of the hand of God in the biblical themes of the Dura Europos synagogue frescoes poses various questions regarding the function of the hand and its significance, as well as its contribution to the visual and conceptual fashioning of the biblical story. Many scholars believe that the hand symbolizes Divine revelation in the world, whose most supreme manifestations are found in biblical history.[17] The ambivalence of biblical literature's approach to the question of God's corporeality is well-known: it speaks, on the one hand, of an abstract and hidden deity that must not be seen: 'But He said: you cannot see my face for man may not see me and live' (Exod. 33:20); 'To whom then can you liken God; what form compare to Him?' (Isa. 40:18), and of the abstract and non-visual nature of the revelation at Sinai: 'For your own sake, therefore, you must be careful, since you saw no shape when the Lord your God spoke to you at Horeb out of the fire' (Deut. 4:15).[18] On the other hand, the strong anthropomorphic aspects of the portrayals of God in biblical literature (as well as in rabbinic literature) that endow Him with bodily limbs and movements (sitting, standing) as well as human emotions such as anger, vengeance, compassion, love, etc. cannot be ignored. This anthropomorphic conception is firmly embedded in the depiction of the creation of man in Gen. 1:27: 'And God created man in His image, in the image of God He created him...'. The creation of man in God's image might also be construed as a physical resemblance between creator and created.[19]

In view of these two opposing conceptions, late antique art seems to adopt a middle path between the hidden, formless God, and the God who is represented in human scale. This approach is expressed in the image of a

---

17 See for example: Sukenik, *Ancient Synagogue of Beth Alpha*, p. 40; Kraeling, *The Synagogue*, pp. 57, 83, 145, 192, 229; Hachlili, *Ancient Jewish Art*, pp. 144–46; Revel-Neher, 'Seeing the Voice', pp. 8–16.

18 Hendel, 'Aniconism and Anthropomorphism'. The approach of the Aramaic Targums to the Bible also steers clear of anthropomorphism, see Klein, *Anthropomorphisms*, pp. 48–56.

19 Scholarly research on this topic is vast. See, for example, Miller, '"Image" and "Likeness"'; Stern, 'Imitatio Hominis'; Goshen-Gottstein, 'Body as Image of God'; Lorberbaum, *Image of God: Halakhah and Aggadah*, pp. 83–104; Kleinberg, *The Sensual God*, pp. 47–55. On the hand of God specifically see Fox, '"As if With a Finger"', pp. 278–81; Bar Ilan, 'The Hand of God', pp. 321–31.

heavenly-human hand that is explicitly anthropomorphic but at the same time detached and disembodied, and emanating from the heavens.

The Dura Europos frescoes are an initial and groundbreaking attempt to present biblical history through visual means; the theme that connects many of the biblical topics that adorn the synagogue is individual or collective salvation and deliverance induced by miracles and Divine acts. The contribution of God's hand to the designing of the biblical narrative of deliverance is therefore decisive: it is the visual manifestation of Divine intervention, i.e. the source of salvation. The hand is a dynamic, active, and even expressive limb and for this reason it seems likely that it was chosen — over all other bodily organs — to represent God's actions in the world.

This interpretation — an essential and fundamental layer in the understanding of this motif — requires an additional, specific exegetical layer to hone our discussion of the hands of God in the Exodus panel. The depiction in the panel is based on Exodus chapters 13–15 that abound with references to the hand of God, for example: 'It was with a mighty hand that the Lord brought us out of Egypt... when Israel saw the wonderous power (in Hebrew: יד, literally "hand") which the Lord had wielded against the Egyptians... Your right hand O Lord glorious in power, Your right hand O Lord shatters the foe... You put out Your right hand, the earth swallowed them... Through the might of Your arm they are still as stone... The sanctuary o Lord which Your hands established'.[20] These verses seemingly explain the incorporation of the hand of God in the panel: however, since the painter chose to paint a pair of hands and not a single hand, this explanation is only partial. The plural form of hand appears only in the last quote: 'The sanctuary o Lord which Your hands established', but in a different context: the building of the Temple.

If the hand of God is a visual symbol of God's presence and Divine revelation as we proposed above, the doubling of the hand in the panel might represent an extraordinarily forceful theophany like the one that occurred at the Red Sea, as the homilist in the Mekilta de R. Ishmael phrased it:

> 'This is my God and I will glorify Him': R. Eliezer says: Whence can you say that a maid-servant saw at the Red Sea what Isaiah and Ezekiel and the prophets never saw? It says about them: 'And by the ministry of the prophets have I used similitudes' (Hosea 12:11). And it is also written: 'The heavens were opened and I saw visions of God' (Ezekiel 1:1). To give a parable for this, to what is this like? To the following: A king of flesh and blood enters a province, surrounded by a circle of guards; his heroes stand to the right of him and to the left of him; his soldiers are before

---

20 Exod. 13:16–15:17. A distant echo of these images is apparent in Isaiah's prophecy where he appeals to the hand of God to act swiftly as in the Exodus from Egypt: 'Awake, awake, clothe yourself with splendour, O arm of the Lord. Awake as in days of old, as in former ages. It was you that hacked Rahab in pieces, That pierced the Dragon. It was you that dried up the sea, the waters of the great deep, that made the abyss of the sea a road the redeemed might walk'. (Isa. 51:9–10).

him and behind him — and all the people ask, saying: 'Which one is the king?' Because he is of flesh and blood like those who surround him. But, when the Holy One, blessed be He, revealed Himself at the sea, no one had to ask: 'Which one is the King?' But as soon as they saw Him, they recognized Him, and they all opened their mouth and said: 'This is my God, and I will glorify Him'.[21]

The Divine revelation in the Midrash, as in the painted panel, is sharp and unequivocally clear, in juxtaposition to a public appearance of a human king.

Possibly, the visual image of a pair of Divine hands that replaces the pervasive image of a single hand, seeks to express the singular nature of the revelation in which each of the children of Israel beheld a vision loftier than that beheld by the greatest prophets, and was able to visually identify the God of Israel.[22]

Carl Kraeling contends that the extraordinary depiction of a pair of hands derives from a literal reading of the biblical story that portrays two mighty miracles that occurred at the Red Sea: the drowning of the Egyptians alongside the splitting of the sea and the Israelites' safe passage through it.[23] His suggestion is reinforced by the Midrash:

R. Abbahu said: It is like one who saw robbers coming towards him. His son was with him, so what did he do? He took his son in one hand and with the other fought the robbers. His son said to him: May I never lack [the protection of] those two hands, the one that is holding me and the other which is slaying the robbers. This is what the Israelites said to God: May peace be upon both Thy hands. Both on the one with which You save us from the sea and on the other with which You overthrow the Egyptians, as it says, Your right hand, O Lord, glorious in power, Your right hand, O Lord, dashes in pieces the enemy (Exod. 15: 6).[24]

---

21 *Mekhilta de-R. Ishmael*, tractate Shirata 3, pp. 24–25.

22 An even more audacious depiction appears in Deuteronomy Rabbah, according to which God raised the male children born to the Israelites in contravention of Pharaoh's decree and returned them to their homes after several months. When their mothers would ask them who had raised them, they responded: 'A young man with beautiful curls; there is none like him, He brought me here and is waiting outside. The mother would say: Show him to me. When they went outside, however, though they would search everywhere, they could never find him. When they saw Him at the Sea of Reeds, they pointed with their fingers to show their mothers: This is the one who raised me! "*This* is my God and I will glorify Him!"' (Exod. 15:2). See *Deuteronomy Rabbah*, Devarim 15.

23 Scholars have already discerned that the panel does not depict the Exodus events chronologically since the drowning of the Egyptians occurred after the Israelites' safe passage through the Red Sea: they rightfully attribute this to considerations of composition and balance in the panel. The panel's clear division into three units creates a sense of balance, like a triptych: the drowning Egyptians at the centre of the panel are flanked on either side by the Israelites. On the right they are depicted departing Egypt, and, on the left, they emerge from the Red Sea, leaving their former captors drowning in the sea. See Kraeling, *The Synagogue*, p. 86; Weitzmann and Kessler, *The Frescoes*, pp. 38–39.

24 *Exodus Rabbah*, trans by Lehrman, 22:2, p. 276. See also: Kraeling, *The Synagogue*, p. 83.

R. Abbahu portrays God anthropomorphically as delivering Israel through His two hands, left and right: 'May peace be upon both Thy hands'. This, despite his citing of the verse that reiterates the right hand ('Your right hand ... Your right hand...') as corroboration.[25] The close affinity between the literary image in the Midrash and the visual image in the painting is expressed in the portrayal of a Divine pair of hands — a right hand and a left hand — and in the specific task assigned each hand: the right hand directs the deliverance of Israel, and the left oversees the downfall of the Egyptians.[26] The hands act in complementary concert: the defeat of Egypt enables the deliverance and emancipation of Israel. This notwithstanding, their status is not equal and their actions are not equally important: the important hand — the right hand — operates to save Israel while the left hand orchestrates the downfall of the Egyptians.

To sum up: the literary sources reveal several themes in common with the painting in Dura Europos; their main contribution to our discussion is the light they shed on the enigmatic and mysterious pair of Divine hands that replaces the single hand. The pair of hands acting in complimentary concert alludes to the two dramatic events of the deliverance of Israel as they departed Egypt; additionally, the doubling of the Divine hand expresses the lofty and singular nature of the Divine revelation to an entire nation.

The Exodus in Jewish and Christian Art in Late Antiquity

The innovative aspect of the hand of God in the Dura Europos frescoes manifests in the monotheistic context of the appearance of God's hand and its affinity to biblical literature. These depictions just slightly predate the

---

Midrash Exodus Rabbah comprises two units that were composed at different periods. The homily discussed above appertains to the second unit that is a homiletic Midrash on chapters 12–40. Divergent scholarly opinions regarding the date of this unit's redaction range from the Byzantine period (the fifth–seventh centuries) to the ninth century. However, since it is widely accepted that the Midrash also integrates earlier traditions, the thematic affinity between the paintings at Dura Europos and the traditions in the Midrash might affirm the antiquity of these traditions. See Reizel, *Introduction to the Midrashic Literature*, pp. 117–25.

25 This according to the convention whereby the right hand is the strong and positive of the two hands. See for example: Isa. 62:8; Ps. 20:7; Ps. 98:1. The *Mekilta de R. Ishmael*, tractate Shirata 5, contains an explanation for the reiteration of the right hand: 'Another Interpretation: "Thy Right Hand O Lord, Glorious in Power". When the Israelites do the will of God, they make His left hand as it were, to be like a right hand, as it is said: "Thy right hand, O Lord... Thy right hand, O Lord" — two times. And when the Israelites fail to do the will of God, they make His right hand to be like a left hand, as it is said: "He hath drawn back His right hand"' (Lam. 2:3). The homilist presents a dichotomic conception that views right and left as polar opposites representing good and evil; the redemption of Israel occurs when the left becomes the right and their downfall — when the right becomes the left. See: *Mekhilta de-R. Ishmael*, p. 41.

26 The identification of the hands in the midrash corresponds to the sequence of their appearance: the first is the right hand ('the one with which You save us from the sea') and the second is the left hand ('the other with which You overthrow the Egyptians').

appearance of the hand of God in Christian art, during the fourth century, where it is interpreted as a visual representation of God the Father, often in Old Testament themes.[27] After analysing the sources that influenced the fashioning of the hand of God in the Dura Europos frescoes in general, and specifically in the Exodus panel, the discussion will now move forward in time and address the imprint of this image — if indeed there was one — on Exodus depictions in Jewish and Christian art in Late Antiquity.

Two mosaic carpets that were uncovered in recent years at two Galilean synagogues, Wadi Hammam and Huqoq, include depictions of one episode of the Exodus events: the drowning of the Egyptians in the Red Sea. In Wadi Hammam, the theme occurs in the prayer hall, in a rectangular panel of which only the lower part has survived. At the centre of the panel is a chariot, seemingly out of control and breaking up, that is harnessed to three horses driven by a rider who holds a whip. To the right of the chariot, a soldier is lying at the bottom of the sea: above him is a fish equal to him in size, and at the left of the panel a monumental building and a city wall with a round tower.[28] A similar and more detailed depiction appears on the mosaic floor adorning the prayer hall of the synagogue at Huqoq, at the centre of the nave. A rectangular panel depicting the drowning of the Egyptians in the sea was uncovered, almost intact. The depiction overflows with various haphazardly displayed elements — armed soldiers, threatened by huge predatory fish, collapsing in defeat, cavalry riders on horses and broken chariots — that create a chaotic atmosphere.[29]

The iconographic and stylistic similarity between the two panels indicates that they share a visual tradition that diverges fundamentally from that of Dura Europos: the Exodus events are not depicted as a narrative sequence of events but rather are condensed into a single episode — the downfall of the enemy — that is perceived as the climax.[30] A specific comparison between the depictions of the drowning of the Egyptians at Huqoq and Wadi Hammam

---

27 Kessler, *Spiritual Seeing*, pp. 4–6; Jensen, *Face to Face*, pp. 115–30.

28 Miller and Leibner, 'The Synagogue Mosaic', pp. 144, 164–68. Leibner suggests that the monumental building is the temple of Ba'al-Tzafon, mentioned in several rabbinic traditions. See: Leibner, 'An Illustrated Midrash', pp. 87–96.

29 Magness and others, 'The Huqoq Excavation', pp. 86–87, 102–06, fig. 40. A similarly chaotic depiction appears in the late sixth century Ashburnham Pentateuch that includes Pharoah's armed soldiers, with their horses and chariots, falling in defeat and drowning in the sea. (See note 36 below.) This said, the Ashburnham Pentateuch's depiction lacks the enigmatic and rare portrayal of the fish consuming Pharoah's army. Magness suggests that this enigmatic image is based on rabbinic tradition, and its occurrence in the mosaic reflects an affinity to the rabbinic world, see Magness and others, 'The Huqoq Excavation', p. 106.

30 Miller and Leibner, 'The Synagogue Mosaic', pp. 177–78; Magness and others, 'The Huqoq Excavation', p. 105; It is worth noting that the artist at Dura Europos uses several methods to focus attention on the scene of the drowning Egyptians: first, through its placement at the centre of the panel in contrast to the chronological order of the events and see above, note 23. Second, through the two monumental images of Moses that frame the depiction, and third, through the dark shade of the water that contrasts with the light background in the other two sections of the panel. See Kraeling, *The Synagogue*, p. 86.

BETWEEN HEAVEN AND EARTH   67

on the one hand and Dura Europos on the other also reveals significant discrepancies. At Huqoq and Wadi Hammam, the military character of the drowning figures is stressed by equipping them with weapons and carriages.[31] The fish, which become enormous and predatory, come to Israel's aid by consuming Pharoah's troops. At Dura, the drowning Egyptians are depicted naked, not as soldiers, and the fish are smaller and not aggressive. The divergence most significant to this discussion is the absence of the hand of God in the mosaic carpets: this is especially pertinent to the Huqoq panel which was uncovered almost entirely intact.[32] In summary, the affinity between the depictions of the Exodus at Dura Europos and at Wadi Hammam and Huqoq is extremely weak and the presence of the hand of God is but one of many differences between them.

The Exodus scene occurs in Christian art from the fourth century onwards, yet it does not rank among the most prevalent biblical scenes during this period. It appears most conspicuously in a group of about thirty sarcophagi on which the scene is carved in various levels of detail. The scene extends along the entire length of the side panels of several late fourth-century sarcophagi, and comprises three units displayed from left to right: Egyptian cavalry pursuing the Israelites, Egyptian soldiers drowning in the Red Sea, and the Israelites emerging safely from the sea.[33] The resemblance between these works and the panel at Dura Europos inheres in the widthwise composition and the division of the narrative into three units, two of which are identical: the drowning of the Egyptians and the Israelites exiting the Red Sea. However, the hand of God does not appear in the carved sarcophagi, except for a sarcophagus, now located in Provence but probably from a Roman workshop, in which the artist interwove the image of Moses receiving the Torah from the hand of God into the events of the Exodus, as an anticipatory, foreshadowing event.[34]

Exodus depictions adorn additional structures and objects in the Byzantine sphere of the fourth and fifth centuries: in Rome — a wall mosaic of the nave at the church of Santa Maria Maggiore, and wall paintings in cubicula C and O at the Via Latina Catacomb. At the necropolis of El-Bagawat in Egypt a long and detailed depiction is painted on the dome of the 'Exodus Chapel'; the Exodus is also depicted on swatches of textile — perhaps shroud material — from Egypt[35] and in the Ashburnham Pentateuch illustrations from the late sixth

---

31   This is the prevalent depiction in Christian works of the fourth–sixth centuries; see below.
32   Although the right section of the panel is absent and it is possible that the hand of God appeared precisely in the upper right corner, the absence of the hand from all other panels of the mosaic carpet reinforces the assumption that it was absent from this panel too.
33   For the typological significance of these detailed depictions in the last third of the fourth century see Noga-Banai, *Prolegomena to the Study of Sarcophagus Production*, pp. 9–22.
34   Christern-Briesenick, *Repertorium*, no. 21, pl. 6.3; Elsner, 'Pharoah's Army', p. 17, fig. 1.5.
35   See Brenk, *Die frühchristlichen Mosaiken in S. Maria Maggiore*, figs 2–3; Fakhry, *The Necropolis of El-Bagawat*, pp. 44–56, pl. 15–17; Metropolitan Museum of Art, 'Recent Acquisitions', pp. 14–15.

century.[36] The hand of God is absent from all these works: moreover, at times it is actually present at the same site or manuscript in depictions of other scenes.[37]

The only work which features the hand of God is a carved wooden door that leads to the narthex at the church of Santa Sabina in Rome dated to the first half of the fifth century. The panel that represents the Exodus is an elongated rectangle that will be described from the bottom up: the narrow bottom register of the panel depicts Moses standing before Pharaoh, with two snakes writhing between them, facing Pharaoh. The broad upper register of the panel presents the events of the Exodus: the Red Sea, depicted in expressionist lines that impart storminess, appears in the lower area. An image of a young man driving a broken chariot drawn by four nearly drowned horses bursts out of the water. The head of another man, also drowning in the water, projects out of the stormy waves. A large group of people stand above the sea register: the first image on the right is Moses, with the Israelites on his left and at his rear. Some of the people are depicted from behind, facing a large angel in the upper left corner of the panel. The panel's upper section depicts, from left to right, four images that symbolize Divine Providence: an angel, clouds, a column of fire and a Divine hand that emerges from a cloud in the right corner (Fig. 2.4); all these represent a careful reading of Exodus 13–14 that references these symbols.[38] The hand of God is represented as a right hand: the thumb is sideways, to the left, and the other four fingers are closed and directed downwards towards the Israelites.[39]

This image recurs in two additional doors in the church, in three panels depicting Moses receiving the Law and the miracles wrought by Moses in the wilderness. In the first scene, the hand of God delivers Moses the Law, designed as a scroll, and in the depictions of the miracles, the hand is designed almost identically to that of the Exodus panel.[40] The hand of God is thus present in a series of events from the life of Moses that are carved on the church's doors. Seemingly, the figure of Moses and his special status in Christian theology are the key to understanding the presence of the hand of God in these works in general and in the Exodus scene specifically.[41]

The differences between the carved panel at Santa Sabina and the painted panel at Dura Europos manifest in the lengthwise vs. widthwise composition, the realistic, three-dimensional style as opposed to a flat, schematic style, and

---

36 Verkerk, *Early Medieval Bible Illumination and the Ashburnham Pentateuch*, p. 22, fig. 7; pp. 85–89.

37 Thus, the hand of God appears in a depiction of Moses removing his sandals before the burning bush at the Via Latina catacomb in Rome. At the necropolis at El-Bagawat the hand appears in a depiction of the sacrifice of Isaac in the 'Peace Chapel', and in the Ashburnham Pentateuch it appears in various miniatures including Moses at the burning bush and the Israelites complaining to Moses and Aaron in the wilderness.

38 See for example: Exod. 13:9, 21–22; Exod. 14:19–20, 24.

39 Effacement in an area at the centre of the panel renders its reconstruction uncertain, therefore the depiction above focuses on the details outside this area. See Jeremias, *Die Holztür der Basilika S. Sabina in Rom*, pp. 26–32; pl. 26–29.

40 Jeremias, *Die Holztür der Basilika S. Sabina in Rom*, pl. 20, 30.

41 Jensen, 'Moses Imagery', pp. 389–418.

the different iconography used to portray the biblical narrative, among other differences. Although a direct affinity between the depictions of the hand of God at Dura Europos and Santa Sabina is not readily identifiable, the two works do share a common concept: both transpose the focal point of salvation from the image of Moses to God Himself.[42] The panel at Dura Europos spotlights the Divine deliverance through a pair of Divine hands while at Santa Sabina — by combining a Divine hand with an angel and a column of fire.[43]

In summary, the motif of the hand of God is very unusual in late antique Exodus depictions and, aside from Dura Europos, it appears only at the fifth-century church of Santa Sabina in Rome, in a series of events from the life of Moses. The requisite conclusion therefore is that the hand of God did not penetrate the iconographic repertoire of Exodus depictions in Christian and Jewish Byzantine art.

In this essay I sought to trace the earliest appearance of the hand of God in ancient Jewish art, focusing on the Exodus panel in the Dura Europos synagogue. The analysis of the hand(s) of God in the panel was two-directional: backwards, towards the roots and sources of this visual image, and forwards, to the imprint of this image on later works. Two sources of inspiration were proposed for the unique depiction of the hand of God in the Exodus panel: Syrian reliefs dating to the first centuries CE as well as biblical literature that incorporates midrashic interpretations. The possible and even plausible accessibility of these sources to the world of the Jewish community of Dura Europos in the mid-third century supports their proposed influence on the fashioning of this image.

Many scholars believe that the hand of God functions as a visual representation that replaces the vocal expression: the voice of God.[44] The conception that

FIGURE 2.4. The Exodus, carved wooden door, the church of Santa Sabina, Rome, fifth century. After: Joachim J. Berthier, *La porte de Sainte-Sabine à Rome: étude archéologique* (Fribourg: Librairie de l'Université, 1892), p. 67.

---

42 Regarding the image of Moses, the relief at Santa Sabina presents Moses only once, realistically proportioned and as a typical person, as opposed to the fresco at Dura Europos where his monumental figure is thrice portrayed.
43 Jeremias, *Die Holztür der Basilika S. Sabina in Rom*, p. 30.
44 Goodenough, *Jewish Symbols*, p. 246; Gutmann, 'Sacrifice of Isaac', p. 67; Hachlili, *Ancient*

the voice of God might be materially expressed relies heavily on the biblical depiction of the theophany at Sinai: 'And all the people saw the thunderings, and the lightnings, and the noise of the trumpet' (Exod. 20: 15),[45] and aligns well with stories in which God or an angel of God are revealed to the prophet and converse with him. Thus, in three panels in the synagogue where the hand of God appears: in the sacrifice of Isaac — in the famous command: 'Do not raise your hand against the boy' (Gen. 22:12), in the burning bush theophany to Moses, and in Ezekiel's prophecy over the dry bones.

In the Exodus panel, the hands are outstretched over the drowning of the Egyptians on one side and the deliverance of Israel on the other. Seemingly, both events are also linked to speech — with the Divine command to Moses: 'And you lift up your rod and hold out your arm over the sea and split it […] hold out your arm over the sea that the waters may come back upon the Egyptians and upon their chariots and upon their horsemen'.[46] That said, it seems to me that contrary to the aforementioned events, where speech is the event itself — God talks and the prophet listens — in the Exodus, speech is the medium to propel the action, and the action is a mighty miracle that undermines the worldly order. Therefore, the Divine hands that echo Moses' hands do not represent the Divine voice but rather the actions precipitated by this voice.

Moreover, the pair of hands outstretched in both directions might echo a composition typically employed in imperial depictions such as coronation scenes or portrayals of the emperor receiving Divine inspiration and approval through a visual image — usually the eagle of Zeus — that envelops him with his wings.[47] Possibly, the pair of hands enveloping both figures of Moses is in dialogue with this composition, weaving an additional layer of significance into this depiction that spotlights Divine Providence as the force driving Moses' actions. It is worth noting that this interpretation transposes the main focus of the depiction from the Divine miracle to the figure of Moses.

The additional perspective proposed in this discussion, concerning the persistence of the hand of God in late antique Jewish and Christian art,

---

Jewish Art, pp. 145–46; Kessler, *Spiritual Seeing*, pp. 3–6; Lander, 'Revealing and Concealing God', pp. 208–10.

45 Philo of Alexandria explains that the voice emanated from the flame and that the voice and the fire were one manifestation experienced by both senses simultaneously. A similar conception is attributed to R. Akiva in the *Mekilta de R. Ishmael*, tractate Bahodesh 9: "'And all the people saw the thunderings"… R. Akiva says: They saw and heard that which was visible. They saw the fiery word coming out from the mouth of the Almighty as it was struck upon the tablets, as it is said: "The voice of the Lord hewed out flames of fire"' (Ps. 29:7). See Philo, Decalogue, 46–47; *Mekhilta de R. Ishmael*, p. 266.

46 Exod. 14:16, 26.

47 Thus, for example, in the imperial chamber in the temple at Luxor, renovated in the tetrarchic period. Four imperial portraits of the Tetrarchs are painted in the central niche, above which, in the vaulted conch, a colossal image of the eagle of Zeus is depicted, wings outstretched, holding in its claws a wreath or a crown. I am grateful to the anonymous reviewer who drew my attention to this depiction. See McFadden, 'Luxor Temple Paintings', pp. 126–34

BETWEEN HEAVEN AND EARTH   71

reveals that the hand of God was not included in the iconography of the Exodus depictions. Interestingly, in Christian art, the hand of God often appears in depictions of other scenes from the life of Moses: the theophany at the burning bush, the receiving of the Law and the striking of the rock, while it is absent specifically from the Exodus scene (apart from the door in Santa Sabina). Possibly, over time, artists interpreted the Divine hand as a symbol of an intimate encounter between God and the prophet rather than a large-scale spectacular theophany like the Exodus. In any event, the sophisticated depiction of the Divine revelation in the Exodus panel at Dura Europos remains singular and without successors in late antique visuality.[48]

A panoramic view of the decorative scheme of the Dura Europos frescoes demonstrates a bold and innovative attempt at the mid-third century to concretize the one monotheistic and abstract God through visual form. From the fourth century onwards, similar attempts appear in Byzantine art in the west and in the east, and despite the geographic distance, the possibility that Christian artists were directly or indirectly influenced by the visual tradition that presumably originated at Dura Europos should not be dismissed.[49] Over time, the hand of God became a widespread and well-known motif in Byzantine art alongside other visual images representing God the Father and I believe that this correctly contextualizes its near-complete absence from late antique Jewish art, with the sole exception of Beit Alpha.[50] The identification of the hand of God with Christian visuality, Christian exegesis of the Bible and with corporeal conceptions of Divinity, prompted an attitude of recoil and estrangement which led to its avoidance. The hand of God extended towards Abraham in the Beit Alpha synagogue mosaic seems then to be the exception that proves the rule.

---

48 The image of the hand of God enjoyed a revival in Jewish art in medieval illuminated manuscripts, albeit still infrequently in Exodus depictions. The hand of God appears in an Exodus scene in the London Haggadah of Joel Ben Shimon from the mid-fifteenth century (MS Add. 14762) and in another fifteenth century Haggadah, from the National Library of Frankfurt am Main (Cod.725/17). The image of a Divine pair of hands appears in the Bird's Head Haggadah from early fourteenth-century southern Germany, at the margin of the page containing the *dayenu* poem, beneath the words: 'Had he fed us manna'. Two hands — a right hand and a left hand — protrude downwards, from a thin strip of sky, holding the manna in a benedictory gesture. Mark Epstein contends that this depiction was intended to enhance the special status of the manna as Divine bread, as a polemic response to the bread of the Eucharist. See Wischnitzer, *Symbole und Gestalten*, pp. 10–12; Cahn and Cahn, 'An Illuminated Haggadah', pp. 170–71, fig. 4; Epstein, *The Medieval Haggadah*, pp. 98–101.

49 Gisela Jeremias attributes great significance to the fact that the only parallel to the depiction of the hand of God at the Exodus scene in Santa Sabina is the Dura Europos synagogue, where it appears in four additional scenes. She believes that it is an original Jewish motif and its appearance in Christian art is based on an ancient Jewish model. See Jeremias, *Die Holztür der Basilika S. Sabina in Rom*, p. 30. See also Speyart Van Woerden, 'The Iconography of the Sacrifice of Abraham', p. 224; Jensen, *Face to Face*, pp. 120–21; Revel-Neher, 'Seeing the Voice', p. 15.

50 Sukenik, *The Ancient Synagogue of Beth Alpha*, pp. 40–42; Goodenough, *Jewish Symbols*, pp. 246–48; Lander, 'Revealing and Concealing God', p. 211.

Bibliography

Primary Sources

Deuteronomy Rabbah, ed. by Saul Lieberman, 3rd edn (Jerusalem: Sifre Vahrman, 1974)

Mekilta de R. Ishmael, trans. by Jacob Z. Lauterbach (Philadelphia: The Jewish Publication Society of America, 1933)

Midrash Rabbah: Esther, trans. by Maurice Simon (London: Soncino, 1983)

Midrash Rabbah: Exodus, trans. by S. M. Lehrman, 3rd edn (London: Soncino, 1983)

Mishnah Avodah Zarah <https://www.sefaria.org.il/Mishnah_Avodah_Zarah.3.2> [accessed 21 June 2022]

Secondary Studies

Bar Ilan, Meir, 'The Hand of God: A Chapter in Rabbinic Anthropomorphism', in *Rashi 1040–1990: Hommage a Ephraim E. Urbach*, Congrès européen des juives, ed. by Gabrielle Sed-Rajna (Paris: Editions du Cerf, Congress of Jewish Studies, 1993), pp. 321–35

Brenk, Beat, *Die Frühchristlichen Mosaiken in S. Maria Maggiore zu Rom* (Wiesbaden: Steiner, 1975)

Cahn, Annabelle, and Walter Cahn, 'An Illuminated Haggadah of the Fifteenth Century', *The Yale University Library Gazette*, 41.4 (1967), 166–82

Christern-Briesenick, Brigitte, *Repertorium der Christlich-Antiken Sarkophage III: Frankreich, Algerien, Tunesien* (Wiesbaden: Reichert, 2003)

Davidovitch, David, *Wall-Paintings of Synagogues in Poland* (Jerusalem: Bialik Institute, 1968) (in Hebrew)

Downey, Susan, *The Stone and Plaster Sculpture: Excavations at Dura Europos* (Los Angeles: The Institute of Archaeology, The University of California, 1977)

Elsner, Jas, '"Pharoah's Army Got Drownded": Some Reflections on Jewish Narrative and Christian Meaning in Late Antiquity', in *Judaism and Christian Art: Aesthetics Anxieties from the Catacombs to Colonialism*, ed. by Herbert L. Kessler and David Nirenberg (Philadelphia: University of Pennsylvania Press, 2011), pp. 10–44

Epstein, Marc M., *The Medieval Haggadah: Art, Narrative, and Religious Imagination* (New Haven: Yale University Press, 2011)

Fakhry, Ahmed, *The Necropolis of El-Bagawat in Kharga Oasis* (Cairo: Govt. Press, 1951)

Fishof, Iris, 'The Many Faces of the Zodiac', in *Written in the Stars: Art and Symbolism of the Zodiac* (Jerusalem: Israel Museum 2001), pp. 58–61 (in Hebrew)

Fox, Harry, '"As if With a Finger": The Text History of an Expression Avoiding Anthropomorphism', *Tarbiz*, 49.3–4 (1980), 278–91 (in Hebrew)

Giambrone, Anthony, 'The Coins of Philip the Tetrarch and the Imperial Cult: A View from Paneas on the Fall of Sejanus', *Journal for the Study of Judaism*, 52 (2021), 197–227

Goodenough, Erwin R., *Jewish Symbols in the Greco-Roman Period*, I (New York: Pantheon, 1953)

Goshen-Gottstein, Alon, 'The Body as Image of God in Rabbinic Literature', *The Harvard Theological Review*, 87.2 (1994), 171–95

Gutmann, Joseph, 'The Dura Europos Synagogue Paintings and their Influence on Later Christian and Jewish Art', *Artibus et Historiae*, 9 (1988), 25–29

——, 'The Sacrifice of Isaac in Medieval Jewish Art', *Artibus et Historiae*, 8 (1987), 67–89

Hachlili, Rachel, *Ancient Jewish Art and Archeology in the Diaspora* (Leiden: Brill, 1998)

Hendel, Ronald S., 'Aniconism and Anthropomorphism in Ancient Israel', in *The Image and the Book: Iconic Cults, Aniconism and the Rise of Book Religion in Israel and the Ancient Near East*, ed. by Karel Van der Toorn (Leuven: Peeters, 1997), pp. 205–28

Jensen, Robin M., *Face to Face: Portraits of the Divine in Early Christianity* (Minneapolis: Fortress, 2004)

——, 'Moses Imagery in Jewish and Christian Art: Problems of Continuity and Particularity', *SBL Seminar Papers*, 31 (1992), 389–418

Jeremias, Gisela, *Die Holztür der Basilika S. Sabina in Rom* (Tübingen: Wasmuth, 1980)

Kessler, Herbert, *Spiritual Seeing: Picturing God's Invisibility in Medieval Art* (Philadelphia: University of Pennsylvania Press, 2000)

Klein, Michael L., *Anthropomorphisms and Anthropopathisms in the Targum of the Pentateuch* (Jerusalem: Makor, 1982) (in Hebrew)

Kleinberg, Aviad M., *The Sensual God: How the Senses Make the Almighty Senseless* (New York: Columbia University Press, 2015)

Kraeling, Carl. H., *The Synagogue: The Excavations at Dura-Europos, Final Report*, VIII/I (New Haven: Yale University Press, 1956; repr. New York: Ktav, 1979)

Lander, Shira, 'Revealing and Concealing God in Ancient Synagogue Art', in *Histories of the Hidden God: Concealment and Revelation in Western Gnostic, Esoteric and Mystical Traditions*, ed. by April D. DeConick and Grant Adamson (Durham, NC: Acumen, 2013), pp. 205–16

Leibner, Uzi, 'An Illustrated Midrash of Mekilta de R. Ishmael, Vayehi Beshalah, 1 – Rabbis and the Jewish Community Revisited', in *Talmuda De 'Eretz Yisrael: Archeology and the Rabbis in Late Antiquity*, ed. by Steven Fine and Aaron Koller (Berlin: de Gruyter, 2014), pp. 83–96

Lorberbaum, Yair, *Image of God: Halakhah and Aggadah* (Tel Aviv: Schocken, 2004) (in Hebrew)

Magness, Jodi, and others, 'The Huqoq Excavation Project: 2014–2017 Interim Report', *BASOR*, 380 (2018), 61–131

McFadden, Susanna, 'The Luxor Temple Paintings in Context: Roman Visual Culture in Late Antiquity', in *Art of Empire: The Roman Frescoes and Imperial Cult Chamber in Luxor Temple*, ed. by Michael Jones and Susanna McFadden (New Haven: Yale University Press 2015), pp. 126–34

Meshorer, Yaakov, *A Treasury of Jewish Coins* (Jerusalem: Yad Izhak ben Zvi, 1997) (in Hebrew)

The Metropolitan Museum of Art, 'Recent Acquisitions: A Selection, 2014–2016', *The Metropolitan Museum of Art Bulletin*, 74.2 (2016)

Miller, J. Maxwell, 'In the "Image" and "Likeness" of God', *Journal of Biblical Literature*, 91.3 (1972), 289–304

Miller, Shulamit, and Uzi Leibner, 'The Synagogue Mosaic', in *Khirbet Wadi Hamam: A Roman-Period Village and Synagogue in the Lower Galilee (Qedem Reports 13)* (Jerusalem: Institute of Archaeology, the Hebrew University of Jerusalem; Israel Exploration Society, 2018), pp. 144–86

Moon, Warren G., 'Nudity and Narrative: Observations on the Frescoes from the Dura Synagogue', *Journal of the American Academy of Religion*, 60.4 (1992), 587–658

Noga-Banai, Galit, *Prolegomena to the Study of Sarcophagus Production in Rome under Pope Damasus* (Jerusalem: European Forum at the Hebrew University Center for the Study of Italian Culture, 2007)

Reizel, Anat, *Introduction to the Midrashic Literature* (Alon Shvut: Tevunot, 2011)

Revel-Neher, Elisheva, 'Seeing the Voice: Configuring the Non-Figurable in Early Medieval Jewish Art', *Ars Judaica*, 2 (2006), 7–24

Schröer, Silvia, 'Zur Deutung der Hand unter der Grabinschrift von Chirbet el-Qôm', *Ugarit Forschungen*, 15 (1983), 191–200

Seyrig, Henri, 'Antiquités', *Syria*, 20 (1939), 177–194

——, 'Antiquités syriennes', *Syria*, 26 (1949), 17–41

Smith, Jonathan Z., *Map is Not Territory: Studies in the History of Religions* (Chicago: The University of Chicago Press, 1993)

Speyart van Woerden, Isabel, 'The Iconography of the Sacrifice of Abraham', *Vigiliae Christianae*, 15.4 (1961), 214–55

Stern, David, 'Imitatio Hominis: Anthropomorphism and the Character(s) of God in Rabbinic Literature', *Prooftexts*, 12.2 (1992), 151–74

Sukenik, Eleazar L., *The Ancient Synagogue of Beth Alpha* (Jerusalem: University Press, 1932)

Tronzo, William, *The Via Latina Catacomb: Imitation and Discontinuity in Fourth-Century Roman Painting* (University Park: Pennsylvania State University Press, 1986)

Verkerk, Dorothy, *Early Medieval Bible Illumination and the Ashburnham Pentateuch* (Cambridge: Cambridge University Press, 2004)

Weitzmann, Kurt, and Kessler, Herbert L., *The Frescoes of the Dura Synagogue and Christian Art* (Washington, DC: Dumbarton Oaks Research Library, 1990)

Wischnitzer, Rachel, *Symbole und Gestalten der jüdischen Kunst* (Berlin: Scholem, 1935)

ZEEV WEISS

Shaping Religious Space

Pagans, Jews, and Christians in Ancient Sepphoris

Temples, like other monumental buildings, graced the urban landscapes of the cities in ancient Palestine and beyond. In most places, the temples dedicated to the local pantheon stood in the city centre. In the infrastructure of the Jewish cities of the Galilee, which had mixed yet predominantly Jewish populations in the first centuries CE, it is assumed that the synagogue was the more common cultic building. Assorted finds bearing figural images, some pagan in nature, are known to date in the two Galilean cities of Sepphoris and Tiberias. Yet, the excavation of a temple in Sepphoris or Epiphanius's testimony of the Hadrianeum in Tiberias undoubtedly indicate a constant pagan presence in both cities throughout the Roman period.[1]

Christianity made its first inroads into fourth-century Galilee, which until then was populated largely by Jews. Christian interest in the region was initially motivated by those sites in which Jesus had his ministry and where the Christian community (of undeterminable size) expanded over time.[2] While the archaeological evidence for growing Christian presence in the Galilee comes from such sites or from nearby villages and small towns, modern scholarship has made no recognizable headway in understanding the socio-cultural, religious, and political changes that transpired in the two major Jewish cities under Christian rule — Sepphoris and Tiberias — or in the role of Christian architecture in shaping their cityscapes.[3] This essay will focus on the cult buildings known to date in Sepphoris — a temple, two churches, and several synagogues — and will discuss their implications for

---

1 Weiss, 'From Roman Temple to Byzantine Church'. On the Hadrianeum in Tiberias, see Miller, 'Markers of Pagan Cults'.
2 Walker, *Holy City, Holy Places?*, pp. 133–70; Stemberger, *Jews and Christians in the Holy Land*, pp. 71–81.
3 Aviam, 'Christian Galilee'; Aviam, 'Distribution Maps'; Ashkenazi and Aviam, 'Monasteries, Monks, and Villages'; Ashkenazi, 'Private Family-Church Buildings'.

Zeev Weiss is the Eleazar L. Sukenik Professor of Archaeology at the Hebrew University of Jerusalem. Trained in Classical Archaeology, he specializes in Roman and late antique art and architecture in the provinces of Syria-Palestine.

Essays on Jews and Christians in Late Antiquity in Honour of Oded Irshai, ed. by Brouria Bitton-Ashkelony and Martin Goodman, CELAMA 40 (Turnhout: Brepols, 2023), pp. 75–92
BREPOLS ❧ PUBLISHERS   10.1484/M.CELAMA-EB.5.132484

the study of the architectural development, social structure, and religious behaviour in this city in the Roman period and throughout Late Antiquity.

Sepphoris: A Look at the Roman and Late Antique City

The building of Sepphoris as a Roman city after the Great Revolt attests to the changes taking place in the Galilee in this and the following eras.[4] Owing to its newfound wealth and prosperous economy, Sepphoris grew significantly and its population reached a peak of 15,000 to 20,000 inhabitants. Excavations conducted on the plateau east of the hill indicate that by the end of the first or in the early second century the city had expanded eastward, boasting an impressive network of streets arranged in a grid, with a colonnaded *cardo* and *decumanus* intersecting at its centre. Designed according to Roman guidelines, public buildings and private dwellings — including a temple, forum, basilica, bathhouses, a theatre, and a monumental building identified as a library or archive — sprang up throughout the city. As in any other ancient city, the monumental buildings in Sepphoris were constructed for the benefit of the local population, fulfilling everyday municipal, religious, economic, and public entertainment needs.

Sepphoris sustained damage in the mid-fourth century, most probably incurred by the earthquake of 363 CE. The late antique city (from the mid-fourth to the sixth centuries) expanded and even experienced an extensive building spurt and a flourishing revival.[5] The network of streets and roads as well as several buildings constructed in the Roman period continued to be used in the late antique city. The theatre and western bathhouse were reconstructed while the temple, forum, basilica, city archives, and the House of Dionysos fell into disuse. Late antique Sepphoris witnessed the construction of new buildings adjacent to the main colonnaded streets and elsewhere in the city, including the Nile Festival Building, the open market to its north, a bathhouse, as well as synagogues and churches.

Sepphoris retained its urban plan throughout Late Antiquity, although the data at our disposal is insufficient to determine when and how the city declined, how its magnificent buildings were destroyed, and when its population dwindled. The city plummeted in the early Arab period: structures were abandoned and destroyed, earlier masonry was looted, and simple buildings were constructed throughout the site.

Several cult buildings dominated the urban landscape of ancient Sepphoris in Roman times and throughout Late Antiquity. To date, the temple is the only cultic building known in the Roman city, whereas the two churches excavated along the *cardo* and two or three synagogues were in use simultaneously in

---

4 For further discussion of the archaeological remains from Sepphoris, see Weiss, *Sepphoris: A Mosaic of Cultures*, esp. pp. 52–114, with references to earlier studies.

5 Weiss, *Sepphoris: A Mosaic of Cultures*, pp. 116–51.

Late Antiquity. Remains of a podium uncovered in 1943 on the hill's southern slope amid the houses of the Arab village Saffūriye were associated at the time with a temple located in this part of the city. Since no other cult-related finds were discovered alongside the podium to corroborate this suggested identification, theoretically it could have been used as a base for some other Roman monument — but not a temple.[6]

In what follows, I will present the various cult buildings excavated at the site and then discuss the importance of the finds in demonstrating Sepphoris's distinct character.

The Temple

Construction of the temple in an *insula* south-east of the main intersection in Lower Sepphoris began in the mid-second century CE, continued for several decades, and was completed by the end of the second or early third century (Fig. 3.1). Like other temples in the Roman East, the building at Sepphoris stands in a large courtyard, a *temenos* (measuring 50.49 × 55.75 m) surrounded by a thick wall. A monumental passageway (*propylaeum*) on the northern side of the *temenos* gave direct access from the *decumanus* into the Roman compound. Inside the *temenos*, only the area leading from the street to the temple was paved with stones, while all other parts of the courtyard were plastered.[7]

Only the deep and massive foundations of the temple have been preserved; its superstructure appears to have been completely dismantled with the construction of the church by the late fifth or early sixth century. The temple (measuring 24.32 × 11.91 m) had a decorated façade facing north-east, toward the *decumanus*. It was located south of the courtyard's centre, rendering the area in front of it almost double the size of the area behind it. The size of the building, the thick foundation walls (averaging 2.70 m), the podium (*c.* 1.5 m), and the assortment of decorated elements found in the debris or used in the church's foundation — attic bases, column drums, cornices, and fragments of Corinthian capitals — may suggest that the temple's façade was composed of four slender columns while the walls of the *naos* were decorated with semi-circular engaged columns. Such *tetrastyle prostyle* temples are well known in Roman architecture, and some were constructed in Roman Palestine; the building in Sepphoris finds a close parallel, in both dimensions and construction methods, to a temple constructed on Mt Gerizim outside Neapolis and to some other structures in the Hauran and northern Syria.[8]

---

6 Archive of the Department of Antiquities of Mandatory Palestine (1919–1948), Scientific Record Files 166 (Saffuriya, fig. B-882760).

7 Weiss, 'From Roman Temple to Byzantine Church', pp. 200–09.

8 Neapolis: Magen, *Flavia Neapolis*, i, pp. 226–37, with references to earlier studies; Hauran: Segal, 'Religious Architecture', esp. pp. 105–09; Steinsapir, *Rural Sanctuaries*, pp. 31–35 and 50–51.

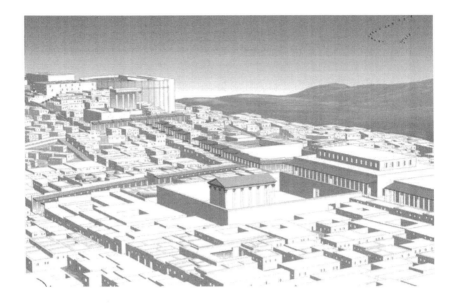

FIGURE 3.1. Suggested reconstruction of Roman Sepphoris, with the temple located in the *insula* south-east of the main intersection in lower Sepphoris. Drawing by Anna Iamim.

No inscriptions, statues, or iconographic evidence were found that could determine to whom the temple was dedicated or which deity was worshipped there. Theoretically, one of the gods portrayed standing in a gabled temple on the coins minted in Sepphoris during the reign of Antoninus Pius, Julia Domna, Caracalla, and Elagabalus could have been worshipped there — be it Tyche and the Capitoline triad, Zeus, Hera, Athena, or even Heracles.[9] However, the temple's monumental size and prominent location next to the *decumanus*, one of the major roads leading into the civic centre, may suggest that the temple was dedicated to a more prominent deity, probably Zeus — a suggestion also befitting the city's new name, Diocaesarea, most probably in the early days of Hadrian's rule.[10] This impressive temple in honour of Zeus, the king of gods, stood in a central location and ensured that anyone who

---

9 Meshorer, 'Sepphoris and Rome'; Meshorer and others, *Coins of the Holy Land*, i, pp. 67–68. On the iconography of temples depicted on coins (including Sepphoris) and their comparison to architecture on site, see Lichtenberger, 'Coin Iconography and Archaeology'.

10 The city was still called Sepphoris when coins were minted under Trajan. The name Diocaesarea appears for the first time on coins minted in the time of Antoninus Pius, however the change of the city's name might have occurred earlier, in the days of Hadrian, either a few years after he ascended to power, *c.* 120 CE, or when he visited the region in 130; see Meshorer and others, *Coins of the Holy Land*, i, p. 68. The city's new name appears on several milestones erected along the new road leading from Legio (= Megiddo), the site of the Roman camp of Legio VI Ferrata, to Sepphoris, constructed in 120 CE, however Benjamin Isaac and Israel Roll ('Judaea in the Early Years') argue that it was a later addition.

SHAPING RELIGIOUS SPACE   79

approached the city, especially from the east, would see it from a distance and be impressed by its grandeur.

The temple at Sepphoris demonstrates the vibrancy of the pagan population, which had the economic, political, and social means to build a large and impressive building in the heart of the civic centre. It was undoubtedly constructed for the benefit of the pagan population, but it is probable that some local wealthy Jews, some of whom even served on the municipal council, participated, at least inconspicuously, in the pagan sacrifices of the city.[11]

Several architectural elements found in conjunction with the temple and its courtyard, primarily at its northern end, indicate significant modifications made in the compound in a later phase.[12] It seems that the new features, mainly the construction of a row of shops south of the *decumanus*, diminished the original functionality of the religious compound and may suggest that the temple was abandoned sometime in the fourth century. It is not clear whether domestic urban circumstances led to the cessation of the pagan cult or, what seems more plausible, if the conversion of the empire to Christianity contributed to the desertion of the cultic site.

Synagogues

Synagogues were built in Roman and late antique Sepphoris, as befitted a city populated largely by Jews. These buildings were in all probability scattered throughout the city, as were other cultic buildings, such as temples and, later on, churches, in other cities of Roman and late antique Palestine.

Although no synagogues are currently known in Roman Sepphoris (second–third centuries), their existence can be cautiously deduced from the rabbinic sources. One of the earliest references to this Jewish public institution in third-century Sepphoris appears in the Palestinian Talmud, where Rabbi Naḥman, in the name of Rabbi Mana, describes Rabbi Judah the Patriarch's funeral. He states that all the towns congregated to eulogize the Patriarch, and that after lying in state in eighteen synagogues, he was brought to Bet She'arim for burial.[13] Even if the number eighteen seems suspect — as argued by some scholars who dismiss the possibility that Sepphoris may have had eighteen synagogues in the time of this patriarch[14] — and even if some of those buildings, as some scholars claim,[15] were located in other villages or towns along the route to Bet She'arim, one would still agree that the early

---

11 According to Sacha Stern ('Babylonian Talmud, Avodah Zarah 16a'), one Palestinian tradition embedded in this talmudic source may allude to such an occasion, suggesting that the members of the house of Rabbi Judah the Patriarch offered regular sacrifices on pagan festival days.

12 Weiss, 'From Roman Temple to Byzantine Church', pp. 209–12.

13 *Jerusalem Talmud, Kil'aim* 9.4.32b; cf. *Jerusalem Talmud, Ketubot* 12.3.35a; *Ecclesiastes Rabbah* 7. 11.

14 Miller, 'On the Number of Synagogues', pp. 59–63.

15 Levine, *Ancient Synagogue*, p. 187.

third-century city boasted a fair number of synagogues, some of which are even known by name, such as 'the Great Synagogue of Sepphoris',[16] 'the Synagogue of Gofnah',[17] and 'the Synagogue of the Babylonians'.[18]

Two synagogues dated to the early fifth century and evidence for a third building are currently known in several areas throughout the site. One building, only partly excavated and of an unknown plan, is located near the western edge of the hill, north of the Crusader church of Saints Joachim and Anna.[19] It has a mosaic floor decorated with a simple interlacing geometric pattern and one of its medallions contains an Aramaic dedicatory inscription.[20]

Traces of coloured mosaics with several letters and fragments of words in Aramaic were found on the western side of the hill, but not in situ. Their palaeography is similar to that of the inscriptions known in the two other synagogues at the site, suggesting that they came from the floor of another synagogue located on the acropolis, however no trace of its exact location has been found yet.[21]

The first completely excavated synagogue at the site, located in the north-eastern part of lower Sepphoris, was in use from the early fifth to the early seventh century. It is a long building (about 7.7 × 20.8 m) oriented away from Jerusalem, as its entrance was in its southern wall and its *bema* was located at the western end of the main hall (Fig. 3.2). The single aisle on the northern side of the main hall distinguishes this building from most other ancient synagogues.[22]

The mosaic in the main hall of this synagogue features figurative scenes while the one in the aisle bears geometric designs and several Aramaic dedicatory inscriptions.[23] The carpet in the main hall (measuring 16.0 × 6.6 m) is divided into seven bands of unequal height, some of which have internal subdivisions. The fourteen panels comprising this mosaic are labelled primarily with Greek dedicatory inscriptions. The zodiac panel dominates the centre of the mosaic; the depictions below it are associated with the biblical patriarchs and illustrate the visit of the angels to Abraham and Sarah at Mamre and the Binding of Isaac; the panels above it portray primarily motifs related to the Tabernacle and the destroyed Temple in Jerusalem. In addition to the well-known Jewish symbols — an architectural façade flanked on either side by a menorah, a shofar, and tongs — these panels display additional themes, such as Aaron's Consecration to the Service of the Tabernacle, the Daily Sacrifice, the Showbread Table, and the Basket of the First Fruits.

---

16 *Pesiqta de-Rav Kahana*, 18. 5, p. 297.
17 *Jerusalem Talmud, Berakhot* 3.1.6a.
18 *Genesis Rabbah*, 52. 4, p. 543.
19 Viaud, *Nazareth et ses deux églises*, pp. 179–84.
20 Naveh, *On Stone and Mosaic*, pp. 51–52.
21 Vilozny, 'Fresco, Secco, Stucco, and Mosaic Fragments', ii, p. 899.
22 Weiss, *Sepphoris Synagogue*, pp. 7–53.
23 Weiss, *Sepphoris Synagogue*, pp. 55–161.

SHAPING RELIGIOUS SPACE 81

FIGURE 3.2. General view of the synagogue uncovered at the north-eastern end of lower Sepphoris, looking north-west. Photo by Gabi Laron.

The variety of depictions and rich iconography assign this mosaic an important place in Jewish art. An analysis of the layout and depictions in this mosaic indicates that it was meant to convey the message of God's promise to the Jewish people and the hope for future redemption.[24] This notion, which also appears in Jewish prayers, rabbinic sermons, and liturgical poetry (*piyyut*), wished to transmit, through art, a clear message to the community about the rebuilding of the Jerusalem Temple and the coming redemption. These themes are understandable in light of the Judaeo-Christian controversy that had reached a new peak at this time, stemming from the centrality of the Bible — the ancient text recognized and revered by Jewish and Christian communities alike and whose vested authority was undisputed by both. The Sepphoris mosaic thus focuses on the main themes that characterized the contemporary Judaeo-Christian controversy and simultaneously served as a Jewish response, via the biblical accounts, claiming that the Jews are the Chosen People.[25]

Sepphoris also had *batei midrash* — houses of study and assembly for the sages and their disciples — that sometimes served as synagogues as well.[26] The Talmud also contains examples of rulings made by sages who lived in Sepphoris that were sometimes directly linked to the city's synagogues. Both the archaeological finds and the literary references attest to the vibrant religious life of the Jews in Sepphoris throughout this period.

Churches

A modestly sized Christian community existed in Sepphoris in the first centuries CE, but it seems to have grown significantly in the late fifth or early sixth century.[27] Its growth was most probably accompanied by the construction of churches in the city and the involvement of the *episcopus*, the head of the Christian community, in municipal affairs. Bishops Marcellinus and Cyriacus, who participated respectively in the ecumenical councils held in 516 in Jerusalem and 536 in Constantinople, were active in the city in the first half of the sixth century,[28] and Bishop Eutropius is attested epigraphically three times, although his dates are unknown (Fig. 3.3).[29]

Sepphoris is not mentioned in the New Testament and is not linked, even indirectly, either to Jesus's activity in the Galilee or to any of his followers. Only in the sixth century, the Christian community established itself in the city, creating new traditions, unknown elsewhere, that associated some New

---

24 Weiss, *Sepphoris Synagogue*, pp. 225–62.
25 Weiss, 'Biblical Stories'.
26 *Jerusalem Talmud, Pe'ah* 7.4.20b; *Jerusalem Talmud, Bava Meṣi'a* 2.13.8d; see also Oppenheimer, 'Beth ha-Midrash'.
27 Freyne, 'Christianity in Sepphoris and in Galilee'.
28 Fedalto, *Patriarchatus Alexandrinus*, p. 1034.
29 Weiss, *Sepphoris: A Mosaic of Cultures*, pp. 47–49, 119.

Testament figures with Sepphoris. The early sixth-century pilgrim Theodosius notes that Simon Magus, mentioned in Acts 8:9–25, came from Diocaesarea whereas the Piacenza Pilgrim who visited the city in the second half of the sixth century (around 570) presumably saw what they said was the jar and bread basket of Saint Mary, mother of Jesus, as well as the chair on which she sat when the angel came to her.[30] The number of pilgrimage sites in ancient Palestine has expanded over time, so it is quite possible that the new traditions were conceived by the city's Christian leaders who sought to establish Sepphoris's status as a Christian city and include it on the pilgrimage map.[31]

By the late fifth or early sixth century, two churches were constructed along the *cardo* in lower Sepphoris, close to the intersection of the city's two main colonnaded streets (Fig. 3.4). These churches, representing the latest construction phase of religious buildings in the city, faced south-east, an orientation derived from the existing urban plan that dictated the alignment of all monumental and public buildings in lower Sepphoris in the Roman period and throughout Late Antiquity.[32]

The church west of the *cardo* is a long building (measuring 27 × 40 m) occupying a large area of the *insula*, from the *decumanus* in the north to the western bathhouse in the south.[33] An 8 × 10-m roofed plaza with a simple mosaic pavement is located between the *decumanus* and the church's long northern wall to its south, providing access to the atrium and, through it, into the church's prayer hall. The church's foundations, composed of different-sized fieldstones (with the exception of the apse, which was built of hewn stones) are all that remain of the building, which contained a prayer hall flanked by several rooms that apparently functioned as chapels. In addition, two large cisterns were exposed inside the building, one located adjacent to the apse, the other south-west of the main hall. The church's foundations, walls, and the fill between them created a sort of podium that raised the building above the level of its immediate surroundings.

The triapsidal church (measuring 62 × 29 m) east of the *cardo* had two entrances leading into it from the nearby thoroughfares.[34] The building followed the typical basilical plan, with a rectangular atrium containing a fountain, narthex, and prayer hall facing east, and additional rooms to their south, two of which contained mosaic floors with geometric patterns. Due to the proximity of the remains to the modern-day surface, nothing of the prayer hall has survived in situ apart from the massive foundations and the

---

30 Theodosius, *De situ Terrae Sanctae*, iv, p. 139. For further discussion on Theodosius and the maps used in his work, see Tsafrir, 'Maps Used by Theodosius'; Antonini Placentini, *Itinerarium*, iv, p. 161.

31 Limor, *Holy Land Travels*, pp. 8–11.

32 The synagogue, for example, faces north-west for the same reasons; Weiss, *Sepphoris Synagogue*, pp. 7–8, 43–45.

33 Weiss, *Sepphoris: A Mosaic of Cultures*, pp. 141–42.

34 Weiss, *Sepphoris: A Mosaic of Cultures*, pp. 142–45.

FIGURE 3.3. Mosaic medallion with a Greek inscription incorporated into the eastern pavement of the *cardo*. It reads: 'In the time of the most pious bishop Eutropius, our father, the entire work of the mosaic was conducted by the provision of Marinus, the most learned head of the doctors, and father (of the city), in the time of the fourteenth indiction'. Photo by Gabi Laron.

floor bedding preserved mainly on its eastern side. Nevertheless, the marble pavers, some opus sectile tiles, and mosaic chunks uncovered in the debris may indicate the nature of the church floors.

The foundation wall (diameter about 7 m) forming the central apse in the eastern church is especially thick (2.40 m) and may suggest that it supported the wall bordering the apse and the synthronon, the bench on which the priests and bishop sat when facing the nave. In the apse, beneath the altar, a rectangular box-shaped depression sealed beneath the floor held a reliquary. The box, which was made of stone, wood, or perhaps a more valuable material, was not preserved in situ, but the depression in the centre of the floor certainly indicates that the church was dedicated to a martyr whose identity is as yet unknown.

The debris covering the destroyed building and the area to its north contained various architectural elements belonging to the church, including bases, pedestals, columns, Corinthian capitals, and three more decorated with crosses. The church had a gable roof supported by a wooden superstructure, as is evident from the large number of roof tiles and nails of various sizes found in the debris. In addition, fragments of stone architectural decorations and shattered pieces of marble from the church had been moved from their original

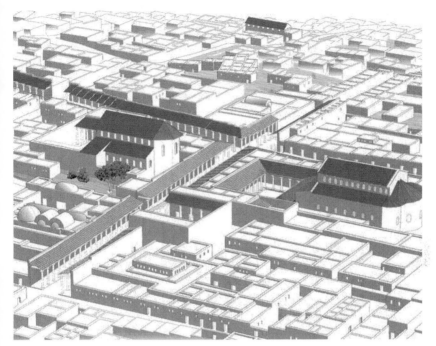

FIGURE 3.4. Reconstruction of late antique Sepphoris. Note the two churches constructed along the *cardo* in the foreground and the synagogue in the background. Drawing by Anna Iamim.

positions to a nearby limekiln. Fragments of marble slabs bearing geometric and floral patterns, including a cross made in low relief in the Champlevé technique, were apparently used as wall revetments decorating the main apse. Other fragments of the liturgical furniture adorning the presbytery include parts of the altar, miniature Corinthian capitals, small columns, and sections of a chancel screen. The high-quality marble elements are consistent with the character of the eastern church, which, judging by its dimensions, was undoubtedly an impressive and lavishly adorned structure.

The close proximity of the two churches to the surface, their poor state of preservation, and the fact that only a few sealed loci were found in conjunction with both buildings make it difficult to ascertain when they were constructed. The stratigraphical analysis of the finds unearthed in the two churches, as well as the architectural development of lower Sepphoris, indicate that these buildings were constructed at the same time, in the late fifth or early sixth century. The western church was constructed on top of the remains of an industrial area, while the eastern church was built on the foundations of the temple, possibly attesting to the preservation of the city's sacred precinct over time. It should be borne in mind, however, that such building activity occurred a century or more after the desertion of the temple and is a known phenomenon elsewhere in the region and in other late antique cities throughout the empire. For example, the Herodian temple at Caesarea Maritima was abandoned in the fourth century, but the construction of the octagonal church uncovered on top of the destroyed structure began only *c.* 500, long after that city embraced Christianity.[35] Similar dates apply to the early sixth-century church with the round plan on the acropolis in Scythopolis, which was built near, and partially covering, the Hellenistic-Roman temple of Zeus Akraios.[36] In Hippos, the temple was destroyed by the earthquake of 363 whereas the north-western church was constructed on top of its ruins in the early sixth century.[37] Similar evidence is known from other cultic sites in the region, such as Mamre and Mt Gerizim.[38] All these examples stand in contrast to the events in Jerusalem and Gaza, for example, where the sources inform us that the churches were constructed immediately after the temples were desecrated and destroyed to accommodate the construction of buildings befitting the incoming religion.[39]

The erection of the two churches representing the latest construction phase in the city is concomitant with the restoration of the adjacent main intersection of the two colonnaded streets and the embellishment of the porticoes with colourful mosaics displaying simple geometric patterns. Three different-sized medallions incorporated in the mosaic floors contain dedicatory inscriptions recording that the renovation was carried out in the days of Eutropius, the bishop of the city. The three inscriptions attest to the role of the bishop of Sepphoris in the late fifth or early sixth century, not only as a religious figure but also as active in the administration of the city and concerned with the welfare of its inhabitants.[40]

Some Concluding Remarks

The archaeological finds unearthed in Sepphoris over the years have provided a wealth of information about this multifaceted urban centre and allow us to draw significant conclusions regarding the city's demographic composition and the cultural relations between the various communities residing there in the first centuries.

The discovery of a pagan temple undoubtedly broadens the scope of our discussion, with the realization that Sepphoris, the Jewish capital of

---

35 Holum and Iamim, 'Octagonal Church'.

36 Tsafrir and Foerster, 'Urbanism at Scythopolis-Beth Shean', pp. 109–11

37 Segal and others, *Hippos-Sussita of the Decapolis*, pp. 129–47, 195–217; Burdajewicz, 'From Pagan Temple to Church'.

38 Mamre: Magen, 'Elonei Mamre'; Mt. Gerizim: Magen, *Flavia Neapolis*, i, pp. 243–55.

39 Wharton, *Refiguring the Post Classical City*, pp. 94–100; Patrich, 'Early Christian Churches in the Holy Land', pp. 359–63.

40 Dan, *The City in Eretz-Israel*, pp. 90–102.

the Galilee in the Roman period, had a significant pagan population that worshipped its god(s) in a large and imposing temple in the heart of its civic centre. The central location of the temple, enclosed within a walled courtyard, its visibility on the urban landscape, and its architectural relationship to the surrounding public buildings and private dwellings emphasize its importance and contribute to our understanding of Sepphoris's urban plan in the Roman era. The temple, which was completed by the end of the second or early third century, flourished at a time when the Jews of Sepphoris enjoyed a vibrant communal, economic, religious, and spiritual life — as we learn from the abundance of traditions in talmudic literature. The diverse archaeological finds uncovered over the years in Roman Sepphoris and their distribution throughout the site — over fifty *miqva'ot* (ritual baths), chalkstone vessels, domestic wares, objects featuring Jewish symbols, inscriptions, sarcophagi, ossuaries, and more — further corroborate the Jewish character of this ancient city.[41] And yet, the temple and assorted finds unearthed at the site are indicative not only of the religious and cultural life in Roman Sepphoris, but also of the way in which both Jews and pagans coexisted and built impressive buildings in the city.[42]

Two or possibly three synagogues dated to the fifth century and two churches dated to the late fifth–early sixth centuries are currently known to have stood on the site. The construction of these synagogues in the early fifth century and their continued existence indicate that the Jewish community preserved its status, place, and architectural visibility in the city — even after the conversion of the empire to Christianity and despite the increased power of the church in the provincial government and the imperial legislation voiced against the Jews.

In the early fourth century, the church father Eusebius, who lived in Caesarea, described Sepphoris as a large city populated by Jews.[43] This view was expressed in the course of Late Antiquity by several ecclesiastic members, such as Peter of Alexandria who, in 373, composed a letter, preserved by the bishop Theodoretus, that tells of the exile of eleven bishops from Egypt in the days of the Arian Emperor Valens, and states that they were banished to 'a city called Diocaesarea, inhabited by the Jews, killers of the Lord'.[44]

---

41 Weiss, *Sepphoris: A Mosaic of Cultures*, pp. 96–99, 206–09, with references for earlier studies. According to David Amit and Yonatan Adler, the existence of ritual baths and stone vessels at various sites in the first centuries of the Common Era throughout the Galilee and Judaea indicates a continual interest in ritual purity for generations after 70 CE; see Amit and Adler, 'Observance of Ritual Purity'. On the finds known to date from Sepphoris's local necropolis, see Weiss, 'Urban Necropoleis'.

42 According to Belayche, Jews and pagans coexisted harmoniously in the two Galilean cities — Sepphoris and Tiberias — however, while the rabbis set up various constraints in order to face this complex reality, the pagans were not affected by Jewish presence; see Belayche, *Iudaea-Palaestina*, pp. 82–95.

43 Cureton, *History of the Martyrs in Palestine, by Eusebius*, p. 29.

44 Theodoret, *Kirchengeschichte*, 4.22.35 (GCS n.s., 5. 259–260). For further discussions on the

This is undoubtedly an overstatement, since the talmudic sources and the archaeological and numismatic finds bear witness to the presence of both pagans and Christians in Sepphoris in the first centuries.[45] Christianity's inroads into Sepphoris in the late fifth and sixth centuries had a marked effect on the city's demography, yet its Jewish community continued to constitute a relative majority there throughout Late Antiquity.[46] Thus, the decision to establish the two churches in lower Sepphoris — close to the main intersection of the city's two colonnaded streets in the heart of the civic centre — was not coincidental, nor did it derive from the fact that these two spots were vacant, even partially, when it was decided to erect them in the late antique city. The construction of the two churches reflects, at first glance, the natural expansion of the Christian community and its establishment within the Jewish city, however it should also be viewed as a political-religious act of the imperial authorities, emphasizing to the local population, through architectural symbols, who the ruler and true victor was. This is true in Tiberias as well, where a large church was constructed in its civic centre sometime in the fifth century.[47]

The temple, synagogues, and churches are extremely important to the study of ancient Sepphoris, shedding light on the architectural developments, religious behaviour, and cultural connections between the various populations residing in the city during the Roman period and throughout Late Antiquity. The finds also stand on a par with similar evidence from other cities in the region, providing noteworthy information for the study of urbanism in ancient Palestine or how the Jewish population conducted its affairs in a period of transition and change — from Rome to Byzantium and from paganism to Christianity.

---

exile of the bishops to Sepphoris, their implications for the Christian discourse, and the connections between Jews and Christians in the city, see Newman, 'Bishops of Sepphoris'; Mratschek, 'Melania'.

45 Safrai, 'Jewish Community in the Galilee and Golan', pp. 145–58; Miller, *Studies in the History and Traditions of Sepphoris*, pp. 31–59; Freyne, *Galilee, Jesus and the Gospels*, pp. 167–75; Meyers, 'Jesus and His Galilean Context'.

46 Dan, *The City in Eretz-Israel*, pp. 24–28; Levine, 'Palaestina Secunda'.

47 Cytryn-Silverman, 'Tiberias', pp. 199–201.

Bibliography

Manuscripts and Archival Resources

Archive of the Department of Antiquities of Mandatory Palestine (1919–1948), Scientific Record Files 166 (Saffuriya, fig. B-882760) <http://iaa-archives.org.il/zoom/zoom.aspx?id=61394&folder_id=7626&type_id=&loc_id=4207> [accessed 19 June 2022]

Primary Sources

Antonini Placentini, *Itinerarium*, iv, ed. by Paul Geyer, *Itinera Hierosolymitana: saeculi III–VIII*, Corpus Scriptorum Ecclesiasticorum Latinorum, 39 (Prague: Tempsky, 1898)

Cureton, William (ed. and trans.), *History of the Martyrs in Palestine, by Eusebius, Bishop of Caesarea: Discovered in a Very Ancient Syriac Manuscript* (Piscataway: Gorgias, 2013)

Fedalto, Giorgio, *Patriarchatus Alexandrinus, Antiochenus, Hierosolymitanus*, Hierarchia Ecclesiastica Orientalis, 2 (Padua: Edizioni Messaggero Padova, 1988)

Genesis Rabbah, 2 vols, ed. by Judah Theodor and Chanoch Albeck (Jerusalem: Wahrmann, 1965) (in Hebrew)

Meshorer, Ya'akov, Gabriela Bijovsky, and Wolfgang Fischer-Bossert, *Coins of the Holy Land: The Abraham and Marian Sofaer Collection at the American Numismatic Society and the Israel Museum*, 2 vols, Ancient Coins in North American Collections, 8 (New York: American Numismatic Society, 2013)

Naveh, Joseph, *On Stone and Mosaic: The Aramaic and Hebrew Inscriptions from Ancient Synagogues* (Jerusalem: Israel Exploration Society, 1978) (in Hebrew)

Pesiqta de-Rav Kahana, 2 vols, ed. by Bernard Mandelbaum (New York: Jewish Theological Seminary of America, 1962) (in Hebrew)

Theodoret, *Kirchengeschichte*, ed. by Léon Parmentier, Die griechischen christlichen Schriftsteller, n.s., Band 5 (Berlin: de Gruyter 1911)

Theodosius, *De situ Terrae Sanctae*, iv, ed. by Paul Geyer, *Itinera Hierosolymitana: saeculi III–VIII*, Corpus Scriptorum Ecclesiasticorum Latinorum, 39 (Prague: Tempsky, 1898)

Secondary Studies

Amit, David, and Adler, Yonatan, 'The Observance of Ritual Purity after 70 c.e.: A Reevaluation of the Evidence in Light of the Archaeological Discoveries', in *'Follow the Wise' (B Sanhedrin 32b): Studies in Jewish History and Culture in Honor of Lee I. Levine*, ed. by Zeev Weiss, Oded Irshai, Jodi Magness, and Seth Schwartz (Winona Lake: Eisenbrauns, 2010), pp. 121–43

Ashkenazi, Jacob, 'Private Family-Church Buildings in Late-Antiquity Rural Palestine and the Competition in the "Field of Religious Goods"', in *Between*

Sea and Desert: On Kings, Nomads, Cities and Monks, Essays in Honor of Joseph Patrich, ed. by O. Peleg-Barkat, Jacob Ashkenazi, Uzi Leibner, Mordechai Aviam, and Rina Talgam, Land of Galilee, 5 (Tzemach: Kinneret Academic College and Ostracon, 2019), pp. 233*–42* (in Hebrew)

Ashkenazi, Jacob, and Mordechai Aviam, 'Monasteries, Monks, and Villages in Western Galilee in Late Antiquity', *Journal of Late Antiquity*, 5.2 (2013), 269–97

Aviam, Mordechai, 'Christian Galilee in the Byzantine Period', in *Galilee through the Centuries: Confluence of Cultures*, ed. by Eric M. Meyers, Duke Judaic Studies, 1 (Winona Lake: Eisenbrauns, 1999), pp. 281–300

——, 'Distribution Maps of Archaeological Data from the Galilee: An Attempt to Establish Zones Indicative of Ethnicity and Religious Affiliation', in *Religion, Ethnicity, and Identity in Ancient Galilee: A Region in Transition*, ed. by Jürgen Zangenberg, Harold W. Attridge, and Dale B. Martin, Wissenschaftliche Untersuchungen zum Neuen Testament, 210 (Tübingen: Mohr Siebeck, 2007), pp. 115–32

Belayche, Nicole, *Iudaea-Palaestina: The Pagan Cults in Roman Palestine (Second to Fourth Century)*, Religion der römischen Provinzen, 1 (Tübingen: Mohr Siebeck, 2001)

Burdajewicz, Mariusz, 'From Pagan Temple to Church in Late Antiquity Palestine: A View from Hippos-Sussita', *Études et Travaux*, 30 (2017), 181–207

Cytryn-Silverman, Katia, 'Tiberias, from its Foundation to the End of the Early Islamic Period', in *Galilee in the Late Second Temple and Mishnaic Periods, ii: The Archaeological Record from Cities, Towns, and Village*, ed. by David A. Fiensy and James R. Strange (Minneapolis: Fortress, 2015), pp. 186–210

Dan, Yaron, *The City in Eretz-Israel during the Late Roman and Byzantine Periods* (Jerusalem: Yad Izhak Ben-Zvi, 1984) (in Hebrew)

Freyne, Seán, 'Christianity in Sepphoris and in Galilee', in *Sepphoris in Galilee: Crosscurrents of Culture*, ed. by Rebecca M. Nagy, Eric M. Meyers, and Zeev Weiss (Winona Lake: Eisenbrauns, for the North Carolina Museum of Art, 1996), pp. 67–73

——, *Galilee, Jesus and the Gospels* (Dublin: Gill and Macmillan, 1988)

Holum, Kenneth G., and Anna Iamim, 'The Octagonal Church: Excavated Evidence', in *Caesarea Maritima Excavations in the Old City 1989–2003 Conducted by the University of Maryland and the University of Haifa: Final Reports, i*, ed. by Kenneth G. Holum, ASOR Archaeological Reports, 27 (Alexandria, VA: American Schools of Oriental Research, 2020), pp. 197–247

Isaac, Benjamin, and Israel Roll, 'Judaea in the Early Years of Hadrian's Reign', *Latomus*, 38 (1979), 54–66

Levine, Lee I., *The Ancient Synagogue: The First Thousand Years*, revised edn (New Haven: Yale University Press, 2005)

——, '*Palaestina Secunda*: The Geohistorical Setting for Jewish Resilience and Creativity in Late Antiquity', in *Strength to Strength: Essays in Appreciation of Shaye J. D. Cohen*, ed. by Michael L. Satlow (Providence: Brown University Press, 2018), pp. 511–35

Lichtenberger, Achim, 'Coin Iconography and Archaeology: Methodological Considerations of Architectural Depictions on City Coins of Palestine', in *Expressions of Cult in the Southern Levant in the Greco-Roman Period: Manifestations in Text and Material Culture*, ed. by Oren Tal and Zeev Weiss, Contextualizing the Sacred, 6 (Turnhout: Brepols, 2017), pp. 197–220

Limor, Ora, *Holy Land Travels: Christian Pilgrims in Late Antiquity* (Jerusalem: Yad Izhak Ben-Zvi, 1998) (in Hebrew)

Magen, Yitzhak, 'Elonei Mamre: A Cultic Site from the Time of Herod', in *Judea and Samaria: Researches and Discoveries*, ed. by Yitzhak Magen, Judea and Samaria Publications, 6 (Jerusalem: Staff Officer of Archaeology, Civil Administration for Judea and Samaria and Israel Antiquities Authority, 2008), pp. 95–114

——, *Flavia Neapolis: Shechem in the Roman Period*, 2 vols, Judea and Samaria Publications, 11 (Jerusalem: Israel Antiquities Authority, Staff Officer of Archaeology-Civil Administration of Judea and Samaria, 2009)

Meshorer, Ya'akov, 'Sepphoris and Rome', in *Greek Numismatics and Archaeology: Essays in Honor of Margaret Thompson*, ed. by Otto Mørkholm and Nancy M. Waggoner (Wetteren: Editions NR, 1979), pp. 159–71

Meyers, Eric M., 'Jesus and His Galilean Context', in *Archaeology and the Galilee: Texts and Contexts in the Graeco-Roman and Byzantine Periods*, ed. by Douglas R. Edwards and C. Thomas McCollough, South Florida Studies in the History of Judaism, 143 (Atlanta: Scholars, 1997), pp. 57–66

Miller, Stuart S., 'Markers of Pagan Cults in a Jewish City: Rethinking the Hadrianeum of Tiberias', in *Expressions of Cult in the Southern Levant in the Greco-Roman Period: Manifestations in Text and Material Culture*, ed. by Oren Tal and Zeev Weiss, Contextualizing the Sacred, 6 (Turnhout: Brepols, 2017), pp. 95–107

——, 'On the Number of Synagogues in the Cities of 'Erez Israel', *Journal of Jewish Studies*, 49.1 (1998), 51–66

——, *Studies in the History and Traditions of Sepphoris*, Studies in Judaism in Late Antiquity, 37 (Leiden: Brill, 1984)

Mratschek, Sigrid, 'Melania and the Unknown Governor of Palestine', *Journal of Late Antiquity*, 5.2 (2013), 250–68

Newman, Hillel I., 'The Bishops of Sepphoris: Christianity and Synagogue Iconography in the Late Fourth and Early Fifth Centuries', in *'Follow the Wise' (B Sanhedrin 32b): Studies in Jewish History and Culture in Honor of Lee I. Levine*, ed. by Zeev Weiss, Oded Irshai, Jodi Magness, and Seth Schwartz (Winona Lake: Eisenbrauns, 2010), pp. 85–99

Oppenheimer, Aharon, 'Beth ha-Midrash – An Institution Apart', *Cathedra*, 18 (1981), 45–48 (in Hebrew)

Patrich, Joseph, 'Early Christian Churches in the Holy Land', in *Christians and Christianity in the Holy Land: From the Origins to the Latin Kingdoms*, ed. by Ora Limor and Guy G. Stroumsa, Cultural Encounters in Late Antiquity and the Middle Ages, 5 (Turnhout: Brepols, 2006), pp. 355–99

Safrai, Shmuel, 'The Jewish Community in the Galilee and Golan in the Third and Fourth Centuries', in *Eretz Israel from the Destruction of the Second Temple* to the Muslim Conquest, i, ed. by Zvi Baras, Shmuel Safrai, Yoram Tsafrir, and Menahem Stern (Jerusalem: Yad Izhak Ben-Zvi, 1982), 144–79 (in Hebrew)

Segal, Arthur, 'Religious Architecture in the Roman Near East: Temples of the Basalt Lands (Trachon and Hauran)', in *The Variety of Local Religious Life in the Near East in the Hellenistic and Roman Periods*, ed. by Ted Kaizer, Religions in the Graeco-Roman World, 164 (Leiden: Brill, 2008), pp. 97–132

Segal, Arthur, Michael Eisenberg, Jolanta Młynarczyk, Mariusz Burdajewicz, and Mark Schuler, *Hippos-Sussita of the Decapolis: The First Twelve Seasons of Excavations 2000–2011*, i (Haifa: Zinman Institute of Archaeology, University of Haifa, 2013)

Steinsapir, Ann I., *Rural Sanctuaries in Roman Syria: The Creation of Sacred Landscape*, BAR International Series, 1431 (Oxford: Hedges, 2005)

Stemberger, Günter, *Jews and Christians in the Holy Land: Palestine in the Fourth Century* (Edinburgh: T & T Clark, 2000)

Stern, Sacha, 'Babylonian Talmud, Avodah Zarah 16a – Jews and Pagan Cults in Third-Century Sepphoris', in *Talmuda de-Eretz Israel: Archaeology and the Rabbis in Late Antique Palestine*, ed. by Steven Fine and Aaron J. Koller, Studia Judaica, 73 (Boston: de Gruyter, 2014), pp. 205–24

Tsafrir, Yoram, 'The Maps Used by Theodosius: On the Pilgrim Maps of the Holy Land and Jerusalem in the Sixth Century CE', *Dumbarton Oaks Papers*, 40 (1986), 129–45

Tsafrir, Yoram, and Gideon Foerster, 'Urbanism at Scythopolis-Beth Shean in the Fourth to Seventh Centuries', *Dumbarton Oaks Papers*, 51 (1997), 85–146

Viaud, Prosper, *Nazareth et ses deux églises de l'Annonciation et de Saint-Joseph, d'après les fouilles récentes pratiquées* (Paris: Picard, 1910)

Vilozny, Naama, 'Fresco, Secco, Stucco, and Mosaic Fragments', in *The Architecture, Stratigraphy, and Artifacts of the Western Summit of Sepphoris*, 2 vols, ed. by Eric M. Meyers, Carol L. Meyers, and Benjamin D. Gordon, Duke Sepphoris Excavation Reports, 3 (University Park: Eisenbrauns, 2018), pp. 889–901

Walker, Peter W. L., *Holy City, Holy Places? Christian Attitudes to Jerusalem and the Holy Land in the Fourth Century*, Oxford Early Christian Studies (Oxford: Clarendon Press, 1990)

Weiss, Zeev, 'Biblical Stories in Early Jewish Art: Jewish-Christian Polemic or Intracommunal Dialogue', in *Continuity and Renewal: Jews and Judaism in Byzantine-Christian Palestine*, ed. by Lee I. Levine (Jerusalem: Dinur Center for the Study of Jewish History, Yad Izhak Ben-Zvi and Jewish Theological Seminary of America, 2004), pp. 245–69 (in Hebrew)

——, 'From Roman Temple to Byzantine Church: A Preliminary Report on Sepphoris in Transition', *Journal of Roman Archaeology*, 23 (2010), 196–218

——, *Sepphoris: A Mosaic of Cultures* (Jerusalem: Yad Izhak Ben-Zvi, 2021) (in Hebrew)

——, *The Sepphoris Synagogue: Deciphering an Ancient Message in Its Archaeological and Socio-Historical Contexts* (Jerusalem: Israel Exploration Society, 2005)

——, 'Urban Necropoleis in Roman and Byzantine Galilee', *Eretz-Israel*, 35 (2023), 418-427

Wharton, Annabel J., *Refiguring the Post Classical City: Dura Europos, Jerash, Jerusalem, and Ravenna* (Cambridge: Cambridge University Press, 1995)

PART II

Christian Perspectives

YONATAN LIVNEH

Cyril's New Jerusalem and His Omission of Local Church History

Jerusalem the Holy City and Mother of all Churches

In the beginning of the fourth century, the see of Jerusalem still held no special formal status in the ecclesiastical hierarchy. The council of Nicaea (325 CE) indeed crowned Jerusalem with extraordinary prestige, but still insisted on its subordination to the provincial seat of government, Caesarea. However, by the end of the century, roles in Palestine seem to have reversed, with Jerusalem gaining primacy over the churches of the three Palestinian provinces.[1] While Jerusalem's path to authority coincided with certain favourable circumstances, only persistent efforts on the part of Jerusalemite bishops could turn this opportunity into reality. One of their number, the celebrated Cyril (bishop c. 350–87 CE), will be the focus of our investigation here. This article examines Cyril's arguments for Jerusalem in two of his surviving works from the early years of his episcopacy, namely, his extensive *Catechetical Lectures*[2] and an epistle that he sent to the emperor Constantius II.[3]

1　See Irshai, 'Fourth Century Christian Palestinian Politics'; Rubin, 'The See of Caesarea in Conflict with Jerusalem'; Honigmann, 'Juvenal of Jerusalem'; and Norton, *Episcopal Elections*, pp. 21–25, 119–29.

2　Cyril of Jerusalem, *Catecheses ad illuminandorum*.

3　Cyril of Jerusalem, *Epistula ad Constantium*. Evidence from later parts of Cyril's career is more limited, and, with regards to our interests in this paper, also less conclusive (however, see below, note 17). The *Mystagogical Lectures*, if authored by Cyril at all, were from a later period in his career; see Doval, *Cyril of Jerusalem*, who defends Cyrillian authorship; and Day, *The Baptismal Liturgy of Jerusalem*, pp. 12–23, for the authorship of Cyril's successor, John II. Cyril's *Homilia ad paralyticum ad piscinam jacentem* should not necessarily be dated to Cyril's presbytership and early career; see McCauley and Stephenson, eds, *The Works of Saint Cyril of Jerusalem*, vol. ii, pp. 221–22 n. 69. In any case, all that can be added regarding this sermon is that the work indeed discusses a miracle performed in Jerusalem and is thus another Cyrillian contribution to the sanctification of the city's biblical sites. The work contains no other direct reference to Jerusalem nor any historical traditions regarding the local church.

Yonatan Livneh has a PhD from the Hebrew University of Jerusalem. His dissertation on ethnic identification and social grouping in Church historiography was supervised by Professor Oded Irshai.

Essays on Jews and Christians in Late Antiquity in Honour of Oded Irshai, ed. by Brouria Bitton-Ashkelony and Martin Goodman, CELAMA 40 (Turnhout: Brepols, 2023), pp. 95–117
BREPOLS ❧ PUBLISHERS　　　　　　　　　　10.1484/M.CELAMA-EB.5.132485

In previous periods, Jerusalem bishops relied on two distinct claims for their city's fame. First, the city was the backdrop to the narrative of Jesus's crucifixion, resurrection, and ascension, and its holy sites served as living witnesses to those events. Second, the Jerusalem episcopacy claimed an historical primacy, going back to James, brother of Christ, the first in line of succession to the Church and the first bishop of the Christian world. As we shall see, each of these arguments had its own history in the debate over Jerusalem's status.

As for the first claim, certain local sites in Jerusalem and its vicinity are mentioned as places of prayer from very early on,[4] but a fundamental leap forward in the sanctification of the city was achieved in the 320s by the identification of Golgotha and the purported remains of the Cross, which were followed by grand imperial building projects on the site and its surroundings.[5] This surge in Jerusalem's importance by the mid-fourth century is manifested in the large-scale building in the city, the growing stream of pilgrims, the institution of monasteries in the city and its vicinity, as well as in various church writings of the time, including those of Cyril. The rising importance of Jerusalem in the period has been well surveyed by now, as is the unease with which the sanctification of the city was received by certain church fathers, most notably Eusebius of Caesarea. On a theological level, the consecration of material sites and relics seemed to these teachers of the church to be foreign to the universal and spiritual messages of Christianity. In more practical terms, too, the elevation of Jerusalem threatened to destabilize the church hierarchy that was crystallizing at the time along the Roman administrative borders: Antioch was supervising the churches of the Diocese of the East, while Caesarea supervised those of the province of Palestine. Likewise, and similarly well documented, Jerusalem's growing attraction to pilgrims was loosening the pull of local churches elsewhere, and on these grounds, too, Jerusalem's claim for superiority met with resistance in certain parts.[6]

In comparison to these topics, the Jerusalem episcopacy's assertion of their church's second point of local pride, its early history and prestigious lineage, has been somewhat neglected in scholarship.[7] This lacuna stems mostly from the absence of reliable sources regarding the church's history itself, which in

---

4   See Wilken, *The Land Called Holy*, pp. 108–11; Perrone, 'Jerusalem, a City of Prayer', pp. 5–9; and Bitton-Ashkelony, *Encountering the Sacred*, pp. 18–22.

5   On Helena's pilgrimage and the imperial patronage of Jerusalem, see Wilken, *The Land Called Holy*, pp. 85–97; Bitton-Ashkelony, *Encountering the Sacred*, pp. 22–25; Hunt, 'Constantine and Jerusalem'; Perrone, '"Rejoice Sion, Mother of All Churches"', pp. 147–49. For Constantine's empire-wide Church-building programme see Lenski, *Constantine and the Cities*, pp. 179–96.

6   See further in Irshai, 'The Christian Appropriation of Jerusalem'; Rubin, 'See of Caesarea'; Rubin, 'The Cult of the Holy Places'; Walker, *Holy City, Holy Places*. For the debate over pilgrimage to the earthly Jerusalem later in the fourth century, see Bitton-Ashkelony, *Encountering the Sacred*, esp. pp. 44–64, 71–97.

7   However, see Irshai, 'From Oblivion to Fame'.

turn inhibits understanding of the later use of those historical traditions by the Jerusalem episcopacy. Eusebius is our most significant source for both topics. In his works, he offered a glimpse at the church's history, from which we can also reconstruct the later circulation of this material. For example, Eusebius discussed substantial passages from Hegesippus's *Hypomnemata* regarding two of Jerusalem's founding fathers, James, brother of Christ, and Simeon, son of Clopas, who was also a relative of Christ.[8] Both of these bishops are exalted in Hegesippus's narrative, which would seem to indicate how they were perceived in the Jerusalem church up until Hegesippus's time in the latter half of the second century.

Similarly, Eusebius produced an episcopal succession list for the city that was probably compiled during the late second or early third century, sometime during the reigns of Bishops Narcissus and Alexander.[9] The list begins with James and Simeon and ends with Narcissus, Alexander's predecessor, and co-bishop for a time, and thus maintains a direct lineage of the Jerusalem episcopacy from apostolic times. Moreover, the list is specifically organized in a way that highlights a comparison of contemporary bishops with the holy men of apostolic times in that it consists of fifteen bishops of Hebrew descent mirrored by fifteen later bishops 'of the nations'. This tale of succession was most probably part of a Jerusalemite self-portrayal as the earliest seat of episcopal power, home of the Church's first bishop — James.[10] For second- and third-century Christians, this privileged past of the Jerusalem church was more than just symbolic. It also laid the groundwork for a claim to an apostolic succession superior to any other church, and therefore to a contemporary position as holder of the apostolic teaching in its purest form.[11]

However, Eusebius's record shows that this tradition of succession also opened the door to potential problems of two types. First, especially in periods of heresiological offensives against 'Judaizing' traditions and communities, the cause of the Jerusalem church ran the risk of being harmed by emphasizing its Jewish beginnings. Thus, as Oded Irshai has shown, the active role that the Jerusalemite episcopacy played in the second-century battle against Quartodecimanism may have been an attempt to dissociate their church from its Jewish past.[12] A second difficulty was that the concrete facts of the

---

8 Eusebius, *Historia ecclesiastica*, II. 23, III. 11; vol. i, p. 164, l. 16–p. 174, l. 17; p. 226, l. 20–p. 228, l. 6.

9 Eusebius, *Historia ecclesiastica*, IV. 5, 3, V. 2; vol. i, p. 304, l. 22–p. 306, l. 3; p. 454, ll. 3–14, Eusebius, *Demonstratio evangelica*, III. 5, 109; p. 131, ll. 14–17, and throughout the *Chronicon*. For a useful presentation of the list's appearance in Eusebius's works, see the appendix of Johnson, 'Lists, Originality, and Christian Time', pp. 208–09.

10 See Irshai, 'From Oblivion to Fame', pp. 103–05, 113–20, and the bibliography there.

11 For the conceptualization of Apostolic Succession as an assurance of the integrity of church teaching, see Brent, 'Diogenes Laertius and the Apostolic Succession', and the bibliography there. On the term 'apostolicity', see below, note 29.

12 See Irshai, 'From Oblivion to Fame', pp. 109–12, and the notes there, which also include a survey of the surviving sources on Quartodecimanism, namely, the insistence of certain Christian communities to celebrate Easter on the Jewish calendric date of the 14th of Nisan.

historical succession in Jerusalem were a questionable matter. According to Eusebius, who relied on Jerusalemite sources, the split between Hebrew and non-Hebrew bishops in the Jerusalem succession list was a result of the Bar Kochba war, which brought an end to the Jewish-descendent church of Jerusalem. It seems from his narrative that after the war the church was renewed by non-Jewish Christians.[13] Thus, a decisive break overshadowed the history of the Jerusalem church, and its claims for superior lineage were cast into doubt.[14] Defending Jerusalem's direct lineage from apostolic times, then, could be both disadvantageous and difficult.

The two lines of argumentation that were open to the Jerusalem episcopacy in the promotion of their see thus raise distinct problems. In the following pages, I seek to show, regarding Cyril's early works, that while, as is common knowledge, he highlighted the city's holy topography in line with the first argument of the Jerusalem church,[15] he actually sidestepped the second point of the church's distinction — its early history since James — an intriguing manoeuvre that has largely gone unnoticed.

Cyril's Promotion of Jerusalem

Cyril's turbulent career is often portrayed as an unremitting campaign for the promotion of his see.[16] Cyril received his episcopacy when the see was in poor standing in the face of Caesarean dominance of the province and imperial apathy toward Jerusalem. By the end of his life, after decades of struggle with the metropolitan bishop in Caesarea and several periods of deposition, he had secured his rule in Jerusalem, and his efforts for his church appear to have further borne fruit with Cyril's personal elevation to a high position in the Council of Constantinople (381 CE) and the council's recognition of the city as the 'mother of all churches'.[17]

---

13 An earlier break, the passage to Pella prior to the first Jewish war, was less problematic inasmuch as afterward, Jerusalem was led by Simeon, son of Clopas, a figure of the apostolic age, another relative of Christ, and one nominated by the unanimous consent of all living apostles and relatives of Christ. For the Pella tradition, see Eusebius, *Historia ecclesiastica*, III. 5, 3; vol. i, p. 196, ll. 13–22, and a survey of the scholarship on the matter in Bourgel, 'The Jewish-Christian's Move from Jerusalem'.

14 This problem remains an issue for modern scholarship. Compare Verheyden, 'The Flight of the Christians to Pella', who minimizes the significance of the matter; and Irshai, 'The Jerusalem Bishopric and the Jews', p. 208; Irshai, 'From Oblivion to Fame', pp. 103–04, 112; and Reed, '"Jewish Christianity" as Counter-History?', pp. 203–07, who give it its full weight. I discuss this topic separately in Livneh, 'Historical Ruptures in Eusebius' History of the Jerusalem Church'.

15 See the literature above, note 6.

16 See Telfer, *Cyril of Jerusalem and Nemesius of Emesa*, pp. 19–30; Drijvers, *Cyril of Jerusalem*, pp. 31–49; and Van Nuffelen, 'The Career of Cyril of Jerusalem'.

17 Theodoret of Cyrrhus, *Historia ecclesiastica*, V. 9, 17, p. 294. This phrase draws on the apostolic

Cyril's involvement in the promotion of his see is already apparent in the *Catechetical Lectures* that date to the first years of his episcopacy.[18] In these lectures, Cyril makes constant reference to the holy places of his city and provides some of our earliest hints as to their incorporation in the city's liturgy.[19] Time and again, he returns to the importance of the sites and how privileged the local believers were to be able to visit them.[20] Thus, for example, in Lecture 13: 'One should never grow weary of hearing about our crowned Lord, especially on this holy Golgotha. For others merely hear, but we see and touch.'[21] And again, a few days later, in Lecture 16, Cyril reminds his audience of this extraordinary source of pride: 'The most honored privileges are ours. Here Christ descended from heaven; here the Holy Spirit descended from heaven.'[22]

While Jerusalem's holy places come up frequently in Cyril's lectures, they occupy centre stage in his *Epistle to Constantius II*. In the epistle, Cyril tells the emperor of the appearance of an illuminated cross 'in the sky above holy Golgotha, stretching out as far as the holy Mount of Olives'[23] and celebrates the privilege of his church in witnessing the event: 'we, the dwellers in Jerusalem, have seen with our own eyes this marvelous occurrence.'[24] Cyril portrays Jerusalem ('in this place') as the spot where Christ 'trod death underfoot and wiped away the sins of mankind with his own precious blood, who bestowed life, immortality and spiritual grace from heaven on all who believe in him.'[25]

---

history of Jerusalem in ways that Cyril seems to have avoided in his earlier works, and, thus, its appearance may indicate a transformation of the bishop's rhetoric by the later part of his reign.

18 On the date of the *Catechetical Lectures*, see Doval, 'The Date of Cyril of Jerusalem's *Catecheses*'.

19 Cyril of Jerusalem, *Catecheses ad illuminandorum*, 16, 4; vol. ii, pp. 208–10. In this passage, Cyril accepts it as self-evident that it is best to discuss the biblical events near the holy places of their occurrence. On Jerusalem's evolving stational liturgy, see Buchinger, 'Liturgy and Topography in Late Antique Jerusalem'; Baldovin, *The Urban Character of Christian Worship*, pp. 45–104.

20 This was not only a matter of the promotion of Jerusalem. The holy places are for Cyril also a medium that could bring his listeners closer to divine contemplation; see Doval, *Cyril of Jerusalem*, pp. 27–29; Perrone, 'Jerusalem, a City of Prayer', pp. 13–16; and Kalleres, 'Cultivating True Sight at the Center of the World'.

21 Cyril of Jerusalem, *Catecheses ad illuminandorum*, 13, 22; vol. ii, p. 80 (trans. vol. ii, p. 19): οὐκ ἔστι ποτὲ καμεῖν ἀκούοντας τὰ περὶ τοῦ δεσπότου στεφανουμένου, καὶ μάλιστα ἐν τῷ παναγίῳ τούτῳ Γολγοθᾷ. ἄλλοι μὲν γὰρ ἀκούουσι μόνον, ἡμεῖς δὲ καὶ βλέπομεν καὶ ψηλαφῶμεν. Cyril usually focuses more on the moment of Crucifixion than of Resurrection, and thus also on Golgotha more than on the Sepulchre; see Kalleres, 'Cultivating True Sight at the Center of the World'.

22 Cyril of Jerusalem, *Catecheses ad illuminandorum*, 16, 4; vol. ii, p. 210 (trans. vol. ii, p. 78): πάντων γὰρ παρ᾽ ἡμῖν ἔστι τὰ ἀξιώματα. ἐνταῦθα Χριστὸς ἐξ οὐρανῶν κατῆλθεν. ἐνταῦθα τὸ πνεῦμα τὸ ἅγιον ἐξ οὐρανῶν κατῆλθεν.

23 Cyril of Jerusalem, *Epistula ad Constantium*, 4, p. 288 (trans. p. 69): ἐν οὐρανῷ, ὑπεράνω τοῦ ἁγίου Γολγοθᾶ μέχρι τοῦ ἁγίου Ὄρους τῶν ἐλαιῶν ἐκτεταμένος ἐφαίνετο.

24 Cyril of Jerusalem, *Epistula ad Constantium*, 5, p. 289 (trans. p. 69): ἡμεῖς, οἱ τῆς Ἰερουσαλὴμ οἰκήτορες, τὸ τοῦ θαύματος παράδοξον αὐταῖς ὄψεσι παραλαβόντες.

25 Cyril of Jerusalem, *Epistula ad Constantium*, 7, p. 291 (trans. p. 70): τοῦ πατήσαντος μὲν

Even more importantly, Jerusalem is presented in the epistle as the place of Christ's anticipated second coming, in a reading of Matthew 24:30 regarding the expected appearance of the 'sign of man'.[26] Cyril aims in this letter to convince the emperor of Jerusalem's utility in promoting imperial fame, by reminding Constantius of the earlier discovery of the cross, and the benefit this had for his father, the emperor Constantine.[27]

Thus, in these first years of his bishopric, Cyril was clearly invested in the promotion of his city, and highlighted the sanctity of the city's holy places, most of all Golgotha, 'the very center of the earth'.[28] Noticeably missing from this short survey of Cyril's rhetoric is a pronouncement of Jerusalem's other claim to fame — its succession from James and Simeon, and the ensuing centuries of the church's history. The search for such material will occupy our essay here.

James in Cyril's *Lectures*

Cyril brings up James twice in the *Catechetical Lectures*, and these instances are sometimes cited by scholars as evidence that in his lectures Cyril elevates not only Jerusalem's holy topography but also its 'apostolicity'.[29] However, the two passing remarks regarding James do not support such a reading. James first appears in the fourth of Cyril's lectures, where Cyril discusses the ordinance of the body and goes on to discuss the question of abstinence from meats offered to idols:

ἐνταῦθα τὸν θάνατον, οἰκείοις δὲ τιμίοις αἵμασι τὰς ἀνθρώπων ἁμαρτίας ἐξαλείψαντος, ζωὴν δὲ καὶ ἀφθαρσίαν καὶ πνευματικὴν ἐπουράνιον χάριν τοῖς πιστεύουσιν ἅπασιν παρασχόντος.

26 Cyril of Jerusalem, *Epistula ad Constantium*, 6, p. 290. On Cyril's eschatology, central to the *Epistle* as well as to the *Catechetical Lectures*, see further in Irshai, 'The Jerusalem Bishopric and the Jews'; Irshai, 'Cyril of Jerusalem: The Apparition of the Cross and the Jews'; and Gassman, 'Eschatology and Politics in Cyril of Jerusalem's *Epistle to Constantius*'.

27 Cyril of Jerusalem, *Epistula ad Constantium*, 3, pp. 287–88.

28 Cyril of Jerusalem, *Catecheses ad illuminandorum*, 13, 28; vol. ii, p. 22: τῆς [...] γῆς τὸ μεσώτατον. And see Kalleres, 'Cultivating True Sight at the Center of the World'.

29 'Jerusalem was considered by Cyril to be the first bishopric and his predecessor James, Jesus' brother, the "prototype" of all other bishops. Twice Cyril singles out James in his Catecheses, obviously in order to stress the authority of Jerusalem as an apostolic see' (Drijvers, *Cyril of Jerusalem*, p. 153). The phrase 'apostolic see' may have various meanings. When used to invoke self-identification of a Christian community with the apostolic church of biblical times, it characterizes most churches throughout the period. One may choose to restrict apostolicity to refer only to claims of direct establishment of a church by an apostle, but Jerusalem's apostolicity, even in this restricted sense of the word, was not a matter of special significance, for 'in the East apostolic sees were two-a-penny' (McCauley and Stephenson, eds, *The Works of Saint Cyril*, vol. i, p. 16). What we seek in Cyril's works is a sense of Jerusalem being heir to a 'special apostolicity' or an 'extraordinary apostolicity', as we may put it, i.e., a church not simply established by an apostle, but as 'the church of all the apostles' (in the words of McCauley and Stephenson, *The Works of Saint Cyril*, vol. i, p. 16). See further in Van Deun, 'The Notion ἀποστολικός: A Terminological Survey'.

CYRIL'S NEW JERUSALEM AND HIS OMISSION OF LOCAL CHURCH HISTORY   101

For, in regard to the meats, not only I, at this time, but before now, the Apostles also, and James, once the Bishop of this Church, have shown concern. For the Apostles and the ancients wrote a Catholic epistle to all the Gentiles that they should abstain first of all from things sacrificed to idols, and then from blood and things strangled.[30]

Cyril refers here to the decree of the apostolic council in Jerusalem (*c.* 50 CE) that exempted non-Jewish followers of Christ from circumcision but retained other Jewish prohibitions, among them the ban against the consumption of certain meats. Cyril, relying here on Acts 15:13–21, does single out James from among the apostles and briefly notes James's episcopacy of the Jerusalem church. However, once we compare this short passage with the scriptural source, Cyril's reference to James does not seem like a significant allusion to the apostolic throne of Jerusalem. As Acts itself singles out James from among those present, Cyril's remark does not attest to great authorial intention. Cyril does add to the biblical text that James was a Jerusalem bishop, but does not mention his relation to Jesus, nor does he emphasize his role as first in the line of Jerusalem bishops. More importantly, in the biblical narrative, James appears to have a special position in the assembly. He closes the debate and suggests a final verdict and a course of action that are adopted by the council.[31] Cyril mentions nothing of this. In his paraphrase, the apostolic decree was written by all the apostles and ancients together, and no mention is made of it being the work of an assembly that took place at Jerusalem. Certainly, the apostolic council in Jerusalem and its decree were sources of local pride, and Cyril, in other lectures, makes use of them as such.[32] However, my point here is that his mention of James, in this specific place and form, should not be read as an instance of Cyrillian promotion of Jerusalemite apostolicity. Cyril, here, quite to the contrary, only casually follows the biblical text in front of him. If he intended to highlight James and his importance as a father of the Jerusalem church, this is a missed opportunity.

In comparison, Cyril's second mention of James, from the 14th lecture, appears on the surface to be a better example of an exaltation of James and of the lineage of the Jerusalem see. In this lecture Cyril discusses Christ's resurrection, and presents the evidence for the actuality of the event, quoting from Paul's First Epistle to the Corinthians:

---

30   Cyril of Jerusalem, *Catecheses ad illuminandorum*, 4, 28; vol. i, p. 120 (trans. vol. i, p. 133, with minor alterations): Περὶ γὰρ [τούτων] τῶν βρωμάτων, οὐκ ἐμοὶ νῦν μόνον, ἀλλ' ἤδη καὶ τοῖς ἀποστόλοις καὶ Ἰακώβῳ τῷ ταύτης τῆς ἐκκλησίας ἐπισκόπῳ σπουδὴ γέγονεν. Καὶ γράφουσιν οἱ ἀπόστολοι καὶ οἱ πρεσβύτεροι πᾶσι τοῖς ἔθνεσι καθολικὴν ἐπιστολήν, προηγουμένως τῶν εἰδωλοθύτων ἀπέχεσθαι, ἔπειτα δὲ καὶ αἵματος, καὶ πνικτοῦ.

31   On James's role in the council, see Dunn, *Beginning from Jerusalem*, pp. 446–69; Myllykoski, 'James the Just in History and Tradition'; and Painter, *Just James: The Brother of Jesus in History and Tradition*, pp. 48–53, esp. p. 49 n. 9 and the bibliography there.

32   For example, Cyril of Jerusalem, *Catecheses ad illuminandorum*, 17, 29; vol. ii, p. 286.

'And he [Christ] appeared to Cephas; and after that to the twelve' (for if you disbelieve one witness, you have twelve witnesses); 'then he was seen by more than five hundred brethren at once' (if they disbelieve the twelve, let them heed the five hundred); 'after that, he was seen by James' His own brother, and first bishop of this diocese. Since such a bishop originally saw (πρωτοτύπως ἰδόντος) the risen Christ, as his disciple, do not disbelieve. But you may say that His brother is a biased witness; thereafter 'he was seen by me', Paul, His enemy; can testimony be doubted when it is proclaimed by an enemy? 'I formerly was a persecutor', but now preach the glad tidings of the Resurrection.[33]

Here too, we should begin the inspection of Cyril's passage by comparing it to the scriptural verses he cites, i Cor. 15:5–8 (NIV):

He appeared to Cephas, and then to the Twelve. After that, he appeared to more than five hundred of the brothers and sisters at the same time, most of whom are still living, though some have fallen asleep. Then he appeared to James, then to all the apostles, and last of all he appeared to me also, as to one abnormally born.

Paul lists here the series of appearances of Christ in a curious order, giving Peter precedence, and later naming James as one among the apostles, but only following mention of the appearances witnessed by the twelve and the five hundred.[34] Cyril follows the same order of appearances, but deviates in certain relevant respects from the epistle: he mentions James's relation to Christ, his role as first bishop of Jerusalem, presents him as of a certain special importance (Τοιούτου... ἐπισκόπου), and emphasizes his privilege in 'originally seeing' (πρωτοτύπως ἰδόντος) the risen Christ.[35] Lastly, Cyril depicts Christ's appearance

---

33 Cyril of Jerusalem, *Catecheses ad illuminandorum*, 14, 21; vol. ii, p. 136 (trans. vol. ii, p. 46, with minor alterations): ὤφθη Κηφᾷ, ἔπειτα τοῖς δώδεκα. εἰ γὰρ τῷ ἑνὶ μάρτυρι οὐ πιστεύεις, ἔχεις δώδεκα μάρτυρας. ἔπειτα ὤφθη ἐπάνω πεντακοσίοις ἀδελφοῖς ἐφάπαξ. εἰ τοῖς δώδεκα ἀπιστοῦσι, τοὺς πεντακοσίους δεχέσθωσαν. ἔπειτα ὤφθη Ἰακώβῳ, τῷ ἑαυτοῦ μὲν ἀδελφῷ, ἐπισκόπῳ δὲ πρώτῳ τῆς παροικίας ταύτης. Τοιούτου τοίνυν ἐπισκόπου πρωτοτύπως ἰδόντος ἀναστάντα τὸν Χριστὸν Ἰησοῦν σὺ ὁ τούτου μαθητὴς μὴ ἀπιστήσῃς. ἀλλὰ λέγεις ὅτι ὁ ἀδελφὸς Ἰάκωβος πρὸς χάριν ἐμαρτύρησεν· ἔπειτα καὶ ἐμοὶ ὤφθη Παύλῳ τῷ ἐχθρῷ. ποία δὲ παρὰ ἐχθροῦ μαρτυρία κηρύσσοντος ἀμφιβάλλεται.

34 The Pauline verses, an early creed of sorts, are probably a compilation of several textual layers. This may explain some of the peculiarities of the list of appearances of Christ, and see Fitzmyer, trans. and comm., *First Corinthians*, pp. 539–54, and the bibliography there.

35 That is, in contrast to Cyril's congregation, who must rely on scriptural testimony. The word πρωτοτύπως is variously recorded in the manuscripts, and in a few of them appears as an adjective describing James as a prototypical bishop (first bishop, first in importance, or first in line), or in plural, 'prototypical bishops', referring to all the witnesses. This reading is adopted, e.g., by Drijvers, *Cyril of Jerusalem*, p. 153 n. 5, providing him with further evidence for Cyril's exaltation of James; see above, note 29. However, other manuscripts testify to the adverb πρωτοτύπως that describes the verb 'to see' (originally saw, saw at first hand), and this reading was chosen by Reischl and Rupp and adopted here as well. On the manuscript variants see *Cyrilli Hierosolymorum*, vol. i, pp. 136–37 n. 11.

to James as one made to him alone, by glossing over the second part of the original Pauline verse — 'and the apostles', an omission that seems to further support a reading of this passage as a celebration of James's unique sanctity.

Such a list of alterations from the original text certainly indicates that Cyril was deliberately rephrasing the biblical passage. However, in searching for Cyril's intent in these changes, there is no need to import an external agenda (a promotion of his see), for Cyril's writing here is simple to follow on its own terms. As mentioned earlier, in this part of the lecture, Cyril moves to convince his catechumens that the post-resurrection appearances were true events and not mere fantastic tales of the Church. James's significance is, first, that he is another witness to the events, and second, that his episcopacy of the Jerusalem church gives his testimony authority over the congregation seated in front of Cyril and listening to his lecture. Finally, in Cyril's framing of the argument, James is used in this passage as a foil to the most convincing testimony of them all, that of Paul who was previously hostile to the Christians. Thus, we can explain Cyril's intervention in the biblical text merely on the basis of the context of his argument. James is not the focus of Cyril's rhetoric here, but simply a useful example, one of several that prove the reality of the resurrection of Christ. Cyril follows the biblical verses in their original order, naming all the preceding appearances of Christ, before arriving at James. When James's name does come up, Cyril highlights his special significance for his congregation ('first bishop of this diocese') and moves on to present the most convincing witness of all, Paul. To this end, James's relation to Christ is presented not in exaltation, but in expectation of criticism that might be raised against him as a biased witness. And so too, Cyril omits the words 'and the apostles' to achieve without interruption the juxtaposition of James and Paul.[36] Once again, if it was Cyril's intention to promote Jerusalem's importance by emphasizing James's special place among the apostles, there were many effective ways open to him in this reading of the Pauline epistle. The fact that James is singly named among the apostles in the original epistle gave Cyril more to build on and was a good opportunity to discuss James's later deeds for his church, and his martyrdom. That this was not his intention here is seen also from his choice to follow strictly the Pauline epistle and honour Peter, the acknowledged founder of the Caesarean church, as the first to witness the appearance of Christ.[37] All in all, this passage too seems unconvincing as proof of a Cyrillian advocation of an elevated apostolicity of the Jerusalem church; this is the more celebratory of only two mentions of the forefather of the Jerusalem church in the *Lectures* (the *Epistle to Constantius* holds none), and here too, Cyril remains measured.

---

36 It is also possible that Cyril avoided the phrase 'then to all the apostles' to limit the possible confusion regarding the relation between 'the twelve' and the apostles, and regarding the question of James's and Paul's apostolicity, and see above, note 34.

37 On Caesarea's claim for authority from Peter, see Eusebius, *Theophania*, IV. 6; p. 20, ll. 9–19, p. 173, l. 30–p. 174, l. 5.

The Early Jerusalem Bishops in Cyril's *Lectures*

Another passage in the *Catechetical Lectures* is directly relevant to our discussion here. In the *Lectures*, Cyril goes to great lengths to equip his audience with apologetic arguments in the face of Jewish criticism of the Christian creed. In one of these instances, the bishop attacks Jewish scepticism of the testimonies regarding Christ's resurrection, and briefly brings up the line of succession of his church:

> Hebrews wrote them [the Biblical testimonies]; the Apostles also were all Hebrews. Why, therefore, do you disbelieve Jews? Matthew, who wrote the Gospel, wrote it in the Hebrew tongue;[38] and Paul the preacher was a Hebrew of the Hebrews; and the twelve Apostles were of the Hebrews; besides, fifteen bishops of Jerusalem in succession were appointed from the Hebrews. Why do you accept your own accounts[39] but reject ours, though these too were written by Hebrews among you?[40]

There is much to say about this short passage. Here, I focus only on Cyril's casual mention of Jerusalem's first bishops, and his confirmation of the Eusebian episcopal list. It is, of course, only natural that Cyril repeats the information supplied by Eusebius. Cyril knew Eusebius's historiography well, and in any case, Eusebius's sources on the topic were derived from Jerusalemite archives and probably known to Cyril independently. And yet, while it is self-evident that Cyril was in a good position to emphasize the local church's distinguished heritage, its presence in his oratory is a very rare event. Moreover, here too, as in the two passages above concerning James, even where Cyril makes mention of historical material it is only in passing, and not employed to promote Jerusalem's unique apostolicity. Cyril met here another good opportunity to name some of the early bishops of his see and mention some historical traditions regarding the early Jewish-descendent church, and yet he chose to gloss over this point and quickly return to his topic at hand, the disputation with the Jews.

Holy Relics and Holy Men

This same inclination to narrowly focus on the biblical past of his city appears also in Cyril's references to holy relics. In the *Lectures*, Cyril makes many

---

38 On this common tradition in patristic writing, see Luz, *Matthew 1–7: A Commentary*, pp. 22, 46–47.

39 Cyril refers to the biblical stories of the rising of the dead by the prophets Elisha and Elijah. His point is that Jews who accept those stories should not dismiss as improbable the testimonies regarding Christ.

40 Cyril of Jerusalem, *Catecheses ad illuminandorum*, 14, 15; vol. ii, pp. 126–28 (trans. vol. ii, pp. 41–42, with minor alterations): Ἑβραῖοι ἔγραψαν ἐκεῖνα. καὶ οἱ ἀπόστολοι πάντες Ἑβραῖοι. διὰ τί οὖν τοῖς Ἰουδαίοις ἀπιστεῖτε; Ματθαῖος ὁ γράψας τὸ εὐαγγέλιον ἑβραΐδι γλώσσῃ τοῦτο ἔγραψε, καὶ Παῦλος ὁ κῆρυξ Ἑβραῖος ἐξ Ἑβραίων, καὶ οἱ δώδεκα ἀπόστολοι ἐξ Ἑβραίων. εἶτα δεκαπέντε ἱεροσολυμῖται ἐπίσκοποι ἐξ Ἑβραίων κατὰ διαδοχὴν κατέστησαν. τίνι τοίνυν τῷ λόγῳ ἀποδέχεσθε μὲν τὰ οἰκεῖα, τὰ δὲ ἡμέτερα ἀποδοκιμάζετε, καὶ ταῦτα ὑπὸ τῶν παρ' ὑμῖν Ἑβραίων γεγραμμένα.

elaborate remarks regarding the remains of the Holy Cross, that were for Cyril a crucial proof of the Gospels and of Christ's crucifixion. This idea is central also to Cyril's message in his letter to Constantius. However, the Cross was not the only holy relic that Jerusalem boasted. For example, Eusebius repeatedly mentions the 'Throne of James', the episcopal chair of the Jerusalem church that was shown with pride to visitors to the city.[41] Of less importance, but still relevant to our comparison, Eusebius tells also of a measure of sacred oil that was kept in Jerusalem — remnant of a blessed miracle performed by the second-century Jerusalem bishop Narcissus, the fifteenth bishop of 'those of the nations'.[42] Neither of these relics are mentioned by Cyril in his works, even though they could have easily found their place in his rhetoric. The same tendency to overlook post-apostolic information is true of Cyril's silence regarding the famed bishops and martyrs of the Jerusalem church, of whom we learn to some extent from Eusebius,[43] but who never appear in Cyril's lectures (and surely the local records in Jerusalem could have supplied Cyril with even more material). We must ask what led Cyril to dismiss this material. Why did he choose to concentrate so intensely on the sanctity of the city's biblical sites and sidestep evidence of his see's post-biblical prestige?

Sozomen's Witness to Cyril

Before we move on to discuss these questions it is necessary to make a short digression to introduce a related passage in Sozomen's *Church History*, for it appears to contradict our conclusions thus far, and may have influenced earlier scholarly assessments of Cyril's works. In this passage, Sozomen mentions Cyril's first deposition from office (357 CE)[44] and presents it as a result of the growing tension between Jerusalem and Caesarea over provincial authority:

> After being entrusted with the bishopric of Jerusalem, Cyril quarrelled with Acacius of Caesarea concerning Metropolitan rights, on the grounds that he ruled an apostolic see (ἀποστολικοῦ θρόνου).[45]

---

41 On the apostolic throne of Jerusalem, see Irshai, 'From Oblivion to Fame', pp. 100–02. More generally, on Eusebius's depiction of James, see Irshai, 'Jews and Judaism in Early Christian Historiography'.

42 Eusebius, *Historia ecclesiastica*, VI. 9, 1–3; vol. ii, p. 538, ll. 1–15.

43 Some mentioned above — the bishops Symeon son of Clopas, Narcissus, and Alexander. See Irshai, 'From Oblivion to Fame', for a full treatment of these traditions of the Jerusalem Church.

44 On the context of this early stage of Cyril's struggle with Acacius, see Van Nuffelen, 'The Career of Cyril of Jerusalem', pp. 135–37.

45 Sozomen, *Historia ecclesiastica*, IV. 25, 2; p. 181, ll .23–28, English translation of the passage taken from McCauley and Stephenson, eds, *The Works of Saint Cyril of Jerusalem*, vol. i, p. 22: ἐπειδὴ <γὰρ> ἐπετράπη τὴν Ἱεροσολύμων ἐπισκοπήν, περὶ μητροπολιτικῶν δικαίων διεφέρετο πρὸς Ἀκάκιον τὸν Καισαρείας ὡς ἀποστολικοῦ θρόνου ἡγούμενος.

This portrayal of Cyril's battle with Acacius has already been identified as anachronistic.[46] Sozomen, whose work was compiled in Constantinople sometime between the years 439 and 450,[47] was aware of the debates of his own days, in which Juvenal of Jerusalem made the most of Jerusalem's apostolicity,[48] a category that grew in that time to acquire a more precise meaning than it had in Cyril's days.[49] Moreover, as a native of Palestine, Sozomen may have also known of the role of James in the liturgy and life of the contemporary Jerusalem church, which had grown significantly since Cyril's early career.[50] As there is no indication that Sozomen was relying in this passage on specific evidence that is now lost, it is best to consider this passage as indicative not of Cyril's argumentation for his see in the early part of his career, but rather of the terms of the debate over Jerusalem in the ensuing century. It directs us once again to view the Jerusalemite campaign for authority as a dynamic process that transformed with the changing circumstances of the Church.

The Argument from Silence

As we approach the question of Cyril's possible reasons for evading the historical traditions of his church, we are essentially drawing conclusions from silence. Such an investigation is of course problematic, yet still has

---

46 McCauley and Stephenson, eds, *The Works of Saint Cyril*, vol. i, p. 23.

47 On the date of Sozomen's work, see Argov, 'A Church Historian in Search of an Identity', p. 368 n. 5.

48 Juvenal at the council of Ephesus (431 CE) named Jerusalem an apostolic see, mentioned it second only to Rome, and demanded Antioch's subjugation to the two, see Concilium Ephesinum anno 431, *actiones*, CPG 8716 = *Collectio Veronensis*, 20, 11, pp. 77–78 = *Collectionis Casinensis*, 39, 1, p. 102 = *Collectio Vaticana* 89, 6 pp. 18–19. On the changing landscape of the debate regarding the prestige of the Jerusalem church up to, and during, Juvenal's episcopacy, see Honigmann, 'Juvenal of Jerusalem'.

49 On 'apostolicity' see above, note 29.

50 James's place in the life and liturgy of the Jerusalem church is too large a topic to be dealt with here, but it is indeed of relevance. The fragments of Hegesippus concerning James, Eusebius's mention of the 'throne of James', and Cyril's mention of James in his lectures are but few examples of the reverence with which James was treated throughout the period. However, his tomb was marked only since the mid-fourth century, and maybe only later. A single source, which is both late and dubious, gives the year 351 for the discovery of the tomb, on which see Drijvers, *Cyril of Jerusalem*, pp. 163–64; Buchinger, 'Liturgy and Topography in Late Antique Jerusalem', p. 134 n. 94; and Mimouni, 'La tombe de Jacques le Juste', pp. 127–54. Egeria does not mention the tomb in the surviving excerpts of her work, and while Jerome does bring up the subject, it is only to contest the tomb's supposed location, indicating that the tradition of its place was still quite new. All this points to a rather late integration of James into the liturgy of the city, supporting in a way my conclusions regarding Cyril's low interest in these matters of his Church's history in the early part of his career. See also Eliav, 'The Tomb of James, Brother of Jesus', and Buchinger, 'Liturgy and Topography in Late Antique Jerusalem', pp. 133–34: 'In the case of James, "the brother of the Lord", considered as the first bishop of the local Church, it perhaps took until as late as the 6th century that a deposition of relics allegedly found in the mid-4th century was incorporated into the stational liturgy'. But see Mimouni, 'La tombe de Jacques le Juste', for an alternative view.

its place in historical research.[51] Thus, in our case, until other evidence appears, it seems disadvantageous to leave Cyril's silence on Jerusalemite church history unstudied. Special caution is of course expected in such an examination and so it is important first to evaluate the significance of this absence of information: should we indeed expect to find historical material in Cyril's surviving work?

In this discussion, let us concentrate on the *Catechetical Lectures*, the larger and more elaborate of Cyril's works, as our findings here will be applicable also to the *Letter to Constantius*. The breadth of historical material in the *Lectures* is restricted by three considerations. First, Cyril's oratory in them is not propelled by historiographical intentions and does not follow a chronology from Creation to the End of Days. Rather, the lectures are organized in a progression that follows the Church's creed — Father, Son, Holy Spirit, and so on.[52] As the Creed merely declares the Church 'one' and 'Catholic' and offers nothing else on the historical formation of the Church after the Ascension, so too Cyril is not expected to delve into post-biblical information. Moreover, Cyril's theological lectures are, in a way, an exegetical teaching of the Creed and so even when he reaches in *Lectures* 12–14 the topics of the Birth, Crucifixion, and Resurrection, he does not introduce the biblical episodes in detail for their own sake, but only cursorily refers to them and quickly moves on to explore their role in Christian dogma and in the Creed. Thus, if we were to find any historical material in Cyril's lectures it would be only in digressions and expansions outside the stated goals of his teaching.

Second, Cyril takes pains to base his teaching first and foremost on scriptural evidence. In the fourth lecture, he declares this agenda straightforwardly:

> For in regard to the divine and holy mysteries of the faith, not even a casual statement should be delivered without the Scriptures, and we must not be drawn aside merely by probabilities and artificial arguments. Do not believe even me merely because I tell you these things, unless you receive from the inspired Scriptures the proof of the assertions. For this saving faith of ours depends not on ingenious reasonings but on proof from the inspired Scriptures.[53]

---

51 See Lange, 'The Argument from Silence', and Duncan, 'The Curious Silence of the Dog and Paul of Tarsus'.

52 On the Jerusalem Baptismal Creed that is reconstructed from these very lectures, see McCauley and Stephenson, eds, *The Works of Saint Cyril*, vol. i, pp. 60–65.

53 Cyril of Jerusalem, *Catecheses ad illuminandorum*, 4, 17; vol. i, p. 108 (trans. vol. i, pp. 127–28): Δεῖ γὰρ περὶ τῶν θείων καὶ ἁγίων τῆς Πίστεως μυστηρίων, μηδὲ τὸ τυχὸν ἄνευ τῶν θείων παραδίδοσθαι γραφῶν· καὶ μὴ ἁπλῶς πιθανότησι καὶ λόγων κατασκευαῖς παραφέρεσθαι. Μηδὲ ἐμοὶ τῷ ταῦτά σοι λέγοντι, ἁπλῶς πιστεύσῃς· ἐὰν τὴν ἀπόδειξιν τῶν καταγγελλομένων ἀπὸ τῶν θείων μὴ λάβῃς γραφῶν. Ἡ σωτηρία γὰρ αὕτη τῆς πίστεως ἡμῶν, οὐκ ἐξ εὑρεσιλογίας, ἀλλὰ ἐξ ἀποδείξεως τῶν θείων ἐστὶ γραφῶν.

Cyril intended his lectures to present the tenets of faith, using the Creed as his template and the Scriptures as his proof,[54] and largely remains true to this goal, rarely presenting information outside the scriptural canon.

A third relevant aspect of Cyril's lectures is that they were meant to follow earlier teaching of the catechumens. The lectures were given consecutively, every morning, during the weeks leading up to the Easter baptism of the new initiates of the church.[55] Thus, they were delivered to a fairly stable audience (not only of catechumens, but also of members of the community) as a summary, divided into daily portions, of the full scope of Christian theology, and as the concluding portion of a lengthier initiation process. And indeed, it is clear from the lectures that the catechumens had already received ample introduction to biblical stories and the founding narrative of Christianity. So, for example, we see that Cyril only mentions, but nowhere expands upon, the stories of Adam, his nakedness in Eden, his expulsion from the Garden, his interaction with the serpent and so on.[56] Similarly, the flood in the days of Noah is mentioned only briefly,[57] and so are Abraham's trials and many other biblical stories that run throughout the lectures.[58] This is true, as noted above, also with regard to the events of Jesus's life and the beginnings of the apostolic mission — which are mentioned, but never dwelled upon. All in all, the lectures attest to the breadth of Christian teaching in Jerusalem at the time. Even if we accept that Cyril's teaching was sometimes beyond his audience's reach, or that some of his points were not understood fully, his mention of so many biblical figures and stories tells of a thorough instruction programme of initiates in the Jerusalem church that preceded the final lectures leading up to baptism.[59] For our purposes, this extended programme may have included also some historical teachings regarding the Jerusalem church and its early fathers, and for this reason Cyril may have found it redundant to repeat this material in his lectures.

Nevertheless, while these characteristics of Cyril's oratory do limit our expectations when mining the lectures for historical teachings, they are in no way severe constraints. The surviving work, a redaction of Cyril's lectures that reflects their extemporaneous character,[60] is in fact rich with stories and imagery that take Cyril off the track of his theological teaching. The lectures

---

54 See further in Jackson, 'Cyril of Jerusalem's Use of Scripture in Catechesis', pp. 431–37.

55 See Doval, *Cyril of Jerusalem*, pp. 42–49 (and the bibliography there), esp. p. 47 n. 100.

56 Cyril of Jerusalem, *Catecheses ad illuminandorum*, 2, 4; 6, 30; 9, 15; vol. i, pp. 42–44, 196–98, 256 (trans. vol. i, pp. 98–99, 166, 193). For more examples, see 'Adam' in the indexes of the two volumes of McCauley and Stephenson, eds, *The Works of Saint Cyril*.

57 Cyril of Jerusalem, *Catecheses ad illuminandorum*, 2, 8; vol. i, p. 48 (trans. vol. i, p. 100), the ark is mentioned in the *Procatechesis*, 14, vol. i, p. 18, but, here too, with very few details.

58 See further in the indexes of the two volumes of McCauley and Stephenson, eds, *The Works of Saint Cyril*.

59 For a similar conclusion, see Jacobsen, 'Catechetical Exegesis', pp. 159–60. On the changing catechetical syllabus during the fourth century see Doval, *Cyril of Jerusalem*, pp. 29–49.

60 See Doval, *Cyril of Jerusalem*, pp. 49–53; and Drijvers, *Cyril of Jerusalem*, p. 53.

also include some extra-scriptural evidence and anecdotes.[61] This is most apparent, as we already saw, in Cyril's frequent exaltation of the holy places of his city, and in his celebration of the symbol of the cross and its remains.[62] For example, in the course of his lecture on the crucifixion, Cyril teaches that Christ's death was real and that he truly suffered on the Cross, and brings proof of this (extra-scriptural proof, we should note) — in Golgotha and in the remains of the Cross:

> He was crucified and we do not deny it, but rather do I glory in speaking of it. For if I should now deny it, Golgotha here, close to which we are now gathered, refutes me; the wood of the Cross, now distributed piecemeal from Jerusalem over all the world, refutes me.[63]

Cyril goes here beyond the simple teaching of the Creed, to remind his listeners of his church's assets, and its role as the radiating centre of the Christian world. Certainly, the holy places of his city and the sanctity of the symbol of the Cross were two dominant topics in Cyril's teaching, to the extent that it is difficult to consider them foreign to the lectures' main thrust, but this is exactly the point. While they are central to Cyril's thought and oratory, they are not the focus of the Creed that guided Cyril in his teaching, and with regard to the reservations just introduced, they too were probably discussed earlier in the initiation process of the catechumens. Cyril's audience knew they were gathered near Golgotha, and that the wood of the Cross was distributed to faraway churches. This information was in fact repeatedly mentioned by Cyril himself in his earlier lectures, and there was no need, other than Cyril's will, to proclaim it again. Cyril's liberty to incorporate varied information in his lectures, including more recent history, surely extended also to other historical material relating to his see. The fact that this opportunity was not seized, I suggest, shows that publicizing his church's history was not among his objectives in this period of his career.

As we saw earlier, it is not only that Cyril could have added such historical information in a way that would fit his oratorical style, but that this would in certain respects contribute to his teaching. For example, Cyril nowhere names any local martyr (other than Stephen),[64] even though martyrdom comes up several times in his lectures.[65] So too, while Cyril repeatedly attacks the Jews

---

61 For example, bishop Archelaus of Carrhae is celebrated in the context of his disputation with Mani in Cyril of Jerusalem, *Catecheses ad illuminandorum*, 6, 27–30; vol. i, pp. 190–94.

62 See the notes of Drijvers, *Cyril of Jerusalem*, pp. 154–58 for mentions of these two matters in Cyril's lectures.

63 Cyril of Jerusalem, *Catecheses ad illuminandorum*, 13, 4; vol. ii, p. 54 (trans. vol. ii, p. 6): ἐσταυρώθη, καὶ οὐκ ἀρνούμεθα, ἀλλὰ μᾶλλον καυχῶμαι λέγων. κἂν γὰρ ἀρνήσωμαι νῦν, ἐλέγχει με οὗτος ὁ Γολγοθᾶς, οὗ πλησίον νῦν πάντες πάρεσμεν. ἐλέγχει με τοῦ σταυροῦ τὸ ξύλον τὸ κατὰ μικρὸν ἐντεῦθεν πάσῃ τῇ οἰκουμένῃ λοιπὸν διαδοθέν.

64 Cyril of Jerusalem, *Catecheses ad illuminandorum*, 17, 24; vol. ii, pp. 278–80.

65 Cyril of Jerusalem, *Catecheses ad illuminandorum*, 3, 10; 15, 17; 16, 20–21; 18, 27; vol. i, pp. 76–78, 176, 230–32, 330.

in his lectures, he nowhere brings up their blame for the death of James. And, for but one final example, consider the following brief supersessionist history that Cyril brings forward, toward the closing of his final lecture:

> Since the Jews for their plots against the Savior were cast down from grace, the Savior built out of the Gentiles a second holy Church, the Church of us Christians […] after the rejection of the first Church in Judea, the Churches of Christ are multiplied throughout the whole world.[66]

The omission of historical material is especially striking in this instance, as Cyril brings up the events in Judea of the first centuries but passes over the question that begs to be asked, regarding how the transformation of the Jerusalem church happened. Here too, Cyril could certainly have moulded a narrative that would extol his church's role in the period of transition from the first Church of the Jews to the churches of Christ.

To conclude, our conjecture that Cyril intentionally sidestepped historical material is not based on silence per se, but rather on a comparison between Cyril's many digressions regarding the city's topography and his practically complete elision of its history. From this comparison, his silence appears both significant and systematic enough to warrant further investigation into the possible reasons behind it. What were Cyril's concerns in the early part of his reign, and what role could the history of his church take under these circumstances?

Cyril and the History of the Jerusalem Church

Cyril rose to the episcopal throne of Jerusalem in difficult times. Earlier in the century, under Constantine, the city enjoyed immense imperial attention and investment that also offered its bishopric internal ecclesiastical influence.[67] After Constantine's death and the rise to power of Constantius II, this situation changed. Caesarean bishops, who enjoyed continuous access to imperial circles, led an effective attack on the Nicaean Christological formula; Jerusalemite

---

66 Cyril of Jerusalem, *Catecheses ad illuminandorum*, 18, 25; vol. ii, pp. 326–28 (trans. vol. ii, 133–34): ἀφ' οὗ δὲ διὰ τὰς γενομένας κατὰ τοῦ σωτῆρος ἐπιβουλὰς ἀπεβλήθησαν Ἰουδαῖοι τῆς χάριτος, δευτέραν ᾠκοδόμησεν ἐξ ἐθνῶν ὁ σωτὴρ τὴν τῶν χριστιανῶν ἡμῶν ἁγίαν ἐκκλησίαν […] τῆς γὰρ ἐν τῇ Ἰουδαίᾳ μιᾶς ἀποβληθείσης κατὰ πάσης τῆς οἰκουμένης λοιπὸν αἱ τοῦ Χριστοῦ πληθύνουσιν ἐκκλησίαι.

67 For example, the fact that the council of Nicaea devoted time to enact the seventh canon specifically on behalf of Jerusalem (even if the decision was unfavourable to it on a practical level) hints to the church's significant standing in the council. Canons 4 and 6 of the council fortified the prevailing jurisdiction of the churches of provincial capitals over the other churches of their province. Canon 7 did not reverse this arrangement with regard to Palestine but did separate the question of jurisdiction from symbolic honour, and conferred, separately — metropolitan authority to Caesarea, ecclesiastic fame to Jerusalem. See the literature above, note 1.

bishops, on the other hand, were slow to identify the changing tides, and supported the champion of the Nicaean cause, Athanasius of Alexandria.[68] The rift between the sees was unbridgeable, and was accompanied by imperial indifference toward Jerusalem, and perhaps even hostility.[69]

Under these circumstances, Cyril, whose nomination was imposed on the Jerusalem church by Acacius of Caesarea, in another sign of Caesarea's dominance in the province, took several steps to forge a new path for his city. First, where earlier bishops were eager to take sides on the Christological battlefield, Cyril attempted to limit his involvement.[70] His lectures and letter to Constantius stay safely behind traditional scriptural language, avoiding the term *Homoousios*, and nowhere commenting directly on the Christological debates of the time.[71] Second, Cyril made an urgent attempt to patch up Jerusalem's relations with the imperial court, as we can see in his epistle to Constantius. In the epistle he presents the emperor with a gift, as he puts it — a proof of divine approval of the emperor's reign, in the hope that the emperor would be drawn to renew the accord of his father with the Jerusalem church.[72] Third, Cyril's *Letter* and *Lectures* — both works that were expected to circulate widely beyond their immediate audience — attempted to reignite Christian interest in Jerusalem. Following Jerusalem's successes during the Constantinian period, Cyril was naturally drawn to emphasize Jerusalem's unique honour as the site of Christ's final days and its role as the place of his expected second coming. By the mid-fourth century, the sanctification of physical sites and relics was already the norm in Palestine and elsewhere, even if certain younger church theologians still shared Eusebius's unease with the phenomenon.[73] This was the domain in which there was no worthy rival to Jerusalem, and so Cyril was determined to leverage it as best as he could.

Jerusalem's early history, on the other hand, remained a minefield. Eusebius's historical and chronographic works circulated quickly throughout the Christian world and established an authoritative history of the Jerusalem church. In these writings, Caesarea received systematic precedence over Jerusalem as we can see, for example, in comparison of the number of martyrs that represent each city in the *Martyrs of Palestine*,[74] and in the primacy that

---

68 The Caesarea–Jerusalem split along the lines of the Arian dispute go back as far as to the time of Arius's refuge in Palestine, *c.* 319, and see Irshai, 'Fourth Century Christian Palestinian Politics', pp. 28–30.

69 More on these historical developments see in the literature mentioned above, note 1.

70 That he was unsuccessful in disengaging from the theological disputes of his days is another matter; see the literature above, note 16.

71 On Cyril's 'cautious middle path', see Doval, *Cyril of Jerusalem*, pp. 23–25 (cited phrase from p. 24); Drijvers, *Cyril of Jerusalem*, pp. 181–86 ('Appendix I: Cyril and Arianism').

72 Cyril of Jerusalem, *Epistula ad Constantium*, 1–3, pp. 286–88.

73 See Bitton-Ashkelony, *Encountering the Sacred*.

74 See Irshai and Rance, 'Holy Cartography Engraved with Blood'.

Caesarea's bishops usually receive in the *Church History* over their Jerusalem counterparts.[75] This was a true obstacle for Cyril. For example, in his fourth lecture, Cyril discusses the transmission of Scriptures, and describes it as the work of 'the Apostles and the ancient bishops, the rulers of the Church, who passed them down'.[76] Certainly, Jerusalem was home to a most important theological library, where some of the process of replicating and disseminating the New Testament had taken place at least since the beginning of the third century.[77] However, it would be impossible for Cyril to single out Jerusalem in this context, when comparison with Caesarea's library and scriptorium would dwarf any local Jerusalemite pride. Armed with much stronger assets (the holy sites and the Cross), Cyril probably found Jerusalem's history of the preceding centuries far less useful, and thought it better left unaddressed.

Moreover, as noted above, it is not only that the church of Jerusalem was of an unremarkable position for long parts of its history, but also that its transition from a church of Jewish believers to a church of Gentiles was a thorny matter. On the one hand, it was necessary to imagine this transformation as continuous and gradual enough to sustain the idea of an apostolic succession in the church; on the other, it was necessary to portray a complete removal of Jewish traditions in the church's teachings to defend the church's orthodoxy. This difficulty was intensified in the mid-fourth century with the crystallization of anti-Jewish polemics and the heightening of Christian anti-Judaizing heresiology.[78] Celebrating the Hebrew roots of the church was impossible at this time, and the whole matter may have seemed to Cyril better left untouched, as he was equipped with the much safer argument of the city's superior holy topography.[79]

Another consideration could have also been at play. The fourth-century Constantinian discoveries in the city indeed propelled Jerusalemite ambitions, but at the same time highlighted the gap between the city's present and its past. While the finding of the True Cross signified the local Jerusalemite roots of Christianity, it could also indicate a desertion of the city and its holy places for the period between Jerusalem's fall in the punishment of the Jews, to its restoration as an increasingly Christian city in Constantine's reign. Such a revival was celebrated in imperial propaganda, and is a major theme in Eusebius's later works, for example, in his *Life of Constantine*:

---

75 See Levine, *Caesarea Under Roman Rule*, p. 115.

76 Cyril of Jerusalem, *Catecheses ad illuminandorum*, 4, 35; vol. i, p. 128 (trans. vol. i, p. 136, with minor alterations): οἱ ἀπόστολοι καὶ οἱ ἀρχαῖοι ἐπίσκοποι, οἱ τῆς Ἐκκλησίας προστάται, οἱ ταύτας παραδόντες.

77 Eusebius, *Historia ecclesiastica* VI, 20, 1; vol. ii, pp. 566, ll. 5–9, and see Carriker, *The Library of Eusebius of Caesarea*, pp. 69–72.

78 See Bay, 'Writing the Jews out of History', and the vast literature there.

79 On the persistence of Jewish Christians in Jerusalem up until, at least, the fourth century, see Perrone, '"Rejoice Sion, Mother of All Churches"', p. 145, and the bibliography there.

New Jerusalem was built at the very Testimony to the Saviour, facing the famous Jerusalem of old, which after the bloody murder of the Lord had been overthrown in utter devastation, and paid the penalty of its wicked inhabitants. Opposite this then the emperor erected the victory of the Saviour over death with rich and abundant munificence, this being perhaps that fresh new Jerusalem proclaimed in prophetic oracles, about which long speeches recite innumerable praises as they utter words of divine inspiration.[80]

By the names Old Jerusalem and New Jerusalem, Eusebius correspondingly refers to the destroyed temple of the Jews and to the new Church of the Holy Sepulchre,[81] a theme that Cyril adopts in his *Lectures*, for example in a passage regarding the Matthean episode about the guard at the tomb of Christ:

> Christ has risen and come back from the dead, and by a bribe they persuade the soldiers; but they do not persuade the kings of our day. The soldiers then betrayed the truth for silver; the emperors of our times have built this holy Church of the Resurrection of God our Savior, inlaid with silver and wrought with gold, where we are assembled, and they have beautified it with treasures of silver and gold and precious stones.[82]

Like Eusebius, Cyril contrasts here the site's biblical past with its recent restoration under Constantine. However, as we saw earlier, by thoroughly passing over the history of his city and of his church in the intervening period, Cyril extends this idea over the city as a whole. The Jerusalem Church, for parts of the second and third centuries, cultivated its image as the enduring successor of the ancient church of the apostles, keeper of the apostolic truths, a local centre of theological learning and regional leadership. In Cyril's early works, we find an abandonment of this claim for local distinction. In his lectures and letter to the emperor, Cyril systematically avoids discussion of his church's historical primacy, and relies solely on its position as the centre of the world, the site of Christ's final days and of his expected second coming.

---

80 Eusebius, *Vita Constantini*, III. 33, 1–2, p. 99 (trans. p. 135): δὴ κατ᾽ αὐτὸ τὸ σωτήριον μαρτύριον ἡ νέα κατεσκευάζετο Ἰερουσαλήμ, ἀντιπρόσωπος τῇ πάλαι βοωμένῃ, ἣ μετὰ τὴν κυριοκτόνον μιαιφονίαν ἐρημίας ἐπ᾽ ἔσχατα περιτραπεῖσα δίκην ἔτισε δυσσεβῶν οἰκητόρων. ταύτης δ᾽ οὖν ἄντικρυς βασιλεὺς τὴν κατὰ τοῦ θανάτου σωτήριον νίκην πλουσίαις καὶ δαψιλέσιν ἀνύψου φιλοτιμίαις, τάχα που ταύτην οὖσαν τὴν διὰ προφητικῶν θεσπισμάτων κεκηρυγμένην καινὴν καὶ νέαν Ἰερουσαλήμ, ἧς πέρι μακροὶ λόγοι μυρία δι᾽ ἐνθέου πνεύματος θεσπίζοντες ἀνυμνοῦσι.
81 See further in Cameron and Hall, trans. and comm., *Life of Constantine*, pp. 284–85.
82 Cyril of Jerusalem, *Catecheses ad illuminandorum*, 14, 14; vol. ii, p. 124 (trans. vol. ii, p. 41): Ἐγήγερται ὁ ἀναστάς, καὶ διὰ δόσιν ἀργυρίου πείθουσι τοὺς στρατιώτας. ἀλλ᾽ οὐ πείθουσι τοὺς νῦν βασιλεῖς. οἱ τότε μὲν στρατιῶται ἀργυρίου προδεδώκασι τὴν ἀλήθειαν, οἱ δὲ νῦν βασιλεῖς δι᾽ εὐσέβειαν ἀργυρένδυτον καὶ χρυσοκόλλητον τὴν ἁγίαν ἐκκλησίαν ταύτην, ἐν ᾗ πάρεσμεν, τῆς τοῦ σωτῆρος θεοῦ ἀναστάσεως ἐξειργάσαντο καὶ τοῖς ἐξ ἀργύρου καὶ χρυσοῦ καὶ λίθων τιμίων κειμηλίοις ἐφαίδρυναν. See note 75 in the translation, regarding Cyril's use of the plural βασιλεῖς. It is tempting to see in this reference to the 'emperors' (and not to Constantine alone) another Cyrillian attempt to rehabilitate ties with the court of Constantius II.

Bibliography

Primary Sources

Concilium Ephesinum anno 431, *actiones*, ed. by Eduard Schwartz, *Collectio Vaticana*, Acta conciliorum oecumenicorum, 1.1.3 (Berlin: de Gruyter, 1960); ed. by Eduard Schwartz *Collectio Veronensis*, Acta conciliorum oecumenicorum, 1.2 (Berlin: de Gruyter, 1960); ed. by Eduard Schwartz, *Collectionis Casinensis*, Acta conciliorum oecumenicorum, 1.3 (Berlin: de Gruyter, 1960)

Concilium Nicaenum anno 325, *Canones*, ed. and trans. by Norman P. Tanner, *Decrees of the Ecumenical Councils*, 1 (Washington, DC: Sheed & Ward, 1990)

Cyril of Jerusalem, *Catecheses ad illuminandorum*, ed. by Karl Wilhelm Reischl and Joseph Rupp, *Cyrilli Hierosolymorum archiepiscopi opera quae supersunt omnia*, 2 vols (Munich: Sumtibus Librariae Lentnerianae, i: 1848; ii: 1860); Eng. trans. by Leo P. McCauley, and Anthony A. Stephenson, *The Works of Saint Cyril of Jerusalem*, 2 vols, The Fathers of the Church, a New Translation 61, 64 (Washington, DC: Catholic University of America Press, i: 1969, ii: 1970)

——, *Epistula ad Constantium*, ed. by Ernest Bihain, 'L'épître de Cyrille de Jérusalem à Constance sur la vision de la Croix', *Byzantion*, 43 (1973), 264–96; Eng. trans. by Edward Yarnold, S. J., *Cyril of Jerusalem*, Early Church Fathers (London: Routledge, 2000)

Eusebius, *Demonstratio evangelica*, ed. by Ivar A. Heikel, Eusebius Werke, 6, Die griechischen christlichen Schriftsteller, 23 (Berlin: de Gruyter, 1913, repr. 2012)

——, *Historia ecclesiastica*, ed. by Eduard Schwartz, Theodor Mommsen and Friedhelm Winkelmann, rev. edn ed. by Friedhelm Winkelmann, Eusebius Werke, 2.3, Die griechischen christlichen Schriftsteller, n.s., 6, 3 vols (Berlin: de Gruyter, 1999)

——, *Theophania*, ed. by Hugo Gressman and Adolf Laminski, Eusebius Werke, 3.2, Die griechischen christlichen Schriftsteller, 11.2, 2nd edn (Berlin: Akademie, 1992)

——, *Vita Constantini*, ed. by Friedhelm Winkelmann, Eusebius Werke, 1.1, Die griechischen christlichen Schriftsteller, 7.1, 2nd edn (Berlin: de Gruyter, 1991); Eng. trans. by Averil Cameron and Stuart G. Hall, *Life of Constantine*, Clarendon Ancient History (Oxford: Clarendon Press, 1999)

Sozomen, *Historia ecclesiastica*, ed. by Joseph Bidez and Günther Christian Hansen, Die griechischen christlichen Schriftsteller, 50 (Berlin: Akademie, 1960)

Theodoret of Cyrrhus, *Historia ecclesiastica*, ed. by Leon Parmentier, rev. edn ed. by Günther Christian Hansen, Die griechischen christlichen Schriftsteller, n.s., 5 (Berlin: Akademie, 1998)

Secondary Studies

Argov, Eran I., 'A Church Historian in Search of an Identity: Aspects of Early Byzantine Palestine in Sozomen's *Historia Ecclesiastica*', *Zeitschrift für Antikes Christentum*, 9 (2006), 367–96

Baldovin, John F., *The Urban Character of Christian Worship: The Origins, Development, and Meaning of Stational Liturgy*, Orientalia Christiana Analecta, 228 (Rome: Pontificium Institutum Orientalium Studiorum, 1987)

Bay, Carson, 'Writing the Jews out of History: Pseudo-Hegesippus, Classical Historiography, and the Codification of Christian Anti-Judaism in Late Antiquity', *Church History*, 90 (2021), 265–85

Bitton-Ashkelony, Brouria, *Encountering the Sacred: The Debate on Christian Pilgrimage in Late Antiquity*, The Transformation of the Classical Heritage, 38 (Berkeley: University of California Press, 2005)

Bourgel, Jonathan, 'The Jewish-Christian's Move from Jerusalem as a Pragmatic Choice', in *Studies in Rabbinic Judaism and Early Christianity*, ed. by D. Jaffé, Ancient Judaism and Early Christianity, 74 (Leiden: Brill, 2010), pp. 107–38

Brent, Allen, 'Diogenes Laertius and the Apostolic Succession', *Journal of Ecclesiastical History*, 44 (1993), 367–89

Buchinger, Harald, 'Liturgy and Topography in Late Antique Jerusalem', in *Jerusalem II: Jerusalem in Roman-Byzantine Times*, ed. by Katharina Heyden and Maria Lissek, Civitatum Orbis Mediterranei Studia, 5 (Tübingen: Mohr Siebeck, 2021), pp. 117–93

Cameron, Averil, and Stuart G. Hall, trans. and comm., *Life of Constantine*, Clarendon Ancient History (Oxford: Clarendon Press, 1999)

Carriker, Andrew, *The Library of Eusebius of Caesarea*, Vigiliae Christianae, Supplements, 67 (Leiden: Brill, 2003)

Day, Juliette, *The Baptismal Liturgy of Jerusalem: Fourth- and Fifth-Century Evidence from Palestine, Syria and Egypt*, Liturgy, Worship and Society (Hampshire: Ashgate, 2007)

Doval, Alexis J., *Cyril of Jerusalem, Mystagogue: The Authorship of the Mystagogic Catecheses* (Washington, DC: Catholic University of America Press, 2001)

——, 'The Date of Cyril of Jerusalem's *Catecheses*', *Journal of Theological Studies*, 48 (1997), 129–32

Drijvers, Jan W., *Cyril of Jerusalem: Bishop and City*, Vigiliae Christianae, Supplements, 72 (Leiden: Brill, 2004)

Duncan, Mike, 'The Curious Silence of the Dog and Paul of Tarsus: Revisiting the Argument from Silence', *Informal Logic*, 32 (2012), 83–97

Dunn, James D. G., *Beginning from Jerusalem*, Christianity in the Making, 2 (Grand Rapids: Eerdmans, 2009)

Eliav, Yaron Z., 'The Tomb of James, Brother of Jesus, as Locus Memoriae', *The Harvard Theological Review*, 97 (2004), 33–59

Fitzmyer, Joseph A., trans. and comm., *First Corinthians*, Anchor Yale Bible, 32 (New Haven: Yale University Press, 2008)

Gassman, Mattias, 'Eschatology and Politics in Cyril of Jerusalem's *Epistle to Constantius*', *Vigiliae Christianae*, 70 (2016), 119–33

Honigmann, Ernest, 'Juvenal of Jerusalem', *Dumbarton Oaks Papers*, 5 (1950), 209–79

Hunt, Edward D., 'Constantine and Jerusalem', *Journal of Ecclesiastical History*, 48 (1997), 405–24

Irshai, Oded, 'The Christian Appropriation of Jerusalem in the Fourth Century: The Case of the Bordeaux Pilgrim', *Jewish Quarterly Review*, 99 (2009), 465–86

——, 'Cyril of Jerusalem: The Apparition of the Cross and the Jews', in *Contra Iudaeos: Ancient and Medieval Polemics Between Christians and Jews*, ed. by Ora Limor, and Guy G. Stroumsa, Texts and Studies in Medieval and Early Modern Judaism, 10 (Tübingen: Mohr Siebeck, 1996), pp. 85–103

——, 'Fourth Century Christian Palestinian Politics: A Glimpse at Eusebius of Caesarea's Local Political Career and its Nachleben in Christian Memory', in *Reconsidering Eusebius: Collected Papers on Literary, Historical, and Theological Issues*, ed. by S. Inowlocki and C. Zamagni, Vigiliae Christianae, Supplements, 107 (Leiden: Brill, 2011), pp. 25–38

——, 'From Oblivion to Fame: The History of the Palestinian Church (135–303 CE)', in *Christians and Christianity in the Holy Land: From the Origins to the Latin Kingdoms*, ed. by Ora Limor and Guy G. Stroumsa, Cultural Encounters in Late Antiquity and the Middle Ages, 5 (Turnhout: Brepols, 2006), pp. 91–139

——, 'The Jerusalem Bishopric and the Jews in the Fourth Century: History and Eschatology', in *Jerusalem: Its Sanctity and Centrality to Judaism, Christianity, and Islam*, ed. by Lee I. Levine (New York: Continuum, 1999), pp. 204–20

——, 'Jews and Judaism in Early Christian Historiography: The Case of Eusebius of Caesarea (Preliminary Observations)', in *The Jews of Byzantium: Dialectics of Minority and Majority Cultures*, ed. by Robert Bonfil, Oded Irshai, Guy G. Stroumsa and Rina Talgam, Scholion Library, 6 (Leiden: Brill, 2011), pp. 799–828

Irshai, Oded, and Osnat Rance, 'Holy Cartography Engraved with Blood: A Historical Political Appraisal of Eusebius of Caesarea's *Martyrs of Palestine*' (forthcoming)

Jackson, Pamela, 'Cyril of Jerusalem's Use of Scripture in Catechesis', *Theological Studies*, 52 (1991), 431–50

Jacobsen, Anders Ch., 'Catechetical Exegesis: Cyril of Jerusalem's Use of Biblical Exegesis in His *Catechetical Lectures*', in *Christian Discourse in Late Antiquity: Hermeneutical, Institutional and Textual Perspectives*, ed. by Anna Usacheva and Anders-Christian Jacobsen (Leiden: Brill, 2020), pp. 145–60

Johnson, Scott F., 'Lists, Originality, and Christian Time: Eusebius' Historiography of Succession', in *Historiography and Identity I: Ancient and Early Christian Narratives of Community*, ed. by Walter Pohl and Veronika Wieser, Cultural Encounters in Late Antiquity and the Middle Ages, 24 (Turnhout: Brepols, 2019), pp. 191–217

Kalleres, Dayna S., 'Cultivating True Sight at the Center of the World: Cyril of Jerusalem and the Lenten Catechumenate', *Church History*, 74 (2005), 431–59

Lange, John, 'The Argument from Silence', *History and Theory*, 5 (1966), 288–301

Lenski, Noel, *Constantine and the Cities: Imperial Authority and Civic Politics* (Philadelphia: University of Pennsylvania Press, 2016)

Levine, Lee I., *Caesarea Under Roman Rule* (Leiden: Brill, 1975)

Livneh, Yonatan, 'Historical Ruptures in Eusebius' History of the Jerusalem Church', *Zeitschrift für Antikes Christentum* (forthcoming)

Luz, Ulrich, *Matthew 1–7: A Commentary*, trans. by James E. Crouch, Hermeneia: A Critical and Historical Commentary on the Bible (Minneapolis: Fortress, 2007)

McCauley, Leo P., and Anthony A. Stephenson, eds, *The Works of Saint Cyril of Jerusalem*, 2 vols, The Fathers of the Church, a New Translation, 61, 64 (Washington, DC: Catholic University of America Press, i: 1969, ii: 1970)

Mimouni, Simon C., 'La tombe de Jacques le Juste, frère de Jésus. État des questions et des recherches', *Transeuphratène*, 44 (2014), 127–54

Myllykoski, Matti, 'James the Just in History and Tradition: Perspectives of Past and Present Scholarship (Part I)', *Currents in Biblical Research*, 5 (2006), 73–122

Norton, Peter, *Episcopal Elections 250–600: Hierarchy and Popular Will in Late Antiquity*, Oxford Classical Monographs (Oxford: Oxford University Press, 2007)

Painter, John, *Just James: The Brother of Jesus in History and Tradition*, Studies on Personalities of the New Testament, 2nd edn (Columbia, SC: University of South Carolina Press, 2004)

Perrone, Lorenzo, 'Jerusalem, a City of Prayer in the Byzantine Era', *Proche-Orient Chrétien*, 64 (2014), 5–30

——, '"Rejoice Sion, Mother of All Churches"': Christianity in the Holy Land during the Byzantine Era', in *Christians and Christianity in the Holy Land: From the Origins to the Latin Kingdoms*, ed. by Ora Limor and Guy G. Stroumsa, Cultural Encounters in Late Antiquity and the Middle Ages, 5 (Turnhout: Brepols, 2006), pp. 141–73

Reed, Annette Yoshiko, '"Jewish Christianity" as Counter-History?: The Apostolic Past in Eusebius' Ecclesiastical History and the Pseudo-Clementine Homilies', in *Antiquity in Antiquity: Jewish and Christian Pasts in the Greco-Roman World*, ed. by Gregg Gardner and Kevin L. Osterloh, Texts and Studies in Ancient Judaism, 123 (Tübingen: Mohr Siebeck, 2008), pp. 173–216

Rubin, Zeev, 'The Cult of the Holy Places and Christian Politics in Byzantine Jerusalem', in *Jerusalem: Its Sanctity and Centrality to Judaism, Christianity, and Islam*, ed. by Lee I. Levine (New York: Continuum, 1999), pp. 151–62

——, 'The See of Caesarea in Conflict with Jerusalem from Nicaea to Chalcedon', in *Caesarea Maritima: Retrospective after Two Millennia*, ed. by Avner Raban and Kenneth G. Holum (Leiden: Brill, 1996), pp. 559–74

Telfer, William, ed., *Cyril of Jerusalem and Nemesius of Emesa*, Library of Christian Classics, 4 (London: S.C.M., 1955)

Van Deun, Peter, 'The Notion ἀποστολικός: A Terminological Survey', in *The Apostolic Age in Patristic Thought*, ed. by Anton Hilhorst, Vigiliae Christianae, Supplements, 70 (Leiden: Brill, 2004), pp. 41–50

Van Nuffelen, Peter, 'The Career of Cyril of Jerusalem (c. 348–87): A Reassessment', *Journal of Theological Studies*, n.s., 58 (2007), 134–46

Verheyden, Joseph, 'The Flight of the Christians to Pella', *Ephemerides Theologicae Lovanienses*, 66 (1990), 368–84

Walker, Peter W. L., *Holy City, Holy Places: Christian Attitudes to Jerusalem and the Holy Land in the Fourth Century* (Oxford: Clarendon Press, 1990)

Wilken, Robert L., *The Land Called Holy: Palestine in Christian History and Thought* (New Haven: Yale University Press, 1992)

This study has profited from the financial support provided by Prof. Daniel R. Schwartz, Herbst Family Chair in Judaic Studies at the Hebrew University of Jerusalem.

JACOB ASHKENAZI

Eudocia, Pulcheria, and Juvenal

Competition in the Field of Religion and the Built Environment of Jerusalem in the Fifth Century CE

Introduction

Under the rule of Theodosius II (408–50) and his successor Marcian (450–57), Jerusalem experienced one of the most turbulent periods in its history, one marked by christological controversies that shook the religious and political stability of the empire and had an important impact on the city and its holy places. At this time, the church of Jerusalem was led by Juvenal, who ascended the throne in 422, and served as the bishop of the Holy City until his death in 457. For a significant part of this period, the empress Eudocia was active alongside Juvenal. She came to Jerusalem as a pilgrim circa 438 and settled there permanently circa 443 until her death in 460. These two figures represent two different elites. Juvenal headed the Church of Palestine, which was empowered by charismatic holy men who took up positions within the highest echelons of the ecclesiastical hierarchy. Eudocia represented the imperial aristocracy, and bore the title 'Augusta', as did her sister-in-law Pulcheria who, like Eudocia and Juvenal, was an active competitor in what Pierre Bourdieu would have called 'the field of religious goods'.

The Bourdieuan field is an arena in which individuals and institutions vie for the production, accumulation, and control of capital, whether material or symbolic, unique to that field.[1] The religious field is capable of responding competitively to demands for its goods, even though the arena in which it operates does not follow standard economic logic. The profits gained in the religious field manifest themselves in capital that can be social, economic, or symbolic. Amassing capital of one type does not necessarily come at the expense of amassing capital of another type; on the contrary, it can strengthen and maximize the profits.[2] Although the symbolic capital accumulated in

---

1 Rey, *Bourdieu on Religion*, pp. 124–26.
2 Bourdieu, *Sociology in Question*, pp. 31–34.

> **Jacob Ashkenazi** is Associate Professor in the Department of Land of Israel Studies at Kinneret Academic College.

Essays on Jews and Christians in Late Antiquity in Honour of Oded Irshai, ed. by Brouria Bitton-Ashkelony and Martin Goodman, CELAMA 40 (Turnhout: Brepols, 2023), pp. 119–139
BREPOLS ❧ PUBLISHERS   10.1484/M.CELAMA-EB.5.132486

the religious field has universal implications, most of the activity within the field is reflected in material investments in specific localities. In what follows, I will address the implications of this competition on the built environment of Jerusalem in the fifth century.

A built environment transforms objectives, desires, and ideals into concrete objects that bear the meanings their builders conferred on them. From the perspective of its organizers, then, the built environment acts as a semiotic system.[3] Monumental buildings can appear to 'mask the will to power beneath signs and surfaces',[4] and they can also be understood as 'an invitation to faith rather than as an attempt to compel assent'.[5] When such invitations are issued by high ecclesiastical officials, under the patronage of and in cooperation with royalty, power becomes the most obvious significance of a given space, and the built environment becomes its 'orthography'.[6]

This chapter examines the actions of Eudocia, Juvenal, and, to a lesser degree, those of Pulcheria in fifth-century Jerusalem. By analysing the symbolic and material significance of their actions, I aim to show how the political status of these actors was derived from their performances, both material and symbolic, within the religious field. I will present the tripartite accord and its material implications on the urban landscape and argue that Eudocia's rivalry with Pulcheria motivated her to act in parallel, and not necessarily in collaboration, with Juvenal in order to establish her status as empress in Jerusalem while turning the Holy City into an imperial religious centre.

Eudocia

Eudocia, who was originally named Athenaïs, was born in either Athens or Antioch to Leontius, a pagan Sophist.[7] According to later and somewhat legendary traditions, Pulcheria, Theodosius II's sister, met Athenaïs in Constantinople, and thought her suitable to be the emperor's bride. In 421 Athenaïs was baptized by the bishop of Constantinople, renamed Eudocia and married to Theodosius II.

As part of her upbringing, Eudocia had received a Classical education, and although she later converted to Christianity, she did not neglect her Hellenic *paideia*, and incorporated her cultural background into her new imperial role.[8]

---

3 Preziosi, *Architecture, Language, and Meaning*, p. 92.

4 Lefebvre, *The Production of Space*, p. 143.

5 Gorringe, *A Theology of the Built Environment*, p. 28.

6 In the words of Gorringe, *A Theology of the Built Environment*, pp. 29–30.

7 For the debate over her place of birth see Holum, *Theodosian Empresses*, pp. 117–18.

8 Whether and to what extent Eudocia's pagan upbringing affected her as a Christian is quite debatable. See Cameron, *Wandering Poets*, p. 64 and compare with Holum, 'Pulcheria's Crusade ad 421–22'.

This is evident in her literary work[9] and in a poem attributed to her that is inscribed at the hot baths of Hammat Gader in Palestine.[10] In 438, Eudocia embarked on a journey to the Holy Land. There are different accounts regarding the catalyst for this journey — it may have been motivated by an oath she took, a desire to escape internal politics at the imperial court, or it may have been a mission on which she was sent by her husband.[11] In any case, on her way she passed through Antioch, where she provided money to renovate the city walls, and delivered a homily to the residents in which she declared the city's special place in her heart.[12] Travelling on from Antioch toward Jerusalem, Eudocia was greeted along the way by Melania the Younger, a Roman noblewoman who had come to Jerusalem with her husband Pinianus a few years earlier, and established monasteries on the Mount of Olives.[13] Melania met Eudocia in Sidon, and accompanied her on her journey to Jerusalem.[14] While in Jerusalem, Eudocia met with Cyril, the bishop of Alexandria, who was visiting the city at the time, and on 15 May 439 she participated in the consecration of her main initiative, the Church of Stephen the protomartyr.[15] The remains of the martyr were discovered during the Church council in Lydda-Diospolis (415) and were thereafter installed in the Church of Holy Zion.[16] Eudocia deposited the saint's foot in the Martyrium of Melania on the Mount of Olives,[17] and took some of the remains of his right arm with her to Constantinople.[18]

---

9   Agosti, 'Eudocia, una poetessa da Atene'; Sandnes, *The Gospel 'According to Homer and Virgil'*, pp. 181–228.

10 Di Segni, 'The Greek Inscriptions of Hammat Gader', pp. 228–33. See also Green and Tsafrir, 'Greek Inscriptions from Ḥammat Gader'.

11 Socrates Scholasticus, *Historia Ecclesiastica*, 7.47, p. 394. See also Gerontius, *Vita Melania*, 56, pp. 238–40. According to a later source it was Eudocia who asked the emperor to let her travel to Jerusalem (Theophanes, *Chronographia*, AM 5942, p. 102).

12 Evagrius, *Historia Ecclesiastica*, I, 20, pp. 28–29.

13 Gerontius, *Vita Melania*, 40–41, pp. 203–06.

14 Gerontius, *Vita Melania*, 58, pp. 240–46.

15 Ioannes Rufus, *Vita Petri Iberii*, 49, p. 33.

16 Lucianus, *Epistola ad omnem ecclesiam*, 8, p. 815. Not all the remains of the martyr were kept in Holy Zion and some, which travelled throughout the Mediterranean, could be found in North Africa, Minorca, and Spain. See Clark, 'Claims on the Bones of Saint Stephen', p. 142. In the ninth century, Theophanes (*Chronographia*, AM 5920, pp. 86–87), relates that Juvenal sent the right hand of St Stephen to Pulcheria and Theodosius in return for the charity they sent for the poor in Jerusalem. Yet, no contemporaneous source reports such an episode.

17 Gerontius, *Vita Melania*, 58, pp. 240–46.

18 *Marcellinus Comes, Chronica Minora*, XIII, p. 303, and followed by Theophanes, *Chronographia*, AM 5920, pp. 86–87. These sources place the relics in the church dedicated to St Laurence, built by Pulcheria. Paul Magdalino dismisses this notion, claiming that it is unlikely that Eudocia deposited the relics in this church because it was completed only in 453 and because the empress would probably not have placed these relics in a church that was built by her rival, Pulcheria. He suggests therefore that the relics were placed in the church of St Polyeuktos that was built by Eudocia and that her great-granddaughter, Anicia Juliana, transferred them to the Church of St Laurence. See Magdalino, 'Aristocratic Oikoi', pp. 56–57.

Four years after returning to Constantinople, Eudocia left the palace for good and returned to Jerusalem, remaining there until her death in the year 460. Eudocia's presence in the cultural, social, political, and religious life of Jerusalem is reflected in the built environment of the city. Michael Avi-Yonah has estimated that the empress invested perhaps one and a half million gold coins into the city, at a time when one person could live on the equivalent of two gold coins per year.[19] Regardless of the accuracy of this calculation,[20] the list of Eudocia's projects and initiatives in Jerusalem, and in other locations in Palestine, during her stay is undeniably impressive.

The fourteenth-century church historian Nicephorus Callistus noted that Eudocia established many monasteries and churches, hospitals, and poorhouses.[21] One of these institutions was probably the hospital known in other sources as the Hospital of the Patriarch,[22] which was built together with the *Episkopeion* (the bishop's residence) to create an ecclesiastical quarter attached to the Holy Sepulchre. Another institution mentioned by Callistus is the home for lepers (the 'sacred disease' in his words) in Phordisia — perhaps Herodium.[23] Despite the span of nine centuries between Eudocia's construction projects and Callistus's writings, the information about Eudocia's imprint on the built environment of the city seems reliable, especially when compared with testimonies closer in time to the events. Cyril of Scythopolis wrote in the mid-sixth century, that 'Blessed Eudocia built a huge number of churches, and more monasteries and houses for the poor and elderly than I am able to count'.[24] He does not list all her enterprises, but he mentions the construction of the Church of St Stephen and the substantial income she allocated for its maintenance,[25] as well as the home for the elderly she built outside the city walls that included an enclosed martyrium dedicated to St George[26] (see Figure 5.1).

Other contemporaneous sources tell us more about Eudocia's investment in religious and civic ventures. John Rufus, the author of Peter the Iberian's Hagiography, notes that upon Peter's arrival in Jerusalem circa 437, he found a sparsely populated city in which the authorities were encouraging land acquisition and construction.[27] This passage serves as an introduction to Peter's contribution to the evolution of the cityscape through the monastery and hostel he established on Mount Zion. If accurate, the description of the city that Peter encountered is probably very similar to what Eudocia saw when

---

19 Avi-Yonah, 'The Economics of Byzantine Palestine', p. 44.

20 As claimed by Hunt, *Holy Land Pilgrimage*, p. 239.

21 Nicephorus Callistus, *Historia Ecclesiastica*, XIV, 50, p. 1240.

22 Cyrillus Scythopolitanus, *Vita Euthymii*, 48, p. 70; Iohannes Moschus, *Pratum Spirituale*, 42, p. 2896. This hospital is mentioned in an inscription from the Hinnom Valley. See Macalister, 'The Rock-Cut Tombs', pp. 233–34.

23 Zias, 'Was Byzantine Herodium a Leprosarium?'.

24 Cyrillus Scythopolitanus, *Vita Euthymii*, 35, p. 53, p. 49.

25 Cyrillus Scythopolitanus, *Vita Euthymii*, 30, p. 49.

26 Cyrillus Scythopolitanus, *Vita Ioanni Hesychastesis*, 4, p. 204.

27 Ioannes Rufus, *Vita Petri Iberii*, 64, p. 44.

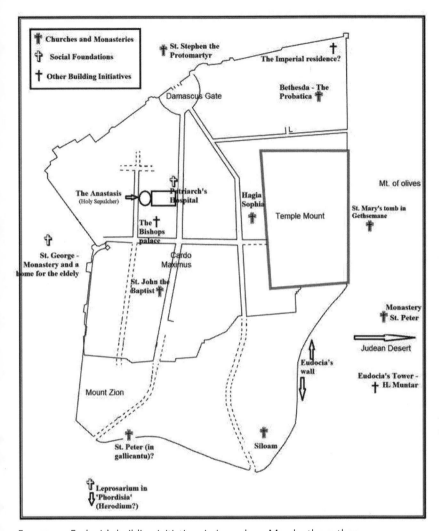

FIGURE 5.1. Eudocia's building initiatives in Jerusalem. Map by the author.

she arrived in Jerusalem shortly thereafter. During her first visit to the city, she set the foundation of the Church of St Stephen, north of the city walls, on the presumed site where the protomartyr was stoned.[28] The construction of the church was completed in 460, only a few months before the empress passed away, and she was buried there beside the martyr's tomb.[29]

---

28 Acts 7:58.
29 Cyrillus Scythopolitanus, *Vita Euthymii*, 35, p. 54. Cyril adds that before the empress passed away, she took care of consecrating and financing all the churches she had built.

The Church of St Stephen was the largest of the churches in Jerusalem, at least until Justinian launched his ambitious project of the *Nea* almost a century later. When an assembly of 10,000 monks convened in the early sixth century to anathematize Severus, the monophysite patriarch of Antioch, and to condemn the religious policy of the emperor Anastasius, the only church that could accommodate such a crowd was the Church of St Stephen.[30] The Itinerary of Theodosius, dating to the middle of the sixth century, also points to the size of the church and mentions that it was built by Eudocia.[31] The nocturnal journey of Peter the Iberian between the holy sites of Jerusalem is worth mentioning here.[32] The point of departure of his journey was not the Holy Sepulchre but the Church of St Stephen built by Eudocia.[33]

Another of Eudocia's projects in Jerusalem, which is mentioned in sources from the sixth century, is the wall she erected around the city. According to Byzantine chronicler John Malalas (*c.* 491–578), in building the walls Eudocia aimed to fulfil the psalm 'Do good to Zion in thy good pleasure (ἐν τῇ εὐδοκίᾳ σου); rebuild the walls of Jerusalem' (*LXX* 50:20).[34] It is possible that the psalm served as inspiration for Eudocia to build Jerusalem's walls as an expression of religious piety;[35] however, at least some of the wall may already have been standing when Eudocia arrived in the city, as recent archaeological excavations south of the city's Ottoman wall seem to indicate.[36] Or perhaps Malalas was referring to the empress's residency in Jerusalem? Given that Eudocia also contributed to building the walls of Antioch,[37] as well as building the Church of Siloam,[38] and perhaps the Church of St Peter (in Gallicantu?) on Mount Zion,[39] it is plausible that an extension of the city walls to the south was initiated by the empress to include these two compounds and the Church of Holy Zion within the city boundaries.

---

30 Cyrillus Scythopolitanus, *Vita Sabae*, 56, p. 151.

31 Theodosius, *De Situ Terrae Sanctae*, 8, pp. 118–19. See also Evagrius, *Historia Ecclesiastica*, I, 22, pp. 32–33.

32 Ioannes Rufus, *Vita Petri Iberii*, 134, pp. 98–100.

33 On the nocturnal tour of Peter and its theological connotations see Kofsky, 'Peter the Iberian', 220–22; Bitton-Ashkelony, '*Imitatio mosis* and Pilgrimage', pp. 67–70. Tsafrir notes that the starting point of the nocturnal voyage was at the village of Beth Tafsha north of the city. This is the reason that the Church of St Stephen was his first station. See Tsafrir, 'Between David's Tower and Holy Zion', p. 248.

34 Ioannes Malalas, *Chronographia*, 14.8, 22, pp. 32–33; *Chronicon Paschale*, i, p. 585; and Nicephorus Callistus, *Historia Ecclesiastica*, p. 1242. See also the mention of Eudocia as the builder of the wall by Antoninus Placentius, *Itinerarium*, 25, p. 142.

35 Klein, 'Do Good in thy good pleasure unto Zion', p. 90.

36 Weksler-Bdolah, 'The Fortifications of Jerusalem in the Byzantine Period', p. 101.

37 Evagrius, *Historia Ecclesiastica*, I, 20, pp. 28–29.

38 Vincent and Abel, *Jérusalem*, ii, p. 861; Avi-Yonah, *The Madaba Mosaic Map*, p. 56. For recent excavations in the area see Reich, 'The Cultic and Secular Use of Water', p. 262.

39 Vincent and Abel, *Jérusalem*, ii, p. 909 (referring to the house of Caiaphas). For a different opinion regarding the St Peter in Gallicantu see Power, 'St Peter in Gallicantu', pp. 421–22.

One might surmise that this enterprise was part of the empress's plan to enclose the holy places of the city within its walls, which would define the city as it was called a century later in the Madaba map: Η ΑΓΙΑ ΠΟΛΙC ΙΕΡΟΥCΑΛΗΜ ('the Holy City Jerusalem'). A look at the map shows many buildings with red roof tiles, an indication of churches. Many of them have been dated to the middle of the fifth century, namely, to the period of Eudocia's stay in Jerusalem.[40] Nonetheless, it would be speculative to attribute the construction of churches such as Hagia Sophia (Praetorium),[41] John the Baptist (near the Church of the Holy Sepulchre),[42] the church at the Pool of Bethesda (Probatica),[43] or monasteries in the area between Holy Zion and the Anastasis,[44] to the empress. Yet, even if Eudocia did not have a hand in constructing these complexes, the permanent residency of an empress in Jerusalem surely impacted the status of the city, and hence its built environment. Thus, it is possible that noblewomen who came to Jerusalem during those years like Bassa, Flavia, or Hikelia, who funded ecclesiastical institutions in the city, did so due to the atmosphere Eudocia had created.[45] In his commentary on the Madaba map, Avi-Yonah identified one of the secular buildings near the Church of Bethesda as 'Eudocia's Palace'.[46] While he qualified this identification as uncertain, it is quite plausible that Eudocia resided within the city walls in a royal residence, such as a governor's house.

Importantly, while in Jerusalem, Eudocia embraced the monastic order, or, as aptly put by Brouria Bitton-Ashkelony: the monastic 'network', of the

---

40 For a conclusive study on Jerusalem in the Madaba map see Tsafrir, 'The Holy City of Jerusalem', pp. 155–63, and see there for further bibliography.

41 Mentioned by Ioannes Rufus as 'the Church of Pilate' (Ioannes Rufus, *Vita Petri Iberii*, 134, p. 99). Both titles (Hagia Sophia and the Praetorium) in Theodosius, *De Situ Terrae Sanctae*, 7, pp. 117–18; in *Breviarius (de Hierosolyma)*, A, 5, pp. 111–12, and in Antoninus Placentius, *Itinerarium*, 23, p. 141. For probable archaeological remains, see Vincent and Abel, *Jérusalem*, ii, pp. 571–77.

42 For identification of a Byzantine church near the Anastasis as the Church of St John the Baptist and for its relation to Eudocia's constructions in Jerusalem, see Dickie, 'The Lower Church of St John'. See also Vincent and Abel, *Jérusalem*, ii, pp. 652–68.

43 Vincent and Abel, *Jérusalem*, ii, pp. 734, 909, suggest, cautiously, that these sanctuaries, which they assume were built during Eudocia's residence in the city, were built by her or at least inspired by her.

44 Antoninus Placentius, *Itinerarium*, 21; see also Tsafrir, 'Between David's Tower and Holy Zion', pp. 255–60.

45 Bassa was a noblewoman who came to Jerusalem probably before the council of Chalcedon and built a monastery and a martyrion for St Menas after the council (Cyrillus Scythopolitanus, *Vita Euthymii*, 30, p. 49). The church was probably located on the northern slopes of Mount Zion in today's Armenian Quarter. See Vincent and Abel, *Jérusalem*, ii, pp. 528–29. For Flavia see Cyrillus Scythopolitanus, *Vita Theognii*, 1, p. 241; for Hikelia see Cyrillus Scythopolitanus, *Vita Theodosii*, 1, p. 236.

46 Avi-Yonah, *The Madaba Mosaic Map*, p. 58, although he states that this cannot be proved. He is followed by Tsafrir who entitles this building with uncertainty as the governor's palace; see Tsafrir, 'The Holy City of Jerusalem', p. 161. Neither refers to any literary or archaeological source. In the *Life of the Monk Barsauma*, the palace of the empress is in Bethlehem. See Nau, 'Résumé', p. 121. For English translation see Palmer, *The Life of the Syrian Saint Barsauma*, p. 80.

city and the surrounding desert.[47] Thus, the empress approached Melania the Younger and Peter the Iberian, who belonged to the aristocratic elite in Rome and Constantinople, before deciding to don the monastic habit and go on a pilgrimage to the holy places and eventually to settle in the Holy City. She also became close to Euthymius, the celebrated monastic father who built his *laura* in the plain of Adumim, near Jerusalem. His hagiographer, Cyril of Scythopolis, associates Eudocia's eventual acceptance of the Chalcedonian creed to the influence of Euthymius.[48] Eudocia also contributed to the promotion of monks from Euthymius's monastery by appointing them to lucrative positions in the Church of Jerusalem.[49] The bond between Eudocia and the monks also had material manifestations, in the form of a tower she built at Jabal Muntar in the Judean Desert, which later became the Monastery of the Scholarius.[50] Additionally, she built a church dedicated to St Peter opposite the Laura of Euthymius, equipped with a large reservoir for the benefit of the monks and pilgrims.[51] The tower on Jabal Muntar served Eudocia in her encounters with the monks. Since she could not enter their monasteries but did not wish to disturb their *hesychia* by forcing them to come to Jerusalem, she erected this tower as a kind of 'forward post'. For the monks of the Judean Desert, Eudocia was a significant patron; they, in turn, played an important part in her efforts to turn Jerusalem into an imperial holy city.[52]

At this point, let us turn to the other two actors in the religious field of Jerusalem. Eudocia had two main competitors: Her influential sister-in-law Pulcheria, and Juvenal, who held the See of Jerusalem almost throughout her stay in the city.

Pulcheria

Pulcheria is portrayed in contemporaneous sources as a pious servant of God and as a devoted sister to her brother, the young emperor Theodosius. Her dominance in the court had repercussions for ecclesiastic affairs in and outside the capital, and played a major role in three ecumenical synods (Ephesus 431, 449, and Chalcedon 451).[53] Although Pulcheria did not embark on a pilgrimage

---

47 Bitton-Ashkelony, 'Monastic Networks in Byzantine Jerusalem'.
48 Cyrillus Scythopolitanus, *Vita Euthymii*, 30, pp. 47–49.
49 Cyrillus Scythopolitanus, *Vita Euthymii*, 30, p. 49.
50 Cyrillus Scythopolitanus, *Vita Euthymii*, 30, p. 48.
51 Cyrillus Scythopolitanus, *Vita Euthymii*, 35, p. 53.
52 Holum, *Theodosian Empresses*, pp. 219–20, emphasizes the efforts of Eudocia to upgrade the status of lesser clerics in Jerusalem's ecclesiastical hierarchy, such as the country bishop Anastasius and the *Staurophylax* (the keeper of the cross), Cosmas, together with the two brothers from Euthymius's *Laura*, Gabriel, and Cosmas. But apart from them, it must be noted that she developed important relations with other great monastic figures in Jerusalem such as Gerontius, Romanus, and Marcian, as well as with the intellectual Hesychius (Cyrillus Scythopolitanus, *Vita Euthymii*, 30, p. 49).
53 For her role in the Christological debates see Holum, *Theodosian Empresses*, pp. 147–74, 195–216.

to the holy places like her sister-in-law Eudocia, she was recognized as a 'new Helena', a title given to her during the synod at Chalcedon for her part in the struggle against the decisions of the 'robber synod' at Ephesus.[54] The roots of this title lay in the days of the First Synod at Ephesus, when she was the driving force behind the excommunication of Nestorius and his party.[55]

Pulcheria's public image as the new Helena was also fuelled by the discovery of relics of the 40 Martyrs of Sebaste and their deposition in a church built in the Helenianai area of Constantinople.[56] Another asset she gained in the religious field was achieved through her building of the Church of St Laurence in an area of the city that was subsequently named Pulcherianai.[57]

Pulcheria's vow of celibacy bestowed an aura of divine holiness on her, as she was perceived as imitating the Mother of God (*Imitatio Mariae*), and she leveraged this image in establishing three 'Marian' churches in Constantinople: a church in Blachernae, the Hodegetria, and the Chalkoprateia — projects that accrued great profit for her in the field of religious goods.[58] Although scholarship has questioned the reliability of such attributions,[59] which originate in local Constantinople traditions,[60] these traditions attest to the strength of Pulcheria's image as the *Magna Mater* or 'Great Mother' of the city, and perhaps of the entire empire.[61]

Pulcheria was also credited with many philanthropic activities in Constantinople,[62] and, like Eudocia, she strengthened her bonds with the growing monastic order. Thus, Pulcheria cultivated close ties with revered figures such as Alexander the Sleepless, Hypatius of Bithynia and Simeon Stylites.[63] Theophanes, writing in the beginning of the ninth century, attributes to her the victory of Chalcedonian Orthodoxy, glorifies and praises her actions in favour of the city and the empire while at the same time treating Eudocia as one who betrayed both her husband and the true faith.[64]

---

54 ACO (*Acta Conciliorum Oecomenicorum*), Tome ii, vol. i. part 2, pp. 155–57.

55 Brubaker, 'Memories of Helena', pp. 60–62. For the materiality of the link between these two Augustae, as reflected in the 'Helenianai' neighbourhood in Constantinople see Angelova, *Sacred Founders*, pp. 141–42.

56 Angelova, *Sacred Founders*, p. 143.

57 Magdalino, 'Aristocratic Oikoi', pp. 56–57.

58 Holum, *Theodosian Empresses*, pp. 130–34.

59 Theodorus Lector, *Historia Ecclesiastica*, pp. 168C.

60 Wortley, 'The Marian Relics at Constantinople'; but see a different view by Twardowska, 'The Church Foundations of Empress Pulcheria', and see there a review of the discussion on the founders of the churches.

61 Herrin, 'The Imperial Feminine in Byzantium', p. 14, suggests that by promoting the cult of Mary in the capital, Pulcheria contributed to the demise of the cult of Tyche. This interpretation may shed light on the way Pulcheria was accepted as the new Helena, transforming the city from darkness to light, as put forward by Theophanes (Theophanes, *Chronographia*, AM 5942, pp. 101–02) some 350 years later.

62 Sozomenus, *Historia Ecclesiastica*, IX, 1. 10–11, p. 391.

63 Holum, *Theodosian Empresses*, pp. 134–35, 170–71.

64 James, 'Making a Name', p. 68.

The building projects initiated by Pulcheria in Constantinople were less significant to the cityscape of the imperial capital than those of Eudocia to Jerusalem. Later chronographers may have attempted to equate the actions of these two empresses in the religious field in order to enhance Pulcheria's reputation and imply that her contributions to Christianity were equal to the kind of material manifestations that Eudocia erected within the walls of Jerusalem.

Juvenal

The third actor in the religious field is Juvenal, who acquired the See of Jerusalem in 422, and was involved in the three tumultuous church councils of his times: the first and second in Ephesus (431 and 449), and the third in Chalcedon (451). However, I shall leave aside Juvenal's manoeuvres in the christological arena and his actions as the head of the ecclesiastic hierarchy of the three provinces of Palestine.[65] Our interest here is in the role that Juvenal played in the field of religious goods, and in the way this role is reflected in the built environment of Jerusalem.

In the period between the first council at Ephesus and the council of Chalcedon, Juvenal was an active member in the party led by Cyril of Alexandria and his successor Dioscuros, who championed the belief in Christ being of one divine nature. At Chalcedon, Juvenal changed his allegiance and sided with Leo of Rome and the camp that believed that Christ had two natures, divine and human. Leo was supported by the new emperor, Marcian, whom Pulcheria had married after the death of her brother Theodosius II.

Juvenal's transition from the monophysite to the dyophysite camp was not well received by his subjects in Palestine, particularly the monks. This was so despite the efforts he made to appease the growing monastic community. Thus, he appointed monks to prime positions in the ecclesiastical hierarchy of his diocese. For example, he appointed the Cappadocians Stephen and Cosmas from the monastery of Euthymius as deacons in the Holy sepulcher, and later promoted Stephen to the bishopric of Iamnia, and Cosmas to the lucrative office of keeper of the Cross.[66] He took these steps, however, prior to the council of Chalcedon. After the synod, the monastic leadership sided with Eudocia who, in effect, controlled the Church of Palestine — through the usurper bishop Theodosius — until Juvenal was reinstalled on his throne two years later.[67] Eudocia turned to the Chalcedonian faith in 454, under the influence of Euthymius, and thus renewed her communion with Juvenal.[68]

---

65 The most extensive study on Juvenal is Honigmann's 'Juvenal of Jerusalem'. He was preceded by two short studies by Vailhé: 'L'erection du Patriarchat de Jerusalem 451', and 'Formation du patriarcat de Jérusalem'.

66 Cyrillus Scythopolitanus, *Vita Euthymii*, 20, pp. 32–33.

67 For a thorough survey of the events in the church of Jerusalem before and after the council of Chalcedon see Perrone, *La chiesa di Palestina*, pp. 89–126.

68 Cyrillus Scythopolitanus, *Vita Euthymii*, 30, pp. 48–49.

According to the anti-Chalcedonian lives of Melania and of Peter the Iberian, Juvenal and Eudocia never met. When Eudocia consecrated the Church of St Stephen and the martyrium in Melania's monastery on the Mount of Olives in the presence of Cyril of Alexandria, Juvenal was not mentioned.[69] In the Church of the Holy Sepulchre, she placed a copper cross instead of a wooden cross that had been burnt in a fire, still with no mention of the bishop's involvement.[70] Juvenal was probably excluded from these narratives due to his earlier anti-Chalcedonian affinity and the authors' resulting abhorrence of the patriarch of Jerusalem.[71]

Other sources, however, point to a connection between Juvenal and Pulcheria. One tradition, presented by Theophanes, relates how Juvenal sent the right hand of St Stephen to Theodosius and Pulcheria in Constantinople as a gift in return for money they had sent to Jerusalem for distribution to the poor, and some precious gifts to the church of the Holy Sepulchre.[72] Though unreliable due to its later date and its contradiction of the much earlier tradition that attributes to Eudocia the sending of the martyr's hand, this tradition is well aligned with Theophanes' adoration of Pulcheria — in parallel to his animosity towards Eudocia — and it also reflects the positive attitude of the later Chalcedonian literature toward Juvenal.

A second tradition, recorded by John of Damascus, writing in the eighth century, tells how Juvenal was asked by the empress Pulcheria and emperor Marcian to send them the body of St Mary. Juvenal replied that according to an ancient tradition it is known that the Mother of God was taken from her tomb by her son and therefore the tomb was empty. In response, the imperial couple asked him to send them the coffin and the shroud, which he did, and they placed them in the church that Pulcheria had dedicated to the Mother of God in Blachernae.[73] This source, like the chronicle of Theophanes, should be taken with caution not only because of its later date of composition but also due to its anti-monophysite tendency that is reflected in Theophanes' positive attitude towards Juvenal and Pulcheria.

As noted above, the construction of three Marian churches in Constantinople was attributed to Pulcheria. Three Marian churches were also built in Jerusalem during the episcopate of Juvenal: the church over Mary's purported tomb in

---

69 Clark, 'Claims on the Bones of Saint Stephen', p. 153; Honigmann, 'Juvenal of Jerusalem', p. 226, who suggests that Juvenal did attend the consecration but played a secondary role in the event. See also Horn, *Asceticism and Christological Controversy*, p. 75.

70 Ioannes Rufus, *Plerophoria*, 9, p. 27.

71 On the hostile attitude of the monophysite literature towards Juvenal see Honigmann, 'Juvenal of Jerusalem', pp. 262–66.

72 Theophanes, *Chronographia*, AM 5920, pp. 86–87.

73 Ioannes Damascenus, *Homiliae*, IX, 18, pp. 748–52. The tradition of Mary's dormition and ascension probably developed towards the middle of the sixth century and perhaps even later. On the origins of the traditions See Honigmann, 'Juvenal of Jerusalem', pp. 268–69; Limberis, *Divine Heiress*, pp. 57–58, and also Shoemaker, *The Ancient Traditions of the Virgin Mary's Dormition*, pp. 68–71.

Gethsemane,[74] the church at Bethesda (the Probatica), where Mary, according to some traditions, was born,[75] and the Church of the Kathisma on the road to Bethlehem, built by the noble Lady Hikelia.[76] The promotion of the Marian cult in Jerusalem by Juvenal was also reflected in his attempts to institute December 25 as the birth date of Jesus instead of the Eastern tradition of celebrating the birth alongside the Epiphany on January 6. These attempts apparently failed due to the opposition of the monophysites, and they bore fruit only toward the end of the sixth century.[77]

The sources describing the religio-political alliance between Juvenal and Pulcheria are late but, in the absence of earlier sources referring to Juvenal's actual role in the religious field, they reflect how the personalities were perceived as defenders of the Chalcedonian creed. Although Cyril of Scythopolis, who wrote about a century after Eudocia's death, had strived to associate her with the 'correct' orthodox faith, he was more interested in glorifying the protagonist of his work, Euthymius, who persuaded the empress to renounce what he calls the 'irrational contentiousness'.[78] In any case, both Theophanes and Cyril, who preceded Theophanes by more than 250 years, wrote their works when the distinction between the two christological camps was sharper and clearer than it was in the first years after the Council of Chalcedon.

Competing in the Fields of Religion and Politics

The christological debate manifested itself both in the local and the global political arenas. Therefore, it can be said that in the case of mid-fifth-century Jerusalem, the competition was not only between two women but also between two cities.[79] While Pulcheria presented herself as the Augusta or empress of the orthodox Chalcedonian Constantinople, Eudocia designed Jerusalem as an alternative imperial centre by building churches and monasteries, constructing social and medical institutions, and strengthening veneration of the holy men and women associated with Jerusalem. By so doing, she augmented the prestige of Jerusalem as the Holy City. Only in Jerusalem, as Konstantin Klein rightly expressed it, could Eudocia present herself as a Christian empress.[80] She made Jerusalem her kingdom, with St Stephen as its favourite saint, and

---

74 For the Byzantine remains see Vincent and Abel, *Jérusalem*, ii, pp. 821–31.
75 Ioannes Rufus, *Plerophoria*, 13, p. 35; Theodosius, *De Situ Terra Sancta*, 8, pp. 118–19; Antoninus Placentius, *Itinerarium*, 27, p. 143. For the Byzantine remains at the site see Vincent and Abel, *Jérusalem*, ii, pp. 698–99.
76 Cyrillus Scythopolitanus, *Vita Theodosii*, 1, pp. 236–37. For the discovery of the site of the Kathisma see Avner, 'The Kathisma: A Christian and Muslim Pilgrimage Site'.
77 See discussion in van Esbroeck, 'La lettre de l'empereur Justinian', pp. 364–65, 370–71.
78 Cyrillus Scythopolitanus, *Vita Euthymii*, 30, p. 48.
79 Hunt, *Holy Land Pilgrimage*, p. 234.
80 Klein, 'Do Good in thy good pleasure unto Zion', p. 88.

left the promotion of the cult of St Mary to Pulcheria in Constantinople and Juvenal in Jerusalem.[81] The cult of Stephen as the choice saint of the Holy City is also reflected in the liturgy of the holy places, as manifested in a panegyric of the Jerusalemite theologian Hesychius, in which he describes Stephen as 'the son of Jerusalem and of the holy places'.[82]

Notably, the remains of St Stephen were held in the Church of Holy Zion after their discovery in 415 and we hear of no opposition to Eudocia taking these relics out of their earlier location (selected by a previous bishop of Jerusalem, John II), and placing them in a church that she had built from her own (or imperial) resources. This act reflects Eudocia's reception in Jerusalem: she was regarded as a queen and the Holy City was her royal capital, rather than as a noble pilgrim dispensing charity. It is for this reason that I question the scholarship that views Eudocia as the new Helena,[83] as this emphasizes one-time tourist discoveries in the city rather than its continued cultivation by a committed royal resident. Although Eudocia arrived in Jerusalem for the first time as a pilgrim, her contribution to the transformation of the urban landscape came during the time she was a permanent resident and not, like Helena, a pilgrim.[84]

We find more clues as to how Eudocia was perceived by her contemporaries in the *Vita* of the monk Barsauma from Samosata.[85] The debate over the historicity of the *vita* should not overshadow its narrative regarding the harsh christological conflicts of the fifth and sixth centuries.[86] According to the *vita*, Barsauma made four visits to the Holy Land during the second quarter of the fifth century. During these visits he had violent confrontations with Jews, Samaritans, and pagans; the most significant of these encounters took place during his fourth visit, after Eudocia had already settled in Jerusalem. This conflict broke out because the empress had given the Jews permission to pray in Jerusalem.[87] Following this gesture, the leaders of the Jews in the

---

81   Klein rightly wonders why Eudocia did not attempt to reproduce Pulcheria's devotion to Maria Theotokos, and suggests that the church built over Mary's tomb in the Kedron Valley was initiated by Theodosius. See Klein, 'Do Good in thy good pleasure unto Zion', p. 90. For the promotion of the Marian cult in Jerusalem and Constantinople by Pulcheria see Mgaloblishvili, 'Regarding One Unknown Ancient Feast', p. 160.

82   Devos, 'Le Panégyrique de Saint Etienne', p. 158. On Hesychius and his works see Perrone, *La chiesa*, pp. 64–79.

83   For instance: Hunt, *Holy Land Pilgrimage*, p. 229; James, 'Making a Name', p. 67; Klein, 'Do Good in thy good pleasure unto Zion', p. 89.

84   In this respect, see Gutfeld, 'The Urban Layout of Byzantine-Period Jerusalem'. Gutfeld analysed the archaeological data from more than 150 years of excavations on the south-western hill of Jerusalem and concluded that the area was extensively cultivated during the fifth century. In the Hebrew version of the article, he attributes the radical change in the cityscape of Jerusalem to Empress Eudocia. See Gutfeld, 'From Aelia Capitolina to Aelia Eudocia', pp. 137–38.

85   Nau, 'Résumé'.

86   Kofsky and Ruzer, 'The Holy Places and the Jewish past in the Fifth-Century Christian Discourse of Appropriation', pp. 225–27.

87   Hagith Sivan emphasizes the similarity to Cyrus's call to the Jews of Babylon in the book of

Galilee sent a letter, cited in the *vita*, to their brothers around the world in which they called on them to return to Jerusalem on the Feast of Tabernacles since 'the kings of the Romans are returning their city to them'.[88]

Barsauma and the monks who accompanied him on this journey reacted violently toward the Jews who arrived in Jerusalem — and toward the local authorities, both sacral and secular. According to the *vita*, the Jews' return to Jerusalem was prevented due to miracles performed by Barsauma and, at the end of the episode, Eudocia recognized the power of the 'holy man' and released the violent monks from prison.[89]

It is Eudocia's depiction in the *vita* that draws our attention. She is the most important figure in the imperial court, a queen to whom Jews and Christians, civil and military authorities, and even high ecclesiastical officials, are subordinate.[90] Given that the *vita* is a monophysite work,[91] the absence of Juvenal, who was considered a Judas by other post-Chalcedonian monophysite sources, is striking.[92]

Barsauma's *Vita* also sheds light on the role of the holy places, and of the Holy City, as tools in the struggle for the true faith; in this case, of the anti-Chalcedonian party.[93] In a letter sent to Juvenal after the Council of Chalcedon, Pope Leo stressed the importance of guarding the holy places as proof of the true faith.[94] Eudocia, at that time still Juvenal's rival, received a similar letter from Leo, begging her to persuade the monks to accept the decisions of the Council of Chalcedon and to reunite with the bishop.[95] Bassa, a noblewoman who built a martyrium to St Menas in Jerusalem, also received a letter from Pulcheria, encouraging her in her right faith.[96] Such correspondence points to the important role that the holy places played in the religious field, especially in times of doctrinal unrest. They also indicate the existence of a 'Chalcedonian' party in Jerusalem that included Bassa, and perhaps also Flavia and Hikelia.[97] In addition to these women, there was a small group of monks, led by Euthymius, who refused to receive communion from the usurper monophysite bishop Theodosius.[98] Confronting this minority stood Eudocia who, at least until her reconciliation with Juvenal in 456, enjoyed the support of the anti-Chalcedonian faction in Palestine.[99]

Ezra 4. See Sivan, 'Subversive Pilgrimages', p. 68.

88 Nau, 'Résumé', p. 119.

89 Nau, 'Résumé', pp. 122–23.

90 On her status in the vita see Holum, *Theodosian Empresses*, p. 218.

91 Sivan, 'Subversive Pilgrimages', p. 70; Kofsky and Ruzer, 'The Holy Places', p. 227.

92 See for instance Ioannes Rufus, *Plerophoria*, 16, pp. 32–33. See also discussion by Honigmann, 'Juvenal of Jerusalem', p. 228.

93 On the theological tensions after Chalcedon and their influence on the narratives of the holy places see Perrone, 'Christian Holy Places and Pilgrimage', pp. 15–20.

94 *ACO*, Tome ii. vol. i. part 2, pp. 63–64.

95 *ACO*, Tome ii. vol. iv, p. 77.

96 *ACO*, Tome ii, vol. i, part 3, pp. 135–36.

97 Perrone, *La chiesa*, p. 97.

98 Cyrillus Scythopolitanus, *Vita Euthymii*, 27, p. 42.

99 Perrone, *La chiesa*, p. 104.

EUDOCIA, PULCHERIA, AND JUVENAL   133

This reality was quite disturbing for Pulcheria, as reflected in the letter she wrote to Bassa. But Pulcheria passed away in 453, and Eudocia continued to enjoy the support and veneration of most of the monks and church officials in Jerusalem, from both sides of the christological fence.

It is difficult to determine what motivated Eudocia in Jerusalem. Maybe it was the defiance of Theodosius, of Marcian or even of Pulcheria, as Hunt has suggested.[100] We do know, however, that Eudocia's departure from the imperial court and move to Jerusalem contributed to a deepening competition between the two Augustae in the field of religious goods.[101] The competition — not necessarily in the sense of hostile confrontation — is reflected in the materiality of religion both in Constantinople and in Jerusalem: churches, monasteries, poor houses, hospitals, palaces, relics of saints that changed hands, and more. All of these have shaped the urban landscape and created a unique built environment in the two cities. Yet, while the cityscape of Constantinople remained relatively unchanged in the face of this rivalry, Jerusalem's built environment was utterly transformed.[102]

Not only did Eudocia shape the built environment of Jerusalem, she left a significant imprint on the human landscape of the Holy city. Having mentioned the strong ties she weaved with the monastic order in the city and its desert, we should emphasize also her contribution to investments in the city that surely gave a boost to the local economy by providing jobs and redistributed imperial wealth to the entire population of the city and its environs.[103] The prosperity that her activities must have generated was presumably another cause for Eudocia's gaining a political stronghold on the city.

Eudocia's choice to be buried in one of these venerated locations — the church she built in honour of the protomartyr Stephen, which became the largest of Jerusalem's churches, showcases Jerusalem as her true kingdom.[104]

The Built Environment of Jerusalem — Concluding Remarks

In the introduction to this study, we put forward the question of how competition in the religious field in which Eudocia, Pulcheria, and Juvenal interacted altered the built environment of Jerusalem in the mid-fifth century. As Pierre Bourdieu argued, the profits gained in the religious field manifest themselves in capital that can be social, economic, or symbolic. It seems that

---

100   Hunt, *Holy Land Pilgrimage*, p. 234. See also Stephens-Falcasantos, 'Christian Religious Symbolism and Pilgrimage', p. 295.
101   Müller, 'Jerusalem als Zentrum von Wohltätigkeit', p. 334.
102   Vincent and Abel, *Jérusalem*, II, p. 906, call the fifth century 'Le siècle d'Eudocie'.
103   See Avi-Yonah, 'The Economics of Byzantine Palestine', pp. 46, 51, who stresses that these were short-term investments that ceased after Eudocia passed away.
104   Ioannes Rufus uses the words 'like a Queen' (ܡܠܟܐ ܒܝ ܗ) to describe Eudocia on her journey (*Vita Petri Iberii*, 71, p. 48).

the religious field in which Eudocia, Pulcheria, and Juvenal competed produced capital that manifested itself in their status. However, the assets gained in these fields demanded significant monetary investments that made their mark on the urban landscape and designed the built environment of both Jerusalem and Constantinople. The construction in Jerusalem of churches, monasteries, martyria, hospitals, poorhouses, and clerical residences, together with a wall to encompass them, are all 'icons of cultural landscape' to use Donald Mitchell's terminology,[105] designed by the empress Eudocia. In the case of fifth-century Jerusalem, these were claims cast in stone for legitimacy, using imperial power to propagate a suitable built environment.[106]

Throughout the long history of Jerusalem, the city's rulers acquired legitimacy by placing their stamp on its built environment of the city. Thus, from Herod the Great[107] to the Mamluks and beyond,[108] these rulers bolstered their authority among the local populace by initiating building projects, mainly religious institutions, which left a lasting mark on the cityscape. So too, Eudocia took steps to inculcate imperial ideology by transforming the built environment of Jerusalem. Through the construction of religious and social projects as well as civil ones, she boosted her imperial legitimacy among the locals, and especially among the highly influential monastic community and the pilgrims who endorsed and disseminated the city's sacred fame throughout the empire and beyond.

---

105 Mitchell, *Cultural Geography*, p. 115.

106 For power and propaganda as manifested in the built environment see Gorringe, *A Theology of the Built Environment*, pp. 29–32.

107 Peleg-Barkat, 'Herodian Jerusalem'.

108 Luz, *The Mamluk City in the Middle East*, p. 150.

Bibliography

Primary Sources

ACO (*Acta Conciliorum Oecomenicorum*), ed. by Edward Schwartz, Tome ii, vol. i, part 2–3 (Berlin: de Gruyter, 1935), Tome ii, vol. iv (Berlin: de Gruyter, 1932)

Antoninus Placentius, *Itinerarium*, ed. by Paul Geyer, *Itineraria et Alia Geographica*, Corpus Christianorum Series Latina, 175 (Turnhout: Brepols, 1965), pp. 129–53

Breviarius (*de Hierosolyma*), ed. by Robert Weber, *Itineraria et Alia Geographica*, Corpus Christianorum Series Latina, 175 (Turnhout: Brepols, 1965), pp. 107–12

Chronicon Paschale, ed. by Ludwig Dindorf, *Corpus Scriptorum Historiae Byzantinae*, 2 vols (Bonn: Weber, 1832)

Cyrillus Scythopolitanus, *Vita Euthymii*, ed. by Eduard Schwartz, *Kyrillos von Skythopolis* (Leipzig: Hinrichs, 1939), pp. 3–84

——, *Vita Ioanni Hesychastesis*, ed. by Eduard Schwartz, *Kyrillos von Skythopolis* (Leipzig: Hinrichs, 1939), pp. 202–21

——, *Vita Sabae*, ed. by Eduard Schwartz, *Kyrillos von Skythopolis* (Leipzig: Hinrichs, 1939), pp. 85–200

——, *Vita Theodosii*, ed. by Eduard Schwartz, *Kyrillos von Skythopolis* (Leipzig: Hinrichs 1939), pp. 236–41

——, *Vita Theognii*, ed. by Eduard Schwartz, *Kyrillos von Skythopolis* (Leipzig: Hinrichs, 1939), pp. 241–43

Evagrius, *Historia Ecclesiastica*, ed. by Joseph Bidez and Léon Parmentier, *The Ecclesiastical History of Evagrius* (London: Bagster and Sons, 1898)

Gerontius, *Vita Melania*, ed. by Denys Gorce, *Vie de Saint Mélanie*, Sources Chrétiennes, 90 (Paris: Cerf, 1962)

Ioannes Damascenus, *Homiliae*, ed. by Jacques-Paul Migne, Patrologiae cursus completus: series graeca, 96 (Paris: Garnier, 1860), pp. 545–814

Ioannes Malalas, *Chronographia*, ed. by Ludwig Dindorf, *Corpus Scriptorum Historiae Byzantinae* (Bonn: Weber, 1831)

Ioannes Moschus, *Pratum spirituale*, ed. by Jacques-Paul Migne, Patrologiae cursus completus: series graecae, 87.3 (Paris: Garnier, 1860), pp. 2951–3116

Ioannes Rufus, *Plerophoria*, ed. by François Nau, 'Jean Rufus, Évèque de Maïouma: Plèrophories, c'est-a-dire témoignages et révélations (contre le concile de Chalcédone)', Patrologia Orientalis, 8 (Turnhout: Brepols, 1912), pp. 11–208

——, *Vita Petri Iberii*, ed. by Richard Raabe, *Petrus der Iberer: Ein Charakterbild zur Kirchen- und Sittengeschichte des 5. Jahrhunderts* (Leipzig: Hinrichs, 1895)

Lucianus, *Epistola ad omnem ecclesiam, de revelatione corporis Stephani martyris*, ed. by Jacques-Paul Migne, Patrologiae cursus completus: series latina, 41 (Paris: Garnier, 1860), pp. 807–16

Marcellinus Comes, Chronica Minora, ed. by Theodor Mommsen, Monumenta Germaniae Historica: Auctorum Antiquissimorum, 13, *Chronicorum Minorum Saec. IV. V. VI. VII* (Berlin: Weidmann, 1898)

Nicephorus Callistus, *Historia Ecclesiastica*, ed. by Jacques-Paul Migne, Patrologiae cursus completus: series graeca, 146 (Paris: Garnier, 1860)

Socrates Scholasticus, *Historia Ecclesiastica*, ed. by Günter Christian Hansen, *Sokrates Kirchengeschichte*, Die griechischen christlichen Schriftsteller der ersten Jahrhunderte, n.s., Band 1 (Berlin: Akademie, 1995)

Sozomenus, *Historia Ecclesiastica*, ed. by Joseph Bidez, *Sozomenus Kirchengeschichte*, Die griechischen christlichen Schriften der ersten Jahrhunderte, n.s., Band 4 (Berlin: Akademie, 1995)

Theodorus Lector, *Historia Ecclesiastica*, ed. by Jacques-Paul Migne, Patrologiae cursus completus: series graeca, 86A (Paris: Garnier, 1863), pp. 165–216

Theodosius, *De Situ Terrae Sanctae*, ed. by Paul Geyer, *Itineraria et Alia Geographica*, Corpus Christianorum Series Latina, 175 (Turnhout: Brepols, 1965), pp. 113–25

Theophanes, *Chronographia*, ed. by Carl de Boor (Leipzig: Teubner, 1883–1885)

Secondary Studies

Agosti, Gianfranco, 'Eudocia, una poetessa da Atene ad Antiochia e a Gerusalemme', *Henoch*, 38 (2016), 320–30

Angelova, Diliana N., *Sacred Founders: Women, Men, and Gods in the Discourse of Imperial Founding, Rome through Early Byzantium* (Oakland: University of California Press, 2015)

Avi-Yonah, Michael, 'The Economics of Byzantine Palestine', *Israel Exploration Journal*, 8 (1958), 39–51

——, *The Madaba Mosaic Map with Introduction and Commentary* (Jerusalem: Israel Exploration Society, 1954)

Avner, Rina, 'The Kathisma: A Christian and Muslim Pilgrimage Site', *ARAM*, 18–19 (2006–2007), 541–57

Bitton-Ashkelony, Brouria, '*Imitatio mosis* and Pilgrimage in the Life of Peter the Iberian', *Le Muséon*, 118 (2005), 51–70

——, 'Monastic Networks in Byzantine Jerusalem', in *Jerusalem II: Jerusalem in Roman-Byzantine Times*, ed. by Katharina Heyden and Maria Lissek with the assistance of Astrid Kaufmann (Tübingen: Mohr Siebeck, 2021), pp. 343–61

Bourdieu, Pierre, *Sociology in Question*, trans. by Richard Nice (London: Sage, 1993)

Brubaker, Leslie, 'Memories of Helena: Patterns in Imperial Female Matronage in the Fourth and Fifth Centuries', in *Women, Men and Eunuchs – Gender in Byzantium*, ed. by Liz James (New York: Routledge, 1997), pp. 52–75

Cameron, Alan, *Wandering Poets and other Essays on Late Greek Literature and Philosophy* (Oxford: Oxford University Press, 2016)

Clark, Elizabeth A., 'Claims on the Bones of Saint Stephen: The Partisans of Melania and Eudocia', *Church History*, 51 (1982), 141–56

Devos, Paul, 'Le Panégyrique de Saint Etienne par Hésychius de Jérusalem', *Analecta Bollandiana*, 86 (1968), 151–72

Dickie, Archibald C., 'The Lower Church of St John in Jerusalem', *Palestine Exploration Fund, Quarterly Statement*, 31 (1899), 43–45

Di Segni, Leah, 'The Greek Inscriptions of Hammat Gader', in Yizhar Hirschfeld, *The Roman Baths of Hammat Gader: Final Report* (The Israel Exploration Society: Jerusalem, 1997), pp. 185–266

Gorringe, Tim J., *A Theology of the Built Environment, Justice, Empowerment, Redemption* (Cambridge: Cambridge University Press, 2004)

Green, Judith, and Yoram Tsafrir, 'Greek Inscriptions from Ḥammat Gader: A Poem by the Empress Eudocia and Two Building Inscriptions', *Israel Exploration Journal*, 32 (1982) 77–96

Gutfeld, Oren, 'From Aelia Capitolina to Aelia Eudocia: Changes in the Urban Plan of Jerusalem', in *Study of Jerusalem Through the Ages*, ed. by Yehoshua Ben-Arieh, Aviva Halamish, Ora Limor, Rehav Rubin, and Ronny Reich (Jerusalem: Yad Ben-Zvi, 2015), pp. 122–38 (in Hebrew)

——, 'The Urban Layout of Byzantine-Period Jerusalem', in *Unearthing Jerusalem: 150 Years of Archaeological Research in the Holy City*, ed. by Katharina Galor and Gideon Avni (Winona Lake: Eisenbrauns, 2011), pp. 327–50

Herrin, Judith, 'The Imperial Feminine in Byzantium', *Past & Present*, 169 (2000), 3–35

Holum, Kenneth G., 'Pulcheria's Crusade ad 421–22 and the Ideology of Imperial Victory', *Greek, Roman and Byzantine Studies*, 18 (1977), 153–72

——, *Theodosian Empresses: Women and Imperial Dominion in Late Antiquity* (Berkeley: University of California Press, 1989)

Honigmann, Ernest, 'Juvenal of Jerusalem', *Dumbarton Oaks Papers*, 5 (1950), 209–79

Horn, Cornelia B., *Asceticism and Christological Controversy in Fifth Century Palestine: The Career of Peter the Iberian* (Oxford: Oxford University Press, 2006)

Hunt, Edward D., *Holy Land Pilgrimage in the Later Roman Empire* (Oxford: Oxford University Press, 1982)

James, Liz, 'Making a Name: Reputation and Imperial Founding and Refunding in Constantinople', in *Female Founders in Byzantium and Beyond*, ed. by Lioba Theis, Margaret Mullett, and Michael Grünbart (Vienna: Böhlau, 2011–2012), pp. 63–72

Klein, Konstantin M., 'Do Good in thy good pleasure unto Zion: The Patronage of Aelia Eudokia in Jerusalem', in *Female Founders in Byzantium and Beyond*, ed. by Lioba Theis, Margaret Mullett and Michael Grünbart (Vienna: Böhlau, 2011–2012), pp. 85–95

Kofsky, Aryeh, 'Peter the Iberian: Pilgrimage, Monasticism and Ecclesiastical Politics in Byzantine Palestine', *Liber Annuus*, 47 (1997), 209–22

Kofsky, Aryeh, and Serge Ruzer, 'The Holy Places and the Jewish Past in the Fifth-Century Christian Discourse of Appropriation', in *Between Sea and Desert: On Kings, Nomads, Cities and Monks, Essays in Honor of Joseph Patrich*, ed. by Orit Pelg-Barkat, Jacob Ashkenazi, Uzi Leibner, Mordechai Aviam, and Rina Talgam (Tzemach: Kinneret Academic College and Ostracon, 2019), pp. 225–34

Lefebvre, Henri, *The Production of Space* (Oxford: Wiley Blackwell, 1991)

Limberis, Vasiliki, *Divine Heiress: The Virgin Mary and the Creation of Christian Constantinople* (New York: Routledge, 1994)

Luz, Nimrod, *The Mamluk City in the Middle East: History, Culture, and the Urban Landscape* (New York: Cambridge University Press, 2014)

Macalister, Robert Alexander Stewart, 'The Rock-Cut Tombs in Wady er Rababi, Jerusalem', *Palestine Exploration Fund Quarterly Statement*, 32 (1900), 225–48

Magdalino, Paul, 'Aristocratic Oikoi in Tenth and Eleventh Regions of Constantinople', in *Byzantine Constantinople: Monuments, Topography and Everyday Life*, ed. by Nevra Necipoğlu (Leiden: Brill, 2001), pp. 53–69

Mgaloblishvili, Tamila, 'Regarding One Unknown Ancient Feast of Jerusalem', in *Between Sea and Desert: On Kings, Nomads, Cities and Monks, Essays in Honor of Joseph Patrich*, ed. by Orit Pelg-Barkat, Jacob Ashkenazi, Uzi Leibner, Mordechai Aviam, and Rina Talgam (Tzemach: Kinneret Academic College and Ostracon, 2019), pp. 159–66

Mitchell, Donald, *Cultural Geography: A Critical Introduction* (Oxford: Blackwell, 2000)

Müller, Andreas, 'Jerusalem als Zentrum von Wohltätigkeit in der Spätantike', in *Jerusalem II: Jerusalem in Roma-Byzantine Times*, ed. by Katharina Heyden and Maria Lissek with the assistance of Astrid Kaufmann (Tübingen: Mohr Siebeck, 2021), pp. 325–44

Nau, Françoise, 'Résumé de monographies syriaques', *Revue de l'Orient chrétien*, ser. II, 9 (1914), 113–34

Palmer, Andrew, *The Life of the Syrian Saint Barsauma: Eulogy of a Hero of the Resistance to the Council of Chalcedon* (Los Angeles: University of California Press, 2020)

Peleg-Barkat, Orit, 'Herodian Jerusalem', in *Routledge Handbook on Jerusalem*, ed. by Suleiman A. Mourad, Naomi Koltun-Fromm, and Bedross Der Matossian (London: Routledge, 2019), pp. 34–46

Perrone, Lorenzo, 'Christian Holy Places and Pilgrimage in the Age of Dogmatic Conflicts', *Proche-Orient Chrétien*, 48 (1998), 5–37

——, *La chiesa di Palestina e le controversie cristologiche* (Brescia: Paideia, 1980)

Power, Edmund, 'St Peter in Gallicantu', *Biblica*, 12 (1931), 411–46

Preziosi, Donald, *Architecture, Language, and Meaning: The Origins of the Built World and its Semiotic Organization* (The Hague: Mouton, 1979)

Reich, Ronnie, 'The Cultic and Secular Use of Water in Roman and Byzantine Jerusalem', in *Jerusalem II: Jerusalem in Roman-Byzantine Times*, ed. by Katharina Heyden and Maria Lissek with the assistance of Astrid Kaufmann (Tübingen: Mohr Siebeck, 2021), pp. 264–43

Rey, Terry, *Bourdieu on Religion Imposing Faith and Legitimacy* (New York: Routledge, 2007)

Sandnes, Karl Olav, *The Gospel 'According to Homer and Virgil': Cento and Canon* (Boston: Brill, 2011)

Shoemaker, Stephen J., *The Ancient Traditions of the Virgin Mary's Dormition and Assumption* (Oxford: Oxford University Press, 2003)

Sivan, Hagith, 'Subversive Pilgrimages: Barsauma in Jerusalem', *Journal of Early Christian Studies*, 26 (2018), 53–74

Stephens-Falcasantos, Rebecca, 'Christian Religious Symbolism and Pilgrimage', in *Routledge Handbook on Jerusalem*, ed. by Suleiman A. Mourad, Naomi Koltun-Fromm, and Bedross Der Matossian (London: Routledge, 2019), pp. 290–300

Tsafrir, Yoram, 'Between David's Tower and Holy Zion: Peter the Iberian and his Monastery in Jerusalem', in *Christ is Here! Studies in Biblical and Christian Archaeology in Memory of Michele Piccirillo, ofm*, ed. by L. Daniel Chrupcała (Milan: Studium Biblicum Franciscanum, 2012), pp. 245–64

——, 'The Holy City of Jerusalem in the Madaba Map', in *The Madaba Map Centenary 1897–1997, Travelling through the Byzantine Umayyad Period*, ed. by Michele Piccirillo and Eugenio Alliata (Jerusalem: Studium Biblicum Franciscanum, 1999), pp. 155–63

Twardowska, Kamilla, 'The Church Foundations of Empress Pulcheria in Constantinople According to Theodore Lector's Church History and Other Contemporary Sources', *Res Gestae, Czasopismo Historyczne*, 5 (2017), 83–94

Vailhé, Siméon, 'Formation du patriarcat de Jérusalem', *Échos d'Orient*, 13 (1910), 325–36

——, 'L'érection du Patriarchat de Jerusalem 451', *Revue de l'Orient chrétien*, 4 (1899), 44–57

Van Esbroeck, Michel, 'La lettre de l'empereur Justinian sur l'annonciacion et la Noël en 561', *Analecta Bollandiana*, 86 (1968), 351–71

Vincent, Hugues L., and Félix-Marie Abel, *Jérusalem. Recherches de topographie, d'archéologie et d'histoire*, ii: *Jérusalem nouvelle* (Paris: J. Gabalda, 1926)

Weksler-Bdolah, Shlomit, 'The Fortifications of Jerusalem in the Byzantine Period', *ARAM*, 18–19 (2006–2007), 85–112

Wortley, John, 'The Marian Relics at Constantinople', *Greek Roman and Byzantine Studies*, 45 (2005), 171–87

Zias, Joe, 'Was Byzantine Herodium a Leprosarium?' *The Biblical Archaeologist*, 49 (1986), 182–86

OSNAT E. RANCE

'Although Their Names Escaped Me'

Local Patriotism and Saints Commemoration in Late Antique Syria[*]

Introduction

In one of his innovative articles, '"The Dark Side of the Moon"',[1] Oded Irshai meticulously examined the political struggle between the two most prominent Palestinian episcopal sees in the fourth century, those of Jerusalem and Caesarea. At the heart of this study lies a composition by the contemporary bishop of Caesarea, Eusebius — *The Martyrs of Palestine*.[2] This work was written at the end of Diocletian's 'Great Persecutions' (303–311 CE) and represents the most detailed account of the combatants and martyrs of this period.[3] Eusebius's account was originally written in Greek, but only a Syriac translation has come down to us in full. This version is part of the famous Syriac codex, dating to the year 411, that contains Syriac translations of Early Christian Greek texts. According to Irshai, a more sophisticated issue lurks behind the immediate façade of this account of Roman brutality and Christian steadfastness — one that served as a launching pad for the creation of a novel Christian conceptual

---

[*] This essay is a token of gratitude to Oded, for sharing his wisdom and for his invaluable guidance throughout my doctoral studies. My thanks to Johannes Hahn and Sergey Minov, and to the peer reviewers, for their reading and for their wise remarks. And thanks as well to all who took part in organizing this volume, and to the editors, Martin Goodman and Brouria Bitton-Ashkelony. From the *Encomium for the Martyrs*, 4: ܪܚܡ ܗܢ ܪܚܡ ܘܡܘܣܐ This text was published by Wright, 'Encomium of the Martyrs'.

[1] Irshai, '"The Dark Side of the Moon"'; Irshai, 'Fourth Century Christian Palestinian Politics'.

[2] For the claim that the composition 'has not really been searched and studied in a systematic way', see Verheyden, 'Pain and Glory', esp. p. 354.

[3] Excluding another of Eusebius's accounts, i.e., the eighth book of his *Church History*, written in Greek.

Osnat Emily Rance has a PhD from the Hebrew University of Jerusalem in 2022. She is a post doctorate fellow at the Centre for Advanced Studies "Beyond Canon" at Universität Regensburg. Her dissertation, on representations of religious violence between Christians and Jews in late antiquity was supervised by Professor Oded Irshai.

Essays on Jews and Christians in Late Antiquity in Honour of Oded Irshai, ed. by Brouria Bitton-Ashkelony and Martin Goodman, CELAMA 40 (Turnhout: Brepols, 2023), pp. 141–157

BREPOLS ❧ PUBLISHERS   10.1484/M.CELAMA-EB.5.132487

map of Palestine, whereby its metropolitan centre, Caesarea Maritima, was being conferred with sacredness via the blood of the martyrs shed in this city.

The Martyrs of Palestine is followed in the same codex by an encomium, entitled *Encomium for the Martyrs*,[4] which is traditionally ascribed to Eusebius of Caesarea as well. This attribution, however, dates to the catalogue of the thirteenth-century bishop, Abdisho of Nisibis[5] and is the only testimony we have regarding the *Encomium*'s authorship.

Several of the martyrs cited in the *Encomium* are nowhere mentioned by Eusebius, either in his *Church History* or in his other testimony on the persecutions, *The Martyrs of Palestine*.[6] Their absence, in and of itself, hardly means that Eusebius was unfamiliar with their stories. However, as we shall see, there are a number of reasons to believe that he was not aware of certain details that were accessible to the author of the *Encomium*. As martyrdom and Eusebius's works are two of Oded's scholarly interests, I would like to contribute to this volume in his honour with an examination of this work. Following in Oded's footsteps with regard to the Caesarean chauvinism demonstrated in *The Martyrs of Palestine*, in the present essay I reconsider, in light of what the saints in this text reveal about its likely authorship.

The Codex

A few words about this famous codex and its historical context are in order. This Syrian manuscript, housed now in the British Library (Add MS 12150), is the oldest codex in any language bearing a date; according to its colophon, it was completed in Edessa in the year 411.

The codex comprises six distinct works: the Pseudo-Clementine *Recognitions*; Titus of Bostra's *Against the Manicheans*; and *The Theophany*, *The Martyrs of Palestine*, and *The Encomium*, all generally recognized as by Eusebius; and the so-called *Syriac Martyrology of 411*. All six are Syriac translations from the Greek of Christian ecclesiastical texts.[7] Luise Marion Frenkel was the first to address the principle of selection that dictated the contents of the codex. In her view, the entire collection was assembled in Edessa during the period of

---

4 However, the Syriac title is: ܩܘܡܗܝܠܬܗܘܢ ܕܝܠܗܘܢ ܕܬܫܒܘܚܬܐ ('a praise for their virtues').

5 Also known as Abdisho of Soba ܒܪ ܒܪܝܟܐ. For Abdisho's catalogue in English, see Badger, *The Nestorians*, pp. 2, 361–79, esp. p. 364. See also Habbi, *Catalogus Auctorum*.

6 In the words of B. H. Cowper: 'As for the authorship, it is undoubted. Among the works of Eusebius, mentioned by Abdisho in his catalogue, the *Martyrs of Palestine* is followed by an oration with exactly the same title as ours'. See Wright, 'Encomium of the Martyrs', p. 406.

7 In regard to our manuscript, it is difficult to determine whether these works were translated from a single earlier Greek source or from multiple sources. For more information about the historical context of the translations from Greek to Syriac see Butts, *Language Change*, esp. ch. 1, pp. 1–8. For a description of the entire codex, see Wright, *Catalogue of Syriac Manuscripts*, pp. 631–33.

the division in the church, due to the Arian controversy, in order to promote the idea of a united-universal Christianity.[8]

The *Encomium*

The *Encomium* opens with a generalized glorification of death in the service of faith, praise of warriors in the name of Christ, elevating martyrs to the status of prophets and apostles, and contrasting them to earthly warriors who sacrifice the grace of Christ and their place in the world to come. The encomiast then enumerates a series of approximately three dozen martyrs, confessors, and saints in three distinct groups. As is customary in such texts, the list enumerates famous ancient martyrs, beginning with Old Testament protagonists, including Noah, Hananiah, Azariah and Mishael, Daniel, Jeremiah, Zechariah, Abel, and the (Maccabean) mother of seven sons. These are followed by the three early apostolic martyrs, Peter, Stephen, and Paul. The concluding list of post-apostolic elect who are commemorated consists of Asclepiades, Serapion, Philetus, Zebinas, Demetrius (Demetrianus), Flavianus (Fabius), Cyrillus(?), Sosipater, Andrew, Babylas, Caerealis(?), Izabenus(?), Zenobius, Paulus, Marinus, Fronto, and Hippolytus.[9]

The Post-Apostolic Martyrs

The logical point of departure for adducing evidence regarding the authorship of such a text is the roster of Church personages, and this inquiry offers insights into the work's programmatic underpinning while also raising questions regarding its attribution to Eusebius. Most notably, at least nine of the named individuals were bishops of Antioch, as Joseph Lightfoot already noted.[10] Their names appear in the following order: Asclepiades, Serapion, Philetus, Zebinas, Demetrius (Demetrianus), Flavianus (Fabius), Cyrillus(?), Babylas,

---

8   Frenkel, 'The "Encomium of the Martyrs"', esp. pp. 92–93. I thank Sergey Minov for referring me to Frenkel's paper.

9   It is interesting to quote here the comment regarding the saints in the *Encomium* offered by B. H. Cowper in his English translation: 'The eminent saints and martyrs whom Eusebius mentions will not, even in name, be all recognized, owing to the loose way in which their names are spelled in the Syriac. A reference to the Martyrs of Palestine supplies the names of Zebinas, and Paulus, but whether they are the same as those in our text does not appear (*Martyrs*, pp. 31, 39, 47). Of the rest, we find the names of two or three in other works of Eusebius, and more in the old martyrologies; but we are not about to investigate them here, and will only remark that all the martyrs mentioned in this part of the oration may be such as suffered in Palestine, but are not named in the larger work'. See Wright, 'Encomium', n. 29.

10   See Lightfoot, 'Eusebius of Caesarea', esp. p. 344. However, Lightfoot's assumption is that this *Encomium* was penned by Eusebius. I claim otherwise and propose a range of dates for its composition.

and Paulus.[11] However, as many scholars have observed, neither all of these bishops nor all of the other figures listed are known to us primarily as martyrs.[12]

Serapeion (190–203), for example, apart from his role as bishop, was a renowned theologian and a fierce combatant against heresies, as evidenced by his writings, which were listed by both Eusebius and Jerome,[13] but there is no record of him being martyred. On the other hand, Babylas figures very prominently as a bishop of Antioch (237–50/1). He was imprisoned during the Decian persecution and died in prison.[14] However, according to Chrysostom, before being martyred, in the days of Emperor Philip the Arabian, Babylas opposed the emperor and forbade him to enter to the church.[15] Thus, Babylas represents the first case of '*parrhesia*',[16] and the first recorded combat between *imperium et sacerdotium*.[17] Babylas is also known for his role in the Christianization in the vicinity of Antioch, and his relics were known for their power to protect the city from the Persians. In the days of Gallus (351–354), Babylas's relics were translated to a martyrium next to the temple of Apollo at Daphne. When, a decade later, Julian the Apostate was advised that Babylas's relics were thwarting the emperor's intent to revive the pagan oracle at the temple, he ordered removal of the remains of Babylas from the martyrium, to a location far from the temple.[18] Subsequently, Babylas's relics were moved

---

11 Peeters notes that some of them are better known for their position on the see of Antioch; see Peeters, 'De S. Demetriano Antiochiae Episcopo'.

12 See, for example, Peeters, 'De S. Demetriano', or Lightfoot, 'Eusebius'. This is not unusual. Other Antiochian bishops were sanctified as well; see, for example, the case of St Meletius of Antioch in Chrysostom's homily: Mayer, with Neil, *The Cult of the Saints*, pp. 39–41. See John Chrysostom, *Homily on Meletios*. It is important to note that despite Meletius's praise in this homily, St Meletius of Antioch was the bishop of the city in the years 360–81 and an ascetic, but not a martyr.

13 Eusebius, *Historia ecclesiastica*, 5.19.1; 6.12 (in Schwartz, *Eusebius Werke* 2, hereafter *Hist. eccl.*); see Schwartz, *Eusebius Werke* 2, pp. 479–80, 544–46 (hereafter 'Schwartz'). For a brief sketch of Serapion's works, see Quasten, *Patrology*, 1, pp. 283–84.

14 Eusebius, *Hist. eccl.*, 6.39.4 (Schwartz, p. 594).

15 For Chrysostom's homily on Babylas see *Homily on Meletios*, PG 1.527–72. Eusebius recorded a similar story about an unidentified bishop at the time of Emperor Philip (Eusebius, *Hist. eccl.*, 6.34; Schwartz, pp. 588–90).

16 *Parrhesia*: from the Greek word παρρησία, meaning 'freedom of speech', more specifically, the possibility of speaking boldly in front of those in power. This was even perceived as an obligation to speak the truth for the common good, even at personal risk. For further reading, see van Renswoude, *The Rhetoric of Free Speech*.

17 The first combat between these two entities is usually ascribed to bishop Ambrose of Milan and Emperor Theodosius I. See, among others, Drake, 'Intolerance, Religious Violence, and Political Legitimacy in Late Antiquity'. According to van Renswoude, *Rhetoric of Free Speech*, 109, 'Bishops found their authority increased if their confrontations (real or staged) with Roman emperors were acknowledged as acts of *parrhesia*'.

18 Socrates Scholasticus, *Historia ecclesiastica*, 3.18; see Sokrates, *Kirchengeschichte*, n.s. 1, pp. 213–14; Sozomenos, *Historia ecclesiastica*, 5.19; see Sozomenos, *Historia ecclesiastica/ Kirchengeschichte*, pp. 643–51; and see Allen and others, '*Let Us Die That We May Live*', pp. 140–41.

several times, until their final deposition in a church built for this purpose and named after him.[19]

Demetrianus (256–260),[20] another long-venerated local martyr, was a bishop of Antioch as well. He was taken captive by the Persians under Shapur I in 256 and remained in prison until his death.[21] A church named after him was erected at Eleusis in Greece, on the site that previously housed a temple of Demeter, the goddess of agriculture. The resemblance between the names of the Greek goddess and the Christian saint to whom the new church was dedicated was seen by some scholars as a contemporary method for the Christianization of paganism: the new shrine undermined the local traditions and offered a substitution for their rituals.[22] Stated otherwise, Demetrius was adopted by the Christian church as a saint in order to undermine the pagan veneration of the goddess Demeter, and his martyrium was established on the site of the earlier temple.[23]

The *Encomium* and Eusebius

There are a number of issues that raise questions regarding the *Encomium*'s attribution to Eusebius. To begin with, several of the referenced Christian martyrs in the *Encomium* — including Sosipater, Andrew, Caerealus, and Fronto — are nowhere mentioned elsewhere by Eusebius, either in his *Church History* or in his other testimony on the persecutions, *The Martyrs of Palestine*.[24]

Second, among those that are common to the unquestioned Eusebian works, the order of saints and martyrs in the *Encomium* is different. Eight of the certainly identifiable Antiochene bishops in the *Encomium* also appear in the *History*, but Eusebius enumerates their order of succession as: Serapion, Asclepiades, Philetus, Zebinas, Babylas, Flavianus (Fabius), Demetrius (Demetrianus), Paul, and Cyril.[25]

---

19 See Allen and others, *'Let Us Die That We May Live'*, pp. 140–48.

20 'Indeed by the seventh century it may have been as impossible to ascertain the facts about the historical figure as it is today'. See Christopher, 'The Origins of the Cult of Saint George', p. 310.

21 See Downey, *A History of Antioch*, p. 309. In the *Chronicle of Séert* his name is Demetrius, rather than Demetrianus; see Scher, 'Histoire Nestorienne Inèdite (Chronicle of Séert)', pp. 232. According to Eusebius, *Hist. eccl.*, 7.13,14 (Schwartz, pp. 666–68), Demetrianus succeeded Fabianus as the bishop of Antioch. According to Peeters, 'De S. Demetriano', this Demetrius was a presbyter in Edessa before being consecrated as the bishop of Antioch.

22 See also Liebeschuetz, *Antioch*, p. 232.

23 Brown, *The Cult of the Saints*, pp. 125–26. The renowned scholar Hippolyte Delehaye took issue with this view, describing it sarcastically as an ingenious theory'. Delehaye, *The Legends of the Saints*, pp. 133–36., esp. p. 133.

24 It is not clear whether the author referenced Andrew the apostle or another figure named Andrew. The same is the case regarding Sosipater.

25 For the order of succession see in Eusebius, *Hist. eccl.*, 5.19.1 (Schwartz, p. 479); 6.11.4 (Schwartz, p. 542); 6.23.3 (Schwartz, pp. 488–90); 6.29.4 (Schwartz, p. 584); 6.39.4

Another issue raised in considering the *Encomium* list of Church elect concerns its inclusion of details that one would have expected to find in related Eusebian works but which, apparently, were unknown to the Caesarean historian. So, for example, Demetrianus is recorded in the *History* as one of Antioch's bishops, but it appears that Eusebius was not aware of the prelate's unfortunate destiny. According to the East Syrian history, the ninth-century *Chronicle of Seert*, Demetrianus was one of the Byzantine captives of Shapur I who was deported to Persia and became the leader of the developing new Christian community there.[26] No reference to Demetrianus's martyrdom appears in other works of Eusebius.

Likewise of note is the case of Hippolytus, who concludes the *Encomium*'s list of saints. A bishop by the name of Hippolytus and the names of several works he authored appears in the *History*, but Eusebius states that he knows neither his origin nor his episcopal see.[27] With the benefit of hindsight, it is difficult to fault the Caesarean historian for his vagueness. Modern scholars have characterized virtually every aspect of the identity, provenance, diocese, and works by one or more ecclesiastical figures named Hippolytus variously as complicated, confusing, puzzling, enigmatic, and irresolvable.[28] The most prominent bishop of this name was a Roman Hippolytus, who was martyred in the persecutions of 235 CE, under Maximinus. We are informed that he and pope Pontianus were sent to 'the island of death' (i.e., Sardinia) and martyred by *damnatio ad metalla*, by slavery and death in the mines.[29] In the *Depositio martirum* of the Chronograph of 354 these two martyrs are listed together, commemorated on 13 August.[30] Complicating matters, the fourth-century poet Prudentius, in his *Liber peristephanon* (Crown of Martyrs), renders a dramatic account of a reformed schismatic Hippolytus whose crypt he visited while in Rome. The tomb painting described in his ekphrasis depicts a prelate who was martyred by being tied to a wild horse and dragged to his death.[31]

(Schwartz, p. 594); 7.14.1 (Schwartz, p. 668); 7.27.1 (Schwartz, p. 702); 7.32.1–2 (Schwartz, p. 716).

26 See n. 22. Although in this text his name is recorded as Demetrius. On this episode see in Downey, *A History of Antioch*, p. 309, and his notes there. Demetrianus has gained a place of importance in the history of this new see, as its founder who brought with him to the church of Gundishapur (Beth Lapat) the prestige of the apostolic Antiochene church and passed it to his successors. See also Wood, *The Chronicle of Seert*, pp. 87–92.

27 Eusebius, *Hist. eccl.*, 6.14.10 (Schwartz, p. 552). He was also mentioned in Jerome, *De viris illustribus*, esp. pp. 671–64.

28 For a summary and bibliography of the recent scholarship, see chapter 3, 'Hippolytus of Rome: A Manifold Enigma', of Vinzent's *Writing the History of Early Christianity*, pp. 162–95. With regard to the numerous works attributed to a single Church Father of Rome, Vinzent states: 'At present the view prevails [...] that the Hippolytus corpus was written not by one man, but by two or more Hippolyti, whose identities remain unclear', p. 165.

29 Quasten, *Patrology*, 2:163–207, esp. 163–65.

30 See Mommsen, *Chronica Minora Saec. IV, V, VI (Vol. 1)*, pp. 71–72. <https://www.tertullian.org/fathers/chronography_of_354_12_depositions_martyrs.htm> [accessed 20 July 2021].

31 Prudentius, 'To the Bishop Valerianus on the Passion of the Most Blessed Martyr

'ALTHOUGH THEIR NAMES ESCAPED ME'   147

Whatever the case may be, it is reasonably certain that the Hippolytus cited by Eusebius was associated, if not one and the same, with the figure in the statue of Hippolytus in the Vatican, as the works listed in the *Church History* partly match those listed on the statue.

The anomaly of a Roman martyr about whom the leading church historians of the fourth century know little appearing in a list of Antiochene bishops is resolved in the very manuscript that contains our *Encomium*. The *Syriac Martyrology of 411* — the last of the five texts in British Library, Add MS 12150[32] — lists 30 'of the Latter Kanun' (January) as the feast day of a saint Hippolytus who was martyred in Antioch. An Antiochene Hippolytus martyred on 30 January is likewise recorded in the Church Calendar of the tenth-century monk of the Mar Saba Monastery, Ioane Zosime, which was largely based on late antique prototypes from Jerusalem.[33] From the context alone, it seems clear that the Hippolytus recorded in the *Encomium* is not a bishop of Rome, but a saint celebrated in the eastern church on a date different from the martyr of 235. Significantly, we have no evidence whatever from Eusebius's writings that he was acquainted with such a person. And certainly, as noted, Hippolytus does not appear in the succession of Antiochene bishops listed in the *History*. The latest bishop of Antioch listed there is Cyril (283–303 CE),[34] which would suggest that the Hippolytus of Antioch was a fourth-century prelate. In sum, these observations further give the lie to Eusebius's authorship of our text.

The veneration accorded to at least eight bishops of Antioch along with our identification of a saint commemorated in the *Encomium* as an Antiochene martyr, warrants consideration of Antioch as the focal point of the Syriac text and may aid in identification of otherwise unspecified figures. Thus, if the Paulus who appears among the enumerated saints is to be connected to the city, we may reasonably surmise that this reference is to the bishop of Antioch, Paul of Samosata (*c.* 260–68). It is most unlikely that Eusebius, were he the author of the *Encomium*, would have included Paulus — assuming the identification is correct — among the saints. In the *History*, Eusebius depicts this Antiochene bishop as a corrupt man, who was deposed in the synod of 268 CE on account of his semi-Arian doctrinal views.[35] Eusebius

---

Hippolytus', in Prudentius, *Crown of Martyrs – Liber Peristephanon*, pp. 140–50.

32 Wright, 'An Ancient Syrian Martyrology'. On the martyrology see Nicholson, ed., s.v. 'Martyrology of 411, Syriac', *Oxford Dictionary of Late Antiquity*, p. 976.

33 See Nikoloz Aleksidze, Cult of Saints, E02896 <http://csla.history.ox.ac.uk/record. php?recid=E02896> [accessed 20 July 2021]. A full bibliography is listed at <https://doi. org/10.25446/oxford.13828313.v1> [accessed 30 November 2022] J. B. Lightfoot for one was unequivocal in his conviction that this martyr was distinct from the Roman (and possibly other) prelates of the same name: 'The publication of Wright's Syriac Martyrology shows that this Antiochene Martyr Hippolytus was a real person celebrated on this day from the beginning [...] This Hippolytus therefore is a real person distinct from any Roman Hipplytus, as the Syriac Martyrology shows'. See Lightfoot, *The Apostolic Fathers*, pp. 371–72.

34 Eusebius, *Hist. eccl.*, 7.32.1–2 (Schwartz, p. 718).

35 Eusebius, *Hist. eccl.*, 7.27.1; 7.29–30 (Schwartz, pp. 702; 705–14).

declares very clearly that he was not among Paul's admirers. Ascribing the *Encomium* — with this controversial protagonist — to Eusebius, therefore, would be highly dubious.

Inserted among the bishops' names in the *Encomium*, we find the names of two other saints who were commemorated as martyrs, Marinus and Fronto. In the *History*, Eusebius recounts only Marinus's martyrdom as having taken place in Caesarea.[36] Surprisingly, however, there is no reference to Marinus in the *Martyrs of Palestine*, which we would expect, given Eusebius's local patriotism and his inclination to 'inflate' the number of the martyrs of his see city, Caesarea, over those of Antioch.[37] Even more noteworthy is that Jerome records that the cult of Marinus *originated* and was active in the vicinity of Antioch, in the martyrium of Saint Julian of Cilicia.[38] Malalas recounts that approximately one hundred years later, in 529, his relics were uncovered and subsequently deposited in St Julian's martyrium.[39] The veneration of Marinus in Antioch, although he was martyred in Caesarea, and although his relics were not yet identified in the late fourth to early fifth century, is somewhat enigmatic.

It appears, therefore, that most of the martyrs commemorated in the *Encomium* had a connection with Antioch, mostly as bishops of that city.[40] In light of this, we may reasonably surmise that the otherwise unidentified saint, Fronto, is likely to have had a connection to Antioch.[41]

The Maccabeans

Compelling evidence that anchors the *Encomium for the Martyrs* in Antioch and supports the improbability of Eusebius's authorship may be adduced from its commemoration of the Maccabees. This part of the text also provides evidence for establishing significant details regarding the likely date of the *Encomium*'s composition.

The most striking feature of the entire *Encomium* is the veneration lavished upon the last of the Old Testament martyrs — 'the mother of

---

36 Eusebius, *Hist. eccl.*, 7.15 (Schwartz, pp. 668–70).

37 Eusebius, *Hist. eccl.*, 7.15 (Schwartz, pp. 668–70). See also Irshai, '"The Dark Side of the Moon"'; Irshai, 'Fourth Century Christian Palestinian Politics'.

38 According to the information at the database of The Cult of Saints in Late Antiquity, a feast of a Marinos was celebrated at this shrine on 26 December. Thus, the feast of Saint Marinus was celebrated near Antioch even before the revelation of his relics. See Oxford Project of Saints <http://csla.history.ox.ac.uk/record.php?recid=E05738> [accessed 20 July 2021].

39 Malalas, *Chronographia*, 18.49 (Ioannis Malalae, *Chronographia*, pp. 379–80), reports that Marinus's relics were found in 529.

40 See Mayer, *The Cult of the Saints*, p. 40, regarding Meletius's sainthood, which Chrysostom attributed to the bishop's asceticism.

41 It is difficult to make a decisive identification regarding Fronto. There was a Fronto among the seventy-two disciples. Early traditions locate him in Antioch while accompanying Peter. See Herrick, 'Studying Apostolic Hagiography'.

seven sons' — who, according to ii Macc. 6:18–8:41 and iv Macc. 1:8–10, were taken captive and suffered martyrdom at the hands of Antiochus IV Epiphanes for their refusal to abandon their ancestral beliefs and embrace Hellenistic religion.[42] It merits observation that while serial execution of the seven sons understandably occupies a very significant part of the Maccabees narrative, and notwithstanding the fact that this extended passage opens with a reference to 'the crown of victory in the great contest *both for men and women who are in confession*', the sole focus of our encomiast is the mother's valour: rearing them by prayer and by milk of the law and heavenly food; crowned on account of all of them; a wise and true mother; a 'blessed woman who didst bring forth with hard pains and without griefs didst restore by prayer the fruit thou didn't rear'.

The veneration of the Maccabean martyrs is not attested before the second half of the fourth century — making this extended passage in the *Encomium* among the earliest.[43] As Martha Vinson persuasively argued, the first recorded Christian prelate to sermonize about the Maccabees as Christian protomartyrs was Gregory of Nazianzus. In response to Emperor Julian's proposal for the Jews to rebuild the Temple in 362 CE, in his Oration 15, *In Praise of the Maccabees*, Gregory sought to sever the association between the Second Temple and the Jews by appropriating the Maccabees as pre-Christian martyrs.[44] Significantly, the oration opens with the acknowledgement that at that point in time, 'not many recognize them because their martyrdom antedates Christ'.

As evidenced by John Chrysostom's homilies of 386, *On the Holy Maccabees and their Mother* [and *Homily on Eleazar and the Seven Boys*], a quarter of a century following Gregory's oration, the Maccabees are firmly established objects of Christian veneration in Antioch.[45] The presentation of 'the mother and seven sons' in the *Encomium* falls quite markedly between these two

---

42 Regarding the veneration of the Maccabean martyrs in Antioch and the confiscation of a synagogue dedicated to the memory of the Maccabean martyrs and its conversion into a martyrium, see Hahn, 'Veneration of the Maccabean Brothers'. See also the discussion in Rutgers, *Making Myths*, pp. 26–32, on the intricate way in which the Maccabean martyrs were appropriated and venerated in Christian liturgy. For traces of traditions about their burial in Antioch, see Schatkin, 'The Maccabean Martyrs', esp. p. 99.

43 On the Maccabean martyrs see van Henten, 'The Maccabean Martyrs as Models'. Concerning the development of Christian veneration of Maccabees, see also Joslyn-Siemiatkoski, *Christian Memories of the Maccabean Martyrs*.

44 See Vinson, 'Gregory Nazianzen's Homily'. However, there are earlier Christian writers who showed interest in the Maccabees, such as Origen and Cyprian. See Hahn, 'Veneration of the Maccabean Brothers', p. 85 and n. 18. Also, many scholars have noted that these Jewish protagonists (the Maccabeans and Daniel and the three young men), among others, are the ones referred to in Hebrews 11. See van Henten, 'The Reception of Daniel 3 and 6 and the Maccabean Martyrdoms'.

45 For Chrysostom's homily, see Mayer, *The Cult of the Saints*, pp. 119–34. In his epistle (Ambrose, *Epist.* 74.16) to Emperor Theodosius I in the year 388, Ambrose depicted the cult of the Maccabeans as 'ancient' (*veteri*). However, this seems to be merely a rhetorical exaggeration.

positions. On the one hand, the Maccabees are patently cited among the Old Testament protagonists; on the other, the encomiast has gone to great lengths to persuade his audience of the Christian virtues of a mother who suffered the martyrdom of her sons. Thus, in his treatment of the mother of the seven sons, our encomiast falls somewhere between Gregory's homily (362) and Chrysostom's sermon (*c.* 386).

There is considerably more to be deduced about the origin of the *Encomium* from this part of the text. While neither of the two Maccabees accounts specifies the locus of the martyrdom of Eleazar and the mother and seven sons, there is a tradition that places their trial and martyrdom at the hands of Antiochus during his residence in Antioch.[46] Chrysostom's sermons — honouring both the Maccabees and Eleazar — attest to a feast honouring the Maccabees in the 380s. But even more significantly, there is an additional testimony that places a shrine of the Maccabees in the city of Antioch.[47] The earliest testimony for the veneration of the mother and seven sons in Antioch comes from the text that accompanies the *Encomium* in our manuscript, the *Syriac Martyrology of 411*.[48] The entry in the *Martyrology*'s liturgical calendar for the month of Ab (= August) reads: 'On the first of the month, according to the Greeks [the commemoration of] the martyrs from among those buried in Antioch, that is to say in [Kerateion],[49] who were the sons of Shamūnī, about whom it was written in [the book of] Maccabees'.[50] Shmuni (or Shamuni) is the Syriac name given to the Maccabean mother of the seven sons.[51]

August is an odd date for the commemoration of the Maccabees, since according to the Jewish tradition they were put to trial in proximity to Hanukkah, which usually falls in December.[52] This unexpected date for their

46 See Hahn, 'Veneration of the Maccabean Brothers', and more below.

47 See Schatkin, 'The Maccabean Martyrs'.

48 Wright, 'An Ancient Syrian Martyrology'.

49 Wright states here ('An Ancient Syrian Martyrology', p. 428 and note n): 'MS. ܒܩܪܛܝܐ, "in Krtia", (Carteia?), probably the name of a place at or near Antioch'. According to Liebeschuetz, *Antioch*, p. 233, the synagogue in which the tomb of the Maccabeans was allegedly situated in Antioch. It was taken and transformed into a Christian church sometime after 363 CE. Carteia was the name of the Jewish quarter in Antioch, and late traditions situated the tomb of the Maccabeans there. Rutgers, *Making Myths*, p. 48, doubts the authenticity of the tradition concerning the Antiochene synagogue (for purity reasons).

50 Translation from Wright, 'An Ancient Syrian Martyrology'. ܒܝܪܚ ܐܒ܂ ܒܚܕ ܒܝܪܚܐ ܒܝܘ̈ܢܝܐ ܣܗ̈ܕܐ ܕܗܘܘ ܡܢ ܗܢܘܢ ܕܩܒܝܪܝܢ ܒܐܢܛܝܘܟܝܐ܂ ܗܢܘ ܕܝܢ ܒܩܪܛܝܐ ܕܐܝܬܝܗܘܢ ܒܢ̈ܘܗ ܕܫܡܘܢܝ܂ ܗܢܘܢ ܕܟܬܝܒܝܢ ܒܡܩܒܝ̈ܐ܀

51 For the name Shamuni see Witakowski, 'Mart(y) Shmuni'. The origin of the mother's name is unclear. Witakowski (pp. 155–57) suggested that it derives from the Hebrew number eight (*shmone*), marking the number of the martyrs, i.e., Shmuni and her seven sons. It could also derive from the name Hasmonean (Ἀσαμωναίος), as they are called by Josephus.

52 According to Vinson, 'Gregory Nazianzen's Homily 15', p. 188, the original feast day of the Maccabean martyrs was celebrated in December, near the Jewish celebration of Hanukkah. However, during the days of Emperor Theodosius I (d. 395), the Christian feast of the Maccabees was shifted to August (Ab), in order to distinguish the Christian celebration from the Jewish one. See also Mayer, *The Cult of the Saints*, p. 119; Allen and others, *'Let Us*

veneration calls for an explanation. It may be the case that Jews commemorated the Maccabees on two occasions during the year: once in the Jewish month of Kislev (equivalent to late November–early December), that is, on Hannukah, and again in the month of Ab, namely, on the ninth of Ab, the day commemorating the destruction of both the First and Second Temples.[53] Thus, for example, traces of the Jewish commemoration of the Maccabees in Ab are to be found in Eichah Rabbah, the midrash aggadah on the book of Lamentations. Among the series of destruction legends cited there (1:50) one finds the tale about the mother of seven sons.

In our context, perhaps a stronger case for the different dates is offered by the Christian evidence. Vinson has reasoned that Gregory's Homily 15 was delivered in December, among other reasons reading the reference to 'these annual processions and festivals' as an allusion to the eight-day Jewish festival.[54] This reading is consistent with our earlier observation that the Maccabees in Gregory are recognized as distinctly Jewish martyrs. Further supporting a December date of the sermon is the link drawn between the Maccabees and Daniel. In his homily, Gregory ascribes the death sentences and martyrdom of the mother and her seven sons, and Daniel and the three Hebrews, to their refusal to eat unclean food.[55] It is therefore telling that Gregory concludes his homily with the commemoration of Daniel and the three Hebrews, combatants whose commemoration falls in December, thus further supporting the conclusion as to the month in which the homily was delivered and that the Maccabees were commemorated in the East in the early 360s.[56]

It is only natural that with the passage of time; untethered from the original, historical reason for the appropriation; and in reaction to the assault of Julian's efforts to rebuild the temple in Jerusalem, Church theologians sought to distinguish the Christian commemoration day of these Jewish protomartyrs from the Jewish feast of dedication and associate it with the commemoration of the Temple's destruction. The *Martyrology of 411*, which records 1 August as the date of veneration and further documents the presence of the martyrs' relics in Antioch, provides a *terminus ante quem* for this shift. And there is indirect evidence that this shift occurred at least by the time of Chrysostom's sermons, as he states that the festival of the Maccabees is

---

Die That We May Live', pp. 111–26, esp. p. 116, regarding veneration of the Maccabean martyrs *within* the city walls of Antioch, already in the time of Chrysostom.

53 Obermann, 'The Sepulchre of the Maccabean Martyrs', p. 250. According to Obermann, 'some calendars of the Oriental church list the memorial day as the Eight of August'. This date demonstrates even more the Christian intention to adopt the Jewish mourning day as the Christian veneration day of the Maccabees, rather than the Jewish feast commemorating the heroic deeds of the Hasmonean family.

54 Vinson, 'Gregory Nazianzen's Homily 15', p. 188.

55 See Vinson, trans., *Gregory of Nazianzus: Selected Orations*, pp. 72–84, and see her comment on Gregory's confusion, p. 83 and n. 37.

56 The commemoration of Daniel falls on December 18.

taking place 'in the sunniest part of the year', i.e., in late summer.[57] Thus, we may conclude that sometime during the years between 362 and the reign of Emperor Theodosius I, the Christian commemoration of the Maccabees shifted from December to August.[58]

As our further study of the *Encomium* will demonstrate, the feast days of most of the named church martyrs fall between mid-November and the end of December. This would indicate that the text was composed sometime before the Christian celebration of the Maccabees was formally moved from December to August. This conclusion is consistent with our earlier positioning of the *Encomium*'s presentation of the Maccabees on a continuum between Jewish prototypes of martyrdom (Gregory) and their celebration as Christianized protomartyrs (Chrysostom).[59] In sum, with the exception of the menology in our codex, there exists no testament that specifies Antioch as the place of the Maccabees' death or veneration.[60] Our *Encomium* offers the first textual exposition regarding their veneration in Antioch. By association with the other martyrs, their commemoration is still in the 'old' date, in proximity to the Jewish feast of Dedication (Hanukkah). In the menology of the same codex a later stage is represented: the commemoration of the Maccabees is dated to the first of Ab, and the link between their martyrdom and the city of Antioch is already well established, while in the *Encomium* the author is exerting efforts to justify their veneration in the first instance.[61]

---

57 See Mayer, *The Cult of the Saints*, p. 119; Allen and others, '*Let Us Die That We May Live*', pp. 111–26, esp. p. 115.

58 Vinson, 'Gregory Nazianzen's Homily 15'.

59 The composition date of this *Syriac Martyrology* is uncertain. Nicholson maintains that it was translated from a Greek recension, and that the most recent saints are dated to the reign of Julian, 'but their names may have been inserted later than the original composition of the text' (Nicholson, ed., 'Martyrology of 411, Syriac', p. 976), However, the commemoration of the Maccabees in August, rather than December, and well-attested veneration in Antioch may evidence a later date than Nicholson's dating of the original Greek composition of this martyrology as a whole.

60 One of the first testimonies we have for the veneration of the Maccabean martyrs is the letter of Ambrose, bishop of Milan (Mediolanum) to emperor Theodosius (I), regarding the burning of a local synagogue in the eastern city of Callinicum in 388 CE. In this letter Ambrose also relates another violent incident, in which a group of monks 'in a certain city' (*in quodam rurali vico*) (= Antioch?) set fire to a Valentinian temple, on the pretext that the Valentinians disturbed the monks in celebrating the festival of the Maccabees (Ambrose, *Epistulae*, 40.16).

61 Both Aphrahat (*c.* 280–345) and Ephrem (*c.* 306–73) — the most famous Syriac Christian authors of antiquity — evidence they have known the Maccabees as martyrs in the fourth century; also Origen (*c.* 185–254 CE) in his *Exhortation to Martyrdom*. For examination of the Maccabean martyrs as models in Origen's work see Van Henten, 'The Maccabean Martyrs as Models'.

The Apostolic Martyrs

The Old Testament martyrs in the *Encomium* are followed by a second group of saints: the earliest apostolic martyrs, Peter, Stephen,[62] and Paul. As the most celebrated of the apostles, inclusion of these three is not surprising, and venerating the apostles Peter and Paul who are credited with establishing the Antiochene church[63] is entirely consistent with the previously established focus of our text. What is noteworthy, however, is that Stephen, the protomartyr, the first to die for his faith just outside of Jerusalem, is not given pride of place in this list — as is almost invariably the case — but, rather, is listed second in order, between Peter and Paul. In addition, the immediately following text refers exclusively (in the singular) to Saul's persecution of the church, and thus ignores Stephen. Thus, we are left with the veneration of two Antiochene martyrs.

The Order of the Martyrs

Given the abundant evidence that situates the *Encomium* in the vicinity of Antioch, we may revisit the earlier observation regarding some anomalies in the order of the church martyrs, including the divergence in the list of bishops from that in Eusebius's *History*. By the nature of the text, we may reasonably assume that the *Encomium* was meant to be delivered in proximity to the martyrs' commemoration date.

So, according to Peeters, Zebinas was commemorated on 12/13 November.[64] After him, Demetrius was commemorated on 14 November. Sosipater was venerated on 10 November, and Andrew's veneration day falls on 29/30 of the same month.[65] In the Church Calendar of Ioane Zosime — although compiled in Georgian in the tenth century, based on a fifth- to seventh-century prototype — the commemoration day of Daniel and the three Hebrews was 18 December.[66]

---

62 Stephanos's commemoration was celebrated in the East, even before the veneration of his relics, on 26 December. See Hunt, *Holy Land Pilgrimage*, p. 218.

63 *Encomium for the Martyrs*, 3: ܘܐܦ ܠܘ ܟܕ ܘ܏ ܟܕ ܢܛܠܗ 'Let Stephen be crowned; and also Paul, no longer persecuting the churches' (Wright, 'Encomium of the Martyrs', p. 132). For the full list of ancient texts claiming the establishment of the church in Antioch to Peter and Paul see Downey, *A History of Antioch*, pp. 583–86.

64 However, in the *Martyrology of 411* he is commemorated on 13 January: '13. At Antioch, Zebennus (Zebenus, Zebinas)'. See Wright, 'An Ancient Syrian Martyrology', p. 423.

65 However, there is another possibility, that the Andrew in the *Encomium* actually refers to Saint Andrew of Antioch (also known as Andreas Stratelates or Andrew the Tribune). For his cult activity, see 'Andrew of Antioch', The Cult of Saints in Late Antiquity <http://csla.history.ox.ac.uk/record.php?recid=S00763> [accessed 21 July 2021].

66 'Daniel', The Cult of Saints in Late Antiquity <http://csla.history.ox.ac.uk/record.php?recid=E03962> [accessed 21 July 2021]. It is interesting to note that there is another trace for this commemoration day, in an excerpt from a Coptic calendar of saints' feast days. See Cult of Saints <http://csla.history.ox.ac.uk/record.php?recid=E05971> [accessed 21 July 2021].

December 26 was the commemoration day of the martyrs Marinus and Fronto[67] and also of the (Maccabean) mother and her seven sons.

Thus, although not all the commemoration days of the saints in the *Encomium* have come down to us, and some of which did were changed over time, the commemoration days of the saints and martyrs that can be identified are concentrated around November–December. Furthermore, in each group of saints (Old Testament, apostolic, early Christian-Antiochene) the figures are organized chronologically within the calendar year, in conformity with their commemoration day in the month.

Conclusion

As noted at the outset, Abdisho of Nisibis's attribution to Eusebius is the only attestation regarding the authorship of *Encomium for the Martyrs*. Perhaps that attribution was rooted in the two preceding treatises in the same codex, authored by him: *The Theophany* and *The Martyrs of Palestine*. It is not difficult to imagine the cataloguer looking for some clues to identify the *Encomium*'s author. Disappointed, he assigned the last, the unknown encomium, to Eusebius, the author of the previous two works.

The foregoing analysis of the personae in the *Encomium*, their relation to works unquestionably authored by Eusebius, and implications of textual material for localization and dating leads to a different conclusion. The work cannot be attributed to Eusebius of Caesarea (d. 349/50). The *Encomium* is well situated in Antioch, as most of the saints in the *Encomium* had strong ties to this city, as bishops and/or local martyrs. This is the first sign for us to look for an author other than Eusebius, who diligently sought to elevate his own city, Caesarea, in the Christian firmament. Without identifying a specific alternative author, we have narrowed the options to a prelate closely connected with Antioch or its environs, active between the years 362 to 380.

---

67   See note 38 above.

Bibliography

Primary Sources

Ambrose, *Epistulae*, Epist. 74, in *Sancti Ambrosii Opera, Pars X: Epistulae et Acta*, ed. by Michaela Zelzer (Vienna: Hoelder, 1982), pp. 54–73

Ioannis Malalae, *Chronographia*, ed. by Ioannes Thurn (Bonn: Weber, 1831)

Jerome, *De viris illustribus*, ed. by Jacques-Paul Migne, Patrologiae cursus completus: series latina, 30 (Paris: Garnier, 1844), pp. 602–712

John Chrysostom, *Homily on Meletios*, ed. by Jacques-Paul Migne, Patrologiae cursus completus: series graeca, 50 (Paris: Imprimerie Catholique, 1862), pp. 515–20

Prudentius, *Prudentius' Crown of Martyrs – Liber Peristephanon*, trans. by Len Krisak (New York: Routledge, 2020)

Sokrates, *Kirchengeschichte*, ed. by Günther Christian Hansen and Manja Sirinjan, Die griechischen christlichen Schriftsteller, n.s., 1 (Berlin: Akademie, 1995)

Sozomenos. *Historia ecclesiastica/Kirchengeschichte*, ed. by Günther Christian Hansen (Turnhout: Brepols, 2004)

Secondary Studies

Allen, Pauline, Boudewijn Dehandschutter, Johan Leemans, and Wendy Mayer, eds, *'Let Us Die That We May Live': Greek Homilies on Christian Martyrs from Asia Minor, Palestine, and Syria c. 350–c. 450 AD* (London: Routledge, 2003)

Badger, George Percy, *The Nestorians and Their Rituals* (London: Masters, 1852)

Brown, Peter, *The Cult of the Saints: Its Rise and Function in Latin Christianity* (Chicago: University of Chicago Press, 1981)

Butts, Aaron Michael, *Language Change in the Wake of Empire* (Winona Lake: Eisenbrauns, 2016)

Christopher, Walter, 'The Origins of the Cult of Saint George', *Revue des études byzantines*, 53 (1995), 295–326

Cross, F. L., and Livingstone, E. A., *The Oxford Dictionary of the Christian Church*, 3rd edn (Oxford: Oxford University Press, 1997)

Delehaye, Hippolyte, *The Legends of the Saints: An Introduction to Hagiography* (London: Chapman, 1962)

Di Berardino, Angelo, ed., *Encyclopedia of the Early Church*, trans. by Adrian Walford, 2 vols (New York: Oxford University Press, 1992)

Downey, Glanville, *A History of Antioch in Syria: From Seleucus to the Arab Conquest* (Princeton: Princeton University Press, 1961)

Drake, Harold A., 'Intolerance, Religious Violence, and Political Legitimacy in Late Antiquity', *Journal of the American Academy of Religion*, 79 (2011), 193–235

Frenkel, Luise Marion, 'The "Encomium of the Martyrs" and the Syriac Reception of Eusebius of Caesarea', in *Überleben im Schatten: Geschichte und Kultur des syrischen Christentums: Beiträge des 10. Deutschen Syrologentages an der FU Berlin 2018*, ed. by S. Talay. Göttinger Orientforschungen, I. Reihe: Syriaca 58 (Wiesbaden: Harrassowitz, 2020), pp. 81–101

Habbi, Yusuf, *Catalogus Auctorum. Abdišo' Sob. († 1318)* (Baghdad: Maṭba'at al-Maǧma' al-'Ilmī al-'Irāqī, 1986)

Hahn, Johannes, 'The Veneration of the Maccabean Brothers in Fourth Century Antioch: Religious Competition, Martyrdom, and Innovation', in *'Dying for the Faith, Killing for the Faith': Old-Testament Faith Warriors (1st and 2 Maccabees) in Historical Perspective*, ed. by Gabriele Signori (Leiden: Brill, 2012), pp. 79–123

Herrick, Samantha Kahn, 'Studying Apostolic Hagiography: The Case of Fronto of Périgueux, Disciple of Christ', *Speculum*, 85 (2010), 235–70

Hunt, Edward D., *Holy Land Pilgrimage in the Later Roman Empire AD 312–460* (Oxford: Oxford University Press, 1984)

Irshai, Oded, '"The Dark Side of the Moon": Eusebius of Caesarea between Theological Polemics and Struggles for Prestige', *Cathedra*, 122 (2006), 63–98 (in Hebrew)

——, 'Fourth Century Christian Palestinian Politics: A Glimpse at Eusebius of Caesarea's Local Political Career and its Nachleben in Christian Memory', in *Reconsidering Eusebius: Collected Papers on Literary, Historical, and Theological Issues*, ed. by Sabrina Inowlocki and Claudio Zamagni (Leiden: Brill, 2011), pp. 25–38

Joslyn-Siemiatkoski, Daniel, *Christian Memories of the Maccabean Martyrs* (New York: Palgrave Macmillan, 2009)

Liebeschuetz, J. H. W. G., *Antioch: City and Imperial Administration in the Later Roman Empire* (Oxford: Clarendon Press, 1972)

Lightfoot, J. B., *The Apostolic Fathers* (Hildesheim: Olms, 1973)

——, 'Eusebius of Caesarea', in *A Dictionary of Christian Biography, Literature, Sects and Doctrines during the First Eight Centuries, Being a Continuation of 'The Dictionary of the Bible'*, ed. by William Smith and Henry Wace, 4 vols (London: J. Murray, 1877–1887), vol. ii, pp. 308–48

Mayer, Wendy, with Bronwen Neil, trans. and annot., *The Cult of the Saints: Select Homilies and Letters of St John Chrysostom* (Crestwood: St Vladimir's Seminary, 2006)

Mommsen, Theodor, *Chronica Minora Saec. IV, V, VI (Vol. 1)*, Monumenta Germaniae Historica: Scriptores Auctores antiquissimi, 9 (Berlin: Weidmann, 1892)

Nicholson, Oliver, ed., 'Martyrology of 411, Syriac', in *The Oxford Dictionary of Late Antiquity* (Oxford: Oxford University Press, 2018) <https://www.oxfordreference.com/view/10.1093/acref/9780198662778.001.0001/acref-9780198662778-e-3036?rskey=9CodSd&result=3189> [accessed 20 November 2022]

Obermann, Julian, 'The Sepulchre of the Maccabean Martyrs', *Journal of Biblical Literature*, 50 (1931), 250–65

Peeters, Paulus, ed., "De S. Demetriano Antiochiae episcopo," *Acta Sanctorum* 4 (1925), 384–91

Quasten, Johannes. *Patrology*, 3 vols (Utrecht: Speculum, 1950–1994)

Rutgers, Leonard V., *Making Myths: Jews in Early Christian Identity Formation* (Leuven: Peeters, 2009)

Schatkin, Margaret, 'The Maccabean Martyrs', *Vigiliae Christianae*, 28 (1974), 97–113

Scher, Addai, 'Histoire Nestorienne Inèdite (Chronicle of Séert)', *Patrologia Orientalis*, 4 (1908), 213–312

Schwartz, E., ed., *Eusebius Werke 2: Die Kirchengeschichte*, Die griechischen christlichen Schriftsteller, 9.2 (Leipzig: Hinrichs, 1903)

Van Henten, Jan Willem, 'The Maccabean Martyrs as Models in Early Christian Writings', in *The Jew as Legitimation: Jewish-Gentile Relations Beyond Antisemitism and Philosemitism*, ed. by David J. Wertheim (London: Palgrave Macmillan, 2017), pp. 17–32

——, 'The Reception of Daniel 3 and 6 and the Maccabean Martyrdoms in Hebrews 11:33–38', in *Myths, Martyrs, and Modernity: Studies in the History of Religions in Honour of Jan N. Bremmer*, ed. by Jitse Dijkstra, Justin Kroesen, and Yme Kuiper (Leiden: Brill, 2010), pp. 359–77

Van Renswoude, Irene, *The Rhetoric of Free Speech in Late Antiquity and the Early Middle Ages*, Cambridge Studies in Medieval Life and Thought, 4th ser., 115 (Cambridge: Cambridge University Press, 2019)

Verheyden, Joseph, 'Pain and Glory: Some Introductory Comments on the Rhetorical Qualities and Potential of the Martyrs of Palestine by Eusebius of Caesarea', in *Martyrdom and Persecution in Late Ancient Christianity: Festschrift Boudewijn Dehandschutter*, ed. by Johan Leemans (Leuven: Peeters, 2010), pp. 353–91

Vinson, Martha, 'Gregory Nazianzen's Homily 15 and the Genesis of the Christian Cult of the Maccabean Martyrs', *Byzantion*, 64 (1994), 166–92

——, trans., *Gregory of Nazianzus: Selected Orations*, Fathers of the Church 107 (Washington, DC: Catholic University of America Press, 2003)

Vinzent, Markus, *Writing the History of Early Christianity: From Reception to Retrospection* (Cambridge: Cambridge University Press, 2019)

Witakowski, Witold, 'Mart(y) Shmuni, the Mother of the Maccabean Martyrs, in Syriac Tradition', in *VI Symposium Syriacum 1992: University of Cambridge, Faculty of Divinity, 30 August–2 September 1992*, ed. by René Lavenant, Orientalia Christiana Analecta, 247 (Rome: Pontificio Inst. Orientale, 1994), pp. 153–68

Wood, Philip, *The Chronicle of Seert: Christian Historical Imagination in Late Antique Iraq* (Oxford: Oxford University Press, 2013)

Wright, William, 'An Ancient Syrian Martyrology', *Journal of Sacred Literature and Biblical Record*, n.s. 8 (1866), 423–32

——, *Catalogue of Syriac Manuscripts in the British Museum Acquired since the Year 1838*, 3 vols (London: British Museum, 1870–1872)

——, 'The Encomium of the Martyrs', *Journal of Sacred Literature and Biblical Record*, 4th series, 5 (1864), 403–08 (Syriac text with introduction by B. Harris Cowper); 4th series, 6 (1865), 129–33 (English translation with introduction by B. Harris Cowper)

ARYEH KOFSKY AND SERGE RUZER

Rethinking the Eschatological Ingathering of Israel in Early Christianity[*]

Introduction

The notions of the sanctity and centrality of Jerusalem are rooted in the conquest of the city by David and its establishment as the capital of the kingdom. The complex history, in various biblical accounts, regarding the conquest, which was accompanied by wondrous events, is tailored to propagate the claim for both the city's sanctification and its transformation into a unifying centre for the tribes of Israel and a metonym for the Land as a whole.[1] The attempts of the tradition — already in the Hebrew Bible (ii Chron 3:1) — to identify Mt. Moriah from the early story of the binding of Isaac with the Temple Mount in Jerusalem enhanced this endeavour.[2]

While pre-exilic prophets were known to voice harsh criticism of the Temple in Jerusalem, they also dreamed of its future universal glorification, including the righteous Gentiles' pilgrimage to Zion.[3] Following the Babylonian exile, biblical prophecy translated the Jerusalem-centred outlook into a longing for return and a vision of the future restoration of the cult in Jerusalem and an ingathering of the exiles there.[4] The ending of 2 Chronicles, destined to become a final statement of the Hebrew Bible, depicts the fulfilment of the hope for return in the days of Cyrus.[5] In case the pre-exilic reservations about the Temple lingered, the whole land of Israel could function as the

---

[*] This study was conducted as part of an ongoing project: 'Late Antique Christian and Jewish Travel Narratives: Patterns and Strategies of Intercultural Exchange' (No. 755/20) under the auspices of the Israel Science Foundation.

1 See e.g, Zakovitch, 'The First Stages of Jerusalem's Sanctification', esp. pp. 27–28.

2 Zakovitch, 'The First Stages of Jerusalem's Sanctification', pp. 30–33.

3 Isa. 2, Mica 4.

4 See Rofé, *Introduction to the Prophetic Literature*, p. 96. On the prophets' role in the Temple, see pp. 76–80.

5 ii Chron. 36:22–23.

> **Aryeh Kofsky**, PhD from the Hebrew University of Jerusalem in 1991, is Professor of Comparative Religion at the University of Haifa.
>
> **Serge Ruzer**, PhD from the Hebrew University of Jerusalem in 1996, is Professor of Comparative Religion at the Hebrew University of Jerusalem.

Essays on Jews and Christians in Late Antiquity in Honour of Oded Irshai, ed. by Brouria Bitton-Ashkelony and Martin Goodman, CELAMA 40 (Turnhout: Brepols, 2023), pp. 159–181
BREPOLS ❧ PUBLISHERS   10.1484/M.CELAMA-EB.5.132488

complementary focus of longing. Sometimes, as in Ezekiel 36, the promise of return to the Land is conjoined with that of a fundamental transformation of the people's hearts and thus acquires a strong eschatological bent:[6]

> For I will take you from the nations, and gather you from all the countries, and bring you into your own land. 25 I will sprinkle clean water upon you, and you shall be clean from all your uncleannesses, and from all your idols I will cleanse you. 26 A new heart I will give you, and a new spirit I will put within you; and I will take out of your flesh the heart of stone and give you a heart of flesh. 27 And I will put my spirit within you, and cause you to walk in my statutes and be careful to observe my ordinances. 28 You shall dwell in the land which I gave to your fathers; and you shall be my people, and I will be your God (Ezek. 36:24–28).

One notes that the eschatological outpouring of the Spirit is likewise intrinsically connected to the return to the Land in Joel:[7]

> And it shall come to pass afterward, that I will pour out my spirit on all flesh; your sons and your daughters shall prophesy, your old men shall dream dreams, and your young men shall see visions. Even upon the menservants and maidservants in those days, I will pour out my spirit [...] And it shall come to pass that all who call upon the name of the LORD shall be delivered; for in Mount Zion and in Jerusalem there shall be those who escape, as the LORD has said, and among the survivors shall be those whom the LORD calls (Joel 3:1–5 (2:28–32)).

And immediately thereafter:

> For behold, in those days and at that time, when I restore the fortunes of Judah and Jerusalem, I will gather all the nations and bring them down to the valley of Jehoshaphat, and I will enter into judgment with them there, on account of my people and my heritage Israel, because they have scattered them among the nations, and have divided up my land (Joel 4:1–2 (3:1–2)).

The late Second Temple period, distinguished by a rise in an end-of-days orientation,[8] produced a variety of eschatological scenarios, some of which did not emphasize the final ingathering,[9] whereas others eagerly embraced it.[10] Even the Qumran Covenanters — with all their animosity towards the Temple and the city around it, and their perception of the desert as the place of preparing God's triumph — fancied themselves sojourning there on the way to the ultimate conquest of Jerusalem and the establishment of its eschatological

---

6 See discussion in Greenberg, *Ezekiel 21–37*, pp. 729–31.
7 We are inclined here to follow the view regarding Joel as a post-exilic prophet.
8 See, for instance, Talmon, 'The Concept of Mašiah'.
9 See discussion in Baumgarten, 'The Role of Jerusalem and the Temple'.
10 E.g. Jub. 1:14–17.

ESCHATOLOGICAL INGATHERING OF ISRAEL IN EARLY CHRISTIANITY

sanctuary.[11] The hope for Jerusalem's restoration would be enhanced — *mutatis mutandis* — in the late first-century post-destruction accounts in 2 Baruch and 4 Ezra.[12] The Second Temple period, or more precisely the second century BCE, also witnessed — as part of the Hasmonean propaganda — the rise of the idea of Jerusalem as the 'navel of the earth.'[13]

Early Christianity inherited the perception of the centrality of Jerusalem and the Land.[14] The tradition's biblical roots were greatly enhanced by the reverence accorded the geographical space as the arena of Jesus's life and mission. Early Christian pilgrimage tendencies to map the Land's holy sites and create its sacred topography have been amply investigated.[15] The range of attitudes about these processes expressed by prominent ecclesiastical writers, including sidestepping the distant Holy Land for the sake of local centres of pilgrimage, have also received scholarly attention.[16] Strategies of appropriating the Land, *inter alia*, by marginalizing its Jewish past, have likewise been discussed, notably in an innovative study by Oded Irshai.[17] Apart from adoration of earthly Jerusalem,[18] later development of Christian political and spiritual attitudes would produce the notions of 'alternative Jerusalems' — either Europocentric or mystical.[19] Leaving all these avenues aside, this essay, while making no claim whatsoever to exhaust the issue, will highlight some representative variations and transmutations of the inherited notion of the eschatological ingathering of Israel. We will thus focus on the patterns of Christian rethinking of the idea of that ultimate pilgrimage.

Earliest Christian Adaptations

The book of Acts, penned in the late first century, embraces — via adaptation — the common Jewish pattern of eschatological anticipation.[20] The theme of the programmatic passage in Acts 1:6–11 promising the swift return of the messiah to Jerusalem is further confirmed in Acts 2:46, where the disciples are described as regularly present in the Temple, awaiting the messiah's second coming.[21] This is accompanied by the appointment of the twelfth apostle to

---

11 See Brooke, 'Moving the Mountains'.
12 For instance, iv Ezra 7:26; ii Baruch 6:9.
13 As attested in Jub. 8:19, see Alexander, 'Jerusalem as the *Omphalos* of the World'.
14 See Sanders, 'Jerusalem and its Temple', who distinguishes between Jesus's, Paul's, and Luke's attitudes.
15 See, for example, Bowman, '"Mapping History's Redemption"'.
16 See Bitton-Ashkelony, 'The Attitudes of Church Fathers toward Pilgrimage'; Bitton-Ashkelony, *Encountering the Sacred*.
17 See Irshai, 'The Christian Appropriation of Jerusalem'. See also e.g. Jacobs, *Remains of the Jews*; Kofsky and Ruzer, 'The Holy Places and the Jewish Past'.
18 Cf. Wilken, 'Loving the Jerusalem Below'.
19 Stroumsa, 'Mystical Jerusalems'.
20 For a recent discussion of Acts' eschatology, see Oliver, *Luke's Jewish Eschatology*.
21 See discussion in Ruzer, 'The Land of Israel at the Center of Messianic Redemption'.

fill the void left by Judas Iscariot (Acts 1:15–26), which converses with the preordained institution of the twelve as end-of-days judges of the tribes of Israel, spelled out by the same author in the Gospel of Luke:[22]

> You are those who have continued with me in my trials; and I assign to you, as my Father assigned to me, a kingdom, that you may eat and drink at my table in my kingdom, and sit on thrones judging the twelve tribes of Israel (Luke 22:28–30, cf. Matt. 19:28).

The Israel-centred aspect of Acts' eschatological outlook therefore includes not only a geographical but also an ethnic component — Jerusalem representing the Land and the twelve tribes as standing for the people as a whole, including Jews in the Diaspora.[23]

The collation of these two aspects, the geographic and the ethnic, finds its natural resolution in yet another foundational motif pertaining to the final redemption, inherited by the author from biblical prophecy — that of the future ingathering of the exiles.[24] Acts 2 presents what may be viewed as a preliminary enacting of such an ingathering by an assembly of Jewish pilgrims, who arrive in Jerusalem from around the world to celebrate the Feast of the Weeks/*Shavuot*. A number of suggestions regarding the sources and the ideas behind the list of diaspora locations whence the pilgrims come (Acts 2:5–11) have been raised.[25] Most interesting perhaps, is Justin Taylor's proposal that this view of *oikoumene* was inspired by the biblical scene of the Jewish return from Babylonia as seen from the perspective of Cyrus (ii Chron. 36:23).[26] This appraisal strengthens the view that Acts sought to indicate the imminence of the ultimate messianic ingathering.[27] We may note that at this stage, the narrative of Acts still focuses exclusively on the Jews (and 'proselytes'), thus retaining both ethnic and geographical Israel-centred emphases.[28]

The narrative of Acts not only presents a general rehearsal of the final ingathering, as preconceived in the broad Jewish anticipation, but characteristically connects it with the Spirit- and land-centred prophecy of Joel addressed above. Moreover, the cleansing of the hearts enacted by the Spirit related further on in Acts 15 converses with the aforementioned passage in Ezekiel 36, where that cleansing is intrinsically linked to the ingathering of the exiles. The author of Acts thus adopts the general Jewish pattern of eschatological belief and uses it to indicate the proximity of redemption. In the author's messianic reworking, however, those participating in the

---

22 Thus, for example, Conzelmann, *Acts of the Apostles*, p. 12: 'The apostles are considered to be representatives of the eschatological Israel'. Cf. Rev. 21:14.

23 Cf. James 1:1, where the twelve tribes are explicitly described as dwelling in the Diaspora.

24 This anticipation has a multiple attestation; see, for instance, Isa. 27:13.

25 For a review, see Fitzmyer, *The Acts of the Apostles*, pp. 240–43; cf. Conzelmann, *Acts of the Apostles*, commentary on pp. 14–15.

26 Taylor, 'The List of the Nations'.

27 Taylor, 'The List of the Nations', p. 420.

28 Fitzmyer, *Acts of the Apostles*, commentary on pp. 244, 248.

preliminary ingathering will be providentially exposed to the Jesus-centred message, which they will take back home.

From the earliest Christian sources onward, however, one can detect a polemical rethinking of that anticipation. We shall offer two outstanding examples. The Epistle to the Hebrews admonishes its addressees, who might have envisioned such an eschatological assembly in Jerusalem:[29]

> For you have not come to what may be touched [...] But you have come to Mount Zion and to the city of the living God, the heavenly Jerusalem, and to innumerable angels in festal gathering, and to the assembly of the first-born who are enrolled in heaven, and to a judge who is God of all, and to the spirits of just men made perfect, and to Jesus, the mediator of a new covenant, and to the sprinkled blood that speaks more graciously than the blood of Abel (Hebrews 12:18–24).

Paul, in his earliest surviving epistle, seems to prefer the ingathering in heaven over that which will take place in the Land of Israel:

> For the Lord himself will descend from heaven with a cry of command, with the archangel's call, and with the sound of the trumpet of God. And the dead in Christ will rise first; then we who are alive, who are left, shall be caught up together with them in the clouds to meet the Lord in the air; and so we shall always be with the Lord (1 Thessalonians 4:16–17).

From the Return of the Jews to the Ingathering of Jesus Believers

The New Testament texts mentioned above already witness the beginning of the 'Christianization' of the motif which is now related to Jesus followers. This tendency is further spelled out in the early second-century Christian composition *Didache* (The Teaching [of the Twelve Apostles]). It deals mostly with ethical issues and instructions for the ritual practices and social interactions of the community, which appears to have included both Jews and Gentiles.[30] The second part of the *Didache* also contains a vision of the eschatological redemption. This vision comprises the seemingly unharmonized motifs of end-of-days assembly and a catastrophic apocalyptic scenario. Chapter 9, for example, presents the former motif in the context of describing the community meal of thanksgiving:

> And concerning the thanksgiving (περὶ τῆς δὲ εὐχαριστίας) give thanks thus. First, as regards the cup: We give you thanks, our Father, for the holy vine of your son David, which you made known to us through your son Jesus; yours is the glory for ever and ever. Then as regards the broken

---

29 Not unlike the Qumran covenanters; see note 11 above and discussion there.

30 See, e.g., Finlan, 'Identity in the Didache Community'; Gregory, 'Reflections on the Didache'.

bread (περὶ δὲ τοῦ κλάσματος): We give you thanks, our Father, for the life and knowledge which you made known to us through your son Jesus; yours is the glory for ever and ever. As this broken bread was scattered on the mountains and being gathered together (συναχθὲν) became one, so may your community (ἐκκλησία) be gathered together (συναχθήτω) from the ends of the earth into your kingdom (βασιλεία); for yours is the glory and the power through Jesus Christ for ever and ever.

The passage bears witness to a variety of the proto-eucharistic formulas employed by Jesus followers in the early phase of the movement. The thanksgiving instructed by the *Didache* differs sharply from the version known to Paul and reflected in the Synoptic descriptions of the Last Supper:[31]

> The cup of blessing which we bless, is it not a participation in the blood of Christ? The bread which we break, is it not a participation in the body of Christ? Because there is one bread, we who are many are one body, for we all partake of the one bread [...] For I received from the Lord what I also delivered to you, that the Lord Jesus on the night when he was betrayed took bread, and when he had given thanks, he broke it (καὶ εὐχαριστήσας ἔκλασεν), and said, 'This is my body which is for you. Do this in remembrance of me'. In the same way also the cup, after supper, saying, 'This cup is the new covenant in my blood. Do this, as often as you drink it, in remembrance of me'. For as often as you eat this bread and drink the cup, you proclaim the Lord's death until he comes (i Cor. 10:16–17, 11:23–26).

While both sources overlap in their emphasis on thanksgiving and the act of breaking the bread, the radically different interpretation in the *Didache* is most significant in our context. Instead of representing Jesus's crucified body, the broken bread signifies the dispersed community of Jesus's followers. Moreover, the same bread indicates the hope that this community will be brought together in God's Kingdom. The motif of the bread symbolizing the unity of believers appears also in i Corinthians (10:17), but it is applied there to the current experience and not to a future ingathering.[32] Though the meaning of *ekklesia* in the *Didache* may still be rather loose, it clearly refers to the community of Christ believers, which seems to include both Jews and Gentiles. As for God's Kingdom, the imagery of the ingathering of the scattered pieces of bread, as well as the strong emphasis on King David, may very well refer to the land of David as the geographical setting of that ingathering.[33]

The final chapter of the treatise, however, highlights an apocalyptic end-of-days scenario, whose connection to the ingathering motif discussed above, is not entirely clear:

---

31 See discussion in Fitzmyer, *First Corinthians*, pp. 389–92, 397–400.

32 Cf. the picture of eschatological redemption in 1 Thessalonians 4, which is oriented vertically, not horizontally and completely devoid of the ingathering motif.

33 For a multifaceted discussion of the meal ritual in the *Didache*, see Schwiebert, *Knowledge and the Coming Kingdom*. See also, Clabeaux, 'The Ritual Meal in Didache 9–10'.

And you shall gather yourselves together (συναχθήσεσθε) frequently, seeking what is fitting for your souls [...] For in the last days the false prophets and destroyers shall be multiplied, and the sheep shall be turned into wolves, and love shall be turned into hate. [...] And then the world-deceiver shall appear as a son of God; and shall work signs and wonders, and the earth shall be delivered into his hands; and he shall do unholy things, which have never been since the world began. Then all created mankind shall come to the fire of testing, and many shall be offended and perish; but those who endure in their faith shall be saved through the Curse itself. And then the signs of the truth shall appear; first a sign of a rift in the heaven, then a sign of a voice of a trumpet, and thirdly a resurrection of the dead; yet not of all, but as it was said (Zech. 14:5): 'The Lord shall come and all his saints with him'. Then the world will see the Lord coming upon the clouds of heaven (*Didache* 16:4–17).[34]

If we wish to discern an overall design by the author/redactor of the eschatological scenario in the *Didache*, we may suggest that this scenario comprises two distinct stages. The ingathering (συναχθήτω) of the messiah's faithful in the Land of Israel will be followed by frequent communal gathering (συναχθήσεσθε) there. After that will come the catastrophic phase with the appearance of the Deceiver, and eventually the final redemption with resurrection and the second coming. Not only the eschatological ingathering but also the end-of-days general resurrection is 'Christianized' here, being reserved exclusively for the believers in Christ.[35]

The Delay of the End and Its Ramifications

In the mid-second century, when the feeling of the postponement of the end was widely sensed, Justin Martyr (*c.* 100–*c.* 165) suggests that the end is delayed since the necessary 'quorum of the just' needed for the ushering of the Kingdom has not yet been achieved.[36] The need to reawaken all those destined for redemption may be, in fact, the divine rationale for not bringing the world to destruction.[37] Moreover, since Justin Martyr retains the belief, discussed above in connection to Acts, that Christ's return will take place in Jerusalem,[38] the ushering of the Kingdom acquires a geographical context too.

Justin foresees two phases of the eschatological bliss similar to those in the *Didache*. First, Christ believers will possess the land that was once conquered by Joshua, and will be reconquered for them by Joshua's namesake, Jesus. They

---

34 In reference to Daniel 1:13 and Matt. 24:30, 26:64.

35 Cf. Balabanski, *Eschatology in the Making*, esp. pp. 197–205; Smith, 'The Lord Jesus and His Coming'.

36 Justin Martyr, *First Apology*, 28; 45; Justin Martyr, *Dialogue with Trypho*, 39.

37 Justin Martyr, *Second Apology*, 7.

38 Justin Martyr, *Dialogue with Trypho*, 85.

will rule over it together with the Messiah: 'So also Jesus the Messiah will turn again the dispersion of the people, and will distribute the good land to each one, though not in the same manner'.[39] Justin emphasizes that the 'people' mentioned here stand emphatically for Gentile believers in Christ, the 'sons of Japhet' — they are 'the saints', who will inherit the land.[40] The rule of the saints following their resurrection will last for a thousand years,[41] and they will also be the participants of the second phase with its general resurrection, judgement, and eternal bliss for the righteous.[42] Elsewhere Justin seems to foresee an eternal rule over Jerusalem and the land following the general resurrection,[43] a perception that can complement the millennium-centred one.[44]

According to Irenaeus (*c.* 130–*c.* 200), the consummation of human history is expected soon and described in apocalyptic millenarian terms. Following the appearance of the Antichrist in Jerusalem and the persecution of the Christians gathered there, Jesus's second coming in glory will likewise take place in Jerusalem; he will defeat the Antichrist, casting him into hell.[45] Defending the millenarian stance of Papias and the 'elders',[46] Irenaeus propagates the idea of the two-stage resurrection scenario:

> It is fitting for the righteous first to receive the promise of the inheritance which God promised the fathers, and to reign in it, when they rise again to behold God in this creation which is renewed, and that the judgment should take place afterwards.[47]

The fathers here clearly refer to the patriarchs of Israel and the whole picture indicates the inheritance of the Promised Land by the followers of Jesus, representing the New Israel. Various additional biblical proof texts regarding future redemption of Israel, which is to usher peace and bountiful restoration of earthly existence, enhance this claim.[48] Irenaeus characteristically cautions against those unwilling to accept the apocalyptic vision and unduly allegorizing the picture.[49]

Such a millennial kingdom turns out not only to be indebted to biblical prophesies but instrumental in the plan of salvation, providing a preparatory interval for the just to become ready for 'partaking of the divine nature'.[50] At the

---

39 Justin Martyr, *Dialogue with Trypho*, 113.
40 Justin Martyr, *Dialogue with Trypho*, 139.
41 Justin Martyr, *Dialogue with Trypho*, 81.
42 Justin Martyr, *Dialogue with Trypho*, 113.
43 Justin Martyr, *Dialogue with Trypho*, 80.
44 For an overview of Justin's eschatology, see Barnard, *Justin Martyr*, pp. 157–68; Wilken, *The Land Called Holy*, pp. 55–59.
45 Irenaeus of Lyons, *Against Heresies*, 4.33.1; 5.25; 5.28–30; 5.30.4.
46 Irenaeus of Lyons, *Against Heresies*, 5.33.4.
47 Irenaeus of Lyons, *Against Heresies*, 5.32.1.
48 Irenaeus of Lyons, *Against Heresies*, 5.33–35.
49 Irenaeus of Lyons, *Against Heresies*, 5.35.1–2.
50 Irenaeus of Lyons, *Against Heresies*, 5.32.1.

end of this millennial interlude comes the Day of Judgement along the lines of Revelation 20 and 21. In fact, the physicality of existence will be retained even after the second resurrection, where the redeemed will be rewarded in accordance with their virtues. Those of the highest righteousness will ascend to heaven; the second rank will gain Paradise, viewed as situated in a lofty place between heaven and earth; and, finally, the third category will continue to 'possess the splendor of the (holy) city'.[51] Overall, Irenaeus adapts the inherited Jewish and nascent Christian eschatological motifs to his late second-century Christian agenda, substituting Jesus believers for the historical Israel in his tripartite reworking of the apocalyptic scheme of redemption. However, he retains the real geographical framework of ingathering in the Land of Israel and Jerusalem, even for the last post-resurrection phase.[52]

Origen and Demythologized Eschatology

The eschatological patterns of belief inherited by Christians from earlier Jewish tradition were demythologized by Origen (c. 184–c. 253). Yet, he retains certain traits of the catastrophic apocalyptic scenario as in his interpretation of Matthew 24:3–44. These, though, are played down as pointing to the events of his own time, such as the appearing of false prophets, the persecutions — from which he himself suffered — and the material impoverishment of the world. They all provide the signs that 'the end of the world' was, in fact, a contemporary reality.[53]

However, the more spiritually advanced are called to comprehend the simultaneous and complementary allegorical meaning of the expected eschatology, namely the spiritual growth of those initiated into the esoteric meaning of the external apocalyptic event, which is the revelation of Jesus's divine beauty. So one can in fact speak of another, parallel, 'second coming of Christ', to the souls of the perfect, which in the final accounting will be consummated in the spiritual unification of reality.[54] Thus the various stages of the apocalyptic vision acquire their allegorical sense: the famine becomes the Christian's hunger for the true inner meaning of Scripture; the plagues — the 'malicious harassments' of Gnostics and heretics; the persecutions — the erroneous beliefs of those who distort Christian faith. And the 'abomination of desolation, standing in the holy place' prophesied in Daniel stands for the

---

51 Irenaeus of Lyons, *Against Heresies*, 5.36.1–2.
52 On Irenaeus's general eschatological outlook, see Osborn, *Irenaeus of Lyons*, pp. 136–40; Wilken, *The Land Called Holy*, pp. 59–62.
53 Origen, *Commentariorum Series in Matthaeum*, 32–60. For Eusebius, similarly, in Matthew 24:3–44 the false prophets refer to Dositheus, Simon Magus, Montanus and the like of them (Eusebius, *Theophany*, 4.35) and the persecutions to Eusebius's contemporaneous Diocletian's persecutions. Thus, the second coming provides for him a historical setting to compensate for the prior evil. See Thielman, 'Another Look at the Eschatology of Eusebius'.
54 Origen, *Commentariorum Series in Matthaeum*, 32.

false interpretation of the Holy Writ,[55] while the Antichrist is a symbol for all doctrinal perversions.[56] These disasters are only a prelude to the appearance of the glorified Christ coming on the clouds of heaven, with clouds representing the writings of his apostles and prophets, and heaven — all the books of truth. This glorious messiah's advent will proclaim the gospel — thus the final trumpet — to the whole world.[57]

In light of this general allegorizing tendency, Origen also addresses the issue of ingathering in the Promised Land, while upholding the backdrop motifs of traditional eschatology. One first notices that he rejects an exclusively literal, millenarian understanding of such an ingathering followed by a blissful earthly existence in the thousand-year kingdom, which he brands as a 'Jewish sense' inherited by the chiliasts.[58] However, he retains the importance of the geographical framework of the land — apparently referring both to the biblical conquest and division of the land by the tribes, and to the eschatological ingathering of the believers — as a blueprint for the spiritual heavenly resettlement of the Christians. In accordance with various locations in the earthly Promised Land, 'Jesus our Lord will establish each person in this or that part of heaven to dwell, not without regard for his merits'.[59] In a similar vein, Origen interprets Jesus's pilgrimage from Capernaum to Jerusalem as a kind of roadmap for the spiritual journey of the soul, leading from the material world to its heavenly abode.[60] This is congruent with his insistence on eschatology as a slow collective process: 'This should not be understood to happen suddenly, but gradually and by steps, as the endless and enormous ages slip by, and the process of improvement and correction advances by degrees in different individuals'.[61]

Fourth-Century Evolution

Apollinarius of Laodicaea (*c.* 310–*c.* 390) was accused by Basil of Caesarea and Gregory of Nazianzus for espousing a millenarian vision and thus reintroducing 'a second Judaism', the same Jewish error denounced by Origen and Eusebius, because of his anticipation of the end-of-days kingdom of the righteous.[62] Hence Jerome included him in the same category as Papias,

---

55 Origen, *Commentariorum Series in Matthaeum*, 37–42.

56 Origen, *Commentariorum Series in Matthaeum*, 33.

57 Origen, *Commentariorum Series in Matthaeum*, 50–52.

58 Origen, *De principiis*, 2.111.2; Origen, *Commentariorum Series in Matthaeum*, 17.35. Eusebius espouses Origen's rejection of a literal millenarianism as a Jewish error as well as a folly of Christians who follow them like Papias or Nepos of Arsinoe (Eusebius, *Ecclesiastical History*, 3.39, 7.24–25).

59 Origen, *Hom. in Num*, 28.3.

60 Hermanin de Reichenfeld, 'From Capernaum to Jerusalem'. Cf. Cerioni, '"Mother of Souls"'.

61 Origen, *De principiis*, 3.6.6; cf. 3.6.9. For Origen's general view of individual and collective eschatology, see Daley, *The Hope of the Church*, pp. 47–60.

62 See Basil of Caesarea, *Epistles*, 263.4; 265.2; Gregory Nazianzen, *Epistles*, 102.14.

Irenaeus, and early Latin writers such as Tertullian and Lactantius.[63] He quotes Apollinarius's prediction of the Antichrist's appearance followed by that of Elijah, who will convert the ingathered Jews, and the eschatological restoration of Jerusalem, which will all occur in the 'seventieth week of years' after Jesus's birth (c. 483–90).[64] Others, however, claimed that Apollinarius had not been a staunch millenarian,[65] and the fragmentary remains of his writings reflect in fact a rather traditional eschatology.[66]

Apollinarius's contemporary, Cyril of Jerusalem (c. 315–87), propounds his eschatological views in the catechetical lectures delivered in the 340s. For him, there is already no anticipation of Jews gathering in the land of their fathers followed by their conversion under Elijah. Their ingathering is rather portrayed as part of the Antichrist's ploy, who dissimulates as the Jewish messiah:[67]

> For if he is to come as Christ (Messiah) to the Jews, and wants their worship, with a view to deceiving them further, he will manifest the greatest zeal for the temple; he will create the impression that he is the descendant of David who is to restore the temple of Solomon [...] Antichrist will appear amid all signs and lying wonders, lifting himself up against all idols.

Unlike that, the ingathering of the Christ believers into the earthly kingdom will be ushered by Jesus's second coming with the help of the angelic host:

> Let us look hopefully for the Lord's coming upon the clouds of heaven [...] 'He will send forth his angels with a great trumpet, and they will gather his elect from the four winds' (Matt. 24:31). He did not despise one man, Lot; how then will he despise the multitude of the just? 'Come, blessed of my Father' (Matt. 25:34), he will say to those who will then ride upon chariots of clouds and be gathered together by angels.

Thus, this true ingathering, accomplished by means of heavenly chariots, will take place together with the Kingdom of God established by Christ. Since its destination is to replace the dominion of the Antichrist with its centre in Jerusalem, this new Kingdom appears to retain the same earthly geographical setting. As suggested already by Oded Irshai, followed by Jan Willem Drijvers, the Antichrist-centred part of Cyril's eschatological elaboration belongs to a later revision of the lectures (probably by Cyril himself) after the abortive attempt to rebuild the Jerusalem sanctuary by the emperor Julian (361–63). Irshai furthermore proposes that Cyril identifies the Antichrist with Julian.[68]

---

63 Jerome, *De viris illustribus*, 111.18.

64 Jerome, *Commentary on Daniel*, 9.24 (PL, 25.548B7–549A5). According to Jerome, Apollinarius borrowed this chronology from Julius Africanus (548D10–549A3).

65 Epiphanius, *Panarion*, 77, 36.5.

66 See Apollinarius, *Kata meros pistis*, 12; Apollinarius, *De fide et incarnatione*, 1.

67 Cyril of Jerusalem, *Catechetical Lectures*, 15.12–23.

68 See Irshai, 'Cyril of Jerusalem: The Apparition of the Cross'; Irshai, 'The Jerusalem Bishopric

Jerome (*c.* 345–420) represents a more composite picture. Whereas the starting point of his eschatological elaborations was of an Origenist nature, later — as a reaction to the catastrophic events in Italy — he adopted a more traditional apocalyptic view expressed mainly in his letters and commentaries, which were saturated with the sense of the imminent end of the world. Thus he regards the Antichrist as a human figure, and a Jew of lowly background, who will subdue the Empire and become the supreme ruler.[69] He is sure that the barbarian invasions of 409 signal that 'the Antichrist is close by'.[70] Not unlike Origen, Jerome regarded contemporary heretics as fulfilling certain eschatological prophecies.[71] However, he now includes among them also Arians, in addition to past deviants, and, significantly, the followers of Origen himself.

It is unclear whether the earthly reign of the Jewish Antichrist — apparently with its centre in Jerusalem — will be replaced with the Christian millennium still centred in the Holy Land. Jerome appears to steer here a balanced course between his rejection of literal millenarianism and full-fledged allegorical spiritualization.[72] He thus prefers to interpret Revelation 21, including the description of the eschatological Jerusalem, as referring to the glorification of the historical Church,[73] but rejects the idea that the earthly reality is to disappear altogether. For him, the end of this world means, in fact, its transformation into an ideal version of itself. He even states — in relation to Revelation 21:1 — that 'We shall not see another heaven and another earth […] but only the old, former ones, changed for the better'.[74] In this vein, he also pays homage to the traditional millenarian views of Tertullian, Irenaeus, and Apollinarius, albeit claiming that they have nothing in common with full-bodied earthly Jewish hopes.[75]

Late Antique Apocalyptic Variants

We have observed that the millenarian stance continued, notably represented by Irenaeus, Hippolytus, Lactantius, and Apollinarius and even to a certain extent by Jerome, in tandem with the Origenist spiritual and allegorical tendency maintained by Eusebius and the Cappadocian circle. Other paths of collating, or even somewhat harmonizing, between earthly millenarianism

---

and the Jews'; Drijvers, *Cyril of Jerusalem*, esp. pp. 139–43.

69 Jerome, *Commentary on Daniel*, 2.7.7; 2.7.11; 4.11.21.

70 Jerome, *Epistles*, 123.16.

71 Jerome, *Commentary on Isaiah*, 6.14.1; Jerome, *Commentary on Ezekiel*, 11.36, where he gives his interpretation of Gog and Magog's invasion.

72 Jerome, *Commentary on Daniel*, ed. by Glorie, 2.7.17; Jerome, *Commentary on Isaiah*, ed. by Adriaen, 16.59.14.

73 Jerome, *Commentary on Ezekiel*, ed. by Glorie, 11.36.

74 Jerome, *Commentary on Isaiah*, 18.65.17.

75 Jerome, *Commentary on Ezekiel*, 11.36. For Jerome's overall view of the eschatological fate of the individual soul and the resurrection of the dead, see Daley, *The Hope of the Church*, pp. 101–04.

and a more spiritual, heaven-centred, vision of the blissful existence of the righteous, are exemplified in the late antique apocalyptic compositions, such as the *Apocalypse of Paul* (*c.* end of fourth century), the *Apocalypse of Thomas* (before fifth century) and the *Gospel of Nicodemus* (mid-fifth century).

Thus, following Revelation 21, the *Apocalypse of Paul* envisages a heavenly eschatological Promised Land descending 'like dew' to earth together with Jesus's second coming, where he will establish his millenarian kingdom.[76] In agreement with Jerome, the *Apocalypse* perceives this promised land as a transformed version of the Land of Israel. However, the New Jerusalem and the kingdom are set aside for the Christian just, whose souls have first been purified by repentance and by the archangel Michael in preparation for their resurrection. In addition, the *Apocalypse of Paul* provides picturesque details, portraying the entrance into the eschatological city as a culmination of a wondrous journey that includes purification through immersion in a lake in the Promised Land, on which one sails to Jerusalem on a golden ship:

> This is the [...] Lake where is the City of Christ, but not every man is permitted to enter that city; for this is the journey which leads to God [...] at first when he has gone out of the body, he is brought and worships God, and thence by command of the Lord he is delivered to the angel Michael and he baptizes him in the [...] Lake — then he leads him into the City of Christ alongside those who have never sinned [...] Follow me, and I will lead you into the City of Christ [...] (and the angel put me) into a golden ship and about three thousand angels were singing a hymn before me till I arrived at the City of Christ. Those who inhabited the City of Christ greatly rejoiced over me as I went to them [...]

The description of the city closely follows Revelation 21, with the addition of the triumphal entry of Christ accompanied by his saints. In an ingenious attempt to clothe the messianic procession with the traditional Jewish garb of the end-of-days ingathering, the author brings in King David, who ushers Jesus into Jerusalem:

> This is David; this is the city of Jerusalem, for when Christ the King of Eternity shall come with the assurance of his kingdom, he again shall go before him that he may sing psalms, and all the righteous at the same time shall sing responding 'Hallelujah!'

In light of the dominant role of Michael, who, following Daniel 12, is in charge of the resurrection and purifies here the souls of the just — and the picture of the ideal earthly life in the City of Christ — it appears that the *Apocalypse* envisages the millenarian ingathering as following the first resurrection.

The *Gospel of Nicodemus* embraces the main contours of the scheme in the *Apocalypse of Paul*, such as the leading role ascribed to Michael, though

---

76 *Apocalypse of Paul*, 21–30.

differing in certain important details.[77] The *Gospel of Nicodemus* thus substitutes the River Jordan — apparently alluding to John's baptism — for the lake as the place of the end-of-days immersion. It is tellingly reserved here for those who are not yet baptized — including Old Testament righteous and some Jewish contemporaries represented by the good thief. This inclusion, as well as the terminology of celebrating the Passover in Jerusalem, shows that the backdrop motif of the Jewish eschatological ingathering still lingers. The motif of the millennial kingdom is not spelled out here, yet the text presupposes the interim phase in Jerusalem before the departure into the heavenly realm.

In contrast to the *Apocalypse of Paul* and the *Gospel of Nicodemus*, the *Apocalypse of Thomas* completely ignores the earthly phase of the eschatological scenario, emphasizing instead the angelic likeness of the resurrected and their immediate transfer — lifted up by the angels — into the realm of light, where the Father dwells.[78]

Syriac Idiosyncrasies

Ephrem the Syrian (*c.* 306–73), also known as Ephrem of Edessa (where he dwelled later in life) or Ephrem of Nisibis (where he was born), was a prominent Christian author, who wrote in Syriac and was revered, *inter alia*, as one of the most notable hymnographers of Eastern Christianity. Ephrem was responding to Julian's anti-Christian policies that were part of the emperor's enterprise of restoring paganism. These included the project of rebuilding the Jerusalem Temple, and Ephrem discerned the eschatological implications of this project for the Jews. He thus denounced the supposed expectations of close ingathering of Jewish exiles in the Land, claiming that it would reinstate the early 'pagan' phase of Israel as expressed in the Golden Calf affair and the cult installed by Jeroboam (Exod. 32; 1 Kings 11–15). According to Ephrem, it is in Julian's pagan bull cult that the contemporary Jews were ready to see that divine calf, which once led them out of Egypt and now would bring them back to the Land:[79]

> Perhaps the Jews cried out to that bull,
> 'Behold the gods who will lead your captives
> Up from Babylon into the Land [...]
> As the molten calf led you out of Egypt!' [...]
> They rejoiced that the calves of Jeroboam were revived.

Ephrem thus completely repudiates the traditional Jewish expectation of the eschatological return, presenting it as linked to the figure of Christianity's

---

77 *Gospel of Nicodemus*, 24–27.

78 See Elliott, *The Apocryphal New Testament*, p. 651.

79 Ephrem, *Hymns against Julian* ('Against Julian, the King Who Apostatized, and against the Heretics and the Jews') 1.17–19.

contemporaneous archenemy. The Jewish ingathering as such turns into an anti-Christian affair. Moreover, for Ephrem — in light of the apocalyptic and millenarian visions already probed by his Christian predecessors — Julian may have very well played the part of the Antichrist leading astray the Jews in his attempt to overtake the world and prevent the Christian redemption. Thus, not unlike Origen, Eusebius and later Jerome, Ephrem appears to view the contemporary crises as signs of the apocalyptic script. Nevertheless, Ephrem does not elaborate on the further stages of the apocalyptic scenario with possible Christian ingathering, focusing instead on the personal dimension of the *eschaton*.

Ephrem's resentment of the perspective of Jewish return to the Land is echoed in the later *Vita of Barsauma* (fifth–sixth century). The protagonist, a Syrian ascetic coming to Jerusalem from the East, encounters there the empress Eudocia, who shows sympathy to the plight of the Jews and allows them to make a pilgrimage to the city and celebrate the feast of *Sukkot* (Tabernacles) on the Temple Mount. The Jews interpret Eudocia's permission as not only cancelling the old Hadrianic/Constantinian ban on residing in and around Jerusalem,[80] but as a sign of imminent redemption and the ingathering of the exiles. They therefore send epistles to their brethren throughout the empire, exhorting them to come to Jerusalem for the upcoming holiday, during which the Kingdom of Israel will be re-established:

> To the great and strong people of the Jews from the priests and leaders of Galilee: warm greetings! We write to inform you that the time of the diaspora of our people is past. Behold, the day has arrived on which our tribes shall be reassembled. After all, the emperors of the Romans have decreed that our city, Jerusalem, is to be restored to us. Make haste, then, and come to Jerusalem for the Feast of Tabernacles, because our reign will then be established in Jerusalem![81]

According to the author of the *Vita*, Barsauma vehemently opposed this turn of events, regarding the empress as coming dangerously close to the path probed by Julian, and with the help of a heavenly host violently sabotages the ingathering on the Temple Mount, causing deaths among the Jewish crowd.[82] The historical accuracy of the tradition is still debated,[83] but the narrative strategy of the composition clearly indicates an extremely antagonistic attitude to the Jewish aspirations.

If the following story reflects the agenda of the fifth-century editors of the *Genesis Rabbah* midrashic anthology, and not exclusively its original context,

---

80 See Irshai, 'Constantine and the Jews'. Jews seem to have been allowed to pray there once a year on the Ninth of Av; cf. the description in Jerome, *Commentary on Zephaniah*, 1.15–16. See also Newman, *Jerome and the Jews*, p. 172.

81 *Vita of Barsauma*, 91.4.

82 *Vita of Barsauma*, 91.9.

83 See Nau, 'Deux épisodes', p. 196; Sivan, 'Subversive Pilgrimages'. But cf. Irshai, 'Constantine and the Jews', pp. 217–18.

a comparative reading of the *Vita* and the midrash may indicate that the antagonism towards Jewish eschatological enthusiasm was shared by some roughly contemporaneous rabbinic circles (*Gen. R.* 64.10):[84]

> In the days of R. Joshua b. Hananiah the [Roman] Empire ordered the Temple to be rebuilt. Papos and Lulianos set tables from Acco as far as Antioch and provided those who had come up from the Diaspora with their basic needs. Thereupon the Samaritans went and warned the King: 'Now be it known to the King that if this city is rebuilt and its walls completed, they (the Jews) will stop paying [...] which will eventually harm the kingdom'. [...] Now, when the (emperor's) epistles with the decree [cancelling the rebuilding of the Temple] arrived [...] they burst out weeping, and considered revolting against the Roman power. Thereupon they [the leaders] decided: Let a wise man go and pacify the congregation [...] Let us be satisfied that we entered into dealings with this nation and have emerged in peace.

The plot focuses on the attempt to rebuild the Sanctuary and thus renew Jewish worship on the Temple Mount, with a mass of enthusiastic Jewish pilgrims anticipating the redemptive event. Yet due to the treacherous machinations of the Samaritans, the usual 'other' of the Midrash, the whole project was shelved. To prevent a Jewish revolt and the inevitable bloodshed, the leaders managed to assuage the disappointment of the agitated crowd. The passionately enthusiastic Jews at the beginning of the story in *Genesis Rabbah* find a parallel in the depiction of Jewish enthusiasm in the *Vita*. Both texts highlight the Jewish anticipation of the near end of their dispersion and the role of the Roman Empire in that eschatological development — in *Genesis Rabbah* as in the *Vita*, it is the Romans who order Jerusalem to be restored as the city of the Jewish sanctuary. It is instructive that the Jewish narrators also attest to reservations regarding messianic activism calling for the ingathering in Jerusalem, aspirations which were likely widespread among the (non-rabbinic) Jewish masses.[85]

An illuminating offshoot of the tendency of Syriac Christians to reject the centrality of the Holy Land and Jerusalem as the traditional locus of Jewish

---

84 For the original text, see *Bereshit Rabba*, pp. 710–11. The translation is by Freedman from *Midrash Rabba Genesis*, p. 580, with some alterations.

85 Papadoyannakis, 'A Debate about the Rebuilding of the Temple'. Papadoyannakis shows that in fifth-century Christian compositions, Jews are routinely portrayed as demanding from the imperial authorities to re-establish the Temple at its historical site. This narrative pattern seems to have served certain needs of Christian propaganda of the period. We have seen, however, that a similar motif appears not only in Christian narratives but also in rabbinic tradition — which may indicate its wide currency and/or underlying historical reality. See also Jacobs, *Remains of the Jews*, p. 195. See further our discussion in Kofsky, Ruzer and Kiperwasser, *Reshaping Identities in Late Antique Syria-Mesopotamia*, pp. 181–216. For a discussion of the motif of eschatological return to the Land in rabbinic sources, see, for example, Milikowsky, 'Trajectories of Return'. See also Urbach, *The Sages*, pp. 655, 657.

eschatological ingathering is provided by the fourth–sixth century *Cave of Treasures* (hereafter *CT*).[86] This composition outstandingly exemplifies a double rejection, substituting Syro-Mesopotamia for the Land of Israel as the Christian promised land, where the true followers of messiah will gather in the end of days.[87] The centre of the eschatological nostalgia is here the mythical cave on the holy mountain in the East — in the vicinity of paradise. This locale is perceived as the original homeland of humanity, to which only Syriac Christians, the true Christians, will return from their current exile:

> After the fulfillment of the times which I have allotted that you shall be in exile outside [Paradise], in the land which is under the curse, behold, I will send my Son [...] and through him redemption and a *return* shall be effected for you.[88]

In this context, the *CT* stance on the issue of the sanctity of Jerusalem shows itself as truly extraordinary. Unlike many other documented traditions, from both Greek and Latin Christianity, the text engages an inverted symbolism: not the local shrine as a replica of faraway Golgotha or as a 'new Jerusalem', but the remote Golgotha as the *second cave of treasures*. The *CT* obviously cannot ignore the centrality of Jerusalem for the general Christian narrative. It is there that the atoning and salvific crucifixion will take place. However, the historical journey westward from the blessed mountain to Jerusalem is presented as a chain of exiles, punishment for the sins committed. Tension between what may be termed Syrian 'local patriotism' and obligations toward the Christian focus on the Holy Land informs the entire structure of *CT*. But perhaps nowhere is it reflected with such ironic clarity as in the textual variants of the episode where God addresses Adam before the protoplasts' exit from paradise. It is here (*CT* 5.10–11) that God warns him that, in the future, Adam's descendants will be expelled from the holy mountain to the West, where eventually the Saviour will be born. That distant place is explicitly characterized in some manuscripts as 'the exile of the earth' (*galuthah dar'a*, ܓܠܘܬܐ ܕܐܪܥܐ) — a Syriac pun on Golgotha. Such seems to have been the perception of the Land of Israel by those who dwelled in the vicinity of the true *omphalos* of the earth. The locus of Jerusalem, with Golgotha in its midst, is thus in need of rehabilitation. This will be achieved by establishing a link between Jerusalem and the true primordial sanctity of the Cave of Treasures, as the crucifixion enables the eschatological return to the East.

---

86 See discussion in Minov, *Memory and Identity*, pp. 36–39.
87 For discussion, see Ruzer and Kofsky, *Syriac Idiosyncrasies*, pp. 87–120.
88 *Cave of Treasures*, 5.6–11.

Conclusion

We have traced a spectrum of early Christian responses to the traditional Jewish notion of Israel's eschatological ingathering in the Promised Land. We observed that while some early texts, such as Acts and the *Didache*, continued to entertain the hope of such an ingathering — with its focus already on Jesus believers — others even at that stage played down the motif, emphasizing instead a heavenly eschatological assembly.

Later second-century authors took it for granted that the final ingathering pertains to Christians. So it is in the two-part millenarian vision of Justin Martyr and Irenaeus. The first stage involves the persecution of the Christ believers gathered in the earthly Jerusalem by the Antichrist. This is followed by the second coming and the establishment of millennium rule. The second stage, following the final resurrection, is that of eternal bliss. Origen provides a spiritualizing and allegorizing reaction to the apocalyptic vividness of millenarian dreams branded as 'Jewish' error. Yet even he retains some elements of inherited tradition, applying them to current historical traumatic events. In the process, he tones down their apocalyptic character. The Promised Land is accorded a central role in Origen's overall allegorical scheme; it becomes a blueprint for the spiritual heavenly resettlement of the believers.

Under the towering influence of Origen, such millenarian and spiritualizing tendencies continue to develop both independently and in an intertwined fashion, as witnessed by prominent fourth-century figures. In this context, even the motif of Jewish ingathering lingers on. One discerns a meaningful difference of attitude in these later works. Whereas Apollinarius views the return of the Jews to Jerusalem as part of their conversion, for Cyril of Jerusalem and apparently Jerome, the Jewish ingathering is an intrinsic part of the Antichrist's deceit. Here, Jerome performs a balancing act between rejection of 'Jewish' literal millenarianism and a full-bodied allegorical spiritualization.

We find other modes of intertwining earthly Land of Israel millenarianism with a spiritual or heavenly-centred vision of the end-of-days bliss in late antique apocalyptic compositions. These brim with colourful details of the eschatological geography of the land and the fantastic journey of the believers to the city, led by the archangel Michael and Jesus. Even here, however, one still finds a residue of the traditional Jewish ingathering motif: the way to the land goes through the baptism of both biblical figures and contemporary Jews in the Jordan River, and the festive procession in the city is headed by none other than King David.

In certain fourth–fifth-century Syriac sources, we observed a strong resentment towards the Jewish eschatological hopes of the return to the land, seemingly vis-à-vis historical developments such as Julian's — and apparently later Eudocia's — pro-Jewish policy. Interestingly, neither Ephrem in his attack against Julian's evil influence on the Jews nor the *Vita of Barsauma* refer to the alternative future Christian ingathering as a supersessionist eschatological scenario. And, finally, the *Cave of Treasures* presents a double rejection eschatology. Not only is the Jewish end-of-days ingathering in the Land denied, but also the final redemption of the Christians is transferred to the East, with the Promised Land regarded as the place of the farthest exile.

To sum up, we have seen how the Jewish motif of return to the Land of Israel casts a *longue durée* shadow on early Christian eschatology evolving in various independent directions, in spite of the rationalizing and spiritualizing tendencies that influenced Christian intellectual discourse following Origen. In fact, such tendencies never truly dimmed the attraction of the final ingathering in the Christianized apocalyptic vision of redemption.

Bibliography

Primary Sources

Apocalypse of Paul, ed. by Konstantin Tischendorf, in Tischendorf, *Apocalypses Apocryphae* (Leipzig: Mendelssohn, 1866 (repr. Hildesheim: Olms, 1966)), pp. 34–69

The Apocalypse of Thomas, the Shorter Text, ed. by Paul Bihlmeyer, in Bihlmeyer, 'Un texte non interpolé de 1'Apocalypse de Thomas', *Rev. Ben. 28* (1911), pp. 270–82; the Longer Text, ed. by Friedrich Wilhelm, in Wilhelm, *Deutsche Legende und Legendare* (Leipzig: Hinrichs, 1907), pp. 40–42

Apollinarius, *De fide et incarnatione*, ed. by Hans Lietzmann (Berlin: Mohr, 1904)

——, *Kata meros pistis*, ed. by Hans Lietzmann (Berlin: Mohr, 1904)

Basil of Caesarea, *Epistles*, ed. and trans. by Roy J. Deferrari and Martin R. P. McGuire (Cambridge, MA: Harvard University Press, 1934)

Bereshit Rabba, ed. by J. Theodor and Ch. Albeck (Jerusalem: Wahrmann, 1965)

Book of Jubilees, ed. by Robert Henry Charles (Oxford: Oxford University Press 1895); English translation by Orval S. Wintermute in *The Old Testament Pseudepigrapha*, vol. i, ed. by James H. Charlesworth (New Haven: Yale University Press, 1985), pp. 86–193

The Cave of Treasures, ed. by Andreas Su-Min Ri, *La Caverne des Trésors: Les deux recensions Syriaques* (Louvain: Peeters, 1987) [cited as *CT*]

Cyril of Jerusalem, *Catechetical Lectures*, ed. by Wilhelm Karl Reischl and Joseph Rupp (Hildesheim: Olms, 1967)

Didache, ed. and English trans. by K. Lake (Cambridge, MA: Harvard University Press, 1949)

Ephrem, *Hymns against Julian*, ed. by Edmund Beck (Louvain: Peeters, 1957)

Epiphanius, *Panarion*, ed. by Karl Holl (Berlin: Hinrichs, 1915–1930)

Eusebius of Caesarea, *Ecclesiastical History*, ed. and English trans. by Kirsopp Lake (Cambridge, MA: Harvard University Press, 1926)

——, *The Theophany*, ed. by Samuel Lee (Cambridge: Cambridge University Press, 1842)

The Gospel of Nicodemus, ed. by Konstantin Tischendorf, in Tischendorf, *Evangelia Apocrypha* (Leipzig: Mendelssohn, 1853 (repr. Hildesheim: Olms, 1966)), pp. 210–432

Gregory Nazianzen, *Epistles*, ed. by Paul Gallay (Berlin: Akademie, 1969)

Irenaeus of Lyons, *Against Heresies*, ed. by Adelin Rousseau, Louis Doutreleau, Bernard Hemmerdinger, and Charles Mercier (Paris: Cerf, 1965–1982)

Jerome, *Commentary on Daniel*, ed. by Franciscus Glorie (Turnhout: Brepols, 1964)

——, *Commentary on Ezekiel*, ed. by Franciscus Glorie (Turnhout: Brepols, 1964)

——, *Commentary on Isaiah*, ed. by Marc Adriaen (Turnhout: Brepols, 1963)

——, *Commentary on Zephaniah*, ed. by Marc Adriaen (Turnhout: Brepols, 1964/1969)

——, *De viris illustribus*, ed. by Wilhelm Herding (Leipzig: Teubner, 1924)

——, *Epistles*, ed. by I. Hilberg, Corpus Scriptorum Ecclesiasticorum Latinorum, 56/2 (Vienna: Tempsky, 1910)

Justin Martyr, *First Apology*, ed. by Miroslav Marcovich (Berlin: de Gruyter, 1994)

——, *Second Apology*, ed. by Miroslav Marcovich (Berlin: de Gruyter, 1994)

——, *Dialogue with Trypho*, ed. by Georges Archambault (Paris: Picard, 1909)

Midrash Rabbah, 10 vols, trans. by H. Freedman (London: Soncino, 1992)

Origen, *Commentarium Series in Matthaeum*, ed. by Erich Klostermann (Leipzig: Hinrichs, 1935)

——, *De principiis*, ed. by Paul Koetschau (Leipzig: Hinrichs, 1913)

——, *Hom. in Num.*, ed. by Louis Doutreleau (Paris: Cerf, 1996)

Vita of Barsauma, ed. by François Nau, 'Resumé de Monographies Syriaques', *Revue de l'Orient Chrétien*, 18 (1913), pp. 270–76, 379–89; 19 (1914), pp. 113–34, 278–89; English translation: Andrew Palmer, *The Life of the Syrian Saint Barsauma: Eulogy of a Hero of the Resistance to the Council of Chalcedon* (Oakland: University of California Press, 2020)

Secondary Studies

Alexander, Philip S., 'Jerusalem as the *Omphalos* of the World', in *Jerusalem: Its Sanctity and Centrality to Judaism, Christianity, and Islam*, ed. by Lee I. Levine (New York: Continuum, 1999), pp. 104–19

Balabanski, Vicky, *Eschatology in the Making: Mark, Matthew and the Didache* (Cambridge: Cambridge University Press, 1997)

Barnard, Leslie W., *Justin Martyr: His Life and Thought* (Cambridge: Cambridge University Press, 1967)

Baumgarten, Albert, 'The Role of Jerusalem and the Temple in "End-of-Days" Speculation in Second Temple Period', in *Jerusalem: Its Sanctity and Centrality to Judaism, Christianity, and Islam*, ed. by Lee I. Levine (New York: Continuum, 1999), pp. 77–89

Bitton-Ashkelony, Brouria, 'The Attitudes of Church Fathers toward Pilgrimage to Jerusalem in the Fourth and Fifth Centuries', in *Jerusalem: Its Sanctity and Centrality to Judaism, Christianity, and Islam*, ed. by Lee I. Levine (New York: Continuum, 1999), pp. 188–203

——, *Encountering the Sacred: The Debate on Christian Pilgrimage in Late Antiquity* (Berkeley: University of California Press, 2005)

Bowman, Glenn, '"Mapping History's Redemption": Eschatology and Topography in the *Itinerarium Burdigalense*', in *Jerusalem: Its Sanctity and Centrality to Judaism, Christianity, and Islam*, ed. by Lee I. Levine (New York: Continuum, 1999), pp. 163–87

Brooke, George J., 'Moving the Mountains: From Sinai to Jerusalem', in *The Significance of Sinai: Traditions about Sinai and Divine Revelation in Judaism and Christianity*, ed. by George J. Brooke, Hindy Najman, and Loren Stuckenbruck (Leiden: Brill, 2008), pp. 73–89

Cerioni, Lavinia, '"Mother of Souls": The Holy City of Jerusalem in Origen's Commentary and Homily on the Song of Songs', in *Origeniana Duodecima: Origen's Legacy in the Holy Land – A Tale of Three Cities: Jerusalem, Caesarea and Bethlehem*, ed. by Brouria Bitton-Ashkelony, Oded Irshai, Aryeh Kofsky, Hillel Newman, and Lorenzo Perone (Leuven: Peeters, 2019), pp. 109–21

Clabeaux, John J., 'The Ritual Meal in Didache 9–10: Progress in Understanding', in *The Didache: A Missing Piece of the Puzzle in Early Christianity*, ed. by Jonathan A. Draper and Clayton N. Jefford (Atlanta: SBL, 2015), pp. 209–30

Conzelmann, Hans, *Acts of the Apostles*, Hermeneia – A Critical and Historical Commentary on the Bible (Philadelphia: Fortress, 1987)

Daley, Brian E., *The Hope of the Church: A Handbook of Patristic Eschatology* (Cambridge: Baker Academic, 1991)

Drijvers, Jan W., *Cyril of Jerusalem: Bishop and City* (Leiden: Brill, 2004)

Elliott, J. Keith, *The Apocryphal New Testament* (Oxford: Oxford University Press, 2005)

Finlan, Stephen, 'Identity in the Didache Community', in *The Didache: A Missing Piece of the Puzzle in Early Christianity*, ed. by Jonathan A. Draper and Clayton N. Jefford (Atlanta: SBL, 2015), pp. 17–32

Fitzmyer, Joseph A., *The Acts of the Apostles*, The Anchor Yale Bible Commentaries (New Haven: Yale University Press, 1998)

——, *First Corinthians: A New Translation with Introduction and Commentary* (New Haven: Yale University Press, 2008)

Greenberg, Moshe, *Ezekiel 21–37: A New Translation with Introduction and Commentary* (New York: Anchor Bible, 1997)

Gregory, Andrew, 'Reflections on the Didache and its Community: A Response', in *The Didache: A Missing Piece of the Puzzle in Early Christianity*, ed. by Jonathan A. Draper and Clayton N. Jefford (Atlanta: SBL, 2015), pp. 123–38

Hermanin de Reichenfeld, Giovanni, 'From Capernaum to Jerusalem: Origen's Sacred Geography of the Holy Land in His Commentaries on the Gospels', in *Origeniana Duodecima: Origen's Legacy in the Holy Land – A Tale of Three Cities: Jerusalem, Caesarea and Bethlehem*, ed. by Brouria Bitton-Ashkelony, Oded Irshai, Aryeh Kofsky, Hillel Newman, and Lorenzo Perone (Leuven: Peeters, 2019), pp. 123–37

Irshai, Oded, 'The Christian Appropriation of Jerusalem in the Fourth Century: The Case of the Bordeaux Pilgrim', *The Jewish Quarterly Review*, 99.4 (2009), 465–86

——, 'Constantine and the Jews: The Prohibition against Entering Jerusalem – History and Hagiography', *Zion*, 60 (1995), 129–78

——, 'Cyril of Jerusalem: The Apparition of the Cross and the Jews', in *Contra Iudaeos. Ancient and Medieval Polemics between Christians and Jews*, ed. by Ora Limor and Guy G. Stroumsa (Tübingen: Mohr Siebeck, 1996), pp. 85–104

——, 'The Jerusalem Bishopric and the Jews in the Fourth Century: History and Eschatology', *Jerusalem: Its Sanctity and Centrality to Judaism, Christianity, and Islam*, ed. by Lee I. Levine (New York: Continuum, 1999), pp. 204–20

Jacobs, Andrew S., *Remains of the Jews: The Holy Land and Christian Empire in Late Antiquity* (Stanford: Stanford University Press, 2004)

Kofsky, Aryeh, and Serge Ruzer, 'The Holy Places and the Jewish Past in the Fifth-Century Christian Discourse of Appropriation', in *Between Sea and Desert: On Kings, Nomads, Cities and Monks. Essays in Honor of Joseph Patrich*, ed. by Orit Peleg-Barkat, Jacob Ashkenazi, Uzi Leibner, Mordechai Aviam, and Rina Talgam (Jerusalem: Ostracon, 2019), pp. 215–24

Kofsky, Aryeh, and Serge Ruzer, in collaboration with Reuven Kiperwasser, *Reshaping Identities in Late Antique Syria-Mesopotamia: Christian and Jewish Hermeneutics and Narrative Strategies* (Piscataway: Gorgias, 2016)

Milikowsky, Chaim J., 'Trajectories of Return, Restoration and Redemption in Rabbinic Judaism: Elijah, the Messiah, the War of Gog and the World to Come', in *Restoration: Old Testament, Jewish, and Christian Perspectives*, ed. by James M. Scott (Leiden: Brill, 2001), pp. 265–80

Minov, Sergey, *Memory and Identity in the Syriac Cave of Treasures: Rewriting the Bible in Sasanian Iran* (Leiden: Brill, 2021)

Nau, François, 'Deux épisodes de l'histoire de la Vie de Barsauma le Syrien', *Revue des Études Juives*, 83–84 (1927), 194–99

Newman, Hillel, *Jerome and the Jews* (PhD dissertation, Hebrew University of Jerusalem, 1997)

Oliver, Isaac W., *Luke's Jewish Eschatology: The National Restoration of Israel in Luke-Acts* (Oxford: Oxford University Press, 2021)

Osborn, Eric, *Irenaeus of Lyons* (Cambridge: Cambridge University Press, 2003)

Papadoyannakis, Yannis, 'A Debate about the Rebuilding of the Temple in Sixth-Century Byzantium', in *Antiquity in Antiquity: Jewish and Christian Pasts in the Greco-Roman World*, ed. by Gregg Gardner and Kevin L. Osterloh (Tübingen: Mohr Siebeck, 2008), pp. 372–82

Rofé, Alexander, *Introduction to the Prophetic Literature* (Sheffield: Sheffield Academic, 1992)

Ruzer, Serge, 'The Land of Israel at the Center of Messianic Redemption: Narrative Strategies of Acts Revisited' (Leiden: Brill, forthcoming)

Ruzer, Serge, and Aryeh Kofsky, *Syriac Idiosyncrasies: Theology and Hermeneutics in Early Syriac Literature* (Leiden: Brill, 2010)

Sanders, Ed P., 'Jerusalem and its Temple in Early Christian Thought and Practice', in *Jerusalem: Its Sanctity and Centrality to Judaism, Christianity, and Islam*, ed. by Lee I. Levine (New York: Continuum, 1999), pp. 90–103

Schwiebert, Jonathan, *Knowledge and the Coming Kingdom: The Didache's Meal Ritual and its Place in Early Christianity* (London: T & T Clark, 2008)

Sivan, Hagith, 'Subversive Pilgrimages: Barsauma in Jerusalem', *Journal of Early Christian Studies*, 26 (2018), 53–74

Smith, Murray J., 'The Lord Jesus and his Coming in the Didache', in *The Didache: A Missing Piece of the Puzzle in Early Christianity*, ed. by Jonathan A. Draper and Clayton N. Jefford (Atlanta: SBL, 2015), pp. 363–408

Stroumsa, Guy G., 'Mystical Jerusalems', in *Jerusalem: Its Sanctity and Centrality to Judaism, Christianity, and Islam*, ed. by Lee I. Levine (New York: Continuum, 1999), pp. 349–70

Talmon, Shemaryahu, 'The Concept of Mašîah and Messianism in Early Judaism', in *The Messiah: Developments in Earliest Judaism and Christianity*, ed. by James H. Charlesworth (Minneapolis: Fortress, 1992), pp. 79–115

Taylor, Justin, 'The List of the Nations in Acts 2:9–11', *Revue Biblique*, 106.3 (1999), 408–20

Thielman, Frank S., 'Another Look at the Eschatology of Eusebius of Caesarea', *Vigiliae Christianae*, 41 (1987), 226–37

Urbach, Ephraim E., *The Sages: Their Concepts and Beliefs* (Jerusalem: Magnes, 1987)

Wilken, Robert L., *The Land Called Holy: Palestine in Christian History and Thought* (New Haven: Yale University Press, 1992)

——, 'Loving the Jerusalem Below: The Monks of Palestine', in *Jerusalem: Its Sanctity and Centrality to Judaism, Christianity, and Islam*, ed. by Lee I. Levine (New York: Continuum, 1999), pp. 240–50

Zakovitch, Yair, 'The First Stages of Jerusalem's Sanctification under David: A Literary and Ideological Analysis', in *Jerusalem: Its Sanctity and Centrality to Judaism, Christianity, and Islam*, ed. by Lee I. Levine (New York: Continuum, 1999), pp. 16–35

ORA LIMOR

Divina Vestigia

Tracking the Early History of Jesus's Footprints at the Mount of Olives

In the year 1523, thirty-two-year-old Ignatius of Loyola embarked on a pilgrimage to Jerusalem. Two years earlier, he had been seriously wounded in battle. The pilgrimage is described in his reminiscences as part of a long process of conversion and as a decisive stage in his life: 'All he wanted to do, once he recovered, was to journey to Jerusalem [...], with all the acts of discipline and all the acts of self-denial that a generous spirit, fired with God, generally wants to do'.[1] Ignatius wanted to remain in Jerusalem for life, but his request was denied by the guardian of the Franciscan Monastery of Mount Sion. The Jerusalem visit is described in general terms, with the Mount of Olives receiving particular mention. Ignatius tells about a dangerous night visit to the Mount, an episode that seals his pilgrimage experience and stands apart from the general tone of the text:

> When this was over, there came over him as he was returning to where he was previously a great desire to go back and visit the Mount of Olives again before he left, now that it was not the will of Our Lord that he should remain in those holy places. On the Mount of Olives is a stone, from which Our Lord went up into heaven, and even now the footprints can be seen; this is what he wanted to go back to see. Thus, without saying a thing nor taking a guide (because those who move about without a Turk to guide them run great danger), he slipped away from the others and went off alone to the Mount of Olives. The sentries didn't want to let him in; he gave them a knife from the writing-things he was carrying. And after he had made his prayer with considerable consolation, the desire came to him to go to Bethpage. And as he was there, he came to remember that on the Mount of Olives he hadn't taken a proper look at where the right

---

1 *Saint Ignatius of Loyola*, p. 16. I would like to thank my friends and colleagues Iris Shagrir, Yamit Rachman-Schrire and Moshe Yagur for their help in writing this essay.

> **Ora Limor** is Professor Emerita in the Department of History, Philosophy and Judaic Studies at the Open University of Israel.

Essays on Jews and Christians in Late Antiquity in Honour of Oded Irshai, ed. by Brouria Bitton-Ashkelony and Martin Goodman, CELAMA 40 (Turnhout: Brepols, 2023), pp. 183–203
BREPOLS ❧ PUBLISHERS   10.1484/M.CELAMA-EB.5.132489

foot was or where the left was. And on returning there, I think he gave his scissors to the sentries so that they would let him in.[2]

For Ignatius, the footprints on a stone at the Mount of Olives are undeniable evidence both of Jesus's presence and of his absence, both of his existence in this world and his ascension to heaven.[3] He concluded his pilgrimage and departed from Jerusalem at the very spot from which Jesus departed from Jerusalem and from this world. Metaphorically, one may also say that the direction of Jesus's footprints dictated for Ignatius the direction his life would take from then on.

While Ignatius was interested in the positioning of Jesus's feet, other pilgrims paid special attention to their measure. And while some mentioned two footprints, others had seen only one. According to the Icelandic Guide, written *c.* 1150, one can see the imprint of the Lord's left foot, fourteen inches long, on the stone from which he ascended to heaven, 'as if he has stepped barefoot into clay'.[4] John Poloner, who visited the Holy Land in 1422, wrote that on the Mount of Olives there is a round chapel in which the vestige of Jesus's left foot is discernible, impressed in the stone when he ascended to heaven. Its length is one palm and two middle fingers.[5]

The stone with the footprints is first recorded in the middle of the twelfth century, when Jerusalem was under Christian Frankish rule, and is mentioned

---

2 *Saint Ignatius of Loyola*, p. 35. For another translation of the last sentences, see *The Autobiography of St Ignatius of Loyola*, pp. 50–51: 'While there he remembered that he had not clearly noticed on Mount Olivet in what direction the right foot was pointed nor in what direction the left. Returning there, I believe he gave his scissors to the guards so they would let him enter'. The autobiography was written up from Ignatius's own narrative by the faithful scribe, Luis Gonçalves da Câmara.

3 See recently Bynum, *Dissimilar Similitudes*, pp. 221–58. Bynum maintains that regarding the footprints, absence is the condition of presence. Like the empty tomb, such absence imparts credibility. See also Bynum, *Christian Materiality*, pp. 273–80. For the history of the footprints in general, see Desjardins, 'Les Vestiges du Seigneur au mont des Oliviers'; Kötting, 'Fußspuren als Zeichen göttlicher Anwesenheit'.

4 Wilkinson with Hill and Ryan, *Jerusalem Pilgrimage 1099–1185*, pp. 221–22. The Guide refers to the Ascension Church as 'Michael's Church', perhaps because of the belief that in the end of times it is there that the Archangel Michael will slay the Antichrist. See McGinn, *Visions of the End*, pp. 50, 87. For an example of a pilgrim token of the footprint of Jesus, see Bynum, *Dissimilar Similitudes*, p. 239.

5 *Johannis Poloner descriptio Terrae Sanctae*, in Titus Tobler, *Descriptiones Terrae Sanctae*, p. 235: '... ecclesiam montis Oliveti, in qua est capella rotunda [...] in qua cernitur (pedis) sinistri vestigium Christi, quod lapidi impressit, cum ad coelos ascendebat, et habet in longitudine unum palmum et duos articulos medii digiti'. William Wey, who visited the Holy Land in 1458 and in 1462, left to the chapel of Edington, among many other gifts, a board with the measurements of Jesus's sepulchre, the depth of the mortice of the Cross, and the length of Jesus's foot. See *The Itineraries of William Wey*, p. 224; Arad, 'Pilgrimage, Cartography, and Devotion', p. 307. On the symbolic uses of measurements in the context of Jerusalem pilgrimage, see Shalev, 'Christian Pilgrimage and Ritual Measurement in Jerusalem'. On the direction of the feet, see also Desjardins, 'Les Vestiges', p. 66.

continuously thereafter.[6] The descriptions vary in detail, but all create an imaginary continuity between the Ascension story of the New Testament and the stone the authors observed with their own eyes, as if the footprints were imprinted there at the very moment Jesus ascended. The problem is that when we try to trace the tradition from the twelfth century backwards to the establishment of the tradition of holy places in Jerusalem, we encounter a much hazier situation, one that evokes more questions than answers.

In the following pages, dedicated to my friend and colleague Oded Irshai, an avid scholar of late antique Jerusalem, I shall try to trace the beginnings of the footprints tradition, dwelling on the early stages of its development, before the impression became one of Jerusalem's most celebrated relics. In contrast to the famous tradition known from the twelfth century on, it transpires that in the earlier version of the tradition, the footprints are sealed not in stone but rather in sand, that is in the bare earth at the basilica of the Ascension.

* * *

Imprinted footprints have been venerated in many cultures. The most important were footprints of deities and angels, such as the footprints of Isis and Serapis in Egypt,[7] the many footprints of Michael the archangel in France and Italy,[8] or the foot of Adam in Sri Lanka (Buddhists see in it the foot of Buddha, Hinduists that of Shiva).[9] In the Mediterranean world of antiquity, people were shown the alleged footprints of male pagan gods such as Heracles, Dionysos, Asklepios/Sarapis, and Mithras, as well as those of Christ and the prophet Mohammed.[10] In the fourth book of his *Histories*, Herodotus relates that in Scythia, on a rock by the river Tyras, one could see a footprint left by Heracles. It resembled a man's footprint, but it was two cubits long.[11] In the Egyptian world, usually one foot is seen; in the Graeco-Roman world, mainly (but not only) two.[12] Apart from that, in Egypt especially, there are also instances in which footprints are almost certainly 'intended to be those of the worshippers, to immortalize the believer's visit to the sanctuary and perpetuate his/her prayers'.[13]

---

6 For a list of sources, see Baldi, *Enchiridion Locorum Sanctorum*, pp. 383–426. The list is hardly exhaustive. See also Pringle, *The Churches of the Crusader Kingdom of Jerusalem*, iii, pp. 72–88.

7 Dunbabin, '*Ipsa deae vestigia*... Footprints divine and human on Graeco-Roman monuments'.

8 Donkin, 'Stones of St Michael'; Arnold, 'Arcadia Becomes Jerusalem'.

9 Kötting, 'Fußspuren'; Fritz, 'Empreintes et vestiges dans les récits de pèlerinage', p. 37; Bynum, *Dissimilar Similitudes*, pp. 222–27.

10 Takács, 'Divine and Human Feet'. Takács remarks that goddesses, unlike male gods, do not seem to have left behind such markers (p. 359).

11 Herodotus, *Histories*, 4, 82; 2, 91. See Takács, 'Divine and Human Feet', p. 357; Kötting, 'Fußspuren'.

12 Dunbabin, '*Ipsa deae vestigia*', p. 88.

13 Dunbabin adds that in the Graeco-Roman world, the two customs appear to have merged and the distinction between divine and human footsteps is frequently not clear. ('*Ipsa deae vestigia*', p. 90). See also Castiglione, 'Vestigia', pp. 95–132.

The footprints alluded to the presence of the divine or human in a particular place at a particular moment. They were understood as physical evidence of a godly presence, a site where earth and heaven, human and divine intersected. As a result, the sites of the footprints became sacred and were believed to hold extraordinary, miraculous powers. Sarolta Takács noted that 'even when religious systems changed, these places retained their importance. People kept visiting such sites'.[14]

A few rare traditions of body prints left by mythological heroes can be found in Jewish culture as well. The traveller Petahiah of Regensburg (*c.* 1180) tells about Mount Gaash, where Joshua son of Nun is buried and beside him Caleb son of Jephunneh: 'Near one shrine one can discern a single footprint, like that of a man walking in the snow, so it appears; it was here that the angel stood and the Land of Israel was agitated after the death of Joshua'.[15] And the Florence Scroll, a pictorial pilgrimage of a medieval Jew, probably from the fourteenth century, tells about Moses' body shape left in a cavern in Mount Sinai:

> This is the shape of Mount Sinai. And within it a space has been excavated, in the shape of a man, and it is said of it: When the holy presence passed over Moses, may he rest in peace, the mountain became like pulp or clay, and he entered into it, hence the shape within the mountain.[16]

The tradition of Moses's body imprint pressed in the stone of a cavern on Mount Sinai was a known local tradition. It can be found also in Christian sources, for example in Thietmar's itinerary, written in the thirteenth century.[17] This is an appealing example of a shared tradition and a shared holy place, even if the writers do not necessarily refer to exactly the same place.[18]

Against this backdrop, the existence of traditions regarding Jesus's bodily imprints in Jerusalem is not surprising. The imprints are testimonies to his presence in the city and add to its holiness. They verify the historicity of the events that happened in these places and seal their sacred traditions in stone.[19] Descriptions of Jerusalem attest to several such imprints. Most celebrated was the flagellation column (Matt. 27:26), kept on Mount Zion and mentioned in many Holy Land accounts. Some of them elaborate on the body marks Jesus left on it. In Theodosius's *De Situ Terrae Sanctae* (*c.* 530), we read:

> The column which was in the House of Caiphas, at which my Lord Christ was scourged, has now by my Lord's command found its way into Holy

---

14 Takács, 'Divine and Human Feet', p. 359.

15 *The Itinerary of R. Petahiah of Regensburg*, p. 31 (in Hebrew). See Reiner, 'From Joshua to Jesus', pp. 228–30.

16 Sarfati, *The Florence Scroll*, pp. 41–42.

17 See Pringle, *Pilgrimage to Jerusalem*, pp. 128–29; more examples are brought by Fritz, 'Empreintes', pp. 28–32.

18 To these examples, one should add the imprints of Abraham in Mecca, famous in Muslim tradition. See Kister, 'Maqām Ibrāhīm'.

19 Rachman-Schrire, 'Evagatorium in Terrae Sanctae'.

Sion and you can see the way he clung to it when he was being scourged as if the marks were in wax. His arms, hands, and fingers clove to it. It shows even today. Also he made on it the impression of his whole face, chin, nose, and eyes as if it had been wax.[20]

Similar information is given in the *Breviarius de Hierosolyma* (*c.* 530): 'The column on which the Lord Jesus was struck. There is a mark where he held onto it like an impression on wax'.[21] And the Piacenza Pilgrim (*c.* 570) follows suit:

In this church is the column at which the Lord was scourged, and it has on it this mark: When he clasped it, his chest clove to the marble, and you can see in that stone the marks of both his hands, his fingers, and his palms so that you can take from it 'measures' (*mensura*) for any kind of disease, and people can wear them round their neck and be cured.[22]

The Piacenza Pilgrim also describes in some detail Jesus's footprint in the stone at the Praetorium (Church of Saint Sophia at the time of the pilgrim's visit), where he stood when sentenced by Pilate:

The Lord mounted it when he was heard by Pilate, and the image of his foot remained on it, a beautiful foot, small and delicate [...] From this stone come many blessings (*virtutes*). People take 'measures' from the footprints, and wear them for various diseases and are cured.[23]

The footprints left by Jesus in the place where he stood when judged by Pilate are also mentioned by Epiphanius the Monk in the eighth century, but he locates them on Mount Zion.[24]

Adomnán, the learned abbot of Iona off the shores of Scotland, in his book *De locis sanctis*, written between 679 and 688, mentions another instance of Jesus's body prints. They are marked on a rock in the tomb of Mary situated at the Valley of Jehoshaphat:

---

20 Theodosius, *De Situ Terrae Sanctae*, 7, p. 118; Wilkinson, *Jerusalem Pilgrims*, p. 107. On the metaphor of wax, see Fritz, 'Empreintes'.

21 *Breviarius de Hierosolyma*, 4, p. 111; Wilkinson, *Jerusalem Pilgrims*, p. 119.

22 *Antonini Placentini Itinerarium*, 22, p. 140; Wilkinson, *Jerusalem Pilgrims*, p. 140. In his *Glory of the Martyrs*, Gregory of Tours tells about a stone in Rome with two small indentations in it, where Peter and Paul prayed to the Lord against Simon Magus. 'When rain water has collected in these indentations, ill people gather it; Once they drink it, it soon restores their health'. Gregorius Turonensis, *Liber in Gloria Martyrum*, 27; Gregory of Tours, *Glory of the Martyrs*, p. 45.

23 *Antonini Placentini Itinerarium*, 23, p. 141. The pilgrim had seen also the stain of Jesus's blood at the crucifixion place. *Antonini Placentini Itinerarium*, 19, p. 138.

24 Donner, 'Die Palästinabeschreibung des Epiphanius Monachus Hagiopolita', p. 83; Wilkinson, *Jerusalem Pilgrims*, p. 209. In this context should be mentioned also the Quo Vadis footprints in Rome. See Desjardins, 'Les Vestiges', p. 60; Worm, 'Steine und Fußspuren Christi auf dem Ölberg', p. 312 n. 48.

On it the Lord knelt to pray in the field of Gethsemane just before he was betrayed, on the night when he was 'given up into the hands of wicked men' and to Judas. The marks of his knees are visible, printed deeply in the rock, as if it had been soft wax.[25]

These instances provide ample evidence of the existence of the phenomenon in Jerusalem. Among other miracles and wondrous manifestations of the holy, the city also offered pilgrims and visitors material vestiges of Christ.

* * *

The Ascension footprints can be seen as another instance of the phenomenon described above. As put by Bynum, 'the footprints on the Mount of Olives proved the Ascension: he was here but he has gone up into heaven'.[26] Nevertheless, the early history of these footprints is quite elusive, in contrast to the stability of the Ascension site itself, which appears consistently in Jerusalem descriptions since the fourth century. The Ascension is twice described in the New Testament, and in both cases it takes place on the Mount of Olives. In his gospel, Luke describes how Jesus led his disciples to the vicinity of Bethany, lifted up his hands and blessed them, and was then taken up into heaven (Luke 24:50–51). In the Acts of Apostles, he describes how Jesus was taken up before their very eyes, while they looked intently up into the sky as he went. Afterwards, the apostles 'returned to Jerusalem from the hill called the Mount of Olives, a Sabbath day's walk from the city' (Acts 1:9–12).

According to Christian belief, the Mount of Olives is not only the place of departure but also the place of return. Jesus will come back to the exact same spot to judge all of humanity. The belief in the messianic nature of the Mount as the venue of the Last Judgment is based in essence on the prophecy of Zechariah 14:4, and was shared in different versions with Judaism and Islam as well. It was also manifested in the architecture of the Ascension church, as will be shown below.[27]

In the fourth century, the Mount of Olives became one of Jerusalem's most important holy places. It was part of a topographic triangle commemorating the essential events in the Christian myth: birth (Bethlehem), crucifixion and resurrection (Golgotha and the Holy Sepulchre), and ascension (the Mount of Olives). Soon after the Christianization of the Roman empire under Constantine,

---

25 Adomnán, *De locis sanctis*, 1, 12; Wilkinson, *Jerusalem Pilgrims*, pp. 177–78. The words 'given up into the hands of wicked men' are based on Mark 14:41. Adomnán also tells about the marble column with the image of George the Confessor in Diospolis (Lydda). The fingers of an unbeliever who tried to harm the image penetrated the column and stuck to it 'as if it had been dust or mud [...] The wonder is that to this day one can see the marks where the ten fingers went in up to the knuckles'. (Adomnán, *De locis sanctis*, 3, 4; Wilkinson, *Jerusalem Pilgrims*, pp. 203–04).

26 Bynum, *Dissimilar Similitudes*, p. 227.

27 'On that day his feet will stand on the Mount of Olives, east of Jerusalem, and the Mount of Olives will be split in two from east to west, forming a great valley, with half of the mountain moving north and half moving south'. See Limor, 'The Place of the End of Days'.

DIVINA VESTIGIA 189

a church was erected in each of these places. On the Mount of Olives, however, the Constantinian church was built not at the summit, considered to be the place of the Ascension, but nearby, over a cave where, according to tradition, Jesus delivered his eschatological sermon known as the 'Little Apocalypse' (Mark 13; Matt. 24–25; Luke 21). The church was named Eleona. It would seem that the promise of return was more important to the early Jerusalem church than the departure, or, put otherwise, the departure was just the first step in an eschatological scheme outlined in Jesus's eschatological sermon.

The Eleona, described by the pilgrim Egeria as a very beautiful church ('ecclesia [...] pulchra satis'),[28] played an important role in Jerusalem's liturgy, and was one of the main stations in its 'stational liturgy'. The place of the Ascension itself was described as being some steps away, on a higher spot termed 'Imbomon' by the pilgrim Egeria.[29] As she doesn't mention a church on the site, at the time of her visit it was probably still a roofless spot. According to her description, the Ascension was celebrated there on the fiftieth day after Easter.[30] Shortly after Egeria's departure, a church was built on the spot, as attested by Jerome in his obituary to Paula, dedicated mostly to her pilgrimage journey, which took place in 385. The church was constructed thanks to the generosity of the Roman lady Poemenia, near the place where the wealthy and pious matron Melania the Elder built her monastic establishment and presided over it.[31] A golden cross was erected upon it.[32] This is also the context for the first appearance of the footprints tradition in historical documentation.

* * *

The footprints are first described in a letter of Paulinus, bishop of Nola (near Naples), a kinsman and friend of Melania, to Sulpicius Severus. Paulinus did not visit Jerusalem. Around the year 400, Melania travelled to Rome after twenty years in the East and on her way paid a visit to Paulinus in Nola. She also brought him as a gift a piece of the True Cross.[33] It was on this visit that Melania may have told Paulinus the story of the footprints, which he included in his letter to Sulpicius Severus. It is plausible that with this account she intended to amplify the importance and sacredness of the Mount she chose as the home for her community.[34] Paulinus writes:

---

28 *Itinerarium Egeriae*, 25, 11; Wilkinson, *Egeria's Travels*, p. 127 and index 'Eleona'.
29 *Itinerarium Egeriae*, 31, 1. The Bordeaux Pilgrim speaks of a 'monticulus' ('hillock'). See *Itinerarium Burdigalense*, p. 18; Wilkinson, *Egeria's Travels*, p. 160.
30 *Itinerarium Egeriae*, 43, 5; See Buchinger, 'Liturgy and Topography in Late Antique Jerusalem', p. 122.
31 On Poemenia, see Hunt, *Holy Land Pilgrimage*, pp. 160–63; Devos, 'La "Servante de Dieu" Poemenia'. On Melania the Elder, see Hunt, *Holy Land Pilgrimage*, pp. 168–71; Moine, 'Melaniana'; Murphy, 'Melania the Elder'.
32 Hieronymus, *Epistula 108*, 12, p. 320.
33 Trout, *Paulinus of Nola*, p. 41; Bitton-Ashkelony, *Encountering the Sacred*, pp. 82, 90, 106 n. 1.
34 We can assume that Melania was eager to stress the Mount's sanctity, particularly in light of

In the basilica commemorating the Ascension is the place from which He was taken into a cloud and *ascending on high, led our captivity captive*[35] in His own flesh. That single place and no other is said to have been so hallowed with God's footsteps that it has always rejected a covering of marble or paving. The soil throws off in contempt whatever the human hand tries to set there in eagerness to adorn the place. So in the whole area of the basilica this is the sole spot retaining its natural green appearance of turf. The sand is both visible and accessible to worshippers, and preserves the adored imprint of the divine feet in that dust trodden by God, so that one can truly say: *We have adored in the place where his feet stood.*[36]

Melania's visit to Nola can be seen as the starting point of the 'footprints-in-the-sand' tradition, to be distinguished from the 'footprints-in-the-stone' tradition, which first appears in the twelfth century, as mentioned above. Notably, Paulinus is careful to use the word 'dicitur' — 'is said to have been' — regarding the information he transmitted to Sulpicius Severus.[37] Severus, on his part, was impressed enough to include the information about the footprints in his *Chronicon*:

It is a remarkable fact that the spot on which the divine footprints had last been left when the Lord was carried up in a cloud to heaven could not be joined by a pavement with the remaining part of the street. For the earth, unaccustomed to mere human contact, rejected all the appliances laid upon it, and often threw back the blocks of marble in the faces of those who were seeking to place them. Moreover, it is an enduring proof of the soil of that place having been trodden by God, that the footprints are still to be seen; and although the faith of those who daily flock to that place, leads them to vie with each other in seeking to carry away what had been trodden by the feet of the Lord, yet the sand of the place suffers no injury; and the earth still preserves the same appearance which it presented of old, as if it had been sealed by the footprints impressed upon it.[38]

---

the rivalry with Jerome in Bethlehem. See Desjardins, 'Les Vestiges', pp. 56–57; Hunt, *Holy Land Pilgrimage*, pp. 172–76; Bitton-Ashkelony, *Encountering the Sacred*, pp. 87–90.

35 Eph. 4:8.

36 Cf. Psalms 132:7; 'Mirum vero inter haec quod in basilica ascensionis locus ille tantum de quo in nube susceptus ascendit, captivam in suam carne ducens captivate nostrum, ita sacratus divinis vestigiis dicitur, ut numquam tegi marmore aut paniri receperit semper excussis solo respuente quae manus adorando studio temptavit adponere. Itaque in toto basilicae spatio solus in sui cespitis specie virens permanet et inpressam divinorum pedum venerationem calcati deo pulveris perspicua simul et adtigua venerantibus harena conservat, ut vere dici possit: adoravimus ubi steterunt pedes eius'. Paulinus of Nola, *Epistulae*, 31, 4, pp. 271–72; *The Letters of Saint Paulinus of Nola*, vol. ii, pp. 129–30. See Trout, *Paulinus of Nola*, pp. 129–30.

37 Desjardins, 'Les Vestiges', pp. 56, 58.

38 'Illud mirum, quod locus ille, in quo postremum institerant divina vestigia, cum in caelum Dominus nube sublatus, continuari pavimento cum reliqua stratorum parte non potuit,

Sulpicius Severus added an important detail not included in Paulinus's letter: visitors to the place 'daily' carry away parts of the sanctified earth, but the place remains unscathed, preserving the appearance of the footprints as it was. Notable too is that Severus omitted the word 'dicitur' from his description, thus upgrading it from hearsay to fact. René Desjardins claims convincingly that it was Severus's authority that imparted reliability to the footprints tradition in the Middle Ages.[39]

The footprints are mentioned briefly also by Paulinus's contemporaries Augustine and Prudentius, who probably learned about them from him or from Sulpicius Severus. Augustine sees in the footprints a sign and proof of Jesus's existence in the world in his body: 'ibi sunt vestigiae eius, modo adorantur, ubi novissime stetit, unde ascendit in caelum'.[40] And Prudentius writes: 'Montis Olivifieri Christus de vertice sursum,/ ad Patrem rediit, signans vestigia pacis'.[41]

These four early-fifth-century references (all belong to the same generation and to the same cultural milieu) are our only testimonies of the Ascension footprints previous to the Muslim conquest of Jerusalem in the seventh century. None of these authors visited Jerusalem. At the same time, the footprints are totally absent from texts devoted specifically to Holy Land descriptions, including those that show great interest in traditions of that kind. The *Breviarius de Hierosolyma*, which lists for pilgrims the main attractions of Jerusalem, including the flagellation column, mentions the Mount of Olives in passing but ignores the footprints. Theodosius is much more interested in body imprints. In addition to the flagellation column on Mount Zion, he mentions a place called 'Ancona' situated on the Mount of Olives. There Jesus 'leaned his shoulders on a rock, and both shoulders sank into the rock as if it had been soft wax'.[42] The Ascension footprints are not mentioned by him either. The text of the Piacenza Pilgrim, the most comprehensive, detailed, and colourful of all sixth-century travel narratives, also ignores them. The pilgrim is very interested in relics and sanctified natural materials and also in pilgrimage practices and body gestures performed in the holy places. As noted above, he also mentions Jesus's footprint on the stone where he stood when judged by

---

siquidem quaecumque applicabantur, insolens humana suscipere terra respueret, excussis in ora apponentium saepe marmoribus. Quin etiam calcati Deo pulveris adeo perenne documentum est, ut vestigia impressa cernantur, et cum cotidie confluentium fides certatim Domino calcata diripiat, damnum tamen arena non sentiat, et eandem adhuc sui speciem, velut impressis signata vestigiis, terra custodit'. Sulpicius Severus, *Chronicon*, 2, 33, 6–8; *The Sacred History of Sulpicius Severus*, p. 274.

39 Desjardins, 'Les Vestiges', p. 58.

40 Augustinus, *In Johannis Evangelium Tractatus*, 47, 4, p. 406; See also Augustinus, *De doctrina Cristiana*, 2. 1, 1, p. 32. See Kötting, 'Fußspuren', p. 201.

41 Prudentius, *Carmina*, p. 398.

42 Theodosius, *De Situ Terrae Sanctae*, 21, p. 122. Wilkinson, *Jerusalem Pilgrims*, p. 113. The name 'Ancona' and the tradition it preserves are not mentioned in other sources. The tradition might be based on the apocryphal treatise The Acts of John. See *The Acts of John*, p. 180.

Pilate at the Praetorium, turned into the basilica Saint Sophia. Moreover, the Piacenza Pilgrim was an avid collector of 'blessings', 'measures', and Holy Land souvenirs of all kinds, yet sand from the site of the footprints was not part of his collection.[43] All three texts do refer to the Ascension Church, which was, as already mentioned, one of the most important churches in Jerusalem, but the footprints are missing from their descriptions. Of course, an argument from silence is always problematic. And no Holy Land description can be expected to include an exhaustive list of traditions and places. But the fact that all three sixth-century texts ignore a phenomenon as significant as the Ascension footprints places its very existence at their time into question.

* * *

Like other churches and monasteries in Jerusalem, the Ascension Church was damaged by the Persian capture of the city in 614, but was restored after the city returned to Christian hands. Christian pilgrims visited it throughout the first Muslim period (638–1099) and it was also venerated by Muslims, a fact that may have helped to preserve it.[44] Adomnán of Iona, mentioned above, was the first author to describe the Christian holy places of Jerusalem after the end of Christian rule of the city. In his comprehensive text, written in the late seventh century, he devoted an elaborate chapter to the Ascension church, which seems second in glory and importance only to the Church of the Holy Sepulchre. The chapter includes a detailed architectural description, an account of the celebration in the church on Ascension Day, and a paragraph devoted to the footprints.[45] According to Adomnán, his information about the church derived from both written and oral sources. The oral evidence was that of the pilgrim Arculf, a bishop from Gaul who told Adomnán about his travels to the East. Arculf described a round church with a central area that was open to the sky, without roof or vaulting, and explained that 'from the place where the divine feet rested for the last time when the Lord was raised up to heaven in a cloud, there should always be an open passage leading to the ethereal regions for the eyes of those who pray there'.[46]

While the architectural description and the account of the Ascension celebration seem to be based on oral information (or at least no written source has been thus far found), the account of the footprints is based on the Chronicle of Sulpicius Severus from whom Adomnán copied nearly verbatim. Adomnán writes:

---

43 See Limor, 'Earth, Stone, Water and Oil'.

44 Visits of Muslims to the church raised criticism from Muslim religious authorities. See Elad, *Medieval Jerusalem and Islamic Worship*, pp. 145–46.

45 See Limor, 'Wondrous Nature'.

46 'Ideo itaque interior illa domus cameram supra collocatam non habet ut de illo loco in quo postremum divina institerant vestigia cum in caelum Dominus in nube sublatus est via semper aperta et ad ethera caelorum directa oculis in eodem loco exorantium pateat'. *Adamnan's De locis sanctis*, ed. by Meehan, 1, 23, pp. 64–65 [= Adamnanus, *De locis sanctis libri tres*, ed. by Bieler, p. 199].

DIVINA VESTIGIA   193

Because, when this basilica (of which a few details are now being recorded) was being built, the place of the Lord's footprints (as is found written in other sources) could not be incorporated in a pavement with the rest of the floor. For the ground (unwont to bear anything human) would reject whatever was laid upon it, casting the marble into the faces of those who were laying it. Nay more, so lasting is the proof that the dust was trodden by God that the imprints of the feet are visible; and, though crowds of the faithful daily plunder the earth trodden by the Lord, still the spot suffers no perceptible damage, and the ground goes on keeping the semblance as it were of footprints. Thus, in this spot, as the holy Arculf (a sedulous visitor of it) relates, a huge bronze circular structure has been set up, levelled out on the top [...] In the middle of it is quite a large perforation, and when this is open the footprints of the Lord are pointed out plainly and clearly stamped on the dust. Also, at the western side of the structure, there is a sort of a door always open, so that people entering by it can easily approach the place of the sacred dust and take particles of it by stretching in their hands through the open perforation in the circular structure.[47]

As can be clearly seen, the core of the footprints description is the lines copied from Severus. Arculf corroborates the information gleaned from Severus while adding some architectural details.

Rivers of ink have flowed on the 'problem of Arculf'. Against the old school that ascribed the information in the book to the pilgrim Arculf, scholars have set out to reclaim the book for its author, Adomnán, and also to reduce to a minimum Arculf's contribution to its formation. Some have even gone so far as to claim that a pilgrim named Arculf never existed.[48] The problematic facticity of Arculf also places into question the information ascribed to him. Lawrence

---

47 (The sentences in italics are copied from Sulpicius Severus). 'Nam cum haec de qua nunc pauca commemorantur basilica fabricaretur, idem locus vestigiorum Domini, ut alibi scriptum repertum est, *contenuari pavimento cum reliqua stratorum parte non potuit, siquidem quaecumque adplicabantur insolens humana suscipere terra respueret in ora adponentium excussis marmoribus. Quin etiam calcati Deo pulveris adeo perenne est documentum ut vestigia cernantur inpressa, et cum cotidie confluentium fides a Domino calcata diripiat, damnum tamen arena non sentit et eandem adhuc sui speciem veluti inpraesis signata vestigiis terra custodit.* In eodem igitur loco, ut sanctus refert Arculfus, sedulus eiusdem frequentator, aerea grandis per circuitum rota desuper explanata collocata est, cuius altitudo usque cervicem haberi monstratur mensurata. In cuius medietate non parva patet pertussura, per quam desuper apertam vestigia pedum Domini plane et lucide inpressa in puluere demonstratur. Illa quoque in rota ab occidental parte quasi quaedam semper patet porta, ut per eam intrantes facile adire locum sacrati pulueris possint et per apertum desuper eiusdem rotae foramen de sacro puluere porrectis minibus particulas sumant'. *Adamnan's De locis sanctis,* ed. by Meehan, 1, 23, pp. 64–67. [= Adamnanus, *De locis sanctis libri tres,* ed. by Bieler, pp. 199–200]. It should be noted that Adomnán's concern was a theological one. Through the description of the building, he aimed to teach a lesson about the nature of Jesus. Only as a god could Jesus ascend to heaven through the open roof, and only as a human could he leave behind his footsteps. See Kötting, 'Fußspuren', p. 200.

48 For example: Delierneux, 'Arculfe, *sanctus episcopus gente Gallus*'. See a summary of the issue in Nees, *Perspectives,* pp. 33–57.

Nees has claimed that the evidence of Adomnán's *De locis sanctis* cannot be taken 'as an accurately transmitted eye-witness account and a reliable basis for understanding what was happening in seventh-century Jerusalem'.[49] In the past I have been reluctant to dismiss Arculf as a witness, because it seems clear that Adomnán also relies on an oral report (or reports).[50] Nevertheless, it would seem that in the description of the footprints at the Ascension Church, Arculf plays an ancillary role, namely, to support the account of Severus, who, for Adomnán, is an unquestionable authority. While the architectural component of the description, namely, the 'huge bronze circular structure' marking the place from which Jesus ascended to heaven was indeed part of the church,[51] the details about the believers who take particles from the dust seem to paraphrase and embellish the tale supplied by Severus, with the addition of a bit of 'religious imagination'.[52]

The Venerable Bede is the next link in the chain. In a short text also titled *De locis sanctis* (written in 703 or 704), Bede summarized Adomnán's book in simple language, including only what seemed to him as the most vital information about the holy places.[53] The author's prestige, combined with the modest scope of his book, made it an important source of information about the holy places for hundreds of years. Bede included in his book an abbreviated version of the footprints story:

> The inside of the house because of the route taken by the Lord's body, cannot be roofed or covered. Its altar is on the east protected by a narrow roof, and in the centre the Lord's last footprints are to be seen with sky above into which he went up. And though believers daily take away the earth, none the less it remains there, and retains the same appearance as before as if marked deeply with footprints.[54]

As can be seen, Bede kept Severus's information, omitting Adomnán's additional details. Similar information is given by Bede in his *Ecclesiastical History of the English People*, in a homily on the Ascension and in his *Expositio* on place names in the book of Acts.[55] These early medieval texts by two authors who

---

49 Nees, *Perspectives*, p. 56.

50 Limor, 'Pilgrims and Authors'.

51 See below, Willibald's description of the church..

52 See Aist, *From Topography to Text*, pp. 40–47. Aist writes: '[Adomnán's] interpretation of Arculf's report, his integration of sources and the ways in which the Holy Land material was filtered through the theological perspectives of Iona speak to the *religious imagination* of Adomnán' (p. 43). Italics are mine.

53 Beda Venerabilis, *De locis sanctis*. Bede attached much importance to the Ascension. See O'Neill, 'Imag(in)ing the Holy Places'.

54 'Interior namque domus propter dominici corporis meatum camerari et tegi non potuit; altare ad orientem habens angusto culmine protectum, in cuius medio ultima Domini vestigia caelo desuper patente, ubi ascendit, visuntur. Quae cum cotidie a credentibus terra tollatur, nihilominus manet eandemque adhuc sui speciem veluti inpressis signata vestigiis servat'. Beda Venerabilis, *De locis sanctis*, pp. 262–63; Wilkinson, *Jerusalem Pilgrims*, p. 222.

55 Beda Venerabilis, *Historia ecclesiastica gentis Anglorum*, 5, 15–17; Homily on the Ascension:

did not visit Jerusalem, one of them drawing on the other, are also offshoots of Sulpicius Severus's text, and they gained wide reception. Adomnán's *De locis sanctis* survived in twenty-two manuscripts and fragments, Bede's *De locis sanctis* in forty-seven manuscripts and his *Ecclesiastical History* in 157. This wide distribution secured the embedding of the tradition in Christian culture, both written and visual, in the West.

Apart from Adomnán, none of the Holy Land descriptions written in the first Muslim period mention the footprints. This includes the two eighth-century texts — Hygeburg's *Life of Willibald*, based on the protagonist's report of his pilgrimage, and the *Guide to the Holy Places* by Epiphanius Hagiopolites.[56] Both mentioned the Ascension Church and the place from which Jesus ascended to heaven but not the footprints. Epiphanius writes briefly: 'Not far to the north of the place of teaching is a church, in the middle of which is the stone where Christ stood when he was taken up, and it is called the Holy Stone.'[57] While Epiphanius is the first to mention a stone in that place, he does not mention any footprints. Willibald's description is longer and more detailed:

> From that [Gethsemane] he went to a church on the mountain itself, where the Lord ascended into heaven. In the centre of it is a square brass object which is beautifully engraved. It is in the centre of the church where the Lord ascended into heaven. And in the middle of the brass object is a square lantern with a small candle inside. The lantern encloses the candle on all sides. It is enclosed in this way so it will continue to burn, rain or fine. That church has no roof, and it is open to the sky [...][58]

The 'brass object' seems to be the 'huge bronze circular structure' mentioned by Adomnán as protecting the footprints. According to Willibald, in the middle of it there is a lantern with a candle burning day and night. Willibald was impressed by the open roof and by the two pillars standing in the Ascension Church, but the footprints were not part of his Jerusalem reminiscences.[59]

Beda Venerabilis, *Homilia 9 in Ascensione Domini*, col. 177; Beda Venerabilis, *Expositio in nomine locorum*, col. 1039.

56 Willibald was in the East in the years 722–29. His *Vita*, including the pilgrimage account, was written in 778. Epiphanius's description is dated to the seventh or the eighth century. See Donner, 'Die Palästinabeschreibung des Epiphanius Monachus Hagiopolita', p. 44.

57 Donner, 'Die Palästinabeschreibung des Epiphanius Monachus', p. 88; Wilkinson, *Jerusalem Pilgrims*, p. 214.

58 'Et in medio aecclesiae stat de aere factum sculptum ac speciosum ac est quadrans, illud stat in medio aecclesie, ubi Dominus ascendit in caelum; et in medio aereo est factum vitreum quadrangulum et ibi est vitreo parvum cisindulum, et circa cisindulum est illud vitreum undique clausum, et ideo est undique clausum, ut semper adere possit in pluvia sed et in sole. Illa aecclesia est desuper patula et sine tectu'. Iadanza, *Vita Willibaldi episcopi Eichstetensis*, p. 32; Wilkinson, *Jerusalem Pilgrims*, p. 243. A round roofless church is mentioned also by Bernard the Monk, 15. See Ackermann, *Das 'Itinerarium Bernardi Monachi'*, p. 123; Wilkinson, *Jerusalem Pilgrims*, p. 267.

59 On Willibald's description, see Aist, *The Christian Topography of Early Islamic Jerusalem*, pp. 202–15.

Yet Jerusalem was far away, and authoritative texts written by distinguished scholars were close at hand. Thus, the chain of transmission of the 'footprints-in-the-sand' tradition grew longer and extended into the High Middle Ages and beyond. Following Adomnán and Bede, other Anglo-Saxon authors also mentioned the footprints. The poet Cynewulf, who probably lived in the ninth century, mentions the footprints in his poem 'Christ II' or 'The Ascension'. Like Bede, he, too, seems to rely on Adomnán's description.[60] The Blicking Homily (tenth century), dedicated to the Ascension, also notes them:

> They [the footprints] always remain as complete and of the same appearance as when they were first impressed upon the ground. Our Lord let His holy feet sink into the ground there as an everlasting reminder to humankind when after His holy passion He brought His human nature into heaven, from whence by reason of His eternal Godhead He had never departed. Those footsteps are still imprinted upon the ground until now, as is clearly manifested by their completeness and by numerous wonders of the creator.[61]

The homily, in turn, influenced visual art.[62] Art historian Meyer Schapiro writes that although the footprints motif is a specifically Gothic element, belonging to the later, more developed cult of the physical person of Christ, it has antecedents in Anglo-Saxon art of the tenth century.[63]

The most influential collection of hagiographies, *The Golden Legend* (*Legenda Aurea*), compiled in the mid-thirteenth century, relies on Sulpicius's evidence from the early fifth century about the footsteps in the sand:

> Concerning the place of the Ascension, Sulpicius, the bishop of Jerusalem says, and the Gloss likewise reports, that when at a later time a church was built there, the spot whereon the feet of Christ had rested could not be covered with paving-stones. The marble slabs which were laid there broke in pieces, and burst in the faces of those who were setting them. And he says that in the dust where Christ trod the marks of His step can still be seen, and the earth still bears the print of His foot.[64]

As late as the seventeenth century, the learned Franciscan friar Franciscus Quaresmius describes the footprint in the stone (of the two footprints, only the left one remained) and adds: 'Est ille locus, quem numquam potuisse

---

60 On Cynewulf, see Schapiro, 'The Image', p. 142; Desjardins, 'Les Vestiges', p. 60.

61 *The Blicking Homilies*, p. 89; See Schapiro, 'The Image', pp. 140–41. The theologian Honorius Augustodunensis (*c.* 1080–*c.* 1140) also read Adomnán's description of the footprints and used it in his homily on the Ascension. See Honorius Augustodunensis, *In Ascensione Domini, Speculum Ecclesiae*, col. 958. For other spiritual mentions, see Desjardins, 'Les Vestiges', pp. 64–66.

62 For artistic representations, see Schapiro, 'The Image'; Worm, 'Steine und Fußspuren'. According to Worm, the Ascension stone motif appears in Christian art around 1100 (pp. 297–98). See also Desjardins, 'Les Vestiges', pp. 67–72.

63 Schapiro, 'The Image', p. 143.

64 de Voragine, *The Golden Legend*, p. 287.

concamerari ait Paulinus cum aliis'.[65] For Quaresmius, the tradition of the footprints in the sand described by Paulinus and the footprint in the stone he observed with his own eyes were one and the same.

And thus, Paulinus's information, as phrased and embellished by Sulpicius Severus and echoed by Adomnán and Bede, held fast in the European topographical imagination and became part of the iconographic and literary lexicon of Christianity. Once Jerusalem returned to Christian rule in the twelfth century, the tradition was brought back there. This time, the footprints were imprinted in stone, not in sand, a fact that secured their longevity. This tradition survives until today, despite variants in descriptions and rival traditions.[66]

* * *

We might well ask: Why did the early footprints tradition, that of the footprints in the sand reported by Paulinus, not take root in Jerusalem itself? If the footprints were attested at the Ascension Church in Melania's days, why did they disappear soon afterwards — or at least leave little impression in Holy Land descriptions? I shall offer a few thoughts on the matter, all of them tentative, as absence is much harder to explain than presence.

There is a clear difference between the other body prints of Jesus shown in Jerusalem and the Ascension footprints. While Jesus's hands and face on the flagellation column, his footprint at Saint Sophia, and his knee in the Gethsemane rock, all belong to his human entity and were left behind before his crucifixion and resurrection, the Ascension footprints were impressed by the resurrected Jesus and thus by a divine entity. According to the accepted Christian dogma, in line with the descriptions in Luke and Acts, Jesus resurrected both in body and in soul.[67] However, this contradicted Paul, who maintained that the resurrected would have only a spiritual body.[68] Such considerations bring up the short description in the apocryphal treatise The Acts of John: 'And I often wished, as I walked with him, to see if his footprints appeared on the ground — for I saw him raising himself from the earth — and I never saw it'.[69] Earlier in the same text, the author describes how he once saw Jesus

---

65 Baldi, *Enchiridion locorum sanctorum*, p. 426. Franciscus Quaresmius (1583–1650) travelled to Jerusalem several times. His book, *Historica Theologica et Moralis Terrae Sanctae Elucidatio*, was published in 1639.

66 From the thirteenth century on, there are references to the Ascension stone bearing the footprint of Christ in Westminster Abbey. The last reference dates to 1520, shortly before the Monastery of Westminster was dissolved and the stone disappeared with other relics. See Desjardins, 'Les Vestiges', p. 63.

67 See Luke 24:36–43; Acts 1:3–4; John 20:1–29.

68 See i Cor 15:42–44, 50; Phil. 2:6–7; over time, Jesus's resurrection in the flesh became the dominant doctrine, and Augustine had to defend it against Manichee attacks. See Augustine, *De civitate Dei*, 22: 21; Fredriksen, *When Christians were Jews*, p. 82. I am grateful to my friend and colleague Paula Fredriksen for helping to clarify this point.

69 *The Acts of John*, p. 181. But see, conversely, *Epistula Apostolorum*, 11, p. 256, where Jesus maintains that he was resurrected in the body: 'Andrew, see whether my foot steps on the ground and leaves a footprint'.

praying and 'his feet […] were whiter than snow, so that the ground there was lit up by his feet…'.[70] Bernhard Kötting has explained as follows: 'If the representative of the humanity of Christ, the body, is just a pseudo-body then he cannot leave any impressions while going'.[71]

Following these descriptions, we may wonder whether there were some protagonists of the Jerusalem Church who might have been puzzled by the theological implications of the footprints.

More generally speaking, the attribution of Psalms 132:7 — 'Let us go to his dwelling place. Let us worship at his footstool' — as referring to the footprints implied a drastic hermeneutical move from the allegorical to the material. Such a move created uneasiness in certain circles. As Brouria Bitton-Ashkelony has observed: 'This attribution of a territorial dimension to the verse is new in comparison with earlier Christian allegorical exegesis'.[72]

In her discussion of the footprints, Caroline Walker Bynum relates to the transition of the tradition from sand to stone and maintains that 'the change of medium mattered less than modern theories suggest it should be […] In both cases, part(icle) transfers whole. Although differently malleable, sand and stone equally retain presence, transfer holiness, and endure rather than dissipate'.[73] While from all aspects discussed by Bynum this is indeed true, sand and stone still differ from other perspectives, differences that may explain the endurance of the flagellation column tradition or of the stone footprints, against the short life, if any, of the sand footprints. Stone is solid, tangible, respectable, and static, in contrast to sand, which is elusive, fragile, modest, and dynamic. On the one hand, the footprints in the sand were a much more dramatic phenomenon than the footprints in the stone shown in later centuries. While the footprints in the stone were a memorial to the Ascension, the sand footprints were a miracle that happened constantly, that is, a permanent miracle. The sand, we are told, was taken daily by the believers but never failed, manifesting God's presence in that place. On the other hand, these footprints were also hard to preserve. They assumed the constant intervention of the divine, and thus demanded the constant care of human agents. It was easier to tell about them than to preserve them.

In sum, it would seem that prior to the Crusader period, the footprints tradition was preserved mainly as text, not as texture. While the spot from where Jesus ascended to heaven was marked architecturally and described in most itineraries of the first millennium, the 'footprints-in-the-sand' was a literary tradition that developed outside the Holy Land. Absent from eyewitness descriptions, it remained present in Christian literature, and later also in Christian artistic culture. None of the authorities that transmitted the

---

70 *The Acts of John*, p. 180.

71 Kötting, 'Fußspuren', p. 199 ('Ist der Repräsentant der Menschheit Christi, der Leib, nur ein Scheinleib, dann kann er keine Eindrücke beim Gehen hinterlassen'.).

72 Bitton-Ashkelony, *Encountering the Sacred*, p. 82.

73 Bynum, *Dissimilar Similitudes*, p. 243.

tradition had visited Jerusalem: Paulinus of Nola, Sulpicius Severus, Augustine, Prudentius, Adomnán, Bede, the author of the Blicking Homily, Jacobus da Voragine — all depended on a single informant from the early fifth century who transmitted the story to Paulinus. The informant was likely Melania the Elder herself, who aimed to advertise the place of her monastery at the summit of the Mount of Olives by pitching its unique sacrality and miraculous nature. Paulinus's report, as rephrased by Sulpicius Severus and echoed by other authors and artists, remained alive in European Christian culture. At the same time, the tradition and practice described in this information left no traces in reports of eyewitnesses. One attempt to link this literary tradition with Jerusalem's reality was made by Adomnán, but the account brought by him is problematic. The tradition was upheld in European culture, both verbally and artistically, until it was imported back to Jerusalem by the crusaders, or rather reinvented by them in the twelfth century, and this time imprinted in stone. The stone is documented in many pilgrimage accounts. In some of them, the old literary tradition is recruited to support the credibility of the footsteps and guarantee their veracity. The substantial difference between sand and stone was forgotten.[74]

A different question, which pertains to a later period than the one at hand, is the possible connection between the appearance in the twelfth century of the Ascension stone with the footprints and the footstep of Muhammad that was shown on the Rock at the Temple Mount, a tradition recorded since the late eleventh century.[75] The dialogue between the Muslim and the Christian footprints traditions is an intriguing example of a shared yet competing tradition. However, discussion of it lies beyond the scope of this study.

Today, the Ascension chapel on the Mount of Olives is visited by groups of pilgrims who touch the stone, anoint it, place personal belongings in the concavity supposed to be Jesus's footprint, kiss it, and cry over it. They are a link in a long chain of believers for whom this is the last point on earth touched by divinity, and thus the closest place to heaven on earth.

---

74 See for example the abovementioned description of the Quaresmius.

75 See Elad, *Medieval Jerusalem*, pp. 70–72; Worm, 'Steine und Fußspuren', p. 313; van Ess, "Abd al-Malik and the Dome of the Rock'. The Christians who conquered Jerusalem in 1099 were quick to appropriate this tradition, as attested by Saewulf, who visited the Holy Land shortly after the conquest (1101–1103). He writes: 'There the footprints of the Lord (vestigia domini) still appear in the rock when he hid himself and left the Temple, as we read in the Gospel, in order that the Jews should not throw the stones they were carrying'. Saewulf, in *Peregrinationes Tres*, p. 68; Wilkinson, *Jerusalem Pilgrimage*, p. 105; cf. John 8:59.

Bibliography

Primary Sources

Ackermann, Josef, *Das 'Itinerarium Bernardi Monachi': Edition – Übersetzung – Kommentar*, Monumenta Germaniae Historica: Studien und Texte, 50 (Hannover: Hahn, 2010)

The Acts of John, New Testament Apocrypha, revised edn, vol. ii, ed. by Edgar Hennecke and Wilhelm Schneemelcher, trans. by R. McL. Wilson (Cambridge: James Clarke, 1991), pp. 152–212

Adamnan's De locis sanctis, ed. by Denis Meehan, Scriptores Latini Hiberniae, 3 (Dublin: The Dublin Institute for Advanced Studies, 1958)

Adamnanus, De locis sanctis libri tres, ed. by Ludwig Bieler, Corpus Christianorum Series Latina, 175 (Turnhout: Brepols, 1965), pp. 175–234

Antonini Placentini Itinerarium, ed. by P. Geyer, Corpus Christianorum Series Latina, 175 (Turnhout: Brepols, 1965), pp. 127–174

Augustinus, *De doctrina Cristiana*, ed. by K. D. Daur and J. Martin, Corpus Christianorum Series Latina, 32 (Turnhout: Brepols, 1953)

——, *In Johannis Evangelium Tractatus*, ed. by D. Radbodus Willems, Corpus Christianorum Series Latina, 36 (Turnhout: Brepols, 1954)

The Autobiography of St Ignatius of Loyola, trans. by Joseph F. O'Callaghan, ed. with introduction and notes by John C. Olin (New York: Harper Torchbooks, 1974)

Baldi, Donatus, *Enchiridion Locorum Sanctorum* (Jerusalem: Franciscan Printing, 1955)

Beda Venerabilis, *De locis sanctis*, ed. by J. Fraipont, Corpus Christianorum Series Latina, 175 (Turnhout: Brepols, 1965), pp. 245–280

——, *Expositio in nomine locorum*, ed. by Jacques-Paul Migne, Patrologiae cursus completus: series latina, 92 (Paris: Garnier, 1844–1864), cols 1033–39

——, *Historia ecclesiastica gentis Anglorum*, ed. and trans. by Bertram Colgrave and Roger Aubrey Baskerville Mynors (Oxford: Oxford University Press, 1969)

——, *Homilia 9 in Ascensione Domini*, ed. by Jacques-Paul Migne, Patrologiae cursus completus: series latina, 94 (Paris: Garnier, 1844–1864), cols 174–81

The Blicking Homilies, ed. and trans. by Richard J. Kelly (London: Continuum, 2003)

Breviarius de Hierosolyma, ed. by R. Weber, Corpus Christianorum Series Latina, 175 (Turnhout: Brepols, 1965), pp. 105–112

Donner, Herbert, 'Die Palästinabeschreibung des Epiphanius Monachus Hagiopolita', *Zeitschrift des Deutschen Palästina-Vereins*, 87.1 (1971), 42–91

Epistula Apostolorum, New Testament Apocrypha, revised edn, vol. i, ed. by Wilhelm Schneemelcher, trans. by R. McL. Wilson (Cambridge: James Clarke, 1991), pp. 252–84

Gregory of Tours, *Glory of the Martyrs*, trans. by Raymond Van Dam (Liverpool: Liverpool University Press, 1988)

Gregorius Turonensis, *Liber in Gloria Martyrum*, ed. by Bruno Krusch, Monumenta Germaniae Historica: Scriptores Rerum Merovingicarum, 1, 2 (Hanover: Hahn, 1885)

Hieronymus, *Epistula 108* (Epitaphium sanctae Paulae), ed. by Isidorus Hilberg, Corpus Scriptorum Ecclesiasticorum Latinorum, 55 (Vienna: F. Tempsky, 1912), pp. 306–351

Honorius Augustodunensis, *In Ascensione Domini, Speculum Ecclesiae*, ed. by Jacques-Paul Migne, Patrologiae cursus completus: series latina, 172 (Paris: Garnier, 1844–1864), cols 955–60

Iadanza, Mario, *Vita Willibaldi episcopi Eichstetensis: il vescovo Willibald e la monaca Hugeburc: la scrittura a quattro mani di un'esperienza odeporica del'VIII secolo* (Florence: Edizioni del Galluzzo, 2011)

The Itineraries of William Wey, ed. and trans. by Francis Davey (Oxford: Bodleian Library, 2010)

The Itinerary of R. Petahiah of Regensburg, ed. by Elazar Halevi Grünhut (Frankfurt: Kauffmann, 1905) (in Hebrew)

Itinerarium Burdigalense, ed. by P. Geyer and Otto Cuntz, Corpus Christianorum Series Latina, 175 (Turnhout: Brepols, 1965), pp. 1–26

Itinerarium Egeriae, ed. by E. Franceschini and R. Weber, Corpus Christianorum Series Latina, 175 (Turnhout: Brepols, 1965), pp. 27–90

The Letters of Saint Paulinus of Nola, trans. and annotated by P. G. Walsh, vol. ii (New York: Newman Press, 1966–1967)

Paulinus of Nola, *Epistulae*, ed. by Wilhelm Hartel, Corpus Scriptorum Ecclesiasticorum Latinorum, 29 (Vienna: P. Tempsky, 1894)

Peregrinationes Tres: Saewulf, John of Würzburg, Theodericus, ed. by R. B. C. Huygens, Corpus Christianorum Continuatio Mediaevalis, 139 (Turnhout: Brepols, 1994)

Pringle, Denys, *Pilgrimage to Jerusalem and the Holy Land 1187–1291* (Burlington: Ashgate, 2012)

Prudentius, *Carmina*, ed. by Mauricius Cunningham, Corpus Christianorum Series Latina, 126 (Turnhout: Brepols, 1966)

The Sacred History of Sulpicius Severus, trans. by Philip Schaff, Nicene and Post-Nicene Fathers, 211 (repr. Grand Rapids: Christian Classics Ethereal Library, 1885)

Saint Ignatius of Loyola, Personal Writings, trans. with introduction and notes by Joseph A. Munitiz and Philip Endean (London: Penguin, 1996)

Sulpicius Severus, *Chronicon*, ed. by Karl Halm, Corpus Scriptorum Ecclesiasticorum Latinorum, 1 (Vienna: Karl Gerold d.J., 1866)

Theodosius, *De Situ Terrae Sanctae*, ed. by P. Geyer, Corpus Christianorum Series Latina, 175 (Turnhout: Brepols, 1965), pp. 115–125

Tobler, Titus, *Descriptiones Terrae Sanctae* (Leipzig: Hinrichs, 1874; repr. Hildesheim, 1974)

de Voragine, Jacobus, *The Golden Legend*, trans. by Granger Ryan and Helmut Ripperger (New York: Longmans, Green and Co., 1941)

Wilkinson, John, *Egeria's Travels* (London: S.P.C.K., 1971)

——, *Jerusalem Pilgrims before the Crusades* (Warminster: Aris & Phillips, 2002)

——, with Joyce Hill and W. F. Ryan, *Jerusalem Pilgrimage 1099–1185* (London: Hakluyt Society, 1988)

Secondary Studies

Aist, Rodney, *The Christian Topography of Early Islamic Jerusalem: The Evidence of Willibald of Eichstätt (700–87 CE)* (Turnhout: Brepols, 2009)

——, *From Topography to Text: The Image of Jerusalem in the Writings of Eucherius, Adomnán and Bede* (Turnhout: Brepols, 2018)

Arad, Pnina, 'Pilgrimage, Cartography, and Devotion: William Wey's Map of the Holy Land', *Viator*, 43.1 (2012), 301–22

Arnold, John Charles, 'Arcadia Becomes Jerusalem: Angelic Caverns and Shrine Conversion at Monte Gargano', *Speculum*, 75 (2000), 567–88

Bitton-Ashkelony, Brouria, *Encountering the Sacred: The Debate on Christian Pilgrimage in Late Antiquity* (Berkeley: University of California Press, 2005)

Buchinger, Harald, 'Liturgy and Topography in Late Antique Jerusalem', in *Jerusalem II: Jerusalem in Roman-Byzantine Times*, ed. by Katharina Heyden and Maria Lissek (Tübingen: Mohr Siebeck, 2021), pp. 117–88

Bynum, Caroline Walker, *Christian Materiality: An Essay on Religion in Late Medieval Europe* (New York: Zone, 2011)

——, *Dissimilar Similitudes: Devotional Objects in Late Medieval Europe* (New York: Zone, 2020)

Castiglione, László, 'Vestigia', *Acta Archaeologica*, 22 (1970), 95–132

Delierneux, Nathalie, 'Arculfe, *sanctus episcopus gente Gallus*: une existence historique discutable', *Revue belge de philologie et d'histoire*, 75 (1997), 911–41

Desjardins, René, 'Les Vestiges du Seigneur au mont des Oliviers', *Bulletin de Litterature Ecclesiastique*, 73 (1972), 51–72

Devos, Pierre, 'La "Servante de Dieu" Poemenia', *Analecta Bollandiana*, 87 (1969), 189–212

Donkin, Lucy, 'Stones of St Michael: Venerating Fragments of Holy Ground in Medieval France and Italy', in *Matter of Faith: An Interdisciplinary Study of Relics and Relic Veneration in the Medieval Period*, ed. by James Robinson and Lloyd de Beer with Anna Harnden (London: British Museum, 2014), pp. 23–31

Dunbabin, Katerine M. D., '*Ipsa deae vestigia…* Footprints Divine and Human on Graeco-Roman Monuments', *Journal of Roman Archaeology*, 3 (1990), 85–109

Elad, Amikam, *Medieval Jerusalem and Islamic Worship: Holy Places, Ceremonies, Pilgrimage* (Leiden: Brill, 1999)

Fredriksen, Paula, *When Christians were Jews: The First Generation* (New Haven: Yale University Press, 2018)

Fritz, Jean-Marie, 'Empreintes et vestiges dans les récits de pèlerinage: quand la pierre devient cire', *Le Moyen Âge*, 118 (2012), 9–40

Hunt, E. D., *Holy Land Pilgrimage in the Later Roman Empire (AD 312–460)* (Oxford: Clarendon Press, 1982)

Kister, Meir J., 'Maqām Ibrāhīm: A Stone with an Inscription', *Le Muséon*, 84 (1971), 477–91

Kötting, Bernhard, 'Fußspuren als Zeichen göttlicher Anwesenheit', *Boreas*, 6 (1983), 197–201

Limor, Ora, 'Earth, Stone, Water and Oil: Objects of Veneration in Holy Land Travel Narratives', in *Natural Materials of the Holy Land and the Visual Translation of Place 500–1500*, ed. by Renana Bartal, Neta Bodner, and Bianca Kühnel (London: Routledge, 2017), pp. 3–18

——, 'Pilgrims and Authors: Adomnán's *De locis sanctis* and Hugeburc's *Hodoeporicon Sancti Willibaldi*', *Revue Bénédictine*, 114 (2004), 253–75

——, 'The Place of the End of Days: Eschatological Geography in Jerusalem', *Journal of Jewish Art (The Real and the Ideal Jerusalem in Jewish, Christian and Islamic Art)*, 23 (1997/8), 13–22

——, 'Wondrous Nature: Landscape and Weather in Early Medieval Pilgrimage Narratives', in *Jews and Journeys: Travel and the Performance of Jewish Identity*, ed. by Joshua Levinson and Orit Bashkin (Philadelphia: University of Pennsylvania Press, 2021), pp. 46–62

McGinn, Bernard, *Visions of the End: Apocalyptic Traditions in the Middle Ages* (New York: Columbia University Press, 1998)

Moine, Nicole, 'Melaniana', *Recherches augustiniennes*, 15 (1980), 3–79

Murphy, Francis X., 'Melania the Elder: A Biographical Note', *Traditio*, 5 (1947), 59–77

Nees, Lawrence, *Perspectives on Early Islamic Art in Jerusalem* (Leiden: Brill, 2015)

O'Neill, Patrick P., 'Imag(in)ing the Holy Places: A Comparison between the Diagrams in Adomnán's and Bede's De locis sanctis', *Journal of Literary Onomastics*, 6 (2017), Iss. 1, Article 5

Pringle, Denys, *The Churches of the Crusader Kingdom of Jerusalem: A Corpus*, vol. iii (Cambridge: Cambridge University Press, 2007)

Rachman-Schrire, Yamit, 'Evagatorium in Terrae Sanctae: Stones Telling the Story of Jerusalem', in *Jerusalem as Narrative Space*, ed. by Annette Hoffmann and Gerhard Wolf (Leiden: Brill, 2012), pp. 353–66

Reiner, Elchanan, 'From Joshua to Jesus: The Transformation of a Biblical Story to a Local Myth. A Chapter in the Religious Life of the Galilean Jew', in *Sharing the Sacred: Religious Contacts and Conflicts in the Holy Land*, ed. by Arieh Kofsky and Guy G. Stroumsa (Jerusalem: Yad Izhak Ben-Zvi, 1998), pp. 223–71

Sarfati, Rachel, *The Florence Scroll: A 14th-Century Pictorial Pilgrimage from Egypt to the Land of Israel* (Jerusalem: The Israel Museum and Yad Izhak Ben-Zvi, 2020) (in Hebrew)

Schapiro, Meyer, 'The Image of the Disappearing Christ: The Ascension in English Art around the Year 1000', *Gazette des Beaux-Arts*, 23 (March 1943), 135–52

Shalev, Zur, 'Christian Pilgrimage and Ritual Measurement in Jerusalem', *Max Planck Institute for the History of Science / preprint*, 384 (2009), 10–11

Takács, Sarolta A., 'Divine and Human Feet: Records of Pilgrims Honouring Isis', in *Pilgrimage in Graeco-Roman and Early Christian Antiquity: Seeing the Gods*, ed. by Jaś Elsner and Ian Rutherford (Oxford: Oxford University Press, 2005), pp. 353–69

Trout, Dennis E., *Paulinus of Nola: Life, Letters, and Poems* (Berkeley: University of California Press, 1999)

van Ess, Josef, '"Abd al-Malik and the Dome of the Rock: An Analysis of Some Texts', in *Kleine Schriften*, ed. by Hinrich Biesterfeldt (Leiden: Brill, 2018), pp. 1085–20

Worm, Andrea, 'Steine und Fußspuren Christi auf dem Ölberg: Zu zwei ungewohnlichen Motiven bei der Himmelfahrt Chrisi', *Zeitschrift für Kunstgeschichte*, 66 (2003), 297–320

DANIEL R. SCHWARTZ

Reinach and Stephanus, Philo and Josephus

A Note on the Testimonium Flavianum

Introduction: A Phrase in the *Testimonium*

In historical philology as elsewhere, sometimes it happens that an attempt to track down the genesis of a puzzling scholarly opinion results, disappointingly, only in the determination that it arose out of nothing more than some elementary misunderstanding. Or, perhaps, that it is based on a text that does not really exist. Or both. Even in such an extreme case, however, such as the one identified in this brief study of a famous passage in Josephus that has often been laid at the feet of our honoree's favourite, Eusebius, it can happen that the peregrinations entailed along the way to that determination not only allow us to clear away some debris, but also, positively, point us to something that can move relevant scholarship forward.

Many of the arguments concerning the interpretation and authenticity of Josephus's *Testimonium Flavianum* have been the object of protracted debates over the centuries.[1] This essay will focus, however, on one particular verb in the *Testimonium* and on an argument about it that, in contrast, has usually been ignored — quite justifiably, as we shall see.

According to the received text of the *Testimonium*, at *Antiquities* 18.63, Jesus won over numerous Jews and Greeks (πολλοὺς μὲν Ἰουδαίους, πολλοὺς δὲ καὶ τοῦ Ἑλληνικοῦ ἐπηγάγετο). Numerous scholars have observed that the notion, that Jesus attracted not only Jews but also non-Jews ('Greeks'), contradicts the Gospels, which, whatever the ambiguities,[2] basically have Jesus's mission being only to 'the lost sheep of the house of Israel' (Matthew 10:6; 15:24). There is,

---

1 For surveys of the debates concerning authenticity and interpretation, see Bardet, *Le Testimonium Flavianum*; Chapman and Schnabel, *The Trial and Crucifixion of Jesus*, pp. 187–88; Whealey, 'The *Testimonium Flavianum*'; and Vitelli, 'La più antica testimonianza'.

2 See Jeremias, *Jesus' Promise*, and Bird, *Jesus and the Origins*.

> **Daniel R. Schwartz** is the Herbst Family Professor Emeritus of Judaic Studies in the Department of Jewish History and Contemporary Jewry at the Hebrew University of Jerusalem.

Essays on Jews and Christians in Late Antiquity in Honour of Oded Irshai, ed. by Brouria Bitton-Ashkelony and Martin Goodman, CELAMA 40 (Turnhout: Brepols, 2023), pp. 205–218
BREPOLS 📚 PUBLISHERS   10.1484/M.CELAMA-EB.5.132490

206 DANIEL R. SCHWARTZ

however, an impasse when it comes to deciding whether this contradiction argues for the passage's authenticity or, rather, against it. Should we infer that only an outsider like Josephus could make such a mistake, so the words are likely authentic?[3] Or should we rather assume that the words were written by some Christian writer, perhaps Eusebius (the earliest known writer who cites the *Testimonium*), who, knowing that Gentiles eventually joined the Church, assumed that this was the natural continuation of a process begun by Jesus himself?[4] Or perhaps a Christian forger of Josephus's text sought to enhance its credibility by craftily inserting something that looked as if it must have been written by an outsider? Arguments such as that one cannot be resolved, and one can well understand that the author of a standard work on the *Testimonium*, more than a century ago, after considering the arguments, left the matter completely open,[5] just as most subsequent scholars abstain from building on this issue one way or another.

Reinach, Eisler, and an Innocuous Verb

Here, however, I will consider another argument concerning the words quoted above, one that has elicited even less discussion, although, as we shall see, it continues to pop up here and there. It pertains to the verb, ἐπηγάγετο. Neither Niese (in his editio maior) nor other scholars who have supplied their own detailed critical apparatuses for the *Testimonium*[6] note any variants, and, apart from the observation, nearly a century ago, that Josephus uses ἐπάγεσθαι frequently,[7] the verb has not attracted much notice.

---

3 So, for example, Reinach, 'Josèphe sur Jésus', pp. 14–15; Thackeray, *Josephus*, p. 146 ('The statement about the Greeks would be impossible for a Christian'); Meier, 'Jesus in Josephus', pp. 93–94.

4 For inclusion of this argument in the case for identifying Eusebius as the *Testimonium*'s author, see Olson, 'A Eusebian Reading', pp. 105–08. For doubts about Olson's argument, see Vitelli, 'Più antica testimonianza', p. 12.

5 Linck, *De antiquissimis*, pp. 24–25.

6 See Linck, *De antiquissimis*, 4 (where ἐπηγάγετο is one of the few words in the *Testimonium* that has no annotation) and Levenson and Martin, 'The Latin Translations', p. 21. In n. 24 Levenson and Martin record only Naber's suggestion to emend the verb into ὑπηγάγετο (*Flavii Iosephi Opera*, ed. by Naber, 47 [if it is an emendation and not simply a misprint; note that it is not mentioned in his list of critical notes, p. xviii]). For the middle voice of ὑπάγω meaning 'to win someone's support, bring under one's sway, bring over to one's side, to move to something', see Rengstorf, ed., *The Complete Concordance*, iv, p. 234. Since that meaning is basically the same as the one normally associated with the middle of ἐπάγω and the emendation is not based on any manuscript evidence, I shall ignore it in the present study. Naber was probably motivated by the same consideration as Niese; see below, note 8. Note also that Dubarle's detailed review of the indirect evidence generated no doubt about ἐπηγάγετο; see below, note 9.

7 See van Liempt, 'De testimonio Flaviano', pp. 111–12; he lists forty occurrences of the verb in Josephus's writings and adds that it is not found in ancient Christian literature. That corresponds to von Gutschmid's remark that the phrase πολλοὺς δὲ καὶ τοῦ Ἑλληνικοῦ ἐπηγάγετο has 'ganz Josephische Färbung [...] [and is] ganz Josephisch' (Gutschmid, *Kleine Schriften*, pp. 352–53), just as Thackeray would later comment that 'the repetition of "many",

REINACH AND STEPHANUS, PHILO AND JOSEPHUS 207

Indeed, it does not appear that there is anything problematic about this verb. Usually, Josephus employs it simply in the literal sense of 'bringing someone along with oneself'; so, for example, *Ant.* 12.383; 14.371; 17.219; 19.341; 20.7, 252.[8] In other cases, however, he uses it metaphorically, for 'winning over'. Thus, for example, at *War* 7.164 Josephus explains that the Romans decided to reduce Masada 'lest by its strength it bring many over to rebellion' (μὴ διὰ τὴν ὀχυρότητα πολλοὺς εἰς ἀποστασίαν ἐπαγάγηται), just as at *Ant.* 17.327 he reports that the false Alexander 'won the confidence' (ἐπηγάγετο εἰς πίστιν) of all the Jews he met. So too at *Ant.* 18.63, the translation appears to be straightforward: 'il entraîna beaucoup de Juifs et aussi beaucoup d'Hellènes' (Reinach), 'He won over many Jews and many of the Greeks' (Feldman), 'e attirò molti Giudei, molti anche della grecità' (Troiani).[9] As LSJ notes, this sense of the middle voice ('bring over to oneself, win over') is found in Thucydides and Polybius as well.[10]

Note, however, that, in line with the first rendering in LSJ, several translators prefer explicitly to reflect the use of the middle voice here: 'ex gentilibus [or: gentibus] *sibi* adiunxit' (Rufinus and Latin translation of Josephus); 'He drew over *to him* both many of the Jews and many of the Gentiles' (Whiston); 'il attire *à lui* beaucoup de Juifs et beaucoup de Grecs' (Mathieu and Herrmann); 'he won over *to himself* many Jews and many also of the Greek (nation)' (Thackeray) ; 'הוא משך אחריו יהודים רבים וגם רבים מן ההלנים' (Schalit).[11] By thus making explicit the point that the many who were won over were won over *to the person who won them over*, they might — although need not — suggest there was something self-serving about the winning over.

Perhaps that suggestion had something to do with the fact that, writing in 1897, Théodore Reinach, in a move that has not attracted much scholarly attention, claimed that ἐπηγάγετο was slightly pejorative (has a 'nuance

---

the neuter τὸ Ἑλληνικόν, and the use of ἐπάγεσθαι for "win converts" are all thoroughly Josephan' (Thackeray, *Josephus*, p. 146).

8 For some other cases, see below, note 27. Niese, in fact, was so sure that 'won over' is the meaning required in the *Testimonium*, but also that the literal sense ('bringing someone along with oneself') is the usual one for ἐπάγεσθαι in Josephus, that he suspected that the appearance of ἐπηγάγετο points to an interpolator or editor who was not sufficiently familiar with Josephus's style: 'nam προσαγαγέσθαι apud eum est conciliare, ἐπαγαγέσθαι secum ducere' (Niese, 'De testimonio Christiano', p. v).

9 Reinach, 'Josèphe sur Jésus', p. 3; Josephus, *Jewish Antiquities*, trans. by Feldman, p. 51; Troiani, 'Il Gesù di Flavio Giuseppe', p. 139. As the matter is summarized by the author of a 'linguistic analysis' of the *Testimonium*, the verb 'pare limitarsi alla valenza neutrale di "attrarre a sé" o al proprio insegnamento "persuadendo"' (Gramaglia, 'Il *Testimonium Flavianum*', p. 158). Note especially that Dubarle ('Le témoignage de Josèphe', p. 501), after a detailed review of the evidence, translated the same as Reinach (apart from using 'de Grecs' instead of 'd'Hellènes') not only in his 'texte reçu' but also in his 'texte reconstitué'. Below I shall focus on a revised translation that Reinach suggests later in his article.

10 Liddell, Scott, and Jones, *A Greek-English Lexicon*, p. 603, s.v. ἐπάγω, § II.6.

11 I added the italics into the texts presented by: Levenson and Martin, 'Latin Translations', p. 22; *Works of Flavius Josephus*, trans by Whiston, p. 548; Josephus, *Antiquités Judaiques*, trans. by Mathieu and Herrmann, pp. 145–46; Thackeray, *Josephus*, p. 136; and *Flavii Josephi Antiquitates*, trans. by Schalit, p. 286.

légèrement méprisante') and is always used *in malam partem*.[12] Therefore, he translated 'il séduisit'. Given that such a nuance was what he would expect from a Jew hostile to Christianity, Reinach pointed to this verb as part of his argument that the *Testimonium* as we have it was indeed composed by Josephus. Thirty years later, Robert Eisler, in support of that same general thesis, went further than Reinach and, after evincing some doubt about the cogency of Reinach's inference from ἐπηγάγετο, suggested that the argument be retained and bolstered by emending ἐπηγάγετο into ἀπηγάγετο — in accordance (so he writes) with some late manuscripts of Eusebius's version of the *Testimonium*. If that is the verb, Eisler states, one cannot miss the hostile and scornful tone ('feindselige verächtliche Ton der Stelle').[13]

Surprisingly, however, Reinach adduced no evidence for the nuance he ascribed to ἐπηγάγετο. I shall turn to that below. Before that, however, we should consider Eisler's suggestion to emend the text to ἀπηγάγετο, and note two major difficulties with it: (1) It appears to be impossible to confirm that any text of Eusebius offers that reading;[14] (2) even if we were to consent to read it at *Ant*. 18.63, none of the three Josephan passages that Eisler cites in support of it having a hostile and scornful nuance in fact shows that. Those three passages are *Ant*. 2.322, *Against Apion* 2.271 ('die bezeichnendste Stelle'), and *Ant*. 18.236.

At *Ant*. 2.322 Josephus states, following Exodus 13:17, that Moses ἀπήγαγεν the Hebrews out of Egypt by a circuitous route because of fear of the Egyptians and Philistines. Eisler renders this as a statement that Moses 'die Juden "wegführt" in die öde Wüste'. In his German that indeed sounds like a

---

12 Reinach, 'Josèphe sur Jésus', p. 7: 'qui ne s'emploie qu'en mauvaise part et rappelle l'accusation de séduction portée contre Jésus'. The latter is, as Reinach (fn. 2) explains, a reference to Matthew 27:63 and Luke 19:48, although Reinach's reference to them as if they referred to 'seduction' is somewhat more specific than the texts seem to warrant.

13 Eisler, *ΙΗΣΟΥΣ ΒΑΣΙΛΕΥΣ*, i, p. 39.

14 The manuscripts to which Eisler (*ΙΗΣΟΥΣ ΒΑΣΙΛΕΥΣ*) refers remain a mystery. Eisler points to Reinach ('Josèphe sur Jésus', p. 3) for his knowledge of the reading found in 'einigen jüngeren Eusebiushss.', and Reinach indeed states (p. 3) that ἀπηγάγετο is the reading of 'quelques manuscrits' of Eusebius's *Historia ecclesiastica*. But Reinach gives no further details. Such a variant was already cited, as Eisler notes, by Müller, *Christus bei Josephus*, pp. 17 and 58 — a study that Reinach too cites in his article, although not in this context. But Müller too gives no details: he does not say whether this variant appears in one manuscript or more, nor does he even say in which Eusebian book it is found — which, given the fact that Eusebius offers two versions of the *Testimonium* (see below), suggests that Reinach had some additional source. To make matters murkier, note that Bammel, although referring to Eisler, speaks of only one such manuscript, but he too gives no details (Bammel, 'Zum Testimonium Flavianum', p. 12). No such variant is noted in the apparatus of the Griechischen Christlichen Schriftsteller editions of Eusebius's two versions of the *Testimonium* (*Historia ecclesiastica* 1.11 [ed. by Schwartz, 80] and *Demonstratio* 3.5 [ed. by Heikel, 130]), nor in the works cited above in note 6, nor in any of the many old editions of Eusebius that I have been able to check. The closest I have come, so far, is Georgius Hamartolus's reading of ἀπηγάγετο in his version of the *Testimonium* (Migne, *Patrologia Graeca* 110.388), to which I was kindly referred by Ken Olson. In sum, as a note in the English translation of Eisler's work put it, apart from references by Müller, Reinach, and Eisler, the manuscripts are 'aliter ignoti' (Eisler, *The Messiah Jesus*, p. 60 n. 5).

complaint, in which 'wegführen' means, as often in German, 'mislead', 'lead astray' — a sense Eisler reinforced by going beyond Josephus and characterizing the desert as desolate ('öde').

How, however, could one imagine Josephus condemning Moses for anything at all, much less — for leading the Hebrews into the desert?! And note that Josephus even explains the good reason — the desire to avoid Egyptians and Philistines — that brought Moses to choose the route he chose. Rather, Josephus's use of ἀπήγαγεν at *Ant.* 2.322 means only that Moses *led* the Hebrews *out* of Egypt — and that is the very same simple sense in which he used the very same verb in the preceding context (2.307, 311), where Josephus reports that God commanded Moses to ἀπάγειν the Hebrews from Egypt. So too, already at 2.253, Josephus reported that Moses led the Egyptians back (ἀπήγαγεν) to their own land after a military campaign abroad, with no implication that there was anything misleading or self-serving about that.

At *Against Apion* 2.271, the second passage to which Eisler refers, Josephus emphasizes that neither fear of conquerors nor the desire to emulate others is able to lead the Jews away (ἀπαγαγεῖν) from observing their own laws. Here, indeed, the verb is used of something the author decries, so we might use something like 'divert' or 'deflect', although one need not agree with Eisler's easy move here from 'leading away' all the way to 'seducing' ('wegführen', d.h. 'verführen').

But however that may be, Eisler's argument here raises the objection that was noticed already by Hans (Johanan) Lewy (1901–1945), who at this point (vol. i, p. 39) pencilled 'Medium!' into the margin of his copy of *IHΣOΥΣ BAΣIΛEΥΣ*.[15] Namely, the first two examples cited by Eisler use ἀπάγω in the active voice, but ἀπηγάγετο in *Ant.* 18.63, were we to read it there, would be in the middle. Eisler apparently recognized this problem, and therefore added his third example: at *Ant.* 18.236, Josephus reports that Antonia Minor advised her grandson, Gaius Caligula, when Tiberius died and Gaius succeeded to the imperial throne, not to release Agrippa I immediately from prison, μὴ δόξαν ἀπάγοιτο ἡδονῇ δεχομένου τὴν Τιβερίου τελευτήν: 'lest he bring upon himself the reputation of having received Tiberius's death with pleasure' (for it was Tiberius who had imprisoned Agrippa). Eisler states that this passage illustrates that 'das Medium ἀπάγεσθαι drückt das "wegführen für sich", "zu sich" aus', and translates 'damit er nicht für sich den Anschein davontrage eines, der den Tod des Tiberius mit Vergnügen vernehme'.[16]

As Eisler notes, he took this example from Thackeray's *Lexicon to Josephus*. There, however, Thackeray rendered simply 'gain the reputation of [...] (be

---

15 Now in the Hebrew University of Jerusalem's Bloomfield Library for the Humanities and Social Sciences on Mt. Scopus. The two volumes of Eisler's work are full of Lewy's marginalia, which he used in preparing his detailed review that appeared in *Deutsche Literaturzeitung*, 15 March 1930, cols. 481–94. But the review does not discuss the *Testimonium*, apart from rejecting Eisler's reconstruction out of hand (col. 483).

16 Eisler, *IHΣOΥΣ BAΣIΛEΥΣ*, i, p. 40.

thought to be)'.[17] Eisler, to further his purpose here, added not only 'zu sich' but also 'für sich'. However, at 18.236 the verb cannot entail 'for his own benefit', as Eisler suggests for 18.63, for at 18.236 Antonia means that Gaius would bring such a *bad* reputation upon himself, to his detriment. This passage, accordingly, cannot support the nuance that Eisler needs for 18.63: misleading others for one's own advantage.

So much for the suggestion of emending ἐπηγάγετο into ἀπηγάγετο, which anyway would have been a stretch from deviant late manuscripts to Eusebius (if they ever existed) to the text of Josephus.[18] But what of Reinach's assertion that ἐπηγάγετο is always used *in malam partem*? Perhaps it is enough to note, now that we have a concordance to Josephus, that the list of English and German equivalents that opens the long entry on ἐπάγω includes neither 'mislead' nor 'seduce', neither 'wegführen' nor 'verführen'. Rather, for the middle voice, it offers only 'to send for, bring (for help), to attract, to persuade to, motivate, induce, to have with, take with, bring with (en route)'.[19] Note, indeed, that Steve Mason, in discussing Josephus's statement at *War* 2.162 that the Pharisees ἀπάγοντες the first sect, points to the suggestion (offered by Hudson and again by Thackeray) to read instead ἐπάγοντες, which 'allows for a greater range of *positive* associations'.[20]

True, Reinach's suggestion has reappeared here and there in scholarly discussion (although usually without reference to his study), but most of these discussions either abstain from any argument at all[21] or, if they offer one, disregard the fact that ἐπηγάγετο is in the middle voice. Thus, for a recent example, note the blithe and unexplained move by Chapman and Schnabel, in the first sentence of the following paragraph, from reference to § II of the entry in LSJ to reference to its § I, i.e., from medium to active:

> The verb ἐπηγάγετο which is usually translated 'he won over' means 'bring over to oneself, win over' (LSJ s.v. ἐπάγω II.7 [*read: II.6, DRS*]), but it can

---

17 Thackeray and Marcus, *A Lexicon*, p. 58, s.v. ἀπάγειν, § 6.

18 For strong criticism of Eisler on this point, see Bauer's review, p. 559. Note that the English version of Eisler's *ΙΗΣΟΥΣ ΒΑΣΙΛΕΥΣ* simply skips his discussion (Eisler, *ΙΗΣΟΥΣ ΒΑΣΙΛΕΥΣ*, i, pp. 39–40) of ἐπηγάγετο; see Eisler, *Messiah Jesus*, p. 47. Bauer's critique applies all the more to Ernst Bammel ('Zum Testimonium Flavianum', pp. 11–12), who depends on the same manuscript (*sic*, singular), wrote that ἐπηγάγετο might be a 'mechanischer Schreibfehler' for ἀπηγάγετο, and then asserts that if we read the latter the sense would be different; in his n. 25 he states that the latter could have 'die significatio seditionis', but makes no effort to demonstrate or illustrate that. All he does is point to Linck's discussion (*De antiquissimis*, pp. 23–24) — but Linck denies there is a negative sense at *Ant.* 18.63 ('Sed hic sensus eius verbi nulla re probatur, nedum postuletur').

19 Rengstorf, ed., *Complete Concordance*, ii, pp. 130–32, s.v. ἐπάγω. For similar entries in general lexica of Greek, see below, note 31.

20 I added the italics into Mason, *Flavius Josephus on the Pharisees*, p. 131.

21 So Smith, *Jesus the Magician*: in his translation of the *Testimonium* at p. 46 he simply added '(astray)' after 'he led', and in his note on p. 178 he declared, without argument, that the parenthetical addition 'is implied by the Greek text'.

also mean 'lead on by persuasion, influence' (ibid. I.3). G. N. Stanton suggests the meaning 'bring trouble to' and even 'seduce, lead astray'. While the noun ἐπαγωγή in the LXX means 'calamity, trouble' (LSJ, Muraoka), BDAG has dropped the information that the figurative sense of ἐπάγω is 'bring something bad upon someone' (BAGD; in BDAG we find the following: 'to cause a state or condition to be or to occur, bring on, bring something upon someone, mostly something bad').[22]

Apart from the reference to Septuagintal usage, which is irrelevant here since Josephus uses ἐπαγωγή in other senses[23] (and anyway there was no reason to think that Josephus would use it particularly in the Septuagintal sense, which is only the seventh of the eight LSJ gives for it), all the above amounts to is an assertion that since ἐπάγω, in the active voice, can mean 'lead on, persuade', and often what is brought upon someone is bad, it follows that there is room to build on Stanton's suggestion that Josephus's ἐπηγάγετο, in the middle voice, means 'seduced' or 'led astray'.[24] However, none of these scholars attempts to explain the move from active to middle; Chapman and Schnabel cite no example from Josephus to illustrate the negative nuance of the verb in either voice; and although Stanton cites one, *Life* 18, there the verb is in the active voice.

I have noticed only one recent scholar who has attempted to justify the notion that Josephus's use of the verb, in the middle, has — or could have — such a nuance. Writing in 2014, Fernando Bermejo-Rubio, who was familiar with Reinach's article, reverted to his position and even asserted that Eisler's emendation was unnecessary

> precisely because the verb ἐπάγομαι already has a negative tinge ('bring something bad upon someone') — only slightly less negative than ἀπάγομαι —, and in this context it may carry the meaning of 'lead astray' or 'seduce'. Interestingly, Josephus himself uses the verb ἐπάγομαι in this negative sense elsewhere (e.g., *Ant.* 1.207. 6.196. 11.199. 17.327).[25]

However, although Bermejo-Rubio has been followed by some others,[26] I believe that anyone who checks these four passages will find it difficult to ascribe it a negative nuance, such as 'lead astray' or 'seduce'; they all refer to heroes, to whom Josephus would never impute something so nasty or underhanded.[27] As for the fourth passage, while such a translation is possible,

---

22 Chapman and Schnabel, *Trial and Crucifixion*, pp. 131–32. The references to BAGD and BDAG are to two successive editions (1979 and 2000) of Danker and others' *A Greek-English Lexicon of the New Testament*. The reference to Muraoka is to his *A Greek-English Lexicon*.

23 See Rengstorf, ed., *Complete Concordance*, ii, p. 132, s.v. ('conduit, inducement, cause, attack, accusation').

24 See Stanton, 'Jesus of Nazareth', pp. 133–34.

25 Bermejo-Rubio, 'Was the Hypothetical *Vorlage*', pp. 354–55.

26 See Vitelli, 'Più antica testimonianza', p. 15, also Curran, '"To Be or to Be Thought to Be"', p. 88 n. 78 (where the same list of four passages in *Antiquities* is offered in support of 'seduce, lead astray').

27 At *Ant.* 1.207 the verb's object is Sarah, whom Abraham brought along with him, not those

nothing requires it, for when 17.327 reports that pseudo-Alexander 'won the confidence' of all who met him, it is not the use of ἐπηγάγετο (which translators take to be innocuous),[28] but rather the reader's knowledge that the man was an impostor, that creates the negative meaning.

In sum, while one can well understand why scholars would like to find a negative nuance in Josephus's ἐπηγάγετο as part of a general attempt to make the *Testimonium* negative, and hence authentic, Reinach did not try to justify that assessment, and those who later tried to do so were far from successful, insofar as they based their arguments on emendation, or on ignoring the difference between active and middle voices, and/or, in general, on a lack of familiarity with Josephan usage.

From Reinach to Stephanus

The fact that those later scholars at least tried to defend the case for ἐπάγεσθαι having a 'negative tinge' points up, however, the fact that Reinach did not; he thought he could take it for granted. Of what was Reinach thinking? What could have led him to assert that ἐπηγάγετο has a 'nuance légèrement méprisante' and is always used *in malam partem*? And what could have allowed him to think that those assertions were so obvious that they were not in need of demonstration, or even of illustration?

An answer to those questions seems to emerge from the fact that, a little later in his article, in repeating his assertion that ἐπηγάγετο is 'un des vestiges les plus caractéristiques du ton hostile de la rédaction primitive' of the *Testimonium*, Reinach glosses it, without argument, with the Latin 'pellicere'.[29] That verb has a clearly negative nuance: Lewis and Short give 'allure, entice, inveigle, decoy, coax, wheedle, etc.', and the *OLD* gives 'win over by insidious means, seduce, captivate, charm'.[30] However, there is nothing like that in standard definitions of ἐπάγω; for the middle, they include only innocuous equivalents with no negative overtones,[31]

---

who Abraham misled about her; at 6.196 it is impossible that Josephus meant that David, who was a virtuous hero, 'misled' or 'seduced' God; and at 11.199 it is impossible that Josephus meant that Esther, who was a virtuous heroine, 'misled' or 'seduced' (rather than 'won over') those who saw her.

28 'Gagna la confiance' (Josephus, *Antiquités Judaiques*, trans. by Mathieu and Herrmann, p. 127); 'won the confidence' (*Josephus: Jewish Antiquities*, trans. by Marcus and Wikgren, p. 523).

29 Reinach, 'Josèphe sur Jésus', p. 11.

30 Lewis and Short, *A New Latin Dictionary*, p. 1325, s.v. pellicio; Glare, *Oxford Latin Dictionary*, p. 1320. See also Santoro L'Hoir, *Tragedy*, pp. 149–50 ('The verb *pellicere* […] connotes deceptive enticement, cajoling words, seduction, and therefore sexual magic').

31 See Liddell, Scott, and Jones, *A Greek-English Lexicon*, p. 603, s.v. ἐπάγω, § II [medium]: 'bring to oneself, procure or provide for oneself; bring into, bring in, introduce; call, adduce; bring upon oneself, bring with one, bring over to oneself, win over, induce'. So too, Menge, *Menge-Güthling*, p. 254, s.v. ἐπάγω, § II [medium]: 'zu sich/für sich heranführen; zu Hilfe rufen; anführen; für sich gewinnen'.

REINACH AND STEPHANUS, PHILO AND JOSEPHUS 213

just as we saw above (n. 19) with regard to Josephus's usage. What, then, led Reinach to set ἐπάγεσθαι equivalent to 'pellicere'?

Given the fact that twice in his article (pp. 10, 13), although not in this connection, Reinach refers generally to 'le *Thesaurus*' as his authority for Greek usage, I checked the standard nineteenth-century (Didot) edition of Stephanus's (Henri Estienne's) *Thesaurus graecae linguae*.[32] Sure enough, there I found that although the entry on ἐπάγω first offers, to illustrate use of the verb in the middle, five passages (from Thucydides, Isocrates, and Polybius) for which Stephanus renders the sense by such Latin verbs as 'allicio', 'elicio', 'lacio', 'electo' — all of them roughly equivalent to 'draw to oneself, attract, elicit' although they might range as far as 'entice, allure', after them it adds the following: 'Sic autem Philo V.M. 2: Πάντας γὰρ ἐπάγεται καὶ συνεπιστρέφει, ubi ἐπάγεσθαι exp. Pellicere'. Assuming that 'exp.' represents some form of 'exprimo', this glosses the Greek verb in Philo's *Life of Moses* 2.20 with 'pellicere', the same way Reinach glossed Josephus at *Ant.* 18.63. Here, then, is the apparent basis for Reinach's statement about ἐπηγάγετο; the fact that he could depend on this standard tool, comparable to our use of LSJ, exempted him from the need to justify his glossing of the verb. And we can even understand why Reinach chose this meaning, rather than the other, more innocuous ones first offered by *Thesaurus*: the particular application of the verb in the Philonic passage is, as we shall see, quite similar to that at *Ant.* 18.63.

However, on closer examination one easily notices two problems, one with the flow of this entry itself and one with the way Stephanus seems to have read Philo. First, with regard to the flow of the entry: recall that it is only after citing five passages that illustrate the use of ἐπάγεσθαι in an innocuous sense,[33] and then introducing the passage from Philo with 'Sic autem Philo' (so [too], however, Philo) and quoting it, that the entry goes on to state 'ubi ἐπάγεσθαι exp. Pellicere'. Given that 'pellicere' has a definitely negative nuance while the first five passages do not, any reader of this entry must be puzzled: how can Stephanus say that Philo's use of ἐπάγεσθαι is both innocuous and pejorative?! Second, as for Stephanus's reading of Philo: in the passage cited (*Life of Moses* 2.20), Philo proudly demonstrates the superiority of Mosaic law by pointing to the fact that Jewish practices have won over and gained the attention (ἐπάγεται καὶ συνεπιστρέφει) of non-Jews everywhere. How could Stephanus possibly imagine that Philo meant anything sinister like 'seduce'?!

One logical possibility is that Henri Estienne, as opposed to modern scholars (see note 30), did not ascribe such a negative sense to 'pellicere'. This seems, however, to be a non-starter. I see nothing to support it, and note that already

---

32 H. Estienne, *Thesaurus graecae linguae* (Didot), iii, p. 1369, s.v. ἐπάγω.

33 In support of Stephanus's assessment, note that of the Loeb Classical Library translations of the five passages Stephanus cites here, for three — Thucydides 5.45.1, Isocrates, *Antidosis* 85, and Polybius 7.14.4 — the translators use, respectively, 'win over', 'draw', and 'attract'. For the other two — Polybius 1.84.8 and 5.17.3 — LCL indeed offers nastier verbs ('entice' and 'decoy'), but they refer to luring an enemy into ambush, and in war one is allowed to be deceiving.

the entry on 'pellicio' in the elder Stephanus's Latin dictionary opened with 'blandiendo decipere' (to mislead/deceive/beguile via coaxing/alluring),[34] just as his Latin-French dictionary defined 'pellicere' as 'induire aucun par belles parolles à faire quelque chose'.[35] 'Belles parolles' are, unambiguously, lies.

That leaves, as far as I can see, only one other possibility: that after the *Thesaurus* states that Philo's usage is like that of the passages cited prior to it, it does not, in fact, say that Philo's ἐπάγεσθαι means 'pellicere'. That was a natural reading of the *Thesaurus*, but my friend Prof. Deborah Gera, with whom I shared my puzzlement, checked the 1572 first edition of the *Thesaurus* and discovered that although the exact same passage from Philo is followed there by virtually the same text as in the Didot edition, in the 1572 edition the abbreviated word is spelled out: 'ubi ἐπάγεσθαι exponitur Pellicere'[36] — 'where ἐπάγεσθαι is/has been translated as pellicere'.

That is, Estienne, after illustrating the innocuous sense of ἐπάγεσθαι, is telling us that 'so [too,] however', is its meaning in the Philonic passage, *although it has been rendered* — i.e., by someone else — *by 'pellicere' as if it had a negative sense.* Indeed, with the generous help of a specialist on early translations of Philo it was simple to discover that Philo's *Life of Moses* had been translated into Latin by one of Henri Estienne's teachers, Adrien Turnèbe,[37] and that that translation, published in 1554, uses 'pellicere' to render Philo's ἐπάγεσθαι in the passage from 2.20 cited in the *Thesaurus*.[38] We may well understand that although Estienne wanted to set the record straight about the verb's true meaning, he avoided embarrassing Turnèbe by mentioning his name.

From Philo to Josephus

It thus turns out, on the one hand, that the search for the basis of Reinach's claim about 'quelques manuscrits' (n. 14) raises doubts about their very existence, not to mention about ascribing them any weight, and Reinach's declaration concerning the sense of ἐπάγεσθαι turns out to derive, so it seems, only from his natural but incorrect misunderstanding of an abbreviation in the dictionary he was using. That is surprising, and disappointing, but such things happen. On the other hand, along the way it happened that we were made to focus on Philo, *Life of Moses* 2.20, and now it may be underlined that it seems that that passage, which I do not recall encountering in discussions

---

34 R. Estienne, *Dictionarium, seu Latinae linguae thesaurus*, p. 1058d.

35 R. Estienne, *Dictionarium latinogallicum*, p. 915.

36 H. Estienne, *Thesaurus graecae linguae* (1572), col. 77.

37 That Turnèbe (who replaced Robert Estienne as the royal printer in Paris) was among Henri Estienne's teachers is noted by Reverdin, 'Le "Platon" d'Henri Estienne', p. 239. Poems by Henri Estienne in honour of Turnèbe are cited by Lewis, *Adrien Turnèbe*, pp. 16–17 n. 9.

38 *Philonis Iudaei*, p. 91: 'omnes enim mortales ad se pelliciunt et convertunt'. My thanks to Dr Andrew Taylor, of Churchill College (Cambridge), who referred me to this translation and generously supplied useful additional information.

of *Ant.* 18.63, is in fact a good guide to the sense of the latter. Namely, just as the *Testimonium* underlines that both Jews and Greeks had been 'won over' (ἐπηγάγετο) to Jesus, so too Philo, referring to the spread of Jewish practices, proudly reports that 'all are won over (ἐπάγεται) and made to be attentive: barbarians, Greeks, dwellers of the mainland and of islands, nations from the east and the west, of Europe and Asia, the whole inhabited world, from end to end'. The fact that Philo is obviously proud of what he reports reinforces the tendency to read Josephus the same way. Note, moreover, that another similar passage in Josephus, which too points out that many 'Greeks' have been attracted to Jewish practice and exemplifies that in much the same way (beginning, as does Philo, with the spread of Sabbath-observance), has often been thought to be based either on this very same passage in Philo's *Life of Moses* or on a common tradition.[39] That tendency about the sense of Josephus's statement at *Ant.* 18.63 has been challenged only by scholars' assertions that the verb has a negative tinge, assertions that — whether or not bolstered by arguments — turn out, it appears, to be baseless.

Usually, most scholars have assumed that the *Testimonium*, as it now is, was formulated by a Christian. Since (as virtually all assume) Josephus was not a Christian, they have concluded that, whether or not he wrote anything here about Jesus, he did not formulate the *Testimonium* as it now is. However, that logic is more cogent for the parts of the *Testimonium* that declare Christian dogma, such as Jesus having been the Christ and having been resurrected from death on the third day in accordance with the words of the prophets.

Signing on to Christian dogma is one thing, taking pride in the fact that a movement born out of Judaism was successful on the world stage is another. Here I would not only recall, in conclusion, the observation that Josephus's formulation in this particular passage is 'thoroughly Josephan' (note 7); I will also point to modern scholarship's willingness to suppose that neither Judaism nor Christianity was so well defined, in Josephus's day, as necessarily to entail hostility.[40] Indeed, even if they were well-defined and mutually exclusive, it is not at all impossible to suppose that Josephus would take pride in the worldwide success of a movement that was born out of Judaism. One need only compare, for example, the way Jewish newspapers, today, no matter how tenaciously they inveigh against intermarriage and assimilation, are happy to trumpet the news whenever someone of Jewish descent receives an Oscar or a Nobel Prize or otherwise makes it big on the global stage.

---

39 For the comparison of *Against Apion* 2.277–86 to Philo's *Life of Moses* 2.12–24, and its source- or tradition-critical implications, see Barclay (Josephus, *Against Apion*, trans. and comm. by Barclay, p. 325, n. 1110 and p. 361).

40 For a similar comment in this context, see Whealey, '*Testimonium Flavianum*', p. 353.

Bibliography

Primary Sources

Eusebius, *Kirchengeschichte*, ed. by E. Schwartz, Eusebius Werke, 2, Die griechischen christlichen Schriftsteller, 9.2 (Leipzig: Hinrichs, 1903)
——, *Die Demonstratio evangelica*, ed. by I. A. Heikel, Eusebius Werke, 4, Die griechischen christlichen Schriftsteller, 23 (Leipzig: Hinrichs, 1913)
Flavius Josephus, *Against Apion*, trans. and comm. by John M. G. Barclay, Flavius Josephus: Translation and Commentary, 10 (Leiden: Brill, 2007)
——, *Antiquités Judaiques, Livres XVI–XX*, trans. by G. Mathieu and L. Herrmann, Œuvres complètes de Flavius Josèphe, 4 (Paris: Leroux, 1929)
——, *Flavii Iosephi Opera Omnia post Immanuelem Bekkerum*, iv, ed. by Samuel Adrianus Naber (Lipsiae: Teubner, 1893)
——, *Flavii Josephi Antiquitates Judaicae, Libri XI–XX, in linguam hebraicam vertit annotationibus amplissimis illustravit et prooemio instruxit*, trans. by Abraham Schalit (Jerusalem: Bialik Institute, 1963) (in Hebrew)
——, *Josephus: Jewish Antiquities, Books XVIII–XX*, trans. by Louis H. Feldman, Loeb Classical Library (London: Heinemann, 1965)
——, *Josephus: Jewish Antiquities, Books XV–XVII*, trans. by Ralph Marcus and Allen Wikgren, Loeb Classical Library (London: Heinemann, 1963)
——, *The Works of Flavius Josephus*, ed. by William Whiston (Hartford: Scranton, 1905)
Georgius Monachus, *Chronicon breve*, ed. by Jacques-Paul Migne, Patrologiae cursus completus: series graeca, 110 (Paris: Garnier, 1863)
Philo of Alexandria, *Philonis Iudaei De Vita Mosis Lib. III*, ed. by Adrien Turnèbe (Paris: apud Adr. Turnebum, 1554)

Secondary Studies

Bammel, Ernst, 'Zum Testimonium Flavianum (Jos Ant 18, 63–64)', in *Josephus-Studien: Untersuchungen zu Josephus, dem antiken Judentum und dem Neuen Testament – Otto Michel zum 70. Geburtstag gewidmet*, ed. by Otto Betz, Klaus Haacker, and Martin Hengel (Göttingen: Vandenhoeck & Ruprecht, 1974), pp. 9–22
Bardet, Serge, *Le Testimonium Flavianum: Examen historique, considérations historiographiques*. Josèphe et son temps 5 (Paris: Cerf, 2002)
Bauer, Walter, review of Eisler, *ΙΗΣΟΥΣ ΒΑΣΙΛΕΥΣ ΟΥ ΒΑΣΙΛΕΥΣΑΣ*, in *Theologische Literaturzeitung*, 55 (1930), 557–63
Bermejo-Rubio, Fernando, 'Was the Hypothetical *Vorlage* of the *Testimonium Flavianum* a "Neutral" Text? Challenging the Common Wisdom on *Antiquitates Judaicae* 18.63–64', *Journal for the Study of Judaism*, 45 (2014), 326–65
Bird, Michael F., *Jesus and the Origins of the Gentile Mission*, Library of New Testament Studies, 331 (London: T. & T. Clark, 2006)

Chapman, David W., and Eckhard J. Schnabel, *The Trial and Crucifixion of Jesus: Texts and Commentary*, Wissenschaftliche Untersuchungen zum Neuen Testament, 344 (Tübingen: Mohr Siebeck, 2015)

Curran, John, "'To Be or to Be Thought to Be": The *Testimonium Flavianum* (Again)', *Novum Testamentum*, 59 (2017), 71–94

Danker, Frederick William, ed., *A Greek-English Lexicon of the New Testament and Other Early Christian Literature*, 3rd edn (Chicago: University of Chicago Press, 2000)

Danker, Frederick William, and F. Wilbur Gingrich, eds, *A Greek-English Lexicon of the New Testament and Other Early Christian Literature*, 2nd edn (Chicago: University of Chicago Press, 1979)

Dubarle, A.-M., 'Le témoignage de Josèphe sur Jésus d'après la tradition indirecte', *Revue biblique*, 80 (1973), 481–513

Eisler, Robert, *ΙΗΣΟΥΣ ΒΑΣΙΛΕΥΣ ΟΥ ΒΑΣΙΛΕΥΣΑΣ: Die messianische Unabhängigkeitsbewegung vom Auftreten Johannes des Täufers bis zum Untergang Jakobs des Gerechten nach der neuerschlossenen Eroberung von Jerusalem des Flavius Josephus und den christlichen Quellen*, 2 vols (Heidelberg: Winters, 1929–1930)

——, *The Messiah Jesus and John the Baptist*, ed. and trans. by Alexander Haggerty Krappe (London: Methuen, 1931)

Estienne, Henri, *Thesaurus graecae linguae*, i (Geneva: Stephanus, 1572)

——, *Thesaurus graecae linguae, ab Henrico Stephano constructus*, ed. by C. B. Hase and G. and D. Dindorf, 8 vols in 9 (Paris: Didot, 1831–1865)

Estienne, Robert, *Dictionarium latinogallicum multo locupletius*, 2nd edn (Lutetiae: Stephanus, 1546)

——, *Dictionarium, seu Latinae linguae thesaurus*, ii, 2nd edn (Paris: Stephanus, 1543)

Glare, P. G. W., ed., *Oxford Latin Dictionary* (Oxford: Clarendon Press, 1982)

Gramaglia, P. A., 'Il *Testimonium Flavianum*: Analisi linguistica'. *Henoch*, 20 (1998), 153–77

Gutschmid, Alfred von, *Kleine Schriften*, iv, ed. by F. Rühl (Leipzig: Teubner, 1893)

Jeremias, Joachim, *Jesus' Promise to the Nations* (Philadelphia: Fortress, 1982)

Levenson, David B., and Thomas R. Martin, 'The Latin Translations of Josephus on Jesus, John the Baptist, and James: Critical Texts of the Latin Translation of the *Antiquities* and Rufinus' Translation of Eusebius's *Ecclesiastical History* Based on Manuscripts and Early Printed Editions', *Journal for the Study of Judaism*, 45 (2014), 1–79

Lewis, Charlton T., and Charles Short, *A New Latin Dictionary* (New York: Harper and Brothers, 1891)

Lewis, John, *Adrien Turnèbe (1512–1565): A Humanist Observed* (Geneva: Droz, 1998)

Lewy, Hans, review of Eisler, *ΙΗΣΟΥΣ ΒΑΣΙΛΕΥΣ ΟΥ ΒΑΣΙΛΕΥΣΑΣ*, in *Deutsche Literaturzeitung*, 51 (1930), 481–94

Liddell, Henry George, Robert Scott, and H. Stuart Jones, *A Greek-English Lexicon*, 9th edn (Oxford: Clarendon Press, 1940)

Linck, Kurt, *De antiquissimis veterum quae ad Iesum Nazarenum spectant testimoniis* (Gießen: Töpelmann, 1913)

Mason, Steve, *Flavius Josephus on the Pharisees: A Composition-Critical Study*, Studia Post-Biblica, 39 (Leiden: Brill, 1991)

Meier, John P., 'Jesus in Josephus: A Modest Proposal', *Catholic Biblical Quarterly*, 52 (1990), 76–103

Menge, Hermann, *Menge-Güthling Griechisch-deutsches und deutsch-griechisches Wörterbuch*, i, 2nd edn (Berlin: Langenscheidt, 1913)

Müller, Gustav Adolf, *Christus bei Josephus Flavius: Eine kritische Untersuchung als Beitrag zur Lösung der berühmten Frage und zur Erforschung der Urgeschichte des Christentums* (Innsbruck: Wagner, 1890)

Muraoka, Takamitsu, *A Greek-English Lexicon of the Septuagint* (Leuven: Peeters, 2009)

Niese, Benedictus, 'De testimonio Christiano quod est apud Josephum antiq. Iud. XVIII 63 sq. disputatio', in *Indices lectionum et publicarum et privatarum quae in Academia Marpurgensi per semestre hibernum […] habendae proponuntur* (Marpurgi: R. Friedrich, 1894), pp. iii–x

Olson, Ken, 'A Eusebian Reading of the *Testimonium Flavianum*', in *Eusebius of Caesarea: Tradition and Innovations*, ed. by Aaron Johnson and Jeremy Schott (Cambridge, MA: Harvard University Press for the Center for Hellenic Studies, 2013), pp. 97–114

Reinach, Théodore, 'Josèphe sur Jésus', *Revue des études juives*, 35 (1897), 1–18

Rengstorf, Karl Heinrich, ed., *The Complete Concordance to Flavius Josephus*, 4 vols (Leiden: Brill, 1973–1983)

Reverdin, Olivier, 'Le "Platon" d'Henri Estienne', *Museum Helveticum*, 13 (1956), 239–50

Santoro L'Hoir, Francesca, *Tragedy, Rhetoric and the Historiography of Tacitus's Annales* (Ann Arbor: University of Michigan Press, 2006)

Smith, Morton, *Jesus the Magician* (London: Gollancz, 1978)

Stanton, Graham N., 'Jesus of Nazareth: A Magician and a False Prophet who Deceived God's People?', in Stanton, *Jesus and Gospel* (Cambridge: Cambridge University Press, 2004), pp. 127–47

Thackeray, Henry St John, *Josephus: The Man and the Historian* (New York: Jewish Institute of Religion, 1929)

Thackeray, Henry St John, and Ralph Marcus, *A Lexicon to Josephus*, 4 parts (Paris: Librairie Orientaliste Paul Geuthner, 1930–1955)

Troiani, Lucio, 'Il Gesù de Flavio Giuseppe', *Ricerche storico bibliche*, 17.2 (2005), 137–47

van Liempt, l., 'De testimonio flaviano', *Mnemosyne*, n.s. 55 (1927), 109–116

Vitelli, Marco, 'La più antica testimonianza letteraria non-cristiana su Gesù: Considerazioni sul *Testimonium Flavianum* (*Ant.* XVIII 63–64)', *Mosaico*, 5 (2018), 1–35

Whealey, Alice, 'The *Testimonium Flavianum*', in *A Companion to Josephus*, ed. by Honora Howell Chapman and Zuleika Rodgers (Chichester: Wiley, 2016), pp. 345–55

PART III

Jewish Perspectives

JOSHUA LEVINSON

When in Rome

Introduction

What picture does rabbinic literature present us of the various Jewish communities in the diaspora? To be clear, I am not asking about the modes and expressions of the 'Jewishness' of diasporic identity itself, of which we have much evidence but little scholarly consensus, and in any case rabbinic literature is a problematic resource to rely upon in this regard,[1] nor how pagan authors like Cicero or Juvenal viewed the mores and practices of the local Jewish population. Rather, I wish to address the question of how rabbinic literature itself portrays the behaviour of diaspora Jewry and its relationship to the Palestinian rabbinic sages. How much of themselves did they see in the other — and how much of the other in themselves?

In most cases, as Martin Goodman has remarked, 'the rabbis took it for granted that their view of the world was normative for all Israel'.[2] Thus, we hear of rabbinic travels abroad to collect funds and adjudicate cases while the local Jews are portrayed as willingly accepting rabbinic authority.[3] A good example of this relationship is the tradition about a group of second-century sages who travelled to Antioch to collect funds for themselves (מגבת חכמים). One of their local benefactors, Aba Yehuda, was rewarded handsomely by Providence because he donated to the sages the last half of his possessions in exchange for their prayers. In addition, he was even inscribed 'at the head of the honour scroll' (ראש טימוס) of rabbinic patrons, as they exclaimed before him; 'A man's gift enriches him and gives him access to the great' (Prov. 18:16).[4]

---

1 Goodman, *Judaism in the Roman World*, pp. 233–59. See also: Barclay, ed., *Negotiating Diaspora*; Barclay, *Jews in the Mediterranean Diaspora*; Goodman (ed.), *Jews in a Graeco-Roman World*; Goodman, *A History of Judaism*, pp. 289–300.
2 Goodman, *Judaism in the Roman World*, p. 235.
3 Cf. tShab 15:8; tYev 14:5. It is worth noting that Richard Kalmin has pointed out that in distinction from Babylonian sources that demonstrate separatist tendencies, only Palestinian sources 'encourage non-rabbis to provide sages with food, clothing, and shelter, depict informal interactions between rabbis and non-rabbis' (Kalmin, 'Relationships Between Rabbis and Non-Rabbis', pp. 157, 161. See also Hezser, *Jewish Travel in Antiquity*, pp. 255–62.
4 yHor 3:4 (48a); Leviticus Rabba 5:4. Margulies places this event (חולת אנטוכיה) on the

---

Joshua Levinson is Professor of Rabbinic Literature in the Department of Hebrew Literature, the Hebrew University of Jerusalem.

Essays on Jews and Christians in Late Antiquity in Honour of Oded Irshai, ed. by Brouria Bitton-Ashkelony and Martin Goodman, CELAMA 40 (Turnhout: Brepols, 2023), pp. 221–239
BREPOLS ❧ PUBLISHERS   10.1484/M.CELAMA-EB.5.132491

The co-dependency of this relationship between the sages and their supporters is ostensibly balanced as financial capital is exchanged for the symbolic capital of the sages' prayers and praise, yet the sages' interest in such an 'economy of salvation' is palpable.

A few narratives seem to suggest rabbinic engagement with non-rabbinic or divergent Jewish observance. Not surprisingly, in all of these cases these options are quickly shut down. An illuminating example is the traditions of Todos (תודס = Thaddeus?)[5] of Rome who instructed (הנהיג) the community in Rome to prepare the paschal sacrifice in a manner similar to the Temple ritual. While not called a rabbi, the text assumes that he is in a position of communal leadership and authority. In the earlier version of the Tosephta (tBetzah 2:15) the rabbis merely express their displeasure at this idiosyncratic practice because its similarity to the Temple sacrifice could mislead the ill-informed. In the later talmudic revisions (yPes 7:1 (34a); bPes 53a-b) he is threatened with excommunication. Here, rabbinic hegemony expands by co-opting dissent and otherness. This punitive warning rabbinizes Todos by assuming that he is under the control and regulation of the rabbis in the land of Israel. Interestingly enough, in the *Yerushalmi* version he is forgiven only because he was a fundraiser for the rabbis (משלח פרנסתהון דרבנין).[6]

A further example of this dynamic is the traditions of the late third-century enigmatic figure Jacob of Kefar Nevoraia (again cited without honorific) richly elucidated by Oded Irshai.[7] This sage ruled in Tyre that fish require ritual slaughter and that it is permitted to circumcise the son of a gentile woman on the Sabbath. When R. Haggai rebukes him for these rulings and their mistaken biblical justifications, Jacob prostrates himself before his teacher and exclaims; 'Whip me, for it is good for instruction'.[8] Thus, the wayward sage is portrayed as accepting his own just corporeal punishment for straying from the accepted path, as rabbinic hegemony is graphically inscribed upon his body. As Steven Fine remarked, these cases 'suggest a certain fluidity of Jewish identity among Tyrian Jews [...] Jacob's rulings, and Rabbi Haggai's strong response to them, reflect the complexities of cosmopolitan Greco-Roman life meeting the academic piety of the rabbis in the Land of Israel'.[9]

---

outskirts of Antioch (*Midrash Wayyikra Rabbah, Leviticus Rabba*, p. 111), and Visotzky suggests that it is a reference to 'the hot springs at Daphne, just outside the city of Antioch proper' (Visotzky, *Golden Bells and Pomegranates*, p. 124 n. 22).

5   Such is the spelling in MS Leiden, Scal. 3 (*Talmud Yerushalmi*, p. 536), and the geniza fragment Budapest, KMTA 289 (*Ginze Yerushalmi*, p. 240).

6   For discussions of these traditions see: Tabory, 'The Crucifixion of the Paschal Lamb'; Bokser, 'Todos and Rabbinic Authority'; Ilan, 'Torah of the Jews of Ancient Rome', pp. 386–87.

7   Irshai, 'Ya'akov of Kefar Niburaia'.

8   yYev 2:6 (4a); *Genesis Rabbah*, 7:2 (p. 50); Pesikta de Rav Kahana 4:3 (p. 63); EccR 7:23.

9   Fine, 'Between Texts and Archaeology', p. 11.

On the Road to Rome

In the following pages, I focus on one travel narrative of the sages to Rome that seems to portray how the (rabbinic) centre imagines the diasporic periphery when that periphery is the empire's centre. I suggest that it undermines the strict dichotomy of us and them, here and there, that structures hegemonic identity narratives by displaying a double embeddedness within separate social systems, where otherness is always infiltrating sameness and vice-versa.[10]

Travel narratives are a fruitful vehicle for examining this question because they thematize 'an encounter between self and other that is brought about by a movement through space',[11] and often challenge the manner we see both ourselves and our others. As Tim Whitmarsh has remarked concerning the Greek Novel, a genre of travel writing cotemporaneous with rabbinic literature, 'travels introduce difference into the identity narrative, a deviation both temporal and spatial, from the linearity that constitutes identity (in its root sense of sameness)'.[12] In particular, travel narratives that take place 'on the road', in the liminal space of betwixt-and-between, can become a site for cultures to represent and dramatize its own fissures and fictions of identity in the complex interaction between self and other that is brought about by movement in space. Simon Ward has emphasized the opportunities which roads and similar spaces present: 'To enter a liminal landscape is to open up a space of free play, but also to open up oneself to experiences beyond the boundaries normally set by society, to confrontations with what that society has placed *beyond* its boundaries, with the abject that "disturbs identity, system, order [and] does not respect borders, positions, rules"'.[13]

Going Native in Rome

The following narrative recounts a complex tale of a rabbinic sojourn in Rome in the context of magic contests with gentiles (ySan 7:13 [25d]).[14] There are three dominant cultural functions of travel writing — as a means of acquiring and disseminating knowledge, expressing power, and forming and performing identity — and all three are present in the narrative before us. While this

---

10 See Clifford, 'Diasporas'.
11 Thompson, *Travel Writing*, p. 10.
12 Whitmarsh, *Narrative and Identity*, p. 20. See also, Hezser, 'Strangers on the Road'.
13 Ward, 'The British "Road-Movie"', p. 186, quoting Kristeva, *Powers of Abjection*, p. 4.
14 On the Jewish community in late antique Rome, see Rutgers, *The Jews in Late Ancient Rome*; Barclay, *Jews in the Mediterranean Diaspora*; Williams, 'The Structure of the Jewish Community in Rome'; Williams, 'Being a Jew in Rome'; Noy, *Foreigners at Rome*; Cappelletti, *The Jewish Community of Rome*; Ilan, 'Torah of the Jews of Ancient Rome'; Simonsohn, *The Jews of Italy*. For an analysis of this tale in relation to its context, see Levinson 'Enchanting Rabbis'.

narrative from the Jerusalem Talmud is not, of course, a product of this community, it does provide us with a perspective on how their Palestinian rabbinic compatriots saw them.

The connection between a magic contest and travel narrative is not as unusual as it first appears. Travel narratives thematize boundary crossings, a departure from the known world and an encounter with the unknown. In other words, identity — one's own and that of an other — is always a sub-text of these stories. To this generic mixture is added a third. The tale concludes with the victorious confrontation with a local witch and the subsequent birth of one of the most prominent rabbinic figures of the diaspora, R. Yehuda b. Bathyra who resided in Nisbis, itself a border town between the Roman and Sasanian empires.[15] It is thus also a tale of the birth of a sage and rabbinic continuity. As I hope to show, it is precisely this generic blend that stages the central cultural anxiety represented here.

The narrative plays out in three scenes, and in each the rabbis confront a different diasporic identity and a different identity option. In the first is depicted their arrival, in the second they are hosted by a local Jewish family, and in the third the Roman witch is defeated:

A. R. Eliezer, R. Yehoshua, and Rabban Gamliel traveled to Rome. They came to a place and found some children making piles [of stones or dirt], saying, This is how the people of the Land of Israel (בני ארעא דישראל) do and say, This is for the Heave Offering, and this is for the Tithe. They [the sages] said, It seems that there are Jews here.[16]

In rabbinic cultural cartography, Rome and Jerusalem were thought of as agonistic entities, where the former was a type of dystopian doppelgänger of Israel.[17] Moreover, as Ron Naiweld has argued, the comparison between the two cities is articulated as a zero-sum game that becomes a meta-historical principle, as the ascent of one nation is the result of the decline of the other.[18] Thus, it is understandable that the Rabbis travel with a certain sense of trepidation to the heart of the 'evil empire'.

Upon arrival, their first encounter with the natives is rather bizarre; they see local children playing a game. Feelings of apprehension are relieved when the first thing they encounter are children playing at being Palestinian Jews separating tithes. While not stated explicitly, it seems reasonable to assume that these are local Roman Jewish children playing at being Jews from the Land of Israel, and not gentile children playing at being Jews in Palestine, who

---

15 See, ySan 1:2 (19a); bSan 32b; Dignas and Winter, *Rome and Persia in Late Antiquity*.

16 ySan 7:13 (25d), translated from *Talmud Yerushalmi*, p. 1306.

17 This worldview was actually shared by both nations. See, for example, bMeg 6a; yAZ 1:2, (39c); Genesis Rabba 33:1 (p. 300); Cicero, *Pro Flacco* XXVIII.66–69 in Stern, *Greek and Latin Authors*, I.68; Tacitus, *Hist.*, V.4.1, in Stern, *Greek and Latin Authors*, II:25. See also, Favro, 'The Iconicity of Ancient Rome'.

18 Naiweld, 'Use of Rabbinic Traditions', p. 13; Gribetz, 'A Matter of Time', pp. 66–72.

would not know the laws of tithes. The rather rare phrase 'the people of the Land of Israel' is only recorded as being said by Jews in the diaspora about Jews in Palestine,[19] and the deduction of the Rabbis that 'there are Jews here' is much stronger if we posit the Jewish identity of these children.

While descriptions of children's games are rather rare in rabbinic literature, we know that it is not unusual to find various types of gaming boards cut into the pavements of the fora and sidewalks in any Roman city, as well as frescoes and mosaics portraying gamers and gamblers.[20] There are other examples in contemporaneous literature, as well, of children assuming the identity of religious figures in play. Theodoret describes a group of young girls in fourth-century Syria; some dressed up as monks while others acted as sufferers seeking exorcism. 'One, dressed in rags, would put her little friends into stitches of laughter by exorcising them'.[21] Likewise, John Moschos in *The Spiritual Meadow*, relates an incident on an estate near Apamea in Syria when some children grew bored pasturing animals and decided to play at priests performing the Eucharist. 'They did everything according to the custom of the church; but before they divided the bread, fire came down from heaven and consumed all the offerings', and the children themselves 'fell to the ground and lay there, half dead'.[22] While very different from our narrative in tone, it is interesting to note that like the Eucharist, the separation of tithes is accomplished by performative ritual discourse, through words. As Derek Krueger remarked, 'if there were ever doubts about the results of "ritual play", or the ability to "do things with words", this incident dispels them'.[23] The common dominator between Eucharistic transubstantiation and the separation of tithes is the use of ritual language to affect a material change, and I will return to this matter later on.

The obvious question is, why did our narrator choose to open this tale of a violent magic contest in such an irenic and circuitous manner? The first thing the Rabbis encounter on foreign soil is actually a copy of themselves: a scene of cultural mimicry. Homi Bhabha first coined this phrase to describe internal contradictions and ambivalence ('almost white, but not quite') inherent in colonial discourse. Mimicry is replication with a difference, 'at once resemblance and menace'.[24] He mentions a two-fold menace of mimicry. On the one hand, if mimicry is complete then it threatens to undermine any

---

19 yBer 2:8 (5c); yKil 9:4 (32c); *Genesis Rabbah*, 96 (p. 1240).

20 Schwartz, 'Aspects of Leisure-Time Activities'; DeFelice, 'Inns and Taverns', p. 480; Kellum, 'The Spectacle of the Street', p. 288; Trfiliò, 'Movement, Gaming and the Use of Space'. For an illuminating example of street games, see the discussion of the border of the Megalopsychia Mosaic (mid-fifth century), discovered in Antioch in Hartnett, *The Roman Street*, pp. 2–4; Matthews, *The Journey of Theophanes*, pp. 79–88.

21 Theodoret of Cyrrhus, *A History of the Monks of Syria*, p. 85, quoted in Brown, 'The Rise and Function of the Holy Man', p. 88.

22 Moschos, *The Spiritual Meadow*, p. 173.

23 Krueger, 'The Unbounded Body', p. 268.

24 Bhabha, *The Location of Culture*, p. 86.

essential difference between colonizer and colonized. Therefore, in the drive to refashion the colonized in the image of the colonizer, it must repeatedly create difference in order to sustain the distinction between them on which colonial control depends. 'In order to be effective, mimicry must continually produce its slippage, its excess, its difference.'[25] On the other hand, mimicry can also be a tactic of resistance on the part of the colonized by exposing the artificiality of colonial authority. Mimicry suggests that our constructions of identity are necessarily fluid, imaginary, and contingent.

The mimicry portrayed here is different, and delightfully complicates Bhabha's colonial situation. This is not the case of the colonized or subjugated mimicking their masters as a tactic of resistance, but rather of diasporic Roman Jews mimicking rabbis from the Roman province of *Palaestina Prima*. In other words, a Palestinian rabbinic document portrays how they imagined, or fantasized, that the Jews of the diaspora wished to imitate them. Thus, Palestinian religious practice as an object of emulation is projected upon this diaspora community. This scene also raises the trope of rabbinic propagation and dissemination with which the narrative concludes, as Palestinian mores and practices are spread (*diaspeirein*) abroad. Perhaps it is not coincidental that there is something non-normative ('not quite') in this mimicry, as the laws of tithes are not applicable outside the Land of Israel, so this game playfully undermines spatial difference of centre and periphery.

It is not fortuitous that this encounter itself takes place on the border, not only the border between land and sea, but more importantly between Rabbinic, pagan, and diasporic Jewish identities. As Yuri Lotman has pointed out, the notion of a border is inherently ambivalent and hybrid; it both separates and connects identities. Since any border by its very nature straddles two semiotic spheres at once, it is not only the site where identities are defined and defended but also where they meet and mingle.[26] We can view this scene as an embodiment of what James Clifford has called the 'Squanto effect'. Squanto was the Native American who greeted the pilgrims in 1620 in Plymouth, and speaking English was able to help them survive the harsh winter. 'Think of coming into a new place like that and having the uncanny experience of running into a Patuxet just back from Europe. A disconcertingly hybrid "native" met at the ends of the earth — strangely familiar, and different precisely in that unprocessed familiarity.'[27] Meeting the children playing at being Rabbis at the gates of Rome is much like meeting 'a disconcertingly hybrid native at the ends of the earth'.

It is hard to think of a better way to dramatize the instability of identity, of identity as performance, than as child's play.[28] The menace of this hybrid image is that upon arriving at Rome, perhaps at the *limen* itself, the strange and

---

25 Bhabha, *The Location of Culture*, p. 86.
26 Lotman, *Universe of the Mind*, pp. 131–42.
27 Clifford, *Routes*, p. 19.
28 Butler, 'Performative Acts and Gender Constitution'.

foreign is transformed into something uncannily familiar, as if they had never left home at all. These children embody a hybrid identity that destabilizes the distinction between here and there, Israel and diaspora.

I suggest that this opening scene interrogates and problematizes hegemonic attempts to stabilize an essential identity. The sages travel to the heart of the other culture only to encounter there a refracted image of themselves, an image that undermines any essential difference between here and there, self and other. This becomes the organizing trope of the entire narrative, as in each scene the rabbis expect to confront a strange other and find themselves before a refracted image of the uncannily familiar. We see this same dynamic in the second section:

> B. They entered a certain place and were hosted in a certain home. When they sat down to eat, they noticed that each dish served to them was first brought to a small chamber before it was served to them. They feared that the food was sacrificial offerings to the dead. They asked [their host]; Why is it that each dish you bring us is first brought to that chamber before it is served to us? Their host said; I have an elderly father, and he took an oath (גזר על נפשיה) that he would not leave his room until he saw the Sages of Israel. They said; Go and tell him to come out for they are here. He emerged from the room and they asked him; What are you doing? He said; Pray for my son who cannot produce children.

Here too the sages encounter a strange practice as the behaviour of their presumably Jewish host arouses their suspicion that he has 'gone native' and performs some form of idolatrous or syncretistic ritual. However, once again what first appears to be strange and foreign is domesticated when they learn of the father's oath to seek relief from the 'Sages of Israel' because his son was suffering from impotence due to the sorcery of a local witch. In all likelihood, the mistaken assumption of sacrifices reflects the reality of household shrines, or *lararium*, whether in the form of a simple niche, aedicule or wall painting. These were often situated in the interior of the house, the atrium, or even in bedchambers. They consisted of representations of the images of the family deities and the provision for sacrifice before these images.[29]

There is an interesting analogy between the first two sections of the narrative. On the one hand, the pre-eminence of Palestinian sages is presupposed in both, either as a model to imitate or because of the efficacy of their prayers and magical prowess. And yet, these are both cases of crossing or blurring the borders of identity. Within the parameters of here and there, us and them, so strongly demarcated in the texts presented at the beginning of this essay, the Roman-Jewish children straddle the border of here and there, just as their host appears to blur the border between us and them. The rabbis' presumption of difference is recuperated as sameness.

---

29 Boyce, 'Corpus of the Lararia of Pompeii'; Orr, 'Roman Domestic Religion'; Yegül and Favro, *Roman Architecture*, p. 249; Small, 'Urban, Suburban and Rural Religion', pp. 191–93.

228 JOSHUA LEVINSON

It becomes clear that the hybrid identity of their host is a mistaken assumption on the part of the rabbis, and the appearance of idolatry is recuperated as the normative and even laudable religious behaviour of an oath to see the sages. It is this moment of hesitation in both sections that raises the spectre that forms of identity are neither given nor mutually exclusive, but rather the result of an overdetermined process of closure. There is always the possibility, even if partially silenced, of what could be or might have been. Thus, in each of these two scenes the narrator both presents options of a hybrid double embeddedness that undermines the dichotomy between sameness and difference, and then recuperates them.

After learning that the son's impotence is the result of malicious magic, the narrative culminates with a confrontation and magical exorcism. Here, difference is not only undermined but also internalized, as the identity of the sages themselves is revealed to be disconcertedly hybrid:

> C. R. Eliezer said to R. Yehoshua; Yehoshua b. Hananya show what you can do. He said to them; Bring me flax seeds, and they brought him. He appeared (איתחמי) to sow the seeds on a table, he appeared to sprinkle water on it and it appeared to sprout, and he appeared to uproot it until he drew up a woman by her tresses. He said to her; Release (שרי) [the spell] that you have cast. She said; I will not. He said; If you do not then I will expose you. She said; I cannot because they were thrown into the sea. R. Yehoshua then decreed (גזר) upon the Prince of the Sea and he disgorged them. They then prayed for him [the barren son], and he was merited with the birth of R. Yehudah b. Bathyra. The sages said; If we had only come here to beget this righteous man, it would have been sufficient for us.

Of the three cultural functions of travel writing mentioned above, the tensions between power and identity are most apparent in this final scene. Although their host requested that the sages pray for his son, R. Yehoshua first enacts a full-scale exorcism to force the malevolent witch to release her spell, and only afterwards do they pray, and as a result of their efforts one of the founding figures of diasporic rabbinic Jewry is born. The successful exorcism demonstrates the sages' power, yet once again destabilizes any essential difference between them and their antagonist.

Tales of magical prowess in nullifying curses and saving the bewitched are rather routine motifs in hagiography. These tales, as Peter Brown has remarked, play out as a theatrical script that dramatically display the power of the Holy Man and the superiority of his God to the demonic world.[30] Rabbis and witches are a powerful pair, and because they both manipulate ritual power for various ends one could say that they compete over the means of production of sacred power and prestige. It is not surprising, therefore, that

---

30 Brown, 'The Rise and Function', p. 88.

'long and intimate duels with the local sorcerer were almost *de rigueur* in the life of a successful saint'.[31] Since the magician was a type of rabbinic nemesis he constituted a serious challenge to rabbinic authority and identity, and no one was more aware of this challenge than the rabbis themselves. John Gager has succinctly summarized the threat posed by magicians to the custodians of 'legitimate' power and authority:

> The idea that magoi could dispense power on matters of central importance to human life; the idea that any private person, for nothing but a small fee, could put that power to use in a wide variety of circumstances; the idea that all of these transactions were available to individuals who stood outside and sometimes against the 'legitimate' corporate structures of society — all of these ideas presented a serious threat to those who saw themselves as jealous guardians of power emanating from the center of that society, whether Greek, Roman, Antiochene, or Rabbinic. Here was power beyond their control, power in the hands of freely negotiating individuals.[32]

This threat was felt by rabbis and priests alike as competing purveyors and practitioners of sacred power. Chrysostom castigates those Christians who 'use the cures of the Jews [...] their incantations, their amulets, their charms and spells [...] It is better to die than to run to God's enemies and be cured that way'.[33] Likewise, the fourth-century Synod of Laodicea decreed that 'they who are of the priesthood, or of the clergy, shall not be magicians, enchanters, mathematicians, or astrologers; nor shall they make what are called amulets, which are chains for their own souls. And those who wear such, we command to be cast out of the Church'.[34]

While hagiographic texts often show that exorcisms can be effected by prayer, or even the mere appearance of the holy man, sometimes they take the form of more complex negotiations and interrogations, as in the text before us.[35] Thus, after praying, Peter the Galatian 'ordered the demon to tell all he had done, and like some murderer or burglar standing before the judge's seat he proceeded through everything, compelled by fear to tell the truth, contrary to his wont'.[36] Regardless of the manner of exorcism, all hagiographical expulsions are displays of power that ultimately served to highlight the potent agency of the holy man or sage.

---

31 Brown, *Authority and the Sacred*, p. 67. See also, Dickie, 'Narrative Patterns in Christian Hagiography'; Magoulias, 'Lives of Byzantine Saints'; Kazhdan, 'Holy and Unholy Miracle Workers'.

32 Gager, *Curse Tablets*, p. 24.

33 Chrysostom, *Discourses Against Judaizing Christians*, p. 222. This attitude mirrors that of R. Yishmael who prohibited the curing of a snake-bite in the name of Jesus; 'Happy are you, Ben Dama, for you have departed in peace, and you did not break down the hedge of the Sages' (tHul 2:22).

34 Canon 36, quoted in Trzcionka, *Magic and the Supernatural*, p. 123.

35 Trzcionka, *Magic and the Supernatural*, p. 145.

36 Theodoret of Cyrrhus, *History of the Monks of Syria*, 9.9, p. 85.

There are a number of particularly interesting elements in the exorcism narrated here. Firstly, as mentioned above, the father requested the sages' prayer, yet contrary to what we just saw in the anecdote of Peter the Galatian, they only do so after defeating the witch. It is not entirely clear if we are to understand their prayer as the concluding act of the exorcism or something new connected to the birth of R. Yehuda. Are magic and prayer presented here as essentially different modes of interacting with the supernatural, or, is that an untenable anachronistic distinction?[37] Perhaps the sages' prayer is precisely the 'replication with a difference' mentioned by Bhabha that cultural mimicry must continually produce.

In any case, there is evident irony in the fact that while the diasporic Jew, just now suspected of idolatry, requested prayer from the 'Sages of Israel', the sages themselves engage in (Roman?) magic. This is another reversal of expectations regarding the strange and familiar. And while the impotent son cannot produce offspring, R. Yehoshua enacts a full-scale magical ceremony where he is seen as 'seeding' and 'growing' — in a manner suspiciously similar to birthing — the local sorceress who has bewitched the son, and enables the birth of a diasporic sage.

While magical practices are fairly prevalent in rabbinic literature, texts about magic, unlike magical texts themselves, rarely describe the actual practice itself, and prefer to use oblique and indirect phrases like 'he said what he said', meaning to cast a spell.[38] However, the present narrative is unusually loquacious and exemplifies much of what we know from primary or insider evidence in magical texts and material artifacts.[39] The type of magic portrayed here is most likely a binding tablet (*defixio*), a ubiquitous form of magic in the Graeco-Roman world; as Pliny the Elder stated, 'there is no one who does not fear this type of magic'.[40] The Latin term *defixiones* is derived from the verb 'to bind or fasten' (*defigere*), and may refer either to the physical form of the curses in their rolled up and bound state, or their fundamental function of restraining, or both. David Jordan describes these curious objects as 'inscribed pieces of lead, usually in the form of thin sheets, intended to bring supernatural power to bear against persons and animals against their will', and customarily without their knowledge.[41] The chief magical idiom employed by the texts is one of binding and restraining not only in relation to the tablet itself but also in terms of function.[42] Esther Eidinow has said that, 'the primary form of influence sought in binding spells was to constrain or "bind" the

---

37 Edmonds, *Drawing Down the Moon*, pp. 149–87; Graf, 'Prayer in Magic'.

38 Sperber, *Magic and Folklore*, pp. 60–66.

39 On this important distinction see, Bohak, *Ancient Jewish Magic*, p. 70.

40 Pliny, *Natural History*, 28.4.19. See also, Ogden, 'Binding Spells'; Eidinow, 'Binding Spells on Tablets'. Already three decades ago, Gager mentioned that the number of surviving examples exceeds fifteen hundred (Gager, *Curse Tablets*, p. 3).

41 Jordan, 'Defixiones', p. 206.

42 Ogden, 'Binding Spells', p. 26.

victim',[43] and once they were manufactured, inscribed with text, pictures and *charaktêres*, the final stage of the tablet's activation was its deposition, often in the ground or a body of water. Thus, a recipe for the manufacture of a curse tablet recommends that it be deposited in 'a river or land or sea or stream or coffin or in a well'.[44] So, the Life of St Hilarion tells of the unrequited love of a man in Gaza for a Christian virgin, who travelled to Memphis to learn the magical arts. 'Upon returning he concealed under the threshold of the girl's home certain revolting words of magic and hideous figures engraved on thin sheets of Cyprian copper'. As a result, 'the virgin went mad with desire' until Hilarion succeeded in exorcising the demon from the young lady and restoring her sanity.[45] Likewise, Theophilus of Alexandria was attacked by a witch, and was told in a dream that he must find a chest that was thrown in the sea. Once drawn up from the water, the chest was found to contain 'a small bronze statuette whose hands and feet were pierced by nails'.[46]

Thus, the detail that the curse tablet was thrown into the sea is not a mere narrative embellishment, but part of the ritual itself. Also, the fact that Roman law explicitly forbade harmful magic gives weight to Yehoshua's threat to expose the witch. As a fourth-century rescript in the Theodosian Code records: 'the Chaldeans and wizards (*magi*) and all the rest whom the common people call magicians (*malefici*), because of the multitude of their crimes [...] shall suffer capital punishment, felled by the avenging sword'.[47] In addition, many representations of witches and female demons, both linguistic and pictorial, emphasize their unbound tresses. The Talmud states that one of the curses of Eve was that 'she grows long hair like Lilith' (bEruv 100b), and many of the depictions of female demons in the Babylonian magic bowls have long unbound hair.[48] In fact, one of the prominent characteristics of she-demons portrayed in the bowls with wild unbound hair is that they attack the sexual and reproductive realm of life.[49]

We know from the narrative itself that the curse concerned impotence, although we are left in the dark concerning its circumstances and motivations. Gager has remarked that 'roughly one-quarter of all surviving tablets concern "matters of the heart"'.[50] So, it could be the result of erotic competition where restraining curses would bind and hamper the activities of the competitor in the erotic arena. As Christopher Faraone remarked, 'if a lover or would-be lover feared the outcome of a contest, he might turn to the use of a *defixio* in

---

43 Eidinow, 'Binding Spells on Tablets', p. 351.
44 Gager, *Curse Tablets*, p. 18.
45 Jerome, 'Life of St Hilarion', 21, p. 259.
46 Magoulias, 'Lives of Byzantine Saints', pp. 236–38.
47 *Theodosian Code*, 9.16.4, p. 237. See also, *CTh* 9.16.11, *Twelve Tables* VIII.8a; Barb, 'The Survival of Magical Arts'.
48 Vilozny, *Lilith's Hair and Ashmedai's Horns*, p. 118.
49 Lesses, 'Exe(o)rcising Power', p. 356.
50 Gager, *Curse Tablets*, p. 78. See also, Winkler, *The Constraints of Desire*, pp. 71–98.

order to impede the advances, the flirting, and even the sexual performance of his or her rival'.[51]

The Targum Yonathan on Deut. 24:6 says: 'Let no one bind (אסר) grooms and brides with a spell for he injures the future child'.[52] Similarly, Ovid blames witchcraft for his sexual failure:

> Was I the wretched victim of charms and herbs, or did a witch curse my name upon a red wax image and stick fine pins into the middle of the liver? When damned by charms the corn withers on the sterile stalk, and when a well is damned by charms, its water dries up; through incantations acorns drop from oaks and grapes from vines, and apples fall when no one has touched them. What prevents the cessation of my energy being due to magical practices? It is perhaps from that source that my powers became inadequate.[53]

Theodoret relates that Romanus often drove out serious diseases, and gave to many sterile women the gift of children.[54] Likewise, Jerome records that St Hilarion's first miracle concerned 'a certain woman of Eleutheropolis, finding herself despised by her husband because of her sterility […] When he learned the cause of her grief, raising his eyes to heaven, he commanded her to have faith and to believe. He followed her departure with tears. When a year had gone by, he saw her with her son'.[55] So it is not surprising that the power of rabbinic magic is concerned with reproduction and continuity, but it is unusual that it brings about the birth of a sage.

Refracted Identities

As I alluded above, the key to understanding this text is its complex generic mix; it is a magical contest that is also a travel narrative and relates the birth tale of a sage. Returning to the three cultural functions of travel writing — as a means of acquiring and disseminating knowledge, expressing power, and forming and performing identity — we could say that as a magical contest, it exemplifies the power of the sages who venture forth from the colonized periphery of the empire to its very centre, to Rome, and vanquish there a local witch who threatens Jewish continuity. As an etiological tale recounting the birth of a diasporic sage it also has a polemical sting. Rabbinic continuity and the production of new (diaspora) sages would seem to depend upon the

---

51 Faraone, 'The Agonistic Context', p. 13; Edmonds, *Drawing Down the Moon*, p. 93.

52 See also the extra-talmudic tale cited by Rashi about Yohani b. Rativi who, when acting as a midwife, would bind up the womb of a birthing mother by witchcraft until she cried for help and then she would release her spell (bSot 22a).

53 Ovid, *Amores*, III.7.27–38, p. 477. See also Petronius, *Satyricon*, 131, p. 341 where Encolpius is similarly afflicted and regains his potency from the incantations of an old witch.

54 Theodoret of Cyrrhus, *History of the Monks of Syria*, p. 95.

55 Jerome, 'Life of St Hilarion', 13, pp. 252–53.

magical prowess of the Palestinian rabbis.[56] Thus, it dramatizes the supremacy of rabbinic power and prestige. But as a travel narrative it emphasizes questions of identity. From this perspective we could say that the sages journey not from the periphery of the empire to its centre, but rather from the heart of normative Jewish identity in Palestine to its diasporic margins.

This, to my mind, is the thematic core of this narrative, the problematic fluidity of identity. To be sure, the sages are revealed as master practitioners of magic, but the price they pay for their victory is to destabilize any reified difference between themselves and their opponents. Thus, in this tale, the sages travel to the heart of the other culture only to encounter there a refracted image of themselves. Likewise, in each scene they expect to confront a strange other and find themselves before the uncannily familiar. This motif is played out not only in the encounter with the children, but also with the old man who at first seems to embody the foreign otherness of idolatrous practices but is revealed to be waiting for the prayers of the very sages who suspect him. And the opposite is also the case: the old man puts his trust in the prayers of the sages, but they perform for him a demonic exorcism. Just as the diasporic children appear to separate tithes, and the old man appears to offer sacrifices to the dead, so R. Yehoshua appears (אִיתחמי) to produce a witch. Sorcery itself seems the embodiment of the strange and foreign, and yet it brings about the birth of a rabbinic sage.

This brings us to an additional important matter. The old man binds himself by an oath not to leave his room, just as R. Yehoshua binds the Prince of the Sea. The overt linguistic parallel between the oath of the father (גזר על נפשיה) and the magic of the rabbis (גזר על שריא דימא) collapses the difference between these two illocutionary acts, both of which use the same verb. Both oaths and magical spells have autonomous efficacy and use performative 'illocutionary speech acts that accomplish in the world what they declare verbally'.[57] The well-documented rabbinic aversion to oaths is based precisely upon this similarity.[58] More importantly, Manekin-Bamburger has shown that while tannaitic texts use this verb in quasi-legal contexts of a legal decree or oath, later talmudic texts as well as the magic bowls employ it in the sense of a magical vow or adjuration to force demonic powers to heed to a human will.[59] Once again, our expectations are reversed as the diasporan Jew uses this verb in its 'rabbinic' juridical sense while R. Yehoshua employs the full force of a magical locution.

In each section of this narrative the discourse of power undermines that of identity, as the border between here and there, us and them, becomes

---

56 This theme in connection with Bathyra is also stressed in ySan 1:2 (19a). See Herman, 'The Jews of Parthian Babylonia', p. 148.

57 Frankfurter, 'Spell and Speech Act', p. 609; See also, Tambiah, 'Form and Meaning of Magical Acts', pp. 60–86; Manekin-Bamberger, 'The Vow-Curse'.

58 Lieberman, *Greek in Jewish Palestine*, pp. 115–43.

59 Manekin-Bamberger, 'Intersections Between Law and Magic', pp. 141–69.

dangerously blurred. It embodies in a particularly forceful manner the hybrid nature of any boundary that both connects and separates identities. We saw how the children straddle the spatial border of here and there, and the host blurs the religio-ethnic border between Jew and pagan. Now we can say that even the rabbis themselves are hybrid characters who blur the boundary between normative and non-normative uses of ritual power; magic enables the birth of a sage — and a sage 'gives birth' to a magician.

If, as Freud suggested, the uncanny reveals itself in the return of the repressed — when we unexpectedly meet that which was denied — then perhaps we could say that the sages are struggling here with those repressed aspects of their own identity; the recognition of the inherent hybridity of all identities. This is the otherness within them that haunts the cultural periphery of the narrator and his characters. As Alan Sinfield has remarked, 'all stories comprise within themselves the ghosts of the alternative stories they are trying to exclude'.[60] The journey to the heart of the other culture reveals that the very distinctions that enable identity are more unstable and porous than they may wish to acknowledge. Each side wears the other's mask, employing cultural mimicry in order to establish his own identity. In a wonderfully dialogical manner, neither side here can express his own identity without using that of the other.

What picture does this rabbinic text present us of the diasporian Jewish community in Rome and their interactions with the Sages of Israel? Unsurprisingly, rabbinic hegemony, authority, and power are affirmed. Less predictable is the expression of this affirmation. The diasporic space of the narrative is the point at which boundaries of inclusion and exclusion, of belonging and otherness, of 'us' and 'them', are contested. Identity is constructed out of paradoxical combination of sameness and difference. The identities of both the rabbis and their local hosts display a type of double consciousness where identity 'is defined, not by essence or purity, but by the recognition of a necessary heterogeneity and diversity; by a conception of "identity" which lives with and through, not despite, difference'.[61]

---

60 Sinfield, *Faultlines*, p. 47.
61 Hall, 'Cultural Identity', p. 235.

Bibliography

Primary Sources

Chrysostom, John, *Discourses Against Judaizing Christians*, trans. by Paul Harkins (Washington, DC: The Catholic University of America Press, 1979)

Genesis Rabbah, ed. by Julius Theodor and Chanokh Albeck (Wahrmann: Jerusalem, 1965)

Ginze Yerushalmi, ed. by Yaacov Sussmann (Jerusalem: Yad Izhak Ben-Zvi, 2020)

Jerome, 'Life of St Hilarion', in *Early Christian Biographies*, ed. by Roy Deferrari (Washington, DC: The Catholic University of America Press, 1952)

Midrash Wayyikra Rabbah, Leviticus Rabba, ed. by Mordecai Margulies (Jerusalem: Wharmann, 1972)

Moschos, John, *The Spiritual Meadow*, trans. by John Wortley (Kalamazoo: Cistercian Publications, 1992)

Ovid, *Amores*, trans. by Grant Showerman, Loeb Classical Library, 41 (Cambridge, MA: Harvard University Press, 1914)

Pesikta de Rav Kahana, ed. by Bernard Mandelbaum (New York: Jewish Theological Seminary, 1962)

Petronius, *Satyricon*, trans. by Michael Heseltine, Loeb Classical Library, 15 (Cambridge, MA: Harvard University Press, 2005)

Pliny, *Natural History*, trans. by W. H. Jones, Loeb Classical Library, 418 (Cambridge, MA: Harvard University Press, 1963)

Plutarch, *The Life of Publicola*, trans. by B. Perrin, Loeb Classical Library, 46 (Cambridge, MA: Harvard University Press, 1914)

Talmud Yerushalmi: According to Ms. Or. 4720 (Scal. 3) of the Leiden University Library with Restorations and Corrections, ed. by Yaacov Sussmann (Jerusalem: The Academy of the Hebrew Language, 2001)

Theodoret of Cyrrhus, *A History of the Monks of Syria*, ed. and trans. by R. M. Price (Kalamazoo: Cistercian Publications, 1985)

The Theodosian Code, trans. by Clyde Fharr (Princeton: Princeton University Press, 1952)

Secondary Studies

Barb, A. A., 'The Survival of Magical Arts', in *The Conflict between Paganism and Christianity in the Fourth Century*, ed. by Arnaldo Momigliano (Oxford: Clarendon Press, 1963), pp. 100–25

Barclay, John, *Jews in the Mediterranean Diaspora* (Edinburgh: T&T Clark, 1996)

——, ed., *Negotiating Diaspora: Jewish Strategies in the Roman Empire* (London: T&T Clark, 2004)

Bhabha, Homi, *The Location of Culture* (London: Routledge, 1994)

Bohak, Gideon, *Ancient Jewish Magic: A History* (Cambridge: Cambridge University Press, 2008)

Bokser, Baruch, 'Todos and Rabbinic Authority in Rome', in *Religion, Literature and Society in Ancient Israel, Formative Christianity and Judaism: Formative Judaism*, ed. by Jacob Neusner (Atlanta: Scholars, 1990), pp. 117–30

Boyce, George, 'Corpus of the Lararia of Pompeii', *Memoirs of the American Academy in Rome*, 14 (1937), 5–112

Brown, Peter, 'The Rise and Function of the Holy Man in Late Antiquity', *The Journal of Roman Studies*, 61 (1971), 80–101

Brown, Peter, *Authority and the Sacred: Aspects of the Christianisation of the Roman World* (Cambridge: Cambridge University Press, 1995)

Butler, Judith, 'Performative Acts and Gender Constitution: An Essay in Phenomenology and Feminist Theory', *Theatre Journal*, 40.4 (1988), 519–31

Cappelletti, Silvia, *The Jewish Community of Rome from the Second Century B.C. to the Third Century C.E.* (Leiden: Brill, 2006)

Clifford, James, 'Diasporas', *Cultural Anthropology*, 9.3 (1994), 302–38

——, *Routes: Travel and Translation in the Late Twentieth Century* (Cambridge, MA: Harvard University Press, 1997)

DeFelice, John, 'Inns and Taverns', in *The World of Pompeii*, ed. by John Dobbins and Pedar Foss (New York: Routledge, 2007), pp. 474–86

Dickie, Mathew, 'Narrative Patterns in Christian Hagiography', *Greek, Roman and Byzantine Studies*, 40 (1999), 83–98

Dignas, Beate, and Engelbert Winter, *Rome and Persia in Late Antiquity* (Cambridge: Cambridge University Press, 2007)

Edmonds, Radcliffe, *Drawing Down the Moon: Magic in the Ancient Greco-Roman World* (Princeton: Princeton University Press, 2019)

Eidinow, Esther, 'Binding Spells on Tablets and Papyri', in *Guide to the Study of Ancient Magic*, ed. by David Frankfurter (Leiden: Brill, 2019), pp. 351–87

Faraone, Christopher, 'The Agonistic Context of Early Greek Binding Spells', in *Magika Hiera: Ancient Greek Magic and Religion*, ed. by Christopher Faraone and Dirk Obbink (New York: Oxford University Press, 1991), pp. 3–32

Favro, Diane, 'The Iconicity of Ancient Rome', *Urban History*, 33.1 (2006), 20–38

Fine, Steven, 'Between Texts and Archaeology: Nabratein and Jacob of Kefar Nevoraia in Rabbinic Literature', in *Excavations at Ancient Nabratein: Synagogue and Environs*, ed. by Eric Meyers and Carol Meyers (Winona Lake: Eisenbrauns, 2009), pp. 3–14

Frankfurter, David, 'Spell and Speech Act: The Magic of the Spoken Word', in *Guide to the Study of Ancient Magic*, ed. by David Frankfurter (Leiden: Brill, 2019), pp. 608–25

Gager, John, *Curse Tablets and Binding Spells from the Ancient World* (Oxford: Oxford University Press, 1992)

Goodman, Martin, *A History of Judaism* (Princeton: Princeton University Press, 2018)

——, ed., *Jews in a Graeco-Roman World* (New York: Oxford University Press, 1998)

——, *Judaism in the Roman World: Collected Essays* (Leiden: Brill, 2007)

Graf, Fritz, 'Prayer in Magic and Religious Ritual', in *Magika Hiera: Ancient Greek Magic and Religion*, ed. by Christopher Faraone and Dirk Obbink (New York: Oxford University Press, 1991), pp. 188–213

Gribetz, Sarit Kattan, 'A Matter of Time: Writing Jewish Memory into Roman History', *AJS Review*, 40.1 (2016), 57–86

Hall, Stuart, 'Cultural Identity and Diaspora', in *Identity: Community, Culture, Difference*, ed. by Jonathan Rutherford (London: Lawrence & Wishart, 1990), pp. 222–37

Hartnett, Jeremy, *The Roman Street: Urban Life and Society in Pompeii, Herculaneum, and Rome* (New York: Cambridge University Press, 2017)

Herman, Geoffrey, 'The Jews of Parthian Babylonia', in *The Parthian Empire and its Religions: Studies in the Dynamics of Religious Diversity*, ed. by Peter Wick and Markus Zehnder (Gutenberg: Computus, 2012), pp. 141–50

Hezser, Catherine, *Jewish Travel in Antiquity* (Tübingen: Mohr Siebeck, 2011)

——, 'Strangers on the Road: Otherness, Identification, and Disguise in Rabbinic Travel Tales of Late Roman Palestine', in *Journeys in the Roman East: Imagined and Real*, ed. by Maren Niehoff (Tübingen: Mohr Siebeck, 2017), pp. 239–53

Ilan, Tal, 'The Torah of the Jews of Ancient Rome', *Jewish Studies Quarterly*, 16 (2009), 363–95

Irshai, Oded, 'Ya'akov of Kefar Niburaia – A Sage Turned Apostate', *Jerusalem Studies in Jewish Thought*, 2.2 (1983), 153–68 (in Hebrew)

Jordan, D. R., 'Defixiones from a Well Near the Southwest Corner of the Athenian Agora', *Hesperia*, 54 (1985), 205–55

Kalmin, Richard, 'Relationships Between Rabbis and Non-Rabbis in Rabbinic Literature of Late Antiquity', *Jewish Studies Quarterly*, 5.2 (1998), 156–70

Kazhdan, Alexander, 'Holy and Unholy Miracle Workers', in *Byzantine Magic*, ed. by Henry Maguire (Washington, DC: Dumbarton Oaks, 1995), pp. 73–82

Kellum, Barbara, 'The Spectacle of the Street', *Studies in the History of Art*, 56 (1999), 282–99

Kristeva, Julia, *Powers of Abjection: An Essay on Abjection* (New York: Columbia University Press, 1982)

Krueger, Derek, 'The Unbounded Body in the Age of Liturgical Reproduction', *Journal of Early Christian Studies*, 17 (2009), 267–79

Lesses, Rebecca, 'Exe(o)rcising Power: Women as Sorceresses, Exorcists, and Demonesses in Babylonian Jewish Society of Late Antiquity', *Journal of the American Academy of Religion*, 69 (2001), 343–75

Levinson, Joshua, 'Enchanting Rabbis: Contest Narratives between Rabbis and Magicians in Late Antiquity', *Jewish Quarterly Review*, 100 (2010), 54–94

Lieberman, Saul, *Greek in Jewish Palestine* (New York: Philipp Feldheim, 1965)

Lotman, Yuri, *Universe of the Mind: A Semiotic Theory of Culture* (London: Tauris, 1990)

Magoulias, Harry, 'The Lives of Byzantine Saints as Sources of Data for the History of Magic in the Sixth and Seventh Centuries A.D.: Sorcery, Relics and Icons', *Byzantion*, 37 (1967), 228–69

Manekin-Bamberger, Avigail, 'Intersections Between Law and Magic in Ancient Jewish Texts' (unpublished doctoral thesis, Tel-Aviv University, 2018)

——, 'The Vow-Curse in Ancient Jewish Texts', *Harvard Theological Review*, 112 (2019), 340–57

Matthews, John, *The Journey of Theophanes: Travel, Business and Daily Life in the Roman East* (New Haven: Yale University Press, 2006)

Naiweld, Ron, 'The Use of Rabbinic Traditions about Rome in the Babylonian Talmud', *Revue de l'histoire des religions*, 233 (2016), 1–19

Noy, David, *Foreigners at Rome: Citizens and Strangers* (London: Duckworth, 2000)

Ogden, Daniel, 'Binding Spells: Curse Tablets and Voodoo Dolls in the Greek and Roman Worlds', in *Witchcraft and Magic in Europe: Ancient Greece and Rome*, ed. by Bengt Ankarloo and Stuart Clark (Philadelphia: University of Pennsylvania Press, 1999), pp. 1–90

Orr, David, 'Roman Domestic Religion: The Evidence of the Household Shrines', *ANRW*, II.16.2 (1978), pp. 1557–91

Rutgers, Leonard Victor, *The Jews in Late Ancient Rome: Evidence of Cultural Interaction in the Roman Diaspora* (Leiden: Brill, 1995)

Schwartz, Joshua, 'Aspects of Leisure-Time Activities in Roman Period Palestine: The Evidence of the Talmud Yerushalmi', in *The Talmud Yerushalmi and Graeco-Roman Culture I*, ed. by Peter Schäfer (Tübingen: Mohr Siebeck, 1998), pp. 313–25

Simonsohn, Shlomo, *The Jews of Italy: Antiquity* (Leiden: Brill, 2014)

Sinfield, Alan, *Faultlines: Cultural Materialism and the Politics of Dissident Reading* (Oxford: Clarendon Press, 1992)

Small, Alastair, 'Urban, Suburban and Rural Religion in the Roman Period', in *The World of Pompeii*, ed. by John Dobbins and Pedar Foss (London: Routledge, 2007), pp. 184–211

Sperber, Daniel, *Magic and Folklore in Rabbinic Literature* (Ramat Gan: Bar-Ilan University Press, 1994)

Stern, Menachem, *Greek and Latin Authors on Jews and Judaism* (Jerusalem: Israel Academy of Sciences and Humanities, 1980)

Tabory, Joseph, 'The Crucifixion of the Paschal Lamb', *The Jewish Quarterly Review*, 86.3/4 (1996), 395–406

Tambiah, Stanley, 'Form and Meaning of Magical Acts', in *Culture, Thought, and Social Action: An Anthropological Perspective* (Cambridge, MA: Harvard University Press, 2013), pp. 60–86

Thompson, Carl, *Travel Writing* (Abingdon: Routledge, 2011)

Trfiliò, 'Movement, Gaming and the Use of Space in the Forum', in *Rome, Ostia, Pompeii: Movement and Space*, ed. by Ray Laurence and David Newsome (Oxford: Oxford University Press, 2011), pp. 312–31

Trzcionka, Silke, *Magic and the Supernatural in Fourth-Century Syria* (London: Routledge, 2007)

Vilozny, Naama, *Lilith's Hair and Ashmedai's Horns: Figure and Image in Magic and Popular Art: Between Babylonia and Palestine in Late Antiquity* (Jerusalem: Yad Ben-Zvi, 2017) (in Hebrew)

Visotzky, Burton, *Golden Bells and Pomegranates: Studies in Midrash Leviticus Rabbah* (Tübingen: Mohr Siebeck, 2003)

Ward, Simon, 'The British "Road-Movie" and the Liminal Landscape', in *Liminal Landscapes: Travel, Experience and Spaces In-Between*, ed. by Hazel Andrews and Les Roberts (London: Routledge, 2012), pp. 185–99

Williams, Margaret, 'Being a Jew in Rome: Sabbath Fasting as an Expression of Romano-Jewish Identity', in *Negotiating Diaspora: Jewish Strategies in the Roman Empire*, ed. by John Barclay (London: T&T Clark, 2004), pp. 8–18

——, 'The Structure of the Jewish Community in Rome', in *Jews in Graeco-Roman World*, ed. by Martin Goodman (New York: Oxford University Press, 1998), pp. 215–28

Whitmarsh, Tim, *Narrative and Identity in the Ancient Greek Novel* (New York: Cambridge University Press 2011), p. 20.

Winkler, John, *The Constraints of Desire: The Anthropology of Sex and Gender in Ancient Greece* (New York: Routledge, 1990)

Yegül, Fikret, and Diane Favro, *Roman Architecture and Urbanism: From the Origins to Late Antiquity* (Cambridge: Cambridge University Press, 2019)

EYAL BEN-ELIYAHU

Where Were the Two Huts
of Remus and Romulus in Rome?

The Two Huts in Rome

Rabbinic interest in the founding of Rome was motivated by a theological agenda, which found its literary expression in the midrashic passages about the huts and its practical realization in halakhic standards.[1] The rabbis used these media to convey their view that the world is run by divine plan rather than by happenstance. Through them, they emphasized that even the rise of the mighty Roman superpower was not a random event that could be explained as the logical consequence of political developments, but rather it was the direct result of the sins of the Jewish people, who thus determined their own fate.

This myth about the two huts built by Remus and Romulus as an origin story of the Roman Empire is found in several parallels in rabbinic literature.[2]

---

1 Elsewhere, I have discussed the halakhic aspect and argued that the legal definition and the history of the Roman *pomerium* is a useful prism through which to study the concept of 'walled cities from the days of Joshua' as applied to cities other than Jerusalem that are not mentioned in the book of Joshua but do have a biblical tradition predating the Return to Zion. The attribution of these cities to the days of Joshua, I have suggested, should be examined within the context of the Roman *pomerium* ceremony, which is in fact, a symbolic reestablishment, of a city. See Ben-Eliyahu, 'Cities Surrounded by a Wall from the Time of Joshua bin Nun'.

2 One branch of the tradition refers to the calves erected by Jeroboam as the trigger for the building of the two huts by Remus and Romulus. This tradition appears in y. 'Abod. Zar. 1.3, 39c; Song of Songs Rab. 1–6; b. Šabb. 56b; and b. Sanh. 21b. Another branch does not relate to the sin of Jeroboam but does mention the she-wolf that was sent to nurse the twins; see Midr. Esth Rab. 3.5: 'There were two twins who were left to him, these were Romeyus and Romyulus [according to Cambridge, University Library, MS Add. 495]. You gave them at first to a wolf to nurse, and later they stood and built two great huts in Rome'. So, too, in the later Midr. Ps 10.6, these traditions about Remus and Romulus building the huts in Rome do not link the story to Jeroboam. For parallels, see Funk, Albrecht, and Schlögl, eds, pp. 8–10. On the spread of this tradition about the she-wolf and Remus and Romulus in the Christian east, see Geiger, 'A Christian Mosaic and a Jewish Midrash', pp. 461–63.

Eyal Ben-Eliyahu is Professor in the Department of Jewish History at the University of Haifa.

Essays on Jews and Christians in Late Antiquity in Honour of Oded Irshai, ed. by Brouria Bitton-Ashkelony and Martin Goodman, CELAMA 40 (Turnhout: Brepols, 2023), pp. 241–249
BREPOLS ❧ PUBLISHERS   10.1484/M.CELAMA-EB.5.132492

The parallels in the Jerusalem Talmud, Song of Songs Rabbah, and the Babylonian Talmud tie the two huts built by Remus and Romulus to the sin of Jeroboam, who built altars in Beth-El and Dan so that the people of the Kingdom of Israel would not feel the need to make pilgrimages to the Temple in Jerusalem.[3] As the foundation of Rome is presented in the Jerusalem Talmud:

> Said R. Levi: 'It is the day on which Solomon married into [the family of] Pharaoh Necho, king of Egypt. On that day, [the angel] Michael came down and thrust a reed into the sea, and pulled up muddy alluvium, [and it grew to a large thicket of reeds, and this was the great city of Rome]'.

> On the day on which Jeroboam erected the two golden calves, Remus and Romulus came and built two huts in the city of Rome. [1 Kings 22:48].

> On the day on which Elijah disappeared, a king was appointed in Rome: 'There was no king in Edom; a deputy was king' [1 Kings 22:48] (y. Avodah Zarah 1:2 [39c])[4]

This tradition embodies the belief that the vast, threatening empire of Rome, which destroyed the Temple and ruled over the Land of Israel, was founded as a result of the sins of Solomon and Jeroboam and the disappearance of Elijah.[5] As such, the tradition aligns with the aforementioned tenet of the Jewish faith by which the external events that affect Jewish history directly derive from the spiritual, moral, and religious level of the Jewish people. Thus, the *tzrifim* passages graphically link the iniquitous inadequacies of the Jewish nation to the rise of Rome, which, with its unlimited power, was responsible for the destruction of the Temple and subsequent millennia-spanning exile of the Jewish people.

Specifically, according to this tradition, the act that symbolized the foundation of Rome as a city[6] was the building of two huts in Rome. The

---

3 While in the Jerusalem Talmud and Midrash Song of Songs Rabbah, the link with the sin of Jeroboam is the second of three stages in the foundation of Rome, the Babylonian Talmud mentions only the first and second stages, the sins of Solomon and Jeroboam.

4 Translation by Kattan-Gribetz, *Time and Difference in Rabbinic Judaism*, pp. 68–69. She remarks that there are two partial parallels of this text in several manuscripts and printed editions of b. Šabb. 56b and b. Sanh. 21a, which contain significant variants (the passage is altogether absent in MS Jerusalem — Yad Harav Herzog 1 of b. Sanh. 21a). See also her apparatus in Kattan-Gribetz, 'A Matter of Time', p. 67 n. 29. B. Sanh. 21b is parallel to the first line of this narrative, in which Solomon's intermarriage causes an angel to stick a reed into the sea, which establishes the city of Rome. See also Feldman, 'Abba Kolon and the Founding of Rome'.

5 While it is understandable why the sins of Solomon and Jeroboam led to the construction of Rome, which ultimately harmed Israel, it must be explained why the disappearance of Elijah mentioned in the parallels in the Jerusalem Talmud and in Midrash Song of Songs Rabbah led to the establishment of a king in Rome. The causal connection might lie in the midrash's perception that Elijah's departure was itself a consequence of the sins of the people of Israel in his days.

6 To be precise, the tradition regarding the founding of Rome and the spiritual causes

The Two Roman Pyramids

Given the definition of the word, *tzrif*, Joseph Geiger's identification of the rabbinic reference to the two huts with two pyramids in Rome is surprising.[9] Geiger relied on the identification made by the *Mirabilis Urbis Romae*, a twelfth-century (before 1143) pilgrims' and visitors' guide that described Rome and its special structures. The guide named the Temple of Remus and the *Meta* (pyramid), also called the Sepulchre of Romulus. A later source from the late twelfth or early thirteenth century described the pyramid of Romulus as standing next to the rounded fortress on the banks of the Tiber that is known today as the Castel Sant'Angelo.[10] The Temple of Remus was also known as the Pyramid of Cestius or the Meta or Sepulcrum Remi.[11]

---

therefore is presented in three stages. The first stage, which came about due to Solomon's sin — the marriage to Pharoah's daughter — was the creation of the site on which Rome was built. The second stage, linking the sins of Jeroboam to the huts that are the subject of this article, concerns the foundation of the city, and the third stage, deriving from Elijah's departure, leads to the commencement of the monarchy in Rome.

7   See the entry in Ben-Yehuda, *A Complete Dictionary*, pp. 5636–37, where *tzrif* is rendered as: 'a kind of tent or small house made of reeds'.

8   Krauss suggests that a *tzrif* is a structure that has a roof with two slanted parts, as appears in the illustration attached to Maimonides' Commentary on the Mishnah, or, alternately, a roof that is rounded like a kind of cap; Krauss, *Qadmoniot ha-Talmud*, vol. i, part 2, pp. 236–37.

9   Geiger, 'The Tombs of Remus and Romulus'.

10 To Geiger's source, *Mirabilia Urbis Romae*, which was composed shortly before 1143, and later medieval sources, we should also add *Sefer ha-Qabbalah* by Abraham Ibn Daud (1160), which associates the wide, round structure on the Tiber with the tomb of Romulus and calls it a *tzrif*: 'The great city of Rome was built in the days of Hezekiah king of Judah by two brothers, both of whom were great kings, the first one's name being Romulus, and the second one's name being Remus. Now Romulus plotted against his brother, killed him summarily and then ruled alone. He brought all the west under Roman domination. After his death in Rome, the Romans paid him a great tribute by building a large round structure over his grave. Its diameter was approximately fifty cubits at the base, while its perimeter extended to 120 cubits; at the top it narrowed into a sort of cone (*tzrif* in Hebrew). This structure, of great height, stands intact in Rome until this very day'; *The Book of Tradition*, p. 37. On this tradition, see also Ben-Shalom, *Medieval Jews and the Christian Past*, pp. 71–80. For the connection between the twelfth-century Christian descriptions of buildings and ruins from ancient Rome that relate to Jewish history to Jewish descriptions like that of Benjamin of Tudela, see Boustan and Champagne, 'Walking in the Shadows of the Past'.

11 On this pyramid, see Richardson, Jr., *A New Topographical Dictionary*, pp. 353–54. The pyramid is located in the angle between Via Ostienses and the street skirting the base of the Aventine Hill. According to the inscriptions on the pyramid, it was the tomb of Cestius, which is probably mentioned by Cicero dated to the first century BCE.

According to Geiger's suggestion, the rabbinic account that appears in the Jerusalem Talmud about the two huts that Remus and Romulus built when Jeroboam erected calves in Dan and Beth-El relates to these two pyramids.[12] Geiger theorized that R. Levi, the fourth-century amora whose opinion is the basis for the tradition in the Jerusalem Talmud, provides the earliest testimony to the medieval traditions that identified the tomb of Romulus with the sepulchral pyramid that stood on the right bank of the Tiber west of the Mausoleum of Hadrian (*Meta Romuli*) and the Tomb of Remus with the Pyramid of Cestius. Geiger based his suggestion on the appearance of the two huts in the amoraic tradition and on the interpretation of the tannaitic sources of a *tzrif* as a structure with an inclined roof or a structure whose base is wider than its roof such that its roof is pointed like a pyramid.[13] He built his theory on the references in m. Sukkah 1:11 and t. Sukkah 1:6 to 'One who establishes his sukkah-like hut'.[14] In short, he suggested that *tzrif* in rabbinic literature is a structure that looks like a pyramid.[15] He therefore posited that the two huts that were built in Rome by Remus and Romulus, according to the rabbinic sources, are the two pyramids of Remus and Romulus.

There are three main difficulties with the identification of the two huts as these pyramids. First, the pyramids were historically held to be the tombs of Remus and Romulus. According to the link in the rabbinic literature between Jeroboam's two golden calves and the foundation of Rome, the two huts are meant to symbolize foundations, quite the opposite of tombs. Second, the *tzrif* in rabbinic literature generally relates to temporary structures like sukkot or booths,[16] and certainly not to massive and monumental structures like the tombs that are described in the *Mirabilis Urbis Romanae*. A third difficulty that could be mentioned is the lateness of Geiger's sources and the dearth of evidence from the Roman period.

---

12 On this structure, see Richardson, *A New Topographical Dictionary*, pp. 252–53; Platner, *A Topographical Dictionary*, p. 101; Geiger, 'A Christian Mosaic and a Jewish Midrash'.

13 Ben-Yehuda, *Complete Dictionary*, vol. xi, pp. 5636–37; Fox, 'A Critical Edition of Mishnah Tractate Sukkah', vol. ii, p. 33.

14 My translation.

15 See Krauss, *Talmudische Archäologie*, pp. 275–76. See also Yuditsky, 'Commentary on Genesis D (4Q254a) Scroll'. But see his remark on p. 379 n. 20, about commentators who said that a *tzrif* has two walls, like the Greek letter Λ, while in our case a pyramid has four walls.

16 Like in m. Sukkah 1:10. See also 'Tsrifin, watchtowers, and sheds in the field do not render [produce] liable. A sukkah-hut like those used in Ginnosar, even though it contains millstones and poultry, does not render [produce] liable. As for the potter's sukkah-hut, the inner part renders [produce] liable and the outer part does not. Rabbi Yose says: Anything which is not both a sunny season and rainy season dwelling does not render [produce] liable [to tithes]. A sukkah used on the festival [of Sukkot]: Rabbi Judah says: This renders [produce] liable [for tithes] But the sages exempt'. (m. Ma'aś. 3:7). Translation by Kulp, 'Sefaria', Mishnah Maasrot 3:7.

Casa Romuli

I would therefore like to suggest a new identification for the 'two huts' in Rome and associate them instead with the Casa Romuli, the hut of Romulus. Classical writers predate the rabbinic sources to the huts referred to as Casa Romuli on the Palatine hill. One early Roman source mentioned the Casa Romuli on the Palatine Hill, while another source referred to another Casa Romuli on the Capitoline Hill.

Dionysius of Halicarnassus (*c.* 60 BCE–after 7 CE) located one of the huts on the slope of the Palatine Hill:

> But their life was that of herdsmen, and they lived by their own labour, generally upon the mountains in huts which they built, roofs and all, out of sticks and reeds. One of these, called the hut of Romulus, remained even to my day on the flank of the Palatine hill which faces towards the Circus, and it is preserved holy by those charged with these matters; they add nothing to it to render it more stately, but if any part of it is injured, either by storms or by the lapse of time, they repair the damage and restore the hut as nearly as possible to its former condition.[17]

Vitruvius (*c.* 80/70 bc–after *c.* 15 bc) described a different hut on the Capitoline Hill: 'On the Capitol, the Hut of Romulus, and other temples on the Citadel, with roofs of thatch, can remind us of the ancient customs of Rome.'[18]

These huts, one on the Palatine Hill and the other on the Capitoline Hill, were, on the one hand, simple structures, consistent with the definition of *tzrif* in rabbinic literature, and, on the other, symbolized the foundation of Rome to its earliest visitors. According to Dudley, the Casa Romuli on the Palatine Hill near the house of Augustus was maintained as a state monument.[19] This perception of the function of the Casa Romuli is reflected in Valerius Maximus's description from the time of Tiberius in the first third of the first century CE:

> Military discipline jealously conserved won the leadership of Italy for the Roman empire, bestowed rule over many cities, great kings, mighty nations, opened the jaws of the Pontic gulf, handed over the shattered barriers of the Alps and Taurus, made it from its origin in Romulus's little hut into the summit of the entire globe. (Valerius Maximus 2.8)

---

17 Dionysius of Halicarnassus, *Rom. Ant.* 1.79. See also Plutarch, *Lives. Romulus* 20.4. Dio Cassius, in his *Roman History* (*c.* 230 CE), claimed that Augustus dwelt on the Capitoline Hill because 'Romulus had once lived there' (Dio Cass. 53.16.5). Varro, *Ling.* 5.54, also mentioned an 'Aedis Romuli' on the Palatine Hill, which, according to Richardson is probably to be identified with the Casa. See Richardson, *A New Topographical Dictionary*, p. 74; Jenkyns, *God, Space, & City.*

18 Vitruvius, *On Architecture*, II.1.5., p. 150.

19 Dudley, *Urbs Roma*, p. 151.

Seneca the Elder (*c.* 54 BCE–*c.* 39 CE) also emphasized the role of the hut in symbolizing to the Romans the journey of Rome from its meagre beginnings to the glorious and developed city in which they lived, with its spacious and impressive temples and buildings:

> Once these hills stood bare; among such wide-flung walls, there is nothing more distinguished than a lowly hut, though above it, shines out the Capitol with its sloping roofs, gleaming in pure gold. Can you reproach the Romans? They might cover up their humble beginnings, but instead they make a show of them and do not regard all this as great unless it is made obvious that it rose from a tiny start. (Seneca, *Controv.* 1.6.4)

Recently, Christopher Siwicki, based on Cassius Dio and Seneca, among others, has claimed that the Casa Romuli, both on the Palatine Hill and the Capitoline Hill, were sacred edifices and vivid symbols of Rome's past.[20] These huts were mentioned by sources from the first century BCE until the fourth century CE, with the structure on the Palatine Hill being preserved at least until the fourth century.[21]

Moreover, the location of the Casa Romuli, on the two central ancient hills of Rome, on the Palatine Hill and on the Capitoline Hill, specifically symbolized the foundation of the city of Rome in these hills, perfectly corresponding to the second stage in the rabbinic tradition that associates the foundation of the city of Rome with the sinful worship of the people. Perhaps because the second stage in the rabbinic tradition about the founding of Rome specifically relates to the founding of the city of Rome, the particular terminology that the Sifre employed in its version of the rabbinic tradition regarding the second stage uses the word *krakhin* (cities) instead of *tzrifim*: 'and on the day that Jeroboam erected the two calves, Remus and Romulus stood up and built two *krakhin* in Rome'. Thus, the version in the Sifre confirms the huts as a symbol of the birth of the city of Rome, and the location of the Casa Romuli in the birthplace of the city of Rome confirms that the huts are the Casa Romuli.

---

20 Siwicki, *Architectural Restoration*, pp. 145–46.

21 As attested by both its appearance in the Regionary Catalogues and a reference to it by Jerome (in the preface to his translation of 'On the Holy Spirit' by Didymus of Alexandria; see Didyme l'Aveugle, *Traité du Saint-Esprit*, pp. 36–39. Several cuttings and post holes that were explored in 1946 on the slope of the Palatine Hill toward the Circus Maximus and dated to the Iron Age, the eighth century BCE, were suggested as the remains of the Casa Romuli. See Puglisi, *Gli Abitatori primitivi del Palatino attraverso le Testimonianze archeologiche e le nuove Indagini strarigrafiche sul Germalo*. But see Siwicki, *Architectural Restoration*, pp. 145–46, who rejects this theory, observing that the putative remains of the Casa Romuli should be dated much later than the eighth century BCE despite their being attributed by the people of Rome during the classical period to that earlier age.

Conclusion

The two huts in the rabbinic tradition are clearly the symbol of the beginnings of Rome. When the relevant traditions in rabbinic literature were articulated, the Casa Romuli on the Palatine Hill and on the Capitoline Hill had already been serving as commemorative sites or even sacred loci. The references in classical sources to the Casa Romuli are from the late first century BCE to the fourth century CE, and they relate to structures 'made of sticks and reeds even now by Italian shepherds'.[22] This description accords with the definitions of *tzrif* in rabbinic literature. Thus, there is ample evidence for my identification of the two huts in rabbinic tradition with the Casa Romuli on the Palatine Hill and the Capitoline Hill,[23] structures that symbolized — to the Romans and to the world at large, including the Jewish sages, thereafter — the development of the city of Rome from its humble beginnings to the glorious and advanced city lying stretched out before their eyes.

---

22 Dudley, *Urbs Roma*, p. 151.

23 Like m.'Ohal. 18:10: 'Ten places are not [subject to the laws] of non-Jewish dwelling-places: Arabs' tents, field-huts (sukkot), the *tsrifin*, fruit-shelters, summer shelters, a gate-house, the open spaces of a courtyard, a bath-house, an armory, and the place where the legions [camp]'. Translation by Kulp, 'Sefaria', Mishnah Oholot 18.10.

Bibliography

Manuscripts and Archival Resources

Cambridge, Cambridge University Library, Esther Rabbah, MS Add 495

Primary Sources

The Book of Tradition: Sefer Ha-Qabbalah: by Abraham Ibn Daud, trans. by Gershon D. Cohen (Philadelphia: Jewish Publication Society of America, 1967)

Didyme L'Aveugle, *Traité du Saint-Esprit*, ed. by Louis Doutreleau (Paris: Cerf, 1992)

Dio Cassius, *Roman History, Volume VI*, trans. by Earnest Cary and Herbert B. Foster, Loeb Classical Library, 83 (Cambridge, MA: Harvard University Press, 1914)

Dionysius of Halicarnassus, *Roman Antiquities, Volume I: Books 1-21*, trans. by Earnest Cary, Loeb Classical Library, 319 (Cambridge, MA: Harvard University Press, 1937)

Fox, Harry, 'A Critical Edition of Mishnah Tractate Sukkah with Introduction and Notes' (unpublished doctoral thesis, Hebrew University of Jerusalem, 1979)

Kahana, Menachem, *Manuscripts of the Halakhic Midrashim: An Annotated Catalogue* (Jerusalem: Israel Academy of Sciences and Humanities and Yad Itzhak Ben-Zvi, 1995)

Kulp, Joshua, Mishnah Maasrot <https://www.sefaria.org/Mishnah_Maasrot.3.7?ven=Mishnah_Yomit_by_Dr._Joshua_Kulp&vhe=Torat_Emet_357&lang=bi> [accessed 12 June 0222]

——, Mishnah Oholot <https://www.sefaria.org/Mishnah_Oholot.18.10?ven=Mishnah_Yomit_by_Dr._Joshua_Kulp&vhe=Torat_Emet_357&lang=bi> [accessed 12 June 2022]

Plutarch, *Lives, Volume I: Theseus and Romulus. Lycurgus and Numa. Solon and Publicola*, trans. by Bernadotte Perrin, Loeb Classical Library, 46 (Cambridge, MA: Harvard University Press, 1914)

Seneca the Elder, *Declamations, Volume I: Controversiae, Books 1-6*, trans. by Michael Winterbottom, Loeb Classical Library, 463 (Cambridge, MA: Harvard University Press, 1974)

Valerius Maximus, *Memorable Doings and Sayings, Volume II: Books 6-9*, ed. and trans. by D. R. Shackleton Bailey, Loeb Classical Library, 493 (Cambridge, MA: Harvard University Press, 2000)

Varro, *On the Latin Language, Volume I: Books 5-7*, trans. by Roland G. Kent, Loeb Classical Library, 333 (Cambridge, MA: Harvard University Press, 1938)

Vitruvius, *On Architecture, Volume I: Books 1-5*, trans. by Frank Granger, Loeb Classical Library, 251 (Cambridge, MA: Harvard University Press, 1931)

Secondary Studies

Ashby, T., *Cambridge Library Collection-Archaeology* (Cambridge: Cambridge University Press, 2015)

Ben-Eliyahu, Eyal, '"Cities Surrounded by a Wall from the Time of Joshua bin Nun" as a Rabbinic Response to the Roman Pomerium', *Jewish Quarterly Review*, 106.1 (2016), 1–20

Ben-Shalom, Ram, *Medieval Jews and the Christian Past: Jewish Historical Consciousness in Spain and Southern France* (Oxford: Littman Library of Jewish Civilization, 2016)

Ben-Yehuda, Eliezer, *A Complete Dictionary of Ancient and Modern Hebrew* (Jerusalem: Mosad Bialik, 1950)

Boustan, Ra'anan S., and Marie-Thérèse Champagne, 'Walking in the Shadows of the Past: The Jewish Experience of Rome in the Twelfth Century', *Medieval Encounters*, 17.4–5 (2011), 462–94

Dudley, Donald R., *Urbs Roma* (Aberdeen: Phaidon, 1967)

Feldman, Louis H., 'Abba Kolon and the Founding of Rome', *Jewish Quarterly Review*, 81 (1991), 239–66

Funk, Salomon, Karl Albrecht, and Nivard Schlögl, eds, *Monumenta Talmudica. Fünfter Band. Geschichte. I. Teil: Griechen Und Römer. Bearbeitet Von Samuel Krauss* (Vienna: Wissenschaftliche Buchgesellschaft, Darmstadt, 1972)

Geiger, Joseph, 'A Christian Mosaic and a Jewish Midrash', *Vigiliae Christianae*, 60 (2006), 461–63

Geiger, Joseph, 'The Tombs of Remus and Romulus: An Overlooked Source and Its Implications', *Athenaeum*, 92 (2004), 245–54

Jenkyns, Richard, *God, Space, & City in the Roman Imagination* (Oxford: Oxford University Press, 2013)

Kattan-Gribetz, Sarit, 'A Matter of Time: Writing Jewish Memory into Roman History', *AJS Review*, 40.1 (2016), 57–86

——, *Time and Difference in Rabbinic Judaism* (Princeton: Princeton University Press, 2020)

Krauss, Samuel, *Qadmoniot ha-Talmud* (Berlin: Moriah, 1924)

——, *Talmudische Archäologie*, 3 vols (Leipzig: Fock, 1910–1912)

Platner, S., *A Topographical Dictionary of Ancient Rome*, ed. by T. Ashby, Cambridge Library Collection – Archaeology (Cambridge: Cambridge University Press, 2015)

Puglisi, Salvatore M., *Gli Abitatori primitivi del Palatino attraverso le Testimonianze archeologiche e le nuove Indagini stratigrafiche sul Germalo, Monumenti antichi*, vol. xli, with chapters by Pietro Romanelli, Alberto Davico, and Guglielmo De Angelis (Rome: Accademia Nazionale dei Lincei, 1951)

Richardson, Lawrence, Jr., *A New Topographical Dictionary of Ancient Rome* (Baltimore: Johns Hopkins University Press, 1992)

Siwicki, Christopher, *Architectural Restoration and Heritage in Imperial Rome* (Oxford: Oxford University Press, 2019)

Yuditsky, Alexey Eliyahu, 'Commentary on Genesis D (4Q254a) Scroll', in *Hebrew Texts and Language of the Second Temple Period*, ed. by George J. Brooke (Leiden: Brill, 2021), pp. 375–79

PART IV

Influence and Competition

HILLEL I. NEWMAN

The Hebrew *Book of Elijah* and Commodian's *Carmen de duobus populis*

The crop of Jewish apocalyptic texts from Late Antiquity, all in Hebrew, is small compared to the abundance of surviving Christian apocalypses from the same period.[1] The two most important Jewish apocalypses composed — by all appearances — prior to the emergence of Islam are *Sefer Zerubavel* (the Book of Zerubbabel) and *Sefer Eliyahu* (the Book of Elijah). Elsewhere I have been critical of the haste of scholars to read the former as an apocalyptic reflection, in the manner of *vaticinia ex eventu*, of events in Byzantine Palestine in the stormy period of Sassanian occupation from 614 to 628, and I have argued instead that the earliest text form of that work dates to the sixth century CE.[2] Here I will focus on *Sefer Eliyahu*, the shorter of the two compositions, whose apocalyptic visionary is, as the title indicates, the prophet Elijah, who passes on to the reader cosmic and eschatological mysteries revealed to him by the angel Michael. My main concern here will not be the question of dating per se, but as in the previous case, I offer a critique of what is in my opinion the excessive eagerness of some readers to assume that various passages reflect events of the seventh century, while failing to recognize that these very portions of the text in fact draw on a body of apocalyptic traditions of earlier provenance. Specifically, I offer a close reading of sections of *Sefer Eliyahu* in comparison with Commodian's *Carmen de duobus populis* and related works.

There are few witnesses to the text of *Sefer Eliyahu*.[3] It is found in one medieval manuscript (Munich, Bayerische SB, MS Cod. hebr. 222) and is to date unattested in the Cairo Genizah. The first printed edition appeared in

---

1 Research for this essay was supported by the Israel Science Foundation (grant No. 1317/17).
2 Newman, 'Dating *Sefer Zerubavel*'; Newman, 'Apocalyptic Poems'; Newman, '*Midreshei Ge'ula*'.
3 See Newman, '*Midreshei Ge'ula*', pp. lxxiv–lxxxi. Modern editions of *Sefer Eliyahu* in: Jellinek, *Bet ha-Midrasch*; in Buttenwieser, *Elias-Apokalypse*; and in Deshen, *Yalkut midrashim*; see also Even-Shmuel, *Midreshei Ge'ula*, pp. 31–47. English translation: Reeves, *Trajectories*, pp. 29–39.

Hillel I. Newman is Professor in the Department of Jewish History and Biblical Studies at the University of Haifa.

Essays on Jews and Christians in Late Antiquity in Honour of Oded Irshai, ed. by Brouria Bitton-Ashkelony and Martin Goodman, CELAMA 40 (Turnhout: Brepols, 2023), pp. 253–270
BREPOLS ❦ PUBLISHERS   10.1484/M.CELAMA-EB.5.132493

Ferrara in 1554 or 1555 and is the source of all later editions.[4] A different version of the work, entitled *Perek Eliyahu* — patently a revision composed after the rise of Islam, was published by Even-Shmuel from a single Yemenite manuscript whose whereabouts are today unknown.[5] For the present we remain entirely dependent on his edition of that manuscript, but as with all his transcriptions, it must be used with caution. Small portions of *Sefer Eliyahu* find parallels in verse form in a late antique or medieval liturgical poem in Hebrew, the *piyyut* 'In Those Days and at That Time' (*Ba-yamim ha-hem u-va'et ha-hi*), which is also heavily influenced by *Sefer Zerubavel*.[6]

Elijah's revelations begin with a cosmic journey to the eastern, southern, and western corners of the world, after which Michael turns to what will happen 'at the End of Days, in the days of a future king'.[7] The narrative continues with what is ostensibly a rabbinic discussion concerning the name of that king.[8] At least three of the six names suggested are those of outstanding Persian kings: הרתחשסתא (Artaxerxes), כרש (Cyrus), and הכסרה — probably Khosrow.[9] The three named sages whose opinions are cited date from the middle of the second century to the beginning of the third century CE, but the passage is clearly pseudepigraphic: the two Sassanian kings bearing the name Khosrow reigned in the years 531–79 and 590–628, but that name was supposedly proposed in the mid-second century CE by R. Shimon b. Yohai. The passage is thus significant for dating the work as it has reached us. *Sefer Eliyahu* proceeds to describe an eschatological confrontation between Persia and Rome, persecution of the Jews, and the ingathering of the exiles — all of which are examined in greater detail below. These anticipated events are followed by further battles waged against Israel, the appearance of the Messiah, and the defeat of Gog and Magog. The work concludes with several visions of Elijah, including descriptions of the resurrection of the dead and the descent of the Heavenly Jerusalem.[10]

The first systematic attempt to date *Sefer Eliyahu* was made by Moses Buttenwieser, who believed it to be a product of the third century, reflecting

---

4 This edition has been ignored completely in the literature on *Sefer Eliyahu*. It is also almost certainly the source from which a manuscript now in Paris (Alliance Israelite Universelle, MS H 178 A) was copied in Ferrara in the seventeenth century. See Newman, 'Midreshei Ge'ula', p. lxxvi n. 44.

5 Even-Shmuel, *Midreshei Ge'ula*, pp. 51–54. Cf. Deshen, *Yalkut midrashim*, 31–36.

6 Even-Shmuel, *Midreshei Ge'ula*, pp. 113–16; Newman, 'Midreshei Ge'ula', pp. xc–xci.

7 For a comparison of Elijah's heavenly journey to the *Book of the Watchers* in I Enoch see Himmelfarb, 'Sefer Eliyyahu', pp. 227–28.

8 As Martha Himmelfarb has noted, *Sefer Eliyahu* displays a variety of rabbinic influences in both form and content. See Himmelfarb, 'Revelation and Rabbinization'.

9 For speculation about these names see Buttenwieser, *Elias-Apokalypse*, pp. 77–79; Reeves, *Trajectories*, p. 33; Himmelfarb, 'Sefer Eliyyahu', pp. 228–29; Greisiger, *Messias – Endkaiser – Antichrist*, pp. 38–40. The other three names are הרמלת (identified by some with the Anti-messiah Armilus, who features prominently in *Sefer Zerubavel*), תרמילא, and הכשרת.

10 For a comparison of these visions to the book of Revelation and other sources see Himmelfarb, 'Sefer Eliyyahu', pp. 232–38.

HEBREW *BOOK OF ELIJAH* AND COMMODIAN'S *CARMEN DE DUOBUS POPULIS* 255

the brief but extraordinary triumphs of the Palmyrene kingdom under Odenathus and Zenobia.[11] At the same time, he acknowledged the later date of the 'rabbinic' passage we have mentioned, which he considered an interpolation. Buttenwieser sought to clarify the historical background of the entire work primarily on the basis of several enigmatic passages containing a peculiar string of names of gentile commanders who, we are told, will wage war against the Jews and the Messiah.[12] These he emended and interpreted boldly but unconvincingly. The significance of the names remains an enigma.[13]

The prevailing opinion in current scholarship is that *Sefer Eliyahu* is essentially a product of the early seventh century. This was first proposed by Yehuda Even-Shmuel, who noted the reference to a king — in his opinion an emperor of Rome attacked by a Persian king — disparagingly called 'the least of all kings, the son of a slave woman' (מלך פחות שבמלכים בן שפחה).[14] He took this to be Phocas, the centurion who rose from the ranks of the army to usurp the throne from the emperor Maurice and then reigned in his place from 602 to 610, when he himself was ousted and executed by Heraclius. Phocas was also a contemporary of Khosrow II, perhaps the Khosrow who seems to be mentioned in *Sefer Eliyahu*, though by the same token that reference could be to Khosrow I of the sixth century. Furthermore, Even-Shmuel noted a reference in *Sefer Eliyahu* to persecution of the Jews at the hands of this same 'least of all kings', which he explained as an allusion to the alleged persecution and forced conversion of Jews by Phocas, as reported in the *Chronicle of Zuqnin*. Historians have rejected that claim, however, noting that the supposed campaign of persecution actually took place in the reign of Heraclius.[15] Even-Shmuel was in fact convinced that *Sefer Eliyahu* also contains veiled allusions to Heraclius and the Persian war. Scholars commonly continue to embrace the core of Even-Shmuel's argument, that the 'least of all kings' refers to Phocas in the role of a Roman emperor who came into conflict with the king of Persia, and some also follow him with respect to supposed references to the reign of Heraclius.[16] I believe that rather than search for historical allusions in

---

11 Buttenwieser, *Elias-Apokalypse*, pp. 68–79. For the opinions of earlier scholars see Even-Shmuel, *Midreshei Ge'ula*, p. 35 n. 16.

12 In the Ferrara edition: קירטלוס; and מקץ; אנפיליפוס בן פנפוס; דמיטרוס בן פנפוס; דמיטרוס בן פוריפוס.

13 Buttenwieser proposed to identify these names with those in a different list in *Genesis Rabba* 76, 6, pp. 902–03, where the Little Horn of Daniel 7:8 is identified with Odenathus of Palmyra. On the other three names see Lieberman, 'Palestine in the Third and Fourth Centuries', pp. 37–38. Another equally unsuccessful attempt at interpretation by means of unrestrained emendation was made by Krauss, 'Der römisch-persische Krieg'.

14 Even-Shmuel, *Midreshei Ge'ula*, pp. 35–38.

15 See Baras, 'The Persian Conquest', p. 306; Dagron and Déroche, *Juifs et chrétiens*, pp. 50–51. For critical evaluations of reports of conflicts between Jews and Christians in Antioch at the end of Phocas's reign: Dagron and Déroche, *Juifs et chrétiens*, pp. 18–22; Boustan, 'Immolating Emperors', pp. 225–26.

16 For example: Avi-Yonah, *Jews under Roman and Byzantine Rule*, p. 261; Baron, *Social and Religious History*, p. 19; Baras, 'The Persian Conquest', pp. 320, 322, 326; Reeves, *Trajectories*, p. 33 n. 21; Himmelfarb, '*Sefer Eliyyahu*', p. 230; Tesei, '"The Romans Will Win"'.

these passages, we would do better first to explore further the affinity of *Sefer Eliyahu* to the wealth of apocalyptic traditions in other sources, particularly patristic texts. Several of these have been noted by others, but there remain significant parallels as yet unrecognized or insufficiently appreciated, some of which have bearing on the question of historical context. Such comparisons challenge us to consider the very meaning of dating such a richly composite work, in which we encounter coherent and deliberate thematic progression interrupted by periodic incongruity.

Let us begin by taking a closer look at the opening portion of the text, where we find several references to an eschatological king, beginning with the general pronouncement that Michael revealed to Elijah what will happen 'at the End of Days, at the conclusion of four kingdoms in the days of the fourth king who is yet to be'. Needless to say, 'four kingdoms' brings to mind the Danielic scheme of Four Kingdoms, culminating — for late antique Jews and Christians — with Rome. The notion of the 'fourth king' is, however, more problematic.[17] After Elijah's cosmic journey, we read again that Michael tells him of 'the appointed time that will be at the End of Days, in the days of the king who is to be'. This is followed by the discussion of the name of the eschatological king, from which we are led to understand that he will be a Persian ruler. Indeed, in the very next sentence, which introduces the lengthy drama of the End of Days, we read: 'The last king of Persia will go up to (or: against) Rome for three years, one after the other, till he attacks it for twelve months'.[18] Three years and another twelve months is perhaps suggestive of half a heptomad, the classic three and a half years of Daniel, though I hesitate to insist on it: a neat three and a half years would be more convincing.[19] Nevertheless, it is worth noting that in the long passage from Commodian which we will examine below, it is precisely at this point in the narrative, on the verge of the invasion of Rome by the eastern Antichrist from beyond the Euphrates, that we read:

> Nero will then do these things for a full period of three years, and in half a year he will complete the appointed times. Deadly vengeance will ensue on account of his misdeeds, as the city and the people will be surrendered along with him.[20]

Cf. Shoemaker, *Apocalypse of Empire*, pp. 93–96. Shoemaker reads *Sefer Eliyahu* as a product of the seventh century but refrains from imputing to it references to particular people or events.

17 Since the eschatological king is identified in *Sefer Eliyahu* as Persian, might this be an apocalyptic projection of the fourth and last king of Persia in Daniel 11:2?

18 Ferrara edition: מלך אחרון שבפרס עולה לרומי שלש שנים זה אחר זה עד שפושט בה שנים עשר חדש Reeves, *Trajectories*, p. 33, mistranslates פושט בה as 'expands (his gains)'.

19 Buttenwieser, *Elias-Apokalypse*, p. 73, considers this possibility but rejects it, without reference to Commodian. Cf. the opinion of John Strugnell brought by Himmelfarb, '*Sefer Eliyyahu*', pp. 230–31.

20 All translations from Commodian are my own.

HEBREW *BOOK OF ELIJAH* AND COMMODIAN'S *CARMEN DE DUOBUS POPULIS* 257

The next sentence in *Sefer Eliyahu* is of considerable significance for the interpretation of all that follows. It is also syntactically awkward and probably textually corrupt. This is the reading in the Munich manuscript: ושלשה גיבורי מלחמה עולין לקראתו מן הים והם נמסרין בידו מלך פחות שבמלכים בן שפחה גיגית שמו לקראתו מן הים; literally: 'And three champions of war will rise up to him from the sea,[21] and they will be delivered into his hand, the least of all kings, the son of a slave woman, his name is Gigit, to him from the sea'. To complicate matters, the Ferrara edition lacks the word שמו ('his name is'). What are we to make of this? Working backwards, we encounter the dangling phrase 'to him from the sea', lacking a verb of ascent. If we supply a verb, should it be in the singular or plural? And who exactly is ascending from the sea to whom? The name Gigit (if indeed it is a name) is unparalleled and incomprehensible in context (Hebrew *gigit* refers to a large tub or tank). Most important, does the phrase 'the least of all kings' stand in apposition to what precedes it, or does it stand as a separate subject? In other words, is the Persian king himself the least of all kings, or does that phrase refer to someone else, and if so, to whom? Various readers have chosen to parse the sentence in different ways.[22] For Even-Shmuel, 'the least of all kings' — whom he identifies with Phocas — is the first of the three champions in the preceding clause.[23] For Reeves, who is likewise inclined to identify him with Phocas, he is a distinct, fourth 'mighty warrior'.[24] For both of them he is Roman. That, however, is not the only possibility, and I will make a case for identifying 'the least of all kings' with the last king of Persia himself.

Allusions to the book of Daniel appear throughout *Sefer Eliyahu*, not all of them explicit. We have already seen that the book begins with a reference to Daniel's Four Kingdoms. In what follows we find a physiognomic portrait attributed to a vision of Daniel himself, with a list of signs that is typical of descriptions of the Antichrist/Anti-messiah in apocalyptic literature.[25]

---

21 Reeves's translation, 'will come up to oppose him from the west' (*Trajectories*, p. 33), is incorrect.

22 The Yemenite *Perek Eliyahu* is a liberal revision of *Sefer Eliyahu*, and it is difficult to establish its value as a witness to an earlier reading, though it is interesting in its own right. If we may rely on Even-Shmuel's transcription, *Perek Eliyahu* reads: ומלך אחד פחות שבמלכים בן שהרני יוצא לקראתו מן הים ('and a certain king, the least of all kings, son of Shahrani, will go out to him from the sea'); see Even-Shmuel, *Midreshei ge'ula*, pp. 51, 378. For the reviser, the Anti-messiah is identified throughout as an Ishmaelite, distinct from the Persian king; see Newman, '*Midreshei Ge'ula*', p. lxxvii. I have rendered שהרני as 'Shahrani' because it appears that the Ishmaelite Anti-messiah is identified specifically as a member of the prominent Shahrani tribe of south-western Arabia.

23 Even-Shmuel, *Midreshei Ge'ula*, p. 37; cf. Baron, *Social and Religious History*, p. 19.

24 Reeves, *Trajectories*, pp. 30, 33 n. 21.

25 Several of these other sources are also associated with Elijah, though not enough for us to establish dependence on a specifically 'Elijan' tradition. See: Stone and Strugnell, *Books of Elijah*, pp. 27–39; Frankfurter, *Elijah in Upper Egypt*, pp. 117–25. It is, I believe, more helpful to look in another direction. The ascription to Daniel brings to mind a number of apocryphal works attributed to Daniel in Syriac, Greek, Hebrew, and other languages containing similar

The identity of this Anti-messiah depends on the manner in which we parse the problematic sentence we have just seen. Shortly thereafter we find another reference to the Danielic Anti-messiah, 'who will rise from the sea, and he will destroy the earth and make it tremble, and he will attack the beautiful holy mountain and burn it, most cursed of women is she who bore him, and that horn which Daniel saw'. This is an allusion to the Little Horn of Daniel's vision (Daniel 7:7–8), whose meaning is subsequently revealed to him: 'And the ten horns [mean]: from that kingdom, ten kings will arise, and after them another will arise. He will be different from the former ones and will bring low three kings' (Daniel 7:24).[26] Daniel's Little Horn, so outstanding in Christian typology of the Antichrist, is less well documented in Jewish apocalyptic texts of Late Antiquity as a symbol of the Anti-messiah.[27] It appears here explicitly, but its typology is also implicit in the passage we discussed above:

> And three champions of war will rise up to him from the sea, and they will be delivered into his hand, the least of all kings, the son of a slave woman, his name is Gigit, to him from the sea.

As scholars have noted without reference to *Sefer Eliyahu*, the defeat of three kings by the Little Horn serves as inspiration for an apocalyptic convention, according to which the Antichrist or Anti-messiah is expected to vanquish three foes.[28] We find this in *Sefer Eliyahu* in that clause which, we will recall, plainly refers to conquest by the last king of Persia, and we will encounter it again with reference to the last king of Persia in Commodian's *Carmen de duobus populis*. Finally, we return to 'the least of all kings'. In context, it appears that this too is derived from traditional exegesis of Daniel 7:8: 'While I was gazing upon these horns, a new little horn sprouted up among them; three of the older horns were uprooted to make room for it'. One example of this exegesis is found in the Epistle of Barnabas, where we read that after ten kingdoms rule the world, a 'little king' (μικρὸς βασιλεύς) will arise who will conquer three of them.[29] We find a similar phrase in Jerome's commentary on Daniel 7:8:

---

lists. *Sefer Eliyahu* may reflect their influence. See Henze, *The Syriac Apocalypse of Daniel*, pp. 90–92; 'The Young Daniel', pp. 269, 284; 'The Vision of Daniel', in Vassiliev, *Anecdota graeco-byzantina*, p. 39; Ben-Sasson, 'Inverting the Image of the Redeemer', p. 332.

26 Cf. Daniel 8:9–11. Biblical translations all follow NJPS.

27 Cf. note 13. For an allusion to the Little Horn and the three horns in a Hebrew *piyyut*, 'The Time to Rebuke the Beast of the Forest', see Fleischer, 'Solving the Qiliri Riddle', pp. 405, 415 (in Hebrew); Newman, 'Apocalyptic Poems', p. 245. The author of the *Doctrina Iacobi* portrays Jews speaking at length about the Little Horn and the other three horns; these Jews identify the Little Horn with 'Hermolaos' the Anti-messiah — 'Armilus' of *Sefer Zerubavel*. See Dagron and Déroche, *Juifs chrétiens*, pp. 166–67, 176–77, 186–87.

28 See Bousset, *Antichrist Legend*, pp. 158–60; Collins, 'Sibylline Oracles', p. 422 n. y, on *Sib. Or.* 8, 171. Cf. also Lactantius, *Institutiones*, 7, 16, 3, vol. i, p. 158, and the sources in note 27 above.

29 *Epistle of Barnabas*, 4. 4, pp. 94–96.

HEBREW *BOOK OF ELIJAH* AND COMMODIAN'S *CARMEN DE DUOBUS POPULIS* 259

At the end of the world, when the kingdom of the Romans will be destroyed, there will be ten kings who divide the earth among themselves, and an eleventh, little king (*paruulum regem*) will arise who will conquer three of the ten kings.[30]

To put it simply, the Little Horn represents a little king. Fundamentally, the language of both Barnabas and Jerome is equivalent to the 'the least of all kings' of *Sefer Eliyahu*, and that little king must be identified with the very Persian ruler who defeated three 'champions of war'. There is no need to introduce Phocas or any other historical figure in order to explain this passage or the others associated with it. The picture that emerges is of an Anti-messiah, the last king of Persia, who conquers Rome and then persecutes the Jews in the Land of Israel, where he is ultimately defeated. Such an apocalyptic narrative is, however, not unique to *Sefer Eliyahu*, for there is — *mutatis mutandis* — an earlier Christian equivalent.

Two compositions by the Latin poet Commodian have reached us: the *Instructiones* and the *Carmen de duobus populis* ('Poem about Two Peoples', also known as *Carmen apologeticum*). The following discussion is devoted mainly to the latter work, a polemic against the Jews, which has survived in a single manuscript.[31] Both Commodian's date and place of origin continue to be contested. Some date him to the third century, others to the fifth, and he has been located in North Africa, Rome, and even Gaza of Roman Palestine, among other places.[32] These questions are not trivial, but they are not critical for our purposes. The *Carmen de duobus populis* is of particular significance here, but I will refer also to the *Instructiones*. The apocalyptic portions of Commodian's poems and Book 7 of Lactantius's *Institutiones* have much in common, and I will make use of the latter as well. Though Buttenwieser noted several passages in the *Institutiones* relevant to *Sefer Eliyahu* and made brief mention of Commodian, a far greater contribution was made by David Flusser, in his important article on Hystaspes and John of Patmos.[33] Even Flusser, however, did not exhaust the comparative material, some of which I will present here.

The *Carmen de duobus populis* is of particular interest to us because of elements it shares with *Sefer Eliyahu*. One of these is the anticipation of an Antichrist/Anti-messiah from beyond the Euphrates, though that belief is not unique to Commodian.[34] The affinity between these two works emerges both

---

30 Jerome, *In Danielem*, 7. 8, p. 844.

31 Passages from both these works are cited here according to the edition of Josef Martin. For *Carmen de duobus populis* see also the edition with commentary of Isabella Salvadore. Unfortunately I have not had access to Antonio Salvatore, *Carme apologetico* (Torino: Società editrice internazionale, 1977). For the *Instructiones* see also Poinsotte, *Commodien. Instructions*.

32 See di Berardino, ed., *Patrology*, pp. 259–65.

33 Buttenwieser, *Elias-Apokalypse*, pp. 18–19, 80–82; Flusser, 'Hystaspes'.

34 See sources in Bousset, *Antichrist*, pp. 172–73. We find this tradition linked in patristic exegesis to Revelation 9:14 and 16:12.

in details and in narrative structure. Some differences are not greater than those we find among Christian sources themselves, as between Commodian and Lactantius — or even, for that matter, between Commodian's two poems. Not surprisingly, there are also more substantial differences between the Jewish and Christian texts, some dictated by competing canons of Scripture and conflicting theological premises, as villains and heroes trade places. These differences are considerable enough that it is impossible to speak of unmediated use by both authors of a single shared source. In the absence of a satisfactory model for describing paths of influence, we will have to make do with giving an account of what is nonetheless a striking family resemblance. Commodian concedes in a cryptic passage that he has made use, not surprisingly, of at least one esoteric written source: 'I offer a few secret things that I have read about this' (l. 936). Unfortunately, coming as it does between the account of Nero's downfall and the rise of the Persian Antichrist on the one hand and a lengthy description of the ingathering of the exiles on the other, we can conclude little of substance from this laconic remark. Flusser suggested that John of Patmos, Lactantius, Commodian, and others all draw on the lost Oracle of Hystaspes, which he took to be a Jewish apocalypse of the Second Temple period. He astutely identified shared motifs in these sources, but their ultimate origin in the Oracle of Hystaspes has not been demonstrated conclusively.[35]

Commodian begins his account of the Eschaton from the end of the sixth millennium with an invasion of the empire by hordes of Goths, who ravage Rome itself.[36] He then introduces the first of two Antichrists, the emperor Nero, resurrected from Hell, who in the manuscript is first called 'Cyrus', which Martin proposes to emend to 'Syrus': 'Meanwhile, at that very time Syrus will arise, and he will terrify the enemies and then free the Senate. He will return from the underworld' (ll. 823–25).[37] Commodian then describes at length a Danielic hebdomad, two periods of three and half years each, divided between the prophet Elijah and Nero. Given the presence of Elijah, it may be tempting to begin already at this point to seek a thematic connection to *Sefer Eliyahu*, but that is probably unwarranted. Elijah plays an active role at the End of Days in this account as a prophet of Christ, for which he is persecuted by both Nero and the Jews, not as an apocalyptic visionary, as in *Sefer Eliyahu*. In Commodian's words:

> But before he (Nero) comes, Elijah will prophesy for a split period of time: half of a hebdomad, which is a turning point. When that period of time is complete, the nefarious one (Nero) will follow, he whom the

---

35 Flusser, 'Hystaspes'. On the problem of Hystaspes see Newman, 'Stars', pp. 283–84.

36 The apocalyptic section of the poem begins at l. 791 and continues till the end of the work (pp. 102–09 in Martin's Latin text). We will examine only a portion of it.

37 See Martin, *Studien und Beiträge*, pp. 131–33. Elsewhere I have suggested that the appearance of the name Cyrus among those proposed for the last king of Persia at the beginning of *Sefer Eliyahu* might be reason enough not to emend the text in Commodian (Newman, '*Midreshei Ge'ula*', p. lxxix n. 53), but Martin makes a strong case.

HEBREW *BOOK OF ELIJAH* AND COMMODIAN'S *CARMEN DE DUOBUS POPULIS*   261

Jews together with the (pagan) Romans will revere. Though there will be another one from the East whom (the Jews) await, together with King Nero they will slaughter us (the Christians) furiously. Consequently, when Elijah prophesies in the land of Judea and sets a mark on the people in the name of Christ, he will angrily beseech the Most High that it not rain because so many of (the Jews) refuse to believe. The heavens will be sealed shut, after which they will not even be moist with dew. In anger he will also turn rivers into blood. The land will become barren and will not be wet with spring water, so that famine will strike, and there will be a plague on earth. Because he does these things, the tormented Jews will press many false charges against him. They will first incite the Senate to rise together in anger by saying that Elijah is an enemy of the Romans. Then the Senate, inspired as a body by them, will persuade Nero with entreaties and excessive gifts (saying): Banish the enemies of the people from human affairs, those by whom our gods are trampled and not worshipped. But he, brimming with fury and the entreaties of the Senate, will carry off the prophets from the East in a carriage of the state. In order to satisfy them (the Senate), or at least the Jews, he will first slay them (the prophets), and then he will go forth to the churches (ll. 833–58).

Nero will continue to persecute the Christians of Rome, thousands of whom will die as martyrs, and then, 'Nero, having himself been driven away (in the past), will command that the Christian people be expelled from the very city, and he will appoint two Caesars as his partners, with whom he will persecute the people in dreadful rage' (ll. 869–72). The enlistment of two anonymous Caesars would be odd, to say the least, were it not for the fact that they serve a crucial role in what follows: together with Nero, these three Caesars will be the three kings vanquished by the second Antichrist, the Little Horn whom we met in *Sefer Eliyahu*.[38] There follows a further description of the persecution and martyrdom of the Christians of Rome at the hands of Nero.

It is precisely at this point that our two narratives begin to converge. Though telling us nothing of what will precede the confrontation between Rome and the Persian king, *Sefer Eliyahu* reports: 'The last king of Persia will go up to (or: against) Rome for three years, one after the other, till he attacks it for twelve months'. For his part, Commodian concludes his description of Nero's persecution of the Christians as follows:

Nero will then do these things for a full period of three years, and in half a year he will complete the appointed times. Deadly vengeance will ensue on account of his misdeeds, as the city and the people will be surrendered along with him. His dominion — that which was replenished inequitably and long tormented everyone by exacting wicked tributes — will be

---

38   See Bousset, *Antichrist*, p. 80. It is not clear if Commodian refers also in the *Instructiones* to two Antichrists or only to one. See Poinsotte, *Commodien. Instructions*, pp. 300–04.

abolished. At Nero's downfall, a king from the East will arise in turn, together with four nations from that region.[39] He will invite numerous peoples to join him on the way to the city (of Rome). They will bring aid, though he himself will be exceedingly powerful (ll. 885–94).

Sefer Eliyahu continues with a description of a battle between Rome and the Persian king involving a maritime confrontation:

And three champions of war will rise up to him from the sea, and they will be delivered into his hand, the least of all kings, the son of a slave woman, his name is Gigit, to him from the sea.

Similarly, in the *Carmen de duobus populis* we read:

He (the king of the East) will fill the sea with ships, with many thousands, and if anyone should resist him, he will be slain by the sword. First he will take captive the subdued cities of Tyre and Sidon, so that the neighbouring peoples faint in terror.[40] Then plague, wars, famine, and bad tidings will be mixed together, creating bewilderment. Meanwhile a trumpet from heaven will suddenly blare, its din everywhere shaking people to the core. Then a fiery chariot will be seen in the midst of the stars, and like a flying torch it will announce a fire to the nations. The entire Euphrates River will then run dry, so that a way may be prepared for the king and for those nations. Persians, Medians, Chaldeans, and Babylonians will come together, fierce and nimble men who know no pain.[41] Thus, when (the king) appears and begins to advance from that place, Nero and the Senate will be distressed by the sight close at hand. Those three Caesars will go forth to oppose (the king), but he will deliver them slain as food to the birds (ll. 895–912).

Sefer Eliyahu continues:

And on that very day (of the Persian king's victory over Rome), he will attack the faithful people (עַם נֶאֱמָן). And on that day he will bring about three earthquakes, and all the planets will gather together and go to one place.

The appearance of the Anti-messiah is thus accompanied by portents, including a conjunction of planets.[42] The Jews are thrown into turmoil:

And (people) will pillage houses and steal fields and beat the orphan and the widow in the marketplace. But if they repent, they will be forgiven.[43]

---

39 The king and the four nations, identified below, come from east of the Euphrates.

40 The description of the conquest of Tyre and Sidon draws on apocalyptic tradition. Cf. Hippolytus, *De antichristo*, 52, p. 35.

41 Here too Commodian draws on traditional exegesis of the book of Revelation. See n. 34, and cf. Hippolytus, *In Danielem*, 3, 9, pp. 154–55.

42 On *mazzalot* as planets see Leicht, 'Planets in Ancient Hebrew Literature', pp. 15–38.

43 These lawless acts are expected of the Jews themselves ('the faithful people'), who will turn against each other but may be redeemed by repentance.

HEBREW *BOOK OF ELIJAH* AND COMMODIAN'S *CARMEN DE DUOBUS POPULIS*   263

> On the 20th of Marheshvan the world will tremble, and heaven and earth will quake. On the 20th of Kislev all Israel will stand in prayer before their father in heaven. And on that day a sword will descend and land on the nations of the world, as it is written: 'The sword always takes its toll' (ii Sam. 11:25).

We cannot determine from this passage alone where the Anti-messiah is expected to attack the Jews. Conceivably this is meant to take place in the Land of Israel, but in any case in the subsequent passage *Sefer Eliyahu* anticipates the ingathering of the exiles, followed by the arrival of the Little Horn in the Land of Israel.

At the corresponding point in the narrative, just after the sack of Rome, Commodian writes:

> The victor (the Persian king), however, will proceed from there to the land of Judea, and he whom the Jews themselves expect to vanquish Rome will perform many signs, that they may believe in him, for the foe will be sent to mislead them. Yet the resounding voice of the Most High will rebuke him from heaven. The man from Persia will say that he is immortal (ll. 927–32).

Note that the appearance of the Antichrist is accompanied by performance of signs, though not the foreboding omens of *Sefer Eliyahu*. From a parallel passage in Commodian's *Instructiones* we learn that: 'He will perform many signs [...]. In particular, a likeness of him will speak, that they may believe in him'.[44] In the next passage in the *Carmen de duobus populis* Commodian writes:

> Nero is made the Antichrist for us, that one (the Persian king) — for the Jews. Nero will be the ruin of the city (of Rome), this one — of the entire world. But I offer a few secret things that I have read about this. Eventually even the Jews themselves will be displeased, and they will murmur to each other because they were deceived by guile. They will cry out together to heaven, weeping aloud, so that the true God may assist them from on high (ll. 933–40)

This is followed by a lengthy account of the ingathering of the exiles.

Let us compare the two texts. According to *Sefer Eliyahu*, after the fall of Rome the Persian Anti-messiah will attack the Jews and produce frightening omens. The Jews, in their agitation, will turn against each other, but after their recovery they will 'stand in prayer before their father in heaven', who will come to their aid with his heavenly sword, followed by the restoration of the exiles to the Land of Israel. According to Commodian, the Persian Antichrist does not openly attack the Jews after the fall of Rome, but rather tries to deceive them by coming to Judea, performing signs, and presenting himself as their

---

44   Commodian, *Instructiones* I, 41, ed. by Martin, p. 34. Cf. Revelation 13:12–15; Lactantius, *Institutiones* 7, 17, 4–5, vol. i, p. 162.

Messiah. Eventually, disillusioned and disappointed, the Jews 'cry out together to heaven, weeping aloud, so that the true God may assist them from on high'. Here too, God responds by restoring the exiles.

Sefer Eliyahu and Commodian describe the ingathering of the exiles in narrative contexts that are not identical but are nonetheless similar. They also share the basic conception of the return of exiles from beyond the River Sambatyon or Sabatyon (though Commodian does not use this name), the mythical river east of Persia, where the ten — or nine and a half — 'lost tribes' are confined and await redemption. At the same time, their depictions are strongly coloured by their sources and literary environments. In the words of *Sefer Eliyahu*, which displays the influence of rabbinic traditions concerning the return of the exiles in three waves:

> On the 20th of Nisan the first exile will depart from Babylonia with 18,000 men and women, and not one of them will be lost.

> On the 25th of Tishrei the second exile on the river Sabatyon will depart with 17,000, and of them twenty men and fifteen women will be killed.

> On the 25th of the eighth month the third exile will depart, and they will weep and cry out over their brothers who were killed, and they will cry out in the desert for twenty-five days. They will taste nothing, and they will live off the decrees of the Lord.[45]

On the other hand, Commodian, who evidently made use of at least one apocryphal text, perhaps of Jewish origin, knows of only one wave. His exiles suffer no casualties and are, in fact, invincible.[46]

I have presented and compared those portions of *Sefer Eliyahu* and the *Carmen de duobus populis* in which shared elements are most pronounced, but before concluding we must turn our attention to the work of one more Latin Christian author: the *Institutiones divinae* of Lactantius. The similarities between the apocalyptic sections of Commodian's poems and Book 7 of the *Institutiones* are well known, as is the fact that they draw on a variety of sources that are not always in agreement. Though a complete account of the relationship between Lactantius and *Sefer Eliyahu* falls outside the scope of this essay, it will be fruitful to take one more look at the passage in *Sefer Eliyahu* describing events that follow the victory of the Persian king over Rome.

We saw above that the Anti-messiah of *Sefer Eliyahu* launches an attack against the Jews, followed by fearful portents and the collapse of social order. The righteous, however, are saved, and they turn in prayer to their Father in Heaven, whose sword descends and smites the nations. We also noted differences between this account and that of Commodian, though in both

---

45 See Reeves, *Trajectories*, p. 34.

46 Commodian writes about the ingathering of the exiles not only in the *Carmen de duobus populis*, but also in the *Instructiones*. For translations of both passages with an introduction see Bauckham, 'Nine and a Half Tribes'.

HEBREW *BOOK OF ELIJAH* AND COMMODIAN'S *CARMEN DE DUOBUS POPULIS* 265

cases we read that the Jews, distressed by the Antichrist or Anti-messiah, pray to God in heaven, who responds by restoring the exiles to the Land of Israel. *Sefer Eliyahu*, however, bears a closer resemblance to Lactantius's alternative apocalyptic scenario at this point, even though the latter lacks the ingathering of the exiles.

Like Commodian, Lactantius seems to know of two Antichrists, the second of whom is identified however as a Syrian, not a Persian.[47] Reading the following passages, we must keep in mind that though for Lactantius the righteous victims of the Antichrist are by definition Christian, the natural symmetry of Jewish and Christian apocalypses makes the distinction largely immaterial for our purposes, particularly if Lactantius's source happens to be Jewish. Lactantius says of the Antichrist:[48]

> Then he will try to overthrow the temple of God,[49] and he will pursue the just people,[50] and there will be persecution and pressure such as there has never been, not since the beginning of the world [...]. In that time justice will be in exile and innocence will be hated, and the evil in their hatred will plunder the good as foes. Neither law nor order nor military discipline will survive, none will respect grey hairs or acknowledge the duty of piety or show pity to women or children; everything will be confounded and confused, contrary to right, contrary to the laws of nature. The whole earth will be wasted as if in a single act of communal depredation.

This brings to mind the words of *Sefer Eliyahu* regarding the Anti-messiah: 'And on that very day, he will attack the faithful people [...]. And (people) will pillage houses and steal fields and beat the orphan and the widow in the marketplace'.

Lactantius continues:

> When this happens, the just and those who pursue truth will separate themselves from the evil and will flee to deserts, and when the impious man hears that, he will flare up in anger and will come with a great army, and he will bring up all his forces to surround the mountain where the just are living in order to seize them. When they see themselves hemmed in on every side and under siege, they will cry to God with a loud voice and beg for help from heaven, and God will hear them and will send them a

---

47 On two Antichrists in Lactantius see Flusser, 'Hystaspes', p. 445.

48 *Institutiones* 7, 17, 6–11. See Lactantius, *Institutiones*, i, p. 162; English translations of Lactantius are taken from *Divine Institutes*, trans. by Bowen and Garnsey, pp. 426–27.

49 Freund, *Laktanz*, ii, pp. 473–74, notes that Lactantius often uses the phrase *templum dei* metaphorically to refer to the Church, but Flusser, 'Hystaspes', p. 426, plausibly sees in this passage the appropriation of an older Jewish tradition which referred to the Temple in Jerusalem. On the Antichrist/Anti-messiah and the restoration of the Temple in the first Danielic heptomad see Newman, 'Apocalyptic Poems'.

50 Buttenwieser, *Elias-Apokalypse*, pp. 80–81, proposes a connection between 'the faithful people' (עם נאמן) of *Sefer Eliyahu* and the 'just people' (*iustum populum*) of Lactantius. He takes no notice of the other similarities between the texts here.

great king from heaven to rescue them and to free them, and to destroy all the impious with fire and sword.

We find this divine sword once again in a later chapter of the *Institutiones*, where Lactantius writes in greater detail of the future battle between Christ and the Antichrist:[51]

> Before he (Christ) descends he will give the following sign. A sword will suddenly fall from the sky, so that the just may know that the leader of the holy army is about to descend, and he will come with angels accompanying him to the centre of the earth, and in front of him will go an inextinguishable flame.

All of this is reminiscent of the continuation of the passage in *Sefer Eliyahu*:

> But if they repent, they will be forgiven. On the 20th of Marheshvan the world will tremble, and heaven and earth will quake. On the 20th of Kislev all Israel will stand in prayer before their father in heaven. And on that day a sword will descend and land on the nations of the world, as it is written: 'The sword always takes its toll' (ii Sam. 11:25).[52]

We see that at the point where *Sefer Eliyahu* diverges somewhat from the parallel narrative in the *Carmen de duobus populis*, it nonetheless displays striking affinity with an alternative model, that of Lactantius. These similarities suggest a complex web of shared traditions, a web which remains largely hidden from us.

I have carried out this exercise primarily for exegetical purposes, that is, to challenge commonly proposed interpretations of the plain meaning of several passages in *Sefer Eliyahu*. I have also sought to contribute to the clarification of the place of *Sefer Eliyahu* in the context of apocalyptic literature at large. I wish to stress a methodological principle that guided this study, one that should be familiar but is too often forgotten by readers of apocalyptic texts, especially those who approach these materials determined to uncover in them coded records of historical events. Some texts do contain generous amounts of such information, but too often the use and re-use of traditional motifs go unrecognized, yielding skewed results on all fronts. We should also remember that the significance of migrating literary patterns may evolve from one station to the next, depending on time, place, historical circumstance, and the religious identity of the authors and their audience — all variables that often elude us.

---

51 *Institutiones* 7, 19, 4–5. See Lactantius, *Institutiones*, i, p. 166; *Divine Institutes*, trans. by Bowen and Garnsey, p. 428.

52 On the sword see Flusser, 'Hystaspes', pp. 430–33; Newman, 'Stars', pp. 279–83. The links between *Sefer Eliyahu* and Lactantius extend beyond what we have seen here, but they warrant a separate discussion.

What did the apocalyptic configuration of *Sefer Eliyahu* mean for the final authors and their audience? It is safe to assume that the distinction between the Persian Anti-messiah of *Sefer Eliyahu*, conqueror of Rome, and Armilus, the Anti-messiah of *Sefer Zerubavel*, born of a statue in Rome, is significant.[53] Was this the product of a conscious and deliberate choice made among diverse materials that were all available to the authors, and if so, what does that teach us? For the present, I leave these questions open. But historical questions take many shapes. The manifold connections between Jewish and Christian apocalyptic texts attest to a world of both mutual influence and competition between Jews and Christians in Late Antiquity, and that is a valuable historical conclusion in its own right.

---

53 Cf. Shoemaker, *Apocalypse of Empire*, pp. 93–96.

Bibliography

Manuscripts and Archival Resources

Munich, Bayerische Staatsbibliothek, MS Cod. hebr. 222
Paris, Alliance Israelite Universelle, MS H 178 A

Primary Sources

Commodian, *Carmen de duobus populis*, ed. by Isabella Salvadore (Bologna: Pàtron, 2011)
——, *Instructiones*, ed. by Jean-Michel Poinsotte (Paris: Les Belles Lettres, 2009)
——, *Instructiones* and *Carmen de duobus populis*, ed. by Josef Martin, Corpus Christianorum Series Latina, 128 (Turnhout: Brepols, 1960)
Doctrina Iacobi nuper baptizati, in Gilbert Dagron and Vincent Déroche, *Juifs et chrétiens en Orient byzantine* (Paris: Association des amis du Centre d'histoire et civilisation de Byzance, 2010), pp. 47–273
Epistle of Barnabas, ed. by Pierre Prigent and Robert Kraft, Sources Chrétiennes, 172 (Paris: Cerf, 1971)
Genesis Rabba, ed. by Julius Theodor and Chanokh Albeck, 2nd edn (Jerusalem: Wahrmann, 1965)
Hippolytus, *De antichristo*, ed. by Hans Achelis, *Griechische Christliche Schriftsteller*, 1/2 (Leipzig: Hinrichs, 1897), pp. 1–47
——, *In Danielem*, ed. by Georg Nathanael Bonwetsch and Marcel Richard, *Griechische Christliche Schriftsteller*, n.s., 7 (Berlin: Akademie, 2000)
Jerome, *In Danielem*, ed. by François Glorie, Corpus Christianorum Series Latina, 75 A (Turnhout: Brepols, 1964)
Lactantius, *Divine Institutes*, trans. by Anthony Bowen and Peter Garnsey (Liverpool: Liverpool University Press, 2003)
——, *Institutiones*, ed. by Stefan Freund, 3 vols (Berlin: de Gruyter, 2009)
Sefer Eliyahu, in Adolph Jellinek, *Bet ha-Midrasch*, iii, 3rd edn (Jerusalem: Wahrmann, 1967), pp. 65–68
——, in Moses Buttenwieser, *Die hebräische Elias-Apokalypse* (Leipzig: Eduard Pfeiffer, 1897)
——, in Idan Deshen, *Yalkut midrashim: Otzar midreshei ḥazal*, iv (Tsefat: Or Olam, 2007), pp. 25–36
'The Syriac Apocalypse of Daniel', in Matthias Henze, *The Syriac Apocalypse of Daniel* (Tübingen: Mohr Siebeck, 2001)
'The Vision of Daniel', in Afanassii Vassiliev, *Anecdota graeco-byzantina: pars prior* (Moscow: Universitas Caesarea, 1893), pp. 38–43
'The Young Daniel', ed. by Sebastian Brock, '"The Young Daniel": A Little Known Syriac Apocalyptic Text. Introduction and Translation', in *Revealed Wisdom: Studies in Apocalyptic in honour of Christopher Rowland*, ed. by John Ashton (Leiden: Brill, 2014), pp. 267–85

Secondary Studies

Avi-Yonah, Michael, *The Jews under Roman and Byzantine Rule* (Jerusalem: Magnes, 1984)

Baras, Zvi, 'The Persian Conquest and the End of Byzantine Rule', in *The Land of Israel from the Destruction of the Second Temple to the Muslim Conquest*, i, ed. by Zvi Baras, Shmuel Safrai, Yoram Tsafrir, and Menahem Stern (Jerusalem: Yad Ben-Zvi, 1982), pp. 300–49 (in Hebrew)

Baron, Salo W., *A Social and Religious History of the Jews*, iii, 2nd edn (Philadelphia: Jewish Publication Society, 1962)

Bauckham, Richard, 'The Nine and a Half Tribes', in *Old Testament Pseudepigrapha: More Noncanonical Scriptures*, i, ed. by Richard Bauckham, James R. Davila, and Alexander Panayotov (Grand Rapids: Eerdmans, 2013), pp. 346–59

Ben-Sasson, Menahem, 'Inverting the Image of the Redeemer and His Enemies in the Apocalyptic Literature: An Example of Interreligious Discourse', *Zion*, 87 (2022), 313–33 (in Hebrew)

Bousset, Willhelm, *The Antichrist Legend*, trans. by A. H. Keane (London: Hutchinson, 1896)

Boustan, Ra'anan S., 'Immolating Emperors: Spectacles of Imperial Suffering and the Making of a Jewish Minority Culture in Late Antiquity', *Biblical Interpretation*, 17 (2009), 207–38

Buttenwieser, Moses, *Die hebräische Elias-Apokalypse* (Leipzig: Eduard Pfeiffer, 1897)

Collins, John J., 'Sibylline Oracles', in *The Old Testament Pseudepigrapha*, i, ed. by James H. Charlesworth (Garden City: Doubleday, 1983), pp. 317–472

Dagron, Gilbert, and Vincent Déroche, *Juifs et chrétiens en Orient byzantine* (Paris: Association des amis du Centre d'histoire et civilisation de Byzance, 2010)

di Berardino, Angelo, ed., *Patrology*, iv (Allen: Christian Classics, 1986)

Even-Shmuel, Yehuda, *Midreshei Ge'ula*, 3rd edn (Jerusalem: Carmel-Bialik, 2017) (in Hebrew)

Fleischer, Ezra, 'Solving the Qiliri Riddle', *Tarbiz*, 54 (1985), 383–427 (in Hebrew)

Flusser, David, 'Hystaspes and John of Patmos', in David Flusser, *Judaism and the Origins of Christianity* (Jerusalem: Magnes, 1988), pp. 390–453

Frankfurter, David, *Elijah in Upper Egypt: The Apocalypse of Elijah and Early Egyptian Christianity* (Minneapolis: Fortress, 1993)

Freund, Stefan, *Laktanz. Divinae institutiones. Buch 7: De vita beata*, 3 vols (Berlin: de Gruyter, 2009)

Greisiger, Lutz, *Messias – Endkaiser – Antichrist. Politische Apokalyptik unter Juden und Christen des Nahen Ostens am Vorabend der arabischen Eroberung* (Wiesbaden: Harrassowitz, 2014)

Himmelfarb, Martha, 'Revelation and Rabbinization in *Sefer Zerubbabel* and *Sefer Eliyyahu*', in *Revelation, Literature, and Community in Late Antiquity*, ed. by Philippa Townsend and Moulie Vidas (Tübingen: Mohr Siebeck, 2011), pp. 217–36

——,'*Sefer Eliyyahu*: Jewish Eschatology and Christian Jerusalem', in *Shaping the Middle East: Jews, Christians, and Muslims in an Age of Transition, 400–800 C.E.*, ed. by Kenneth G. Holum and Hayim Lapin (Bethesda: University Press of Maryland, 2011), pp. 223–38

Krauss, Samuel, 'Der römisch-persische Krieg in der jüdischen Elia-Apocalypse', *Jewish Quarterly Review*, 14 (1902), 359–72

Leicht, Reimund, 'Planets in Ancient Hebrew Literature', in *Giving a Diamond: Essays in Honor of Joseph Yahalom on the Occasion of His Seventieth Birthday*, ed. by Naoya Katsumata and Wout van Bekkum (Leiden: Brill, 2011), pp. 15–38

Lieberman, Saul, 'Palestine in the Third and Fourth Centuries', *Jewish Quarterly Review*, 36 (1946), 329–70; 37 (1946), 31–54

Martin, Josef, *Studien und Beiträge zur Erklärung und Zeitbestimmung Commodians* (Leipzig: Hinrichs, 1913)

Newman, Hillel I., 'Apocalyptic Poems in Christian and Jewish Liturgy in Late Antiquity', in *Prayer and Worship in Eastern Christianities, 5th to 11th Centuries*, ed. by Brouria Bitton-Ashkelony and Derek Krueger (London: Routledge, 2017), pp. 239–53

——, 'Dating *Sefer Zerubavel*: Dehistoricizing and Rehistoricizing a Jewish Apocalypse of Late Antiquity', *Adamantius*, 19 (2013), 324–36

——, '*Midreshei Ge'ula*: A Methodological and Historical Critique', in Yehuda Even-Shmuel, *Midreshei Ge'ula* (Jerusalem: Carmel-Bialik, 2017), pp. lii–xcvi (in Hebrew)

——, 'Stars of the Messiah', in *Tradition, Transmission, and Transformation from Second Temple Literature through Judaism and Christianity in Late Antiquity*, ed. by Menahem Kister, Hillel I. Newman, Michael Segal, and Ruth A. Clements (Leiden: Brill, 2015), pp. 272–303

Poinsotte, Jean-Michel, *Commodien. Instructions* (Paris: Les Belles Lettres, 2009)

Reeves, John C., *Trajectories in Near Eastern Apocalyptic: A Postrabbinic Jewish Apocalypse Reader* (Atlanta: Society of Biblical Literature, 2005)

Shoemaker, Stephen J., *The Apocalypse of Empire: Imperial Eschatology in Late Antiquity and Early Islam* (Philadelphia: University of Pennsylvania, 2018)

Stone, Michael E., and John Strugnell, *The Books of Elijah, Parts 1–2* (Missoula: Scholars, 1979)

Tesei, Tommaso, '"The Romans Will Win!" Q 30:27 in Light of 7th c. Political Eschatology', *Der Islam*, 95 (2018), 1–29

ISRAEL JACOB YUVAL

And the Rest is History

Sabbath Versus Sunday

מה היה העולם חסר? מנוחה. באה שבת, באה מנוחה
(רש"י, בראשית ב, ב)

The Sabbath was given for rest
(Aphrahat, Demonstrations 2)

[1]

The course of my life would have been completely different, had I not been
Oded Irshai's friend. At a crucial point in my life, he helped me not only to
get out of a difficult entanglement but also to embark on a new path. It was
in the mid-1990s, when my academic career was challenged by a hostile
article published against me in a prestigious journal, fifty pages of destructive
criticism. The journal's editors offered me the chance to respond in the same
volume, on condition that I met the publication date. I thus entered into a
tight race against time. My saviour was Oded, who was then on sabbatical at
Oxford. Every question I asked was answered with a wealth of bibliographic
references written on yellow pages in his meticulous handwriting, which I
used in my counterarguments against my critics. His erudite scholarship was
matched only by his generous friendship, and I will always be grateful for both.

My friendship with Oded dates back to the early 1970s, when we met at
Yeshivat HaKotel. There, the charismatic Rabbi Yeshayahu Hadari introduced us
to a world of deep religious thought that went beyond the traditional halakhic
study found in most yeshivas. Later, at university, we were both captivated by
the magic of history, which presented us with yet more varieties of Judaism,
varieties that were open and attentive to their cultural environments. We
shared this new ocean of knowledge, but we sailed to different continents:
Oded turned to Late Antiquity, I to the Middle Ages. Our lifelong journey
has never been overshadowed by even a single cloud. Perhaps this is due

Israel Jacob Yuval is the Teddy Kollek Professor (Emeritus) for Cultural Studies
of Vienna and Jerusalem in the Department of Jewish History at the Hebrew
University in Jerusalem.

Essays on Jews and Christians in Late Antiquity in Honour of Oded Irshai, ed. by Brouria Bitton-
Ashkelony and Martin Goodman, CELAMA 40 (Turnhout: Brepols, 2023), pp. 271–293
BREPOLS ❦ PUBLISHERS   10.1484/M.CELAMA-EB.5.132494

to our origin stories: we were both born in the same provincial hospital in Afula, in northern Israel.

I dedicate this essay to Oded. Although it is not yet in its fully formed state — a not-uncommon vagary of Jubilee volume timeframes — I hope to expand its scope in my forthcoming book, 'Sacred Time in Judaism and Christianity'.

[2]

The biblical obligation to rest on the Sabbath raised two fundamental questions among Jews and Christians. The first is: What is rest? Is it abstinence from work and physical exertion, or is it spiritual rest, which include activities such as study, prayer, attending sermons, and even fasting? Second, when should we rest? For Jews, the answer had long been on the seventh day of creation, known as Saturday. Christianity challenged this view and claimed that the day of rest should be 'the Lord's Day', namely, Sunday. The Jewish-Christian debate over these two questions was conducted simultaneously.

The first part of this essay addresses the Christian criticism of the Jewish rest and its timing. In the second part, I will argue that some passages in the Jewish Sabbath liturgy are designed to defend the Jewish concept of rest in light of Christian critiques. Additionally, they reflect the Jewish fear of losing exclusive hold on the idea of rest. The temporal proximity between the two holy days generated tension between Sabbath-keepers. The longer the Sabbath moves towards its ending, the more the tension with the competing alternative grows. Although the aforementioned texts do not explicitly mention Christianity, I suggest reading them as a hidden discourse aimed at establishing identity vis-à-vis exterior critiques.

[3]

In today's world of incessant distractions, the notion of rest has taken on renewed appeal. Industrialization and the resulting consumerism created cultures of leisure, and the pursuit of leisure became part and parcel of capitalism. Increasingly, people are seeking rest not only from work but also from technology. Rest has become a spiritual value, a state of contemplation and reflection to be desired.

The English words 'school' and 'scholar' derive from the Greek word for leisure: *scholé*. There is of course a link between learning and leisure, for only a person who does not have to work ceaselessly for his or her living can afford to go to school. The Mishnah states: 'What is a great city? A place in which there are at least ten *batlanim*'.[1] In modern Hebrew, the term *batlanim* — idle

---

1   Mishnah Megillah 1:3.

people — is pejorative, but the Mishnah had in mind scholars, people who can afford to devote themselves to study. Thus, erudition and the urban go hand in hand. This was also the prevailing view in the aristocratic circles of Greece and Rome, in which one's ability to forgo work conveyed one's elevated social and economic standing.

Leisure is a positive concept, idleness a negative one. One of the first thinkers to discuss leisure in modern society was the British philosopher Bertrand Russell, who in 1932 published an essay entitled 'In Praise of Idleness'.[2] In 1948, the German philosopher and theologian Josef Pieper published his book *Leisure and Culture*.[3] These two philosophers saw in leisure the potential for cultural improvement. While 'leisure culture' had once been reserved for those who Russell defined as the 'leisure class', in contrast to the 'working class', modern technology made it possible, at least in theory, for everyone to be part of a leisure society — a phenomenon which Russell thought could contribute to the creation of a happier and better society.[4]

Against this background, one might mention Abraham Joshua Heschel's seminal book, *The Sabbath: Its Meaning for Modern Man*, which first appeared in 1951.[5] Heschel described the Sabbath as a unique mechanism through which time, rather than place, is sanctified; as he wrote: 'The day of the Lord [i.e., the Sabbath] is more important than the House of the Lord' (i.e., the Jerusalem Temple).[6] This recognition of the universal value of leisure and rest is also expressed in Article 24 of the Universal Declaration of Human Rights of 10 December 1948: 'Everyone has the right to rest and leisure'. How did the idea of rest evolve into a universally acknowledged human right? In the following, I will present some initial thoughts on the long and complex history of rest.

[4]

The idea of rest can be traced back to Mesopotamian literature. According to Enūma Eliš (the Babylonian myth of creation), the noisy games of the young gods disturbed the rest of their parents, the old gods Apsû and Tiamat. To restore calm, Apsû, the father, sought to kill his sons. Before he succeeded in doing so, however, the plot was exposed and the sons killed their father. The desire to gain rest led to murder.

The gods' aspiration for rest is also a recurring motif in the Babylonian story of the flood. To free the gods from their labours, humans blessed with eternal life were created to work in their place. The humans multiplied, and the noise

---

2 Russell, *In Praise of Idleness and other Essays*.
3 Pieper, *Muße und Kult*.
4 Heintzman, *Leisure and Spirituality*, deals with the Christian foundations of leisure culture. See more in Pope John Paul II's apostolic letter 'Dies Domini' of 1998.
5 Heschel, *The Sabbath*, p. 79.
6 Heschel, *The Sabbath*, p. 79.

they made disturbed the rest of the god Enlil, who decided to bring an end to all humanity by flood. The small number of humans who survived the flood no longer possessed eternal life so that their ability to multiply was limited.

In these two myths, tension arises between human activity and the gods' desire to rest. The biblical story of Creation diverges from these stories in that God operates alone for six days and stops working on the seventh day. Exodus 20:8 states that God 'rested', but in Genesis 1–2 the use of this term is avoided, perhaps to distinguish the biblical Creator from the gods of Babylonian mythology.

This trend is also evident in the biblical story of the flood. Unlike in Babylonian mythology, the biblical flood was not caused by the disturbance of divine rest. Rather, it was the result of human evil. The noisy activity of human beings here takes on a moral meaning, a kind of moral noise. However, the idea of rest still resonates in the background. In the three verses that open the story of the flood (Gen. 6:6–8), we hear echoes of the word rest (*mano'ah*) five times: 'כי נחמתי ;'אמחה ה' אמר ה', 'וינחם ה', and then the pun 'ונח מצא חן'. Even the name 'Noah' alludes to rest (*mano'ah*), rest. However, Noah was not a god. To emphasize his human nature and righteousness, his name is repeated four times in two verses (9–10): 'These are the descendants of Noah. Noah was a righteous man […] Noah walked with God. And Noah had three sons'.

According to the biblical conception, rest does not remain within the purview of God alone but is also an essential element of human life. It is for this reason that human beings are commanded to imitate divine rest. The rest of Creation is intrinsically linked to the rest at the end of life and the end of days. When the *homo faber* dies, he will enjoy a 'requiem aeternam' according to the Christian prayer, or a מנוחה נכונה (proper rest) according to the Jewish prayer. In this view, history proceeds from God's rest after the act of Creation to the eternal rest of humanity in the world to come. The innovation of the Jewish Sabbath is that it offers a period of rest during active life and amid the days of the week, a rest that is 'a taste of the world-to-come'.[7]

The duty to rest is mentioned in both versions of the Decalogue, found in Exodus 20 and in Deuteronomy 5. Yet the two differ from one another regarding underlying rationale. In the former, the commandment is framed as a reminder of Creation, whereas in the latter, it is a reminder of Jewish slavery in Egypt. The Israelites were given the commandment to rest on the Sabbath only after they had become free (Exod. 16). It would then seem logical that Deuteronomy would require only free people to observe the Sabbath. However, both versions expanded the obligation of rest to all of one's possessions, including slaves and cattle. The Bible thus rejects the conception that rest is exclusively a privilege of free men.

---

7 BT Berachot 57b.

A fifth-century midrash reports a fictitious dialogue between Moses and Pharaoh, which allegedly took place while the Israelites were still slaves in Egypt. It reads as follows:[8]

> Moses left Pharaoh's house and saw the suffering of his people. What suffering did he see? Moses saw that his people had no rest. Said Moses to Pharaoh, 'He that has a servant, and does not allow him to rest one day a week, kills him. The Israelites are your slaves, and if you do not leave them a day a week, they will die'. Then Pharaoh said to Moses, 'Give them the Sabbath'. And Moses went and gave them the Sabbath for rest.

This midrash has Pharaoh affirm Moses' view, that even slaves have a claim to rest. Their rest is in the interests of their master; today, we would say the interests of their employer. Even Pharaoh, the supreme master of the Israelites, grasped this reasoning.

This concept of rest was incomprehensible to the classical Roman authors, who criticized the Jews for their Sabbath rest. In his famous discourse on the negative qualities of the Jews, the Roman historian Tacitus wrote in the second century that the Jews avoid work on the seventh day, since on this day they ended their wanderings in the desert and reached the Promised Land.[9] According to him, the Jews wandered in the desert for only for a week. He also wrote:

> We are told that the seventh day was set aside for rest because this marked the end of their toils (= the wanderings in the desert). In the course of time, the seductions of idleness made them devote every seventh year to indolence as well.

For Tacitus, the Jewish weekly day of rest and the abandonment of the fields every seventh year were indicative of sloth. And he was far from alone in holding this view. Augustine quotes similar sentiments expressed by the Roman philosopher Seneca:[10]

> Seneca attacks the rites of the Jews, and especially the Sabbath, since by the interposition of this one day in seven they practically lose a seventh part of their life in inactivity, and they suffer because they have urgent tasks to postpone.

In these voices, we hear the gap between the biblical recognition of the social value of rest and the Roman view that rest is a prerogative reserved for the upper classes.

---

8   Shemot Rabbah 1, 28.

9   Tacitus, *Histories*, 5, 4. See Goldenberg, 'The Jewish Sabbath in the Roman World'.

10 Augustine, *The City of God*, Book VI, chapter 11.

[5]

From the outset, Christianity regarded Sunday as the most important day of the week, because the resurrection of Jesus occurred on that day.[11] As Gerard Rouwhorst has pointed out, early Christians did not have other holidays, and it was only natural that they established Sunday as a holiday. It was a day of prayer, and the Eucharist celebration was held to commemorate the resurrection of Jesus on that day. During the first centuries, Sunday resembled ordinary pagan holidays in which public ceremonies were held without imposing a duty of rest.[12] Christian writers adopted the Roman critique of the Jewish rest.

In the second century, Justin Martyr railed against the laziness of the Jews and interpreted the biblical obligation to rest on the Sabbath as a demand for spiritual and moral behaviour on all days.[13] Ignatius of Antioch, one of the earliest Church Fathers, presents a similar opinion.[14] He suggests that the Sabbath no longer be observed according to the Jewish customs so as not to enjoy the 'days of their idleness'. In this regard, he quotes Paul in 2 Thessalonians 3:10: 'If you do not want to work, you should not eat' and Genesis 3:19: 'By the sweat of your brow you shall eat bread'. These two quotations illustrate the crux of his argument: one who indulges in idleness (i.e., the Jew on the Sabbath) has no right to eat and enjoy.

The Epistle to the Hebrews quotes from Psalms 95 the conditional sentence '*today*, if you hear His voice'. He explains that only if you believe in Jesus today — unlike the desert generation that rebelled against God — will you be entitled to 'enter my rest'. The promise has been given, and Jesus has already come, but there is still the fear that the lack of faith demonstrated in the desert might also befall later generations: 'For [only] we who have believed enter that rest, just as God has said "As in my anger I swore, they shall not enter my rest"'.[15]

The 'rest' mentioned here is the eternal rest of the soul at the end of time, a rest that echoes and completes God's rest after Creation. Jesus has already come, but his believers await his return and the eternal rest of the soul. In verses 9–10 the author of Hebrews formulates his conception of eschatological rest: 'A Sabbath rest still remains for the people of God. For those who enter God's rest also cease from their labours as God did from his'. The author discusses only the eschatological rest, not the Sabbath as a day of rest. This

---

11 For a comprehensive review of the issue, see Durst, 'Remarks on Sunday in the Early Church'. I am thankful to him for providing me with a draft of his forthcoming article. For more, see Rordorf, *Sabbat und Sonntag in der Alten Kirche*; and Rordorf, *Der Sonntag: Geschichte des Ruhe- und Gottesdiensttages im ältesten Christentum*; Carson, *From Sabbath to Lord's Day*.

12 Rouwhorst, 'The Reception of the Jewish Sabbath'; Rouwhorst, 'Der Sonntag als originär christliche Schöpfung?'.

13 Justin Martyr, *Dialogue with Trypho*, 12, 3.

14 Pseudo-Ignatius of Antioch, *The Epistle to the Magnesians*, 9. See Cohen, 'Dancing, Clapping, Meditating', pp. 29–51.

15 Hebrews 4:1–3.

position seems to be consistent with Paul's view of the Sabbath in Colossians 2:17. There, in discussing the laws of the Sabbath, he says: 'These are only a shadow of what is to come, but the substance belongs to Christ'.

The eschatological significance of rest is also attested in the Epistle of Barnabas, which establishes a connection between the sanctity of the Temple and the sanctity of the Sabbath, whose roots go back to the Torah.[16] The author (according to Tertullian he is the author of the Hebrews) combines two different verses: Deuteronomy 5: 'Observe the Sabbath day and keep it holy' with Psalm 24: 'Who shall stand in his holy place? Those who have clean hands and pure hearts', thus linking the holiness of time with the holiness of space. At present, he states, there is no one who can have the pure heart necessary to sanctify the rest on the Sabbath:

> Consider: we shall, as it appears, properly rest, and sanctify it then only when we are able to do so after being ourselves justified and having received the promised blessing; when there is no more iniquity, and all things have been made new by the Lord, then at last shall we be able to sanctify it, because we have first sanctified ourselves.

This severe requirement for sanctity postpones the implementation of the Sabbath rest to an eschatological era. The author compares the Sabbath of the Decalogue, given when God spoke face-to-face with Moses, to the Sabbath at the Creation of the world, and reaches the conclusion that the fulfilment of the Sabbath is possible only:

> When His Son returns. He will put an end to the era of the Lawless One, judge the wicked, and change the sun, the moon, and the stars. Then, on the seventh day, He will properly rest.

Since Psalm 95 seems to be the exegetical source of this concept, it is interesting to note that more than a thousand years later, kabbalists in sixteenth-century Safed introduced a new liturgical unit to the Friday evening prayer, called 'Kabbalat Shabbat' ('Welcoming the Sabbath'), which begins with Psalm 95. Their choice was influenced by the Psalm's concluding verse: 'They shall not enter my rest'. For the kabbalists too, this verse alluded to 'the next world that is the true rest'.[17]

[6]

From the fourth century on, new trends in the Christian world sought to implement the idea of rest on Sunday. In 321, the Roman emperor Constantine issued two laws, which prescribed public rest on Sunday:[18]

---

16 The Epistle of Barnabas, 15, pp. 59–60.
17 Kimmelman, *The Mystical Meaning*, p. 28.
18 Justinian Code 3, 12, 3. See Girardet, 'Vom Sonnentag zum Sonntag'.

On the venerable Day of the sun let the magistrates and people residing in cities rest, and let all workshops be closed. In the country, however, persons engaged in agriculture may freely and lawfully continue their pursuits.

It is not certain whether Constantine's motivations were economic or theological. His decision to give Sunday official status may be seen as an expression of the recognition of Christianity in the Roman Empire. The commandment of Sunday serenity was intended to create the public conditions which would enable the faithful to participate in prayer and Eucharistic celebrations. Constantine founded his new laws on an earlier Roman law concerning pagan festivals, not on the biblical commandment. He excluded peasants from the obligation to rest, which indicates that the establishment of rest on Sunday had nothing to do with Mosaic law.[19]

However, in the fifth and even more so in the sixth century, the practice of Sunday serenity became more and more justified by the biblical Sabbath model. This process was accompanied by the decline of the Roman leisure culture of horseracing, gladiator battles, and theatrical performances — events that were not limited to a specific day of the week.[20] Neither the Church Fathers nor the Rabbis had kind words for these activities. In the fifth and sixth centuries, criticism by the municipal bishops succeeded in bringing about the decline of the pagan leisure culture and the gradual abandonment of the public buildings in which these events took place. Private donors increasingly directed their donations to building churches instead of public buildings for sports and games. By the sixth century, churches were replacing theatres, and plays were replaced by Sunday Mass. To secure the participation of as many believers as possible, the need to limit work on Sunday was acknowledged and rest on this day was praised.[21]

[7]

Parallel to the establishment of Sunday as a day of rest, there were also new trends that strove to regard Saturday as an additional day for pursuing spiritual goals. To differentiate the Christian rest on Saturday from the Jewish one, the latter continued to be defined as 'idleness'. The Synod of Laodicea (380) called against keeping the Jewish Sabbath of rest:[22]

For it is not necessary that Christians judaize and have leisure on the Sabbath, but let them work on that day, and give precedence to the Lord's Day.

---

19 Rouwhorst, 'Reception of the Jewish Sabbath'.
20 Weiss, *Public Spectacles in Roman and Late Antique Palestine*, pp. 250–53.
21 The Epistle of Christ from Heaven (mentioned in the sixth century by Licinianus, bishop of Cartagena) opens with the instruction: 'I command you to go to church and keep the Lord's Day holy [...] for I have ordained [it] a day of rest'. See von Esbroeck, 'La lettre sur le dimanche descendue du ciel', pp. 267–84.
22 Synod of Laodicea, canon 29; Kraft, 'Some Notes on Sabbath Observance in Early Christianity'.

Instead, the Synod prescribed reading Gospels along with other Holy Scriptures on Saturdays. Sabbatical rest as an activity of reading and studying is also recommended by the Ignatian Epistles, a text dated to the fourth century:[23]

> Let us no longer observe the Sabbath in a judaistic way and rejoice in idleness [...] But each of you should observe the Sabbath in a spiritual way, rejoicing in study of laws.

For Epiphanius of Salamis, the Sabbath is a day of gathering, and the Syrian Didascalia calls Saturday and Sunday 'days of rejoicing'.[24] In the Apostolic Constitutions, a collection of laws attributed to the Twelve Apostles dated to the fourth century, we read as follows:[25]

> Let the slaves work five days; but on the Sabbath day and the Lord's day let them have leisure to go to church for instruction in piety. We have said that the Sabbath is on account of the Creation, and the Lord's Day of the resurrection.

The ongoing need for Christians to differentiate their rest on Saturdays from the Jewish Sabbath rest can be explained by the contradiction between the nature of the Jewish and Christian Sabbath. The Jewish Sabbath is informed by the notion of *Oneg Shabbat* ('Sabbath delight'), whereas for Christians, the Sabbath evokes the sadness associated with Jesus's crucifixion, which took place on a Saturday. The joy of the Jews thus flies in the face of Christian mourning.[26]

[8]

Indeed, in the Latin West there was a practice of making the Sabbath a day of fasting. It also had an additional objective, which was to endow the concept of rest with spiritual significance. Fasting was regarded as abstinence from worldly pleasures for the purpose of pursuing spiritual goals. This custom seems to have been unknown in the Greek East.

This divergence of practices played an important role in the Great Schism of 1054. The practice in the West to fast on Saturday was sharply criticized by the Greeks in the East. In 1053, two notable churchmen from Constantinople sent a letter to the pope and to the priests in Rome in which they denounced several Roman customs, including fasting on Saturday.[27]

Another learned monk from Constantinople, Nicetas Stethatos, wrote a treatise called *Libellus Contra Latinos*, in which the Catholic Church is

---

23 Cohen, 'Dancing, Clapping, Meditating'; Lewis, 'Ignatius and the "Lord's Day"', p. 50.
24 *Didascalia Apostolorum*, 21.
25 *Apostolic Constitutions*, VIII, 33, 1.
26 This is reflected in the words of Pope Sylvester in the fourth century, who emphasized the tension between the Sabbath delight of the Jews and the reflective sadness of the Christians (quoted by R. L. Odom, 'The Sabbath in the Great Schism of A.D. 1054', p. 78).
27 Odom, 'The Sabbath in the Great Schism of A.D. 1054', pp. 74–80.

accused of violating the fourth-century *Apostolic Constitutions* that prohibited fasting on Saturday. The Romans were accused of being judaizers because they adopted the Jewish concept of rest.[28]

In the spring of 1054, Pope Leo IX sent a delegation to Constantinople to submit a claim for his supreme authority, which ultimately failed. One of the delegates, Cardinal Humbert, wrote a treatise called *Adversus Calumnias Graecorum* (= *Against the Slanders of the Greeks*), which takes the form of a debate between a Roman and a Greek. To refute the Greek accusation that the Romans are judaizers, the Roman asserts that only Jews rest on the Sabbath, whereas Romans do not. The Roman interlocutor argued that fasting on Saturday has nothing to do with the Jewish Sabbath. He made the following accusation:[29]

> You [Greeks], if you do not judaize, tell us why you have something in common with the Jews in a similar observance of the Sabbath? They certainly observe the Sabbath, and you observe it. They dine and always break the fast on the Sabbath.

While it is easy to understand the Western accusation against the Greeks, it is harder to comprehend the Greek argument that the practice of fasting on Saturday resembles the Jewish custom of resting on the Sabbath. After all, the Sabbath is a day of rejoicing, not of fasting.

A clue to the answer may be found in the writings of Pirkoi ben Baboi, a ninth-century Babylonian Talmudic scholar who criticized Jews living in the Land of Israel that fasted on the Sabbath before Yom Kippur.[30] Fasting on the Sabbath was not an unknown custom among some Jewish circles and rabbis, as attested in the Talmud.[31] Historian Gedalyahu Alon has noted that during the Second Temple period, prior to the emergence of Christianity, there were two basic Jewish views concerning the Sabbath. According to the mainstream one, the essence of the Sabbath is delight; thus, one dines well and dresses nicely. According to Philo, however, there were Jews who stressed the purification of the soul on the Sabbath.[32] This old Jewish tradition may explain why fasting was regarded as a higher level of rest, because it encourages contemplation and overcoming physical constraints. This may explain why the custom of Christians in Rome to fast was regarded in the Christian East as a Jewish one.

---

28 Odom, 'The Sabbath in the Great Schism of A.D. 1054', pp. 74–75.

29 Odom, 'The Sabbath in the Great Schism of A.D. 1054', pp. 77–78.

30 Davidson and Ginzberg, *Ginze Schechter*, II, p. 559.

31 Gilat, 'Fasting on Sabbath'; Williams, 'Being a Jew in Rome'; Strand, 'Some Notes on the Sabbath Fast in Early Christianity'.

32 Alon, *Studies in Jewish History*, p. 306; Kister, 'The Prayers of the Seventh Book of the "Apostolic Constitutions"'.

AND THE REST IS HISTORY   281

[9]

What about the Jews? Were they aware of — and if so, did they care — about these internal Christian controversies? How did they respond to the Christian claim that their rest is not sacred and not carried out on the correct day?[33]

In what follows, I present two central liturgical texts that I believe represent Jewish responses to Christian criticism of the Jewish Sabbath. The first is a passage from the Sabbath morning silent prayer (the *Amidah*). It opens with an ode to Moses:

> Moses rejoiced in the gift of his portion,
> for Thou didst call him a faithful servant.
> A diadem of glory didst Thou place upon his head
> when he stood before Thee on Mount Sinai.
> In his hand he brought down the two tablets of stone
> upon which was engraved the command to observe the Sabbath,
> as it is written in Thy Torah: (a quotation from Exod. 31:16–17 follows)

It is difficult to determine when this prayer, as well as the prayer *Ata Echad* which will be discussed below, were composed.[34] Both are later additions to the main blessing of the Sabbath prayer, called the 'Holiness of the Day'. Menachem Zulai and Aharon Mirsky have suggested that this hymn about Moses is an ancient *piyyut* (liturgical poem) that consisted of an acrostic of the letters Yod-Kaf-Lamed (**Y**ishmach Moshe… **K**lil Tiferet… **L**uchot Avanim).[35] The *piyyut* is mentioned by the ninth-century R. Natronai as a prayer that was customarily recited at both the major yeshivas of Babylon but not in all communities, so it can be assumed that it was composed and added to the liturgy before R. Natronai's time but was not accepted immediately.[36]

A particular phrase in the *piyyut* seems to hint at its antiquity: 'klil tiferet' (diadem of glory). This phrase is mentioned in the book of Ben Sira 45. 8 in a hymn about Moses, but the phrase refers to Aaron. It is also mentioned in the *Book of Hekhalot* in reference to God.[37] In ancient sources, the term 'klil' indicates the crown on a king's head. The attribution of 'klil tiferet' to Moses is probably an innovation of this particular *piyyut*. This phrasing, plus the fact that the *piyyut* is not rhymed, point to an ancient provenance for the *piyyut*. No less important is the date of its inclusion in the morning prayer; we learned from R. Natronai's testimony that it was already in regular use, albeit not universally, in the ninth century.

---

33 On the Talmudic defence of the Sabbath rest, see Brezis, *The Sages and Their Hidden Debate with Christianity*, pp. 107–16; Kattan Gribetz, *Time and Difference in Rabbinic Judaism*, pp. 92–134.

34 Wieder, *The Formation of Jewish Liturgy*, pp. 295–322.

35 Wieder, *The Formation of Jewish Liturgy*, p. 299.

36 Wieder, *The Formation of Jewish Liturgy*, p. 296.

37 *Synopse zur Hekhalot-Literatur*, i, p. 36.

The *piyyut* begins with mention of a gift that was given to Moses. The nature of the gift is not specified, but it can be deduced that it is the Sabbath. The Talmud says: 'God said to Moses: I have a good gift in my treasures; the Sabbath is its name. I seek to give it to Israel; go and inform them.'[38] In the Talmud, this gift is given by God to Israel, not to Moses. Moses is the intermediary between God and the people. Some medieval sources have interpreted the gift as referring to the legend mentioned above, according to which Moses advised Pharaoh to give his slaves, the children of Israel, one day off a week so that they would not die from hard labour. Pharaoh agreed, and Moses chose the seventh day of the week. After God also commanded the people to rest on the seventh day, Moses rejoiced that he had chosen the same day that God had. That is why it is said, 'Moses rejoiced in the gift of his portion.'[39]

The *piyyut* goes on to say, 'for Thou didst call him a faithful servant' following Deuteronomy 4:5 and Joshua 1:7, where Moses is described as a servant of God. The phrase 'A diadem of glory didst Thou place upon his head' is unlikely to refer to Genesis 34:35 ('the skin of his face was shining'), where no diadem of glory is mentioned. It is more likely adapted from Ben Sira or the *Book of Hekhalot*, as discussed above. The connection made in the *piyyut* between Moses receiving the two tablets and the observance of the Sabbath can be related to Exodus 31:18 and to the two preceding verses (31:16–17), which are quoted in the prayer immediately after the *piyyut*.

Thus far, we have discussed the linguistic style and sources of the *piyyut*. But if we move on to looking at its content, the emphasis on Moses' status raises a question: Why was this poem introduced into the Sabbath morning prayer? Indeed, Moses' centrality in the *piyyut* aroused perplexity in the halakhic literature of the Middle Ages. Rashi (and before him Saadia Gaon) argued against reciting this *piyyut* because he did not see a connection between Moses and the Sabbath.[40] Those who favoured its recitation argued that 'it is appropriate to recite the praise of Moses in the prayer', since according to the Talmud the Torah was given on Sabbath morning.[41] Another reservation voiced was that the *piyyut* does not contain either praise of God or requests from him, as is customary in prayers.[42] The thirteenth-century R. Yitzchak Or Zarua sought to respond to these two concerns.[43] In his view, the *piyyut* contains a request from God to remember the merit of Israel on the day when the Torah was given by Moses. This and similar explanations seem to be post-factum attempts to justify a *piyyut* whose recitation had already become customary.

---

38 BT Sabbath 10b.
39 Wieder, *The Formation of Jewish Liturgy*, pp. 308–11.
40 *Sepher Ha-Pardes*, p. 310.
41 BT Sabbath 86b.
42 Wieder, *The Formation of Jewish Liturgy*, p. 303.
43 Wieder, *The Formation of Jewish Liturgy*, p. 305.

AND THE REST IS HISTORY   283

The connection between the Sabbath and the giving of the Torah is indeed puzzling, since the Sabbath was given to the people of Israel at Marah, before Israel received the Torah (Exod. 16). The expectation from God to recall the giving of the Torah ostensibly overshadows the specific idea of Sabbath. How did the giving of the Torah to Moses make the Sabbath a gift to Moses? Placing Moses at the centre of the Sabbath prayer does not fit with the biblical signification of the Sabbath as a remembrance of the Creation or the Exodus.

There is another difficulty in the text. The *piyyut* notes that Moses brought down the two tablets of the law from Mount Sinai, which included the commandment to observe the Sabbath. It is followed by the sentence 'as it is written in Thy Torah'. At this point, one would expect to quote the commandment of Sabbath from the Decalogue. Instead, a quote from Exodus 31:16–17 is given, according to which the children of Israel kept the Sabbath as 'as a perpetual covenant'.

I propose that the glorification of Moses was intended to polemicize with Christianity, which saw Sunday as the Lord's Day (*Dies Dominicus*). In this view, Sunday is the day of the proclamation of faith in Jesus, a time when the era of Creation and the Old Testament were over, and the age of salvation began.[44] The resurrection of Jesus marks the beginning of a new era of salvation and joy, as stated in Psalms 118:24: 'This is the day that the Lord has made, let us rejoice and be glad in it'.[45] According to Pope Gregory I, the true Sabbath of Sunday is in the image of the Saviour, Jesus the Messiah.[46] The salvation that Jesus brought is a new Exodus from Egypt that freed men from enslavement to sins.

The transition from the era of Creation to the era of Salvation is not surprising since already in the Torah the meaning attributed to the Sabbath was transferred from the Creation (Exod. 20:11) to the redemption from Egypt (Deut. 5:15), as mentioned above. Just as the biblical Passover became in Christianity a model for Easter and the Lord's Day, so the deliverance from Egypt became a model for the salvation of the believers in Jesus. A similar move exists in medieval halakhic literature, in which it is customary to interpret the evening prayer (*Ma'ariv*) of the Sabbath as an allusion to the Creation, the morning prayer (*Shacharit*) to the Giving of the Torah, and the afternoon prayer (*Mincha*) to the future redemption.[47]

The connection between rest and redemption adds another dimension to the idea of the Sabbath: it can be seen as a covenant or a sign, as attested in Exodus 31:16. For Christians, the salvation delivered by Jesus began the era of a new covenant, thus creating an affinity between Sunday and the abolition of the old covenant. For Augustine, the 'sign' is the circumcision, which is

---

44 ii Corinthians 5:17.
45 Pseudo-Eusebius of Alexandria, *Sermon* 16: PG 86, 416.
46 Gregory the Great, *Registrum Epistolarum*, 13, 1, p. 992.
47 Wieder, *The Formation of Jewish Liturgy*, p. 297 n. 13.

commanded on the eighth day after birth. Circumcision is a prefiguration for the birth of the new man and a sign of faith:[48]

> When the Lord rose from the dead, he put off the mortality of the flesh; his risen body was still the same body, but it was no longer subject to death. By his resurrection he consecrated Sunday, or the Lord's Day. Though the third after his passion, this day is the eighth after the Sabbath, and thus also the first day of the week.

That is, the eighth day of the week, which is Sunday, is given equal status to the circumcision on the eighth day. This symbolism recalls an exegesis of the Mekhilta on the verse 'observing the Sabbath throughout their generations as a perpetual covenant' (Exod. 31:16). R. Eliezer explains how the covenant becomes eternal and final: 'something that the covenant is "cut" for it. And what is this? It is circumcision'.[49] The verb 'to make' a covenant is in Hebrew לכרות (to cut off), hence, an allusion to circumcision. Both religions perceive circumcision as related to the Sabbath.

In light of this thick system of symbols, one can see why the *piyyut* presented Moses as the founder of the Sabbath. Its aim is to oppose the second deliverer, the founder of the Holy Day on Sunday. The Jewish Sabbath-keepers declare their allegiance to the Torah of Moses, and not to the Torah of Jesus. This tacit polemic also explains the mention of the giving of the Torah at Sinai and the two Tablets of the Covenant, a statement that claims the eternity of the Sinai Covenant. Midrashic literature provides rich material on the connection between keeping the Sabbath and the redemption of Israel, a move that is reminiscent of the parallel connection that Christianity made between Sunday and redemption, but that topic is beyond the current discussion.

Considering all this, it is also understandable why the editors of the Siddur preferred, as mentioned above, to quote Exodus 31:16–17, which speaks of the 'covenant' and the 'sign' and not the Decalogue, which even according to Christianity was not abolished. The composers of the *piyyut* preferred a text that presents the Sabbath as an exclusive — and eternal — covenant between God and Israel.

[10]

We now move on to the next passage presented in the Sabbath morning prayer, which runs as follows:

> And You did not give it, O Lord our God, unto the nations of other lands, nor did You, O our King, make it the heritage of worshippers of idols, nor do the uncircumcised dwell in its rest;

---

48 Augustine, *Octave of Easter*, Sermon 8, 4 (following Justin Martyr, *Dialogue with Trypho*, 41).
49 *Mechilta d'Rabbi Ismael*, p. 343.

AND THE REST IS HISTORY   285

but unto Your people Israel, You did give it in love, unto the seed of
Jacob whom You didst choose…
You favoured the seventh day and hallowed it,
calling it the most cherished of days, a reminder of the work of Creation.

Four groups are mentioned here: The nations of other lands, the idolaters, the
uncircumcised, and the people of Israel. The definition of the first group is
ethnic; that of the second, religious. As for the members of the third category,
the uncircumcised, I would argue that they are Christians.

This category is reminiscent of the distinction Paul made between the
Gentiles and the circumcised in Galatians 2:9. As Adi Ophir and Ishay
Rosen-Zvi have shown, it was Paul who invented the category of 'Gentiles'
in the overall sense of those who are not part of the covenant between God
and Israel.[50] This is the background to the Israel/Gentile dichotomy in the
Mishna literature. Even though the terms 'Jew', 'Judea' and 'Palestine' were
in common use at that time, the Mishna never uses 'Jew' but only 'Israel' and
'Eretz Israel'. The exclusive use of Israel also characterizes the Jewish prayer
book.[51] In both cases it reflects a latent controversy with the Christian claim
that only believers in Jesus may claim to be the true Israel (*verus Israel*). This
is the context in which the above passage that excludes the 'uncircumcised'
from the commandments of the Sabbath should be read.

The prayer states that the nations of the earth and the idolaters did not
receive the Sabbath, while the uncircumcised were given the Sabbath but they
do not 'dwell' in it, because their rest is not a proper Sabbath rest. They are
not 'in it' since they are not part of it. This statement can be understood as a
competition over the concept of rest — to whom it belongs, how it should
be practised and when it must be observed, on Saturday or on Sunday. In this
view, the Christian rest does not take place at the right time, and thus fails to
meet the criteria of a proper rest.

The prayer goes on: 'You called it the most cherished of days, a reminder
of the work of Creation'. The Hebrew term for 'the most cherished of days'
is חמדת ימים. Term is found in the midrash Bereshit Rabbati: ויכל אלהים ביום
השביעי, חמד הב"ה באלף השביעי פעולת ידיו אשר בחר, אלו ישראל.[52] The midrash
converts the verse 'God finished (ויכל) the work on the seventh day' (Gen.
2:1) into 'God cherished in the seventh millennium his election of the people
of Israel'. Thus, 'finished' becomes 'cherished',[53] and the 'day' becomes a
'millennium', the divine Day.

---

50 Ophir and Rosen-Zvi, *Israel's Multiple Others*.

51 In the Middle Ages, the use of the terms 'Jew' returned to use, with two exceptions:
    Maimonides' Mishneh Torah and the Zohar. Both works were conceived by their authors as
    a sequel to or substitute for the Mishnah.

52 *Midrash Bereshit Rabbati*, p. 20. Cf. the Aramaic translation of Onkelos to Genesis 2:1
    (Sperber edition); *Ozar Midrashim*, p. 455.

53 It probably understood ויכל in accordance with Ps. 84:3 נפשי כלתה ('my soul yearned').

The transformation of 'finished' to 'cherished' seems to resolve a perplexity that arises from the Masoretic text, which states that God finished His work on the seventh day, whereas He evidently finished it on the sixth day (as stated by the Septuagint and the Samaritan versions of Genesis 2:1 and the Book of Jubilees 2:1). To resolve this problem, the midrash turns the seventh day of Creation into the seventh eschatological millennium, in which God 'cherished' His election of the people of Israel. This may refute the Christian claim that the eschatological Sabbath is on the eighth day, Sunday. Accordingly, the sentence of the prayer 'You called it the most cherished of days, a reminder of the work of Creation' makes the claim that the Sabbath of Creation and the eschatological Sabbath fall on the same day, which is the Jewish Sabbath and not Sunday.[54]

The sacred character of the Sabbath rest is also expressed in the blessing that concludes this prayer: 'Find pleasure in our rest' and immediately afterwards 'sanctify us by your commandments'. The repetitive emphasis given at the end of the prayer to the concept of rest has an exclusive, national character: 'And the Children of Israel who sanctify your name will rest in them' — they, and no others, for only by their observance of the Sabbath will the name of God be sanctified.

[11]

The second liturgical text that I would like to read in this context is a section of the *Amidah* prayer recited as part of *Mincha*, the afternoon prayer, on the Sabbath:

> You are One and Your Name is One.
> and who is like Your people Israel, one nation on the earth?
> Glory of elevation, and crown of salvation
> a day of rest and holiness You have given unto Your people.
> Abraham was glad, Isaac rejoiced, Jacob and his sons rested thereon.
> a rest of love and generosity,
> a rest born of true faith,
> a rest in peace and tranquillity, in quietude and safety,
> a perfect rest wherein You delightest.
> May Your children perceive and know that this their rest is from You,
> and by their rest they sanctify Your Name.

The centrality of the motif of rest stands out. It is mentioned eight times, appearing in almost each line. The uniqueness of Israel is expressed in the Sabbath rest: 'a day of holy rest You have given unto Your people'. This idea also concludes the blessing: 'and by their rest they sanctify Your Name'.

---

54 According to Pseudo-Ignatius, Sunday is the queen of all the days and the most sublime (Pseudo-Ignatius of Antioch, *The Epistle to the Magnesians*, 9, 4).

The favour of Israel is also reflected in the following verse: 'Abraham was glad, Isaac rejoiced, Jacob and his sons rested thereon'. The first two patriarchs, Abraham and Isaac, are mentioned alone, while Jacob is mentioned with his sons. Abraham is also the father of the Ishmaelites, and Isaac is also the father of the Edomites, namely, of peoples who do not keep the Sabbath. Jacob is the only one whose sons belong exclusively to the people of Israel, and his observance of the Sabbath also includes his sons, and them alone.

The re-affirmation of the special status of Jacob is also reflected in the manner of his observance of the Sabbath: 'Abraham was glad, Isaac rejoiced, Jacob and his sons rested thereon'. Abraham and Isaac took joy in the Sabbath but only Jacob rested in it. This rest is not merely the avoidance of labour, but its origin is divine and holy. It is described by a series of positive attributes, which bind the members of the one nation to the one God. Their rest is raised to a sublime status, reflecting the divine rest.

It has been a full century since Arthur Marmorstein suggested that the claim made by the Sages that the patriarchs observed the Sabbath even before the giving of the Torah sought to disprove the Christian view of the abolition of the Sabbath and its replacement with Sunday.[55] Following Marmorstein, I suggest reading this prayer as a polemic in an ongoing rivalry. The question at stake is whose rest is sacred — the Jewish Sabbath or the Christian Sunday? This prayer refutes the Christian criticism of Jewish idleness and lack of spirituality. The introduction of Sunday as an obligatory day of rest became a threat to the singularity of the Jewish Sabbath. The Jewish claim that only the Jews adhered to the Sabbath on the correct day intensified their feeling of religious exclusivity and pride. The prayer rings as a counterargument to Aphrahat's claim against the Jews: 'in vain they take pride in keeping it'. Aphrahat concludes his treatise with the following words: 'I have written this [...] against those who boast because of it'.[56] The Jewish prayer does indeed express pride and exclusivity.

The controversy over rest is thus given a dominant place precisely at the *Mincha* service. Note the phonetic similarity between the Hebrew words '*menucha*' (rest) and '*mincha*'. Another possibility is that the Sabbath afternoon prayer takes place at the end of the day of rest, shortly before the transition to Sunday. This temporal proximity could have raised among Jews an awareness of the menacing Christian competition.

---

55 BT Yoma 28b; *Midrash Bereshit Rabba*, chs. 11 and 79. Marmorstein, 'Quelques problèmes de l'ancienne apologetique juive', pp. 161–74; Marmorstein, 'Juden und Judentum in der Altercatio Simonis Judaei et Theophili Christiani', pp. 379 ff. Paz, '"Prior to Sinai"', discusses the parallels to this tradition in the literature of the Second Temple, the Sages and the Church Fathers. He concludes that the parallels, many of which predate Christianity, render superfluous the claim that they reflect a polemical response (p. 98). In my view, the existence of old ideas does not rule out a renewed, anti-Christian context given to them.

56 Aphrahat, *Demonstrations*, 13, 12–13.

[12]

A sceptic might argue that the main ideas of the Sabbath prayers — the sanctity of rest and the exclusivity of Sabbath observance by Israel — have ancient roots in Exodus 33 and Jubilees 50.[57] As such, these prayers can be seen as reflecting an inner Jewish tradition and one need not resort to the Christian context in order to understand them.

Indeed, had we not known about the intense critique of the Jewish rest in Christian sources, we would not be interrogating the Christian context of these prayers. But the Christian alternative was part of daily life, and the historian should ask him/herself whether Jews were likely to have ignored it. The question is not limited to the textual aspects but also extends to their mediation. Prayers do not need to invent new ideas. They can repurpose old ones, take them off the shelf, dust them off, and turn them into new messages that appeal to their audience. It is thus worth considering how worshippers 'consumed' prayers.

The assumption that the composers, editors, and worshippers of the Sabbath prayers were concerned by Christian ideas invites us to take a second look at the opening sentence of the *Mincha* prayer: 'You are One and Your Name is One; and who is like Your people Israel, one nation on the earth?'. Linguistically, it seems that 'You' and 'Your Name' are two separate entities, which join a third — the people of Israel. But such a reading, which makes God and His Name two separate divine entities, seems implausible. A better reading would take 'You' as referring to the transcendental God, while 'His Name' refers to the revealed God. The phrase claims that the hidden God and the revealed God are one.

This statement differs from the Christian Trinity, which distinguishes between the one 'essentia' of God and his three 'personae' (identities). The corresponding expression for 'persona' in the Jewish prayer is the 'Name' of God, which identifies Him. The prayer declares that the essence of God and His Name, that is, his persona — are one. This idea also concludes the prayer: 'And for their rest shall they sanctify thy Name'. The Sabbath rest sanctifies (namely, proclaims) the Name of the one God, and thus makes known to everyone that He and his Name are one, in clear contrast to Christian doctrine.

The Christian context also helps us to understand another aspect of the prayer. The structure of the Holiness of the Day in the *Mincha* prayer is different from that in the evening and morning prayers of Shabbat. In both prayers, a quote from the Torah confirming the content of the blessing is given — Genesis 2 in the evening and Exodus 31 in the morning prayers. During *Mincha*, there is no quotation from the Torah that complements the blessing. However, in a version found in the Cairo Genizah, there is such a quote from Exodus 33:14: 'My face (= presence) will go with you, and I will

---

57 Doering, 'The Concept of the Sabbath'.

give you rest'. This verse is taken from the incident of the Golden Calf. God sought to wipe out the people of Israel as punishment for their sin, but Moses requested mercy and his prayer was accepted.

It is worth mentioning that, according to Marmorstein, this mention of the Golden Calf is a Jewish response to the Church Fathers, who claimed that the Sinai Covenant was annulled by the sin of the Golden Calf and is no longer binding.[58] The *Mincha* prayer expresses the idea that God forgave his people and restored the Sinaitic Covenant. The quotation from Exodus 33:14 demonstrates that God's grace did not depart from his people, and this is because only Israel keeps the Sabbath on the day of divine rest.

[13]

The idea that the proximity of the Jewish Sabbath to Sunday raised concerns among Jews is borne out in a number of customs and ceremonies, especially in Ashkenazi communities, which lived among Christians. I shall discuss them in my forthcoming book 'Sacred Time in Judaism and Christianity'. Here, I limit myself to just one example.

The *Havdala* is a separation ceremony which marks the transition from sacred time to secular time, and is recited upon the conclusion of the Sabbath. This rite consists of four blessings: on wine, spices, light, and the *Havdalah* itself, in which God is blessed for distinguishing 'between the sacred and the secular, between light and dark, between Israel and the nations, between the seventh day and the six days of labour'.

I propose that this contrast between light and darkness may aim to highlight the 'impure' light of Sunday. In pagan Rome, Sunday was called *Dies Solis*. The resurrection of Jesus is celebrated at Easter with the appearance of fire and light, and the Gospels describe Jesus as the light of the world.[59] Hence, in Rome, the transition from Sunday, the day of the sun, to the Lord's Day was quite natural. Christians perceive their light as holy, and the pagan light as impure. It is easy to imagine a parallel dispute between Jews and Christians regarding the holiness of the light in the transition from Sabbath to Sunday.

Let us take a closer look, then, at the *Havdala* ceremony, which includes a mélange of verses from the books of Isaiah and Psalms, all containing the word 'salvation'.

---

58 Marmorstein, 'Eine liturgische Schwierigkeit'.
59 Matthew 5; John 1.

Behold, God is my salvation, I am safe and I am not afraid	הנה אל ישועתי, אבטח ולא אפחד
for the Lord God is my strength and my psalm and is my salvation	כי עזי וזמרת יה ה׳, ויהי לי לישועה
With joy you will draw water from the wells of salvation[60]	ושאבתם מים בששון, ממעייני הישועה
Salvation is found in the Lord. Your blessings be upon your people...	לה׳ הישועה, על עמך ברכתך סלה...
Save, Lord, the king, and hear us when we call...	ה׳ הושיעה, המלך יעננו ביום קראנו...
I lift up the cup of salvation and call on the name of the Lord.	כוס ישועות אשא ובשם ה׳ אקרא.

Each of these verses has various declinations of the Hebrew ישועה (salvation), which may allude to the Hebrew name of Jesus, ישו. By placing 'salvation' at the core of the *Havdalah*, the ceremony integrates a messianic meaning that refutes the looming Lord's Day. The dispute is over the identity of the Redeemer. In the Middle Ages, another biblical figure was introduced into the *Havdalah* ceremony, namely, the prophet Elijah, who is said to be the herald the messiah. Thus, at the end of the Sabbath, expectations arose for the coming of the Saviour — the Jews expected a Jewish messiah, while Christians awaited the Christos.

[14]

The history of rest is restless. It contains all the components of a living culture: competition, strife, acculturation, and imitation. From the history of rest and leisure we can learn to value the debt we owe to the common Christian and Jewish religious traditions. I shall conclude with a précis of 'Rest', a short story written by the Nobel laureate Shmuel Agnon:[61]

> An old man lived in Moses' neighbourhood, a straight and honest man. God blessed him with sons and daughters, and he lacked nothing but the rest of his soul. When Moses ascended to heaven to receive the tablets, the same old man said to him: 'Moses, when you go up to heaven ask for one more thing: some rest'.

---

60 On the usage of this verse in the Jewish-Christian polemic, see Halbertal and Naeh, 'Ma'ayanei ha-Yeshuah', 179–97.

61 Agnon, 'Rest', p. 410. The translation is mine.

Moses rose to heaven, received the tablets, and when it was time for him to descend, he said to the Holy One, blessed be He: 'There is an old man in my neighbourhood, honest and upright. Please do me a favour and give him rest'.

The Holy One, blessed be He, said to Moses: 'You ask me for something impossible'.

Said Moses: 'Is there anything you cannot do? Have you not written in your Torah "Is the Lord's power limited"'(Num. 11:23)?

The Holy One, blessed be He said to Moses: 'Whatever I created, I created in six days, but rest I did not create'.

Bibliography

Primary Sources

Agnon, S. J., 'Rest', in *Elu Va`elu* [These and Those] (Jerusalem: Shocken, 1998), p. 410

The Apostolic Constitution, trans. by James Donaldson, The Ante-Nicene Fathers, 7 (New York: Christian Literature Publishing Co., 1886)

Augustine, *The City of God*, ed. by B. Dombart and A. Kalb, Corpus Christianorum Series Latina, 47–48 (Turnhout: Brepols, 1954–1955)

——, *Octave of Easter*, sermon 8, 4, ed. and trans. by S. Poque, *Sermon pour la Pâque*, Sources Chrétiennes, 116 (Paris: Cerf, 1966)

Aphrahat, *Demonstrations* 13, 12–13, ed. by J. Parisot, *Aphraatis Sapientis Persae Demonstrationes*, Patrologia Syriaca, 1 (Paris: Firmin-Didot, 1894)

Didascalia Apostolorum 21, ed. and trans. by A. Vööbus, *The Didascalia Apostolorum in Syriac*, Corpus Scriptorum Christianorum Orientalium, 401–02, 407–08 (Louvain: Peeters, 1979)

The Epistle of Barnabas, 15, ed. by M. W. Holmes, *The Apostolic Fathers: Greek Texts and English translations* (Grand Rapids: Baker, 1992), pp. 314–17

Gregory the Great, *Registrum Epistolarum*, 13, 1, Corpus Christianorum Series Latina, 140A (Turnhout: Brepols, 1982)

Justin Martyr, *Dialogue with Trypho*, 12.3, 41, ed. and trans. by Philippe Bobichon, *Dialogue avec Tryphon* (Fribourg: Academic Press, 2003)

Justinian Code 3, 12, 3, ed. by P. Krueger, *Codex Justinianus* (Berlin: Apud Weidmannos, 1877)

Mechilta d'Rabbi Ismael, ed. by H. S. Horovitz and I. A. Rabin (Jerusalem: Wahrmann, 1970)

Midrash Bereshit Rabbati, ed. by C. Albeck (Jerusalem: Mekize Nirdamim, 1940)

Ozar Midrashim, ed. by J. D. Eisenstein, 'Ten Commandments' (Jerusalem: Bibliotheca Midrashica, 1969), p. 455

Pope John Paul II, 'Dies Domini', 1998

Pseudo-Eusebius of Alexandria, *Sermon 16*, ed. by Jacques-Paul Migne, Patrologiae cursus completus: series graeca, 86, 146 (Paris: Garnier, 1860), p. 416

Pseudo-Ignatius of Antioch, *The Epistle to the Magnesians*, 9, ed. by M. W. Holmes, *The Apostolic Fathers: Greek Texts and English translations* (Grand Rapids: Baker Academic, 1992), pp. 154–55

Sepher Ha-Pardes... Attributed to Rashi, ed. by H. L. Ehrenreich (Budapest: 1924)

Synopse zur Hekhalot-Literatur, ed. by Peter Shäfer, i, no. 73 (Tübingen: Mohr Siebeck, 1981)

Tacitus, *Histories*, 5,4, ed. and trans. by Clifford H. Moore and John Jackson, Loeb Classical Library, 249 (Cambridge, MA: Harvard University Press, 1931)

Secondary Studies

Alon, Gedalyahu, *Studies in Jewish History in the Time of the Second Temple, the Mishnah, and the Talmud* (Tel Aviv: Hakibutz Hameuchad, 1957) (in Hebrew)

Brezis, David, *The Sages and Their Hidden Debate with Christianity* (Jerusalem: Carmel, 2018) (in Hebrew)

Carson, D. A., *From Sabbath to Lord's Day: A Biblical, Historical, and Theological Investigation* (Grand Rapids: Zondervan, 1982)

Cohen, Shaye J. D., 'Dancing, Clapping, Meditating: Jewish and Christian Observance of the Sabbath in Pseudo-Ignatius', in *Judaea-Palaestina, Babylon and Rome: Jews in Antiquity*, ed. by Benjamin Isaac and Yuval Shahar (Tübingen: Mohr Siebeck, 2012), pp. 29–53

Davidson, Israel, and Louis Ginzberg, *Ginze Schechter*, ii (New York: JTSA, 1929)

Doering, Lutz, 'The Concept of the Sabbath in the Book of Jubilees', in *Studies in the Book of Jubilees*, ed. by Matthias Albani, Jörg Frey, and Armin Lange (Tübingen: Mohr Siebeck, 1997), pp. 179–205

Durst, Michael, 'Remarks on Sunday in the Early Church', in *From Sun-Day to the Lord's Day. The Cultural History of Sunday in Late Antiquity and the Early Middle-Ages*, ed. by Uta Heil (Turnhout: Brepols, forthcoming)

Gilat, Yitzhak D., 'Fasting on Sabbath', *Tarbiz*, 52 (1983), 1–15 (in Hebrew)

Girardet, Klaus Martin, 'Vom Sonnentag zum Sonntag: Die *dies solis* in Gezetzgebung und Politiuk Konstantins', *Zeitschrift für antikes Christentum*, 11 (2006), 279–310

Goldenberg, Robert, 'The Jewish Sabbath in the Roman World up to the Time of Constantine the Great', in *Aufstieg und Niedergang der Römischen Welt*, ii, 19.1, pp. 414–47

Halbertal, Moshe, and Shlomo Naeh, 'Ma'ayanei ha-Yeshuah: Interpretative Satire and The Rebuke of the Heretics', in *Higayon le-Yonah: New Aspects in the Study of Midrash, Aggadah and Piyut in Honor of Professor Yonah Fraenkel*, ed. by Joshua Levinson and others (Jerusalem: Magnes, 2006) pp. 179–97 (in Hebrew)

Heintzman, Paul, *Leisure and Spirituality: Biblical, Historical, and Contemporary Perspectives* (Grand Rapids: Baker Academic, 2015)

Heschel, Abraham J., *The Sabbath: Its Meaning for Modern Man* (New York: Farrar, Straus and Young, 1951)

Kattan-Gribetz, Sarit, *Time and Difference in Rabbinic Judaism* (Princeton: Princeton University Press, 2020)

Kimmelman, Reuven, *The Mystical Meaning of Lekhah Dodi and Kabbalat Shabbat* (Los Angeles: Magnes Press, 2003)

Kister, Menahem, 'The Prayers of the Seventh Book of the "Apostolic Constitutions" and their Implications for the Formulation of the Synagogue Prayers', *Tarbiz*, 77 (2008), 212–20 (in Hebrew)

Kraft, Robert A., 'Some Notes on Sabbath Observance in Early Christianity', *Andrews University Seminary Studies*, 3 (1965), 23–24

Lewis, Richard B., 'Ignatius and the "Lord's Day"', *Andrews University Seminary Studies*, 6 (1968), 50

Marmorstein, Arthur, 'Eine liturgische Schwierigkeit', *Jeschurun*, 12 (1925), 198–211

——, 'Quelques problèmes de l'ancienne apologétique juive', *Revue des Etudes Juives*, 68 (1914), 161–74

——, 'Juden und Judentum in der Altercatio Simonis Judaei et Theophili Christiani', *Theologische Tijdschrift*, 49 (1915), 379 ff

Odom, R. L., 'The Sabbath in the Great Schism of A.D. 1054', *Andrews University Seminary Studies*, 1 (1963), 74–80

Ophir, Adi, and Ishay Rosen-Zvi, *Israel's Multiple Others and the Birth of the Gentile* (Oxford: Oxford University Press, 2018)

Paz, Yakir, '"Prior to Sinai": The Patriarchs and the Mosaic Law in Rabbinic Literature in View of Second Temple and Christian Literature' (unpublished master's thesis, The Hebrew University of Jerusalem, 2009)

Rordorf, Willy, *Der Sonntag: Geschichte des Ruhe- und Gottesdiensttages im ältesten Christentum* (Zürich: Zwingli, 1962)

——, *Sabbat und Sonntag in der Alten Kirche* (Zürich: Theologisch, 1972)

Rouwhorst, Gerard, 'The Reception of the Jewish Sabbath in Early Christianity', in *Christian Feast and Festival: The Dynamics of Western Liturgy and Culture*, ed. by P. Post, G. Rouwhorst, A. Scheer, and L. van Tongeren (Leuven: Peeters, 2005), pp. 223–66

——, 'Der Sonntag als originär christliche Schöpfung?', *Bibel und Liturgie*, 86 (2013), 164–72

Russell, Bertrand, *In Praise of Idleness and other Essays* (London: Taylor & Francis, 2004)

Pieper, Josef, *Muße und Kult* (Munich: Kösel, 1948)

Strand, Kenneth A., 'Some Notes on the Sabbath Fast in Early Christianity', *Andrews University Seminary Studies*, 3 (1965), 167–74

Von Esbroeck, Michel, 'La lettre sur le dimanche descendue du ciel', *Analecta Bollandiana* 107 (1989), 267–84

Weiss, Zeev, *Public Spectacles in Roman and Late Antique Palestine* (Cambridge, MA: Harvard University Press, 2014)

Wieder, Naphtali, *The Formation of Jewish Liturgy in the East and the West*, i (Jerusalem: Ben-Zvi Institute, 1998), pp. 295–322 (in Hebrew)

Williams, Margaret, 'Being a Jew in Rome: Sabbath Fasting as an Expression of Roman-Jewish Identity', in *Negotiating Diaspora: Jewish Strategies in the Roman Empire*, ed. by John M. G. Barclay (London: T. & T. Clark, 2004), pp. 8–18

List of Contributors

Jacob Ashkenazi is Associate Professor in the Department of Land of Israel Studies at Kinneret Academic College. His fields of interest include rural societies, monasticism, pilgrimage, and Church politics in the late antique Levant. He is the author of *The Mother of all Churches: The Church of Jerusalem from Its Foundation to the Arab Conquest* (Jerusalem: Yad Ben-Zvi, 2009), and co-editor of two Festschrifts, *Between Sea and Desert: On Kings, Nomads, Cities and Monks: Essays in Honor of Joseph Patrich* (Tzemach: Ostracon, 2019), and *Uriel: Papers Submitted to Uriel Rappaport* (Jerusalem: Zalman Shazar Center, 2006).

Brouria Bitton-Ashkelony is Martin Buber Professor in the Department of Comparative Religion at the Hebrew University of Jerusalem. Her research focuses on the histories of late antique eastern Christianities. She is the author of *The Ladder of Prayer and the Ship of Stirrings: The Praying Self in Late Antique East Syrian Christianity* (Leuven: Peeters, 2019), co-author, inter alia, of *The Monastic School of Gaza* (Leiden: Brill, 2006), and the co-editor of *Origeniana Duodecima: Origen's Legacy in the Holy Land* (Leuven: Peeters, 2019).

Eyal Ben-Eliyahu is Professor in the Department of Jewish History at the University of Haifa. His research focuses on perceptions of space and place in the ancient Jewish world. His most recent book, *Identity and Territory: Jewish Perceptions of Space in Late Antiquity*, was published in 2019 by the University of California Press.

Paula Fredriksen, a Fellow of the American Academy of Arts and Sciences, is Aurelio Professor of Scripture emerita at Boston University. In 2009, she became a member of the Department of Comparative Religions at the Hebrew University of Jerusalem, which awarded her an honorary doctorate in 2018. An historian of ancient Christianity, she also writes on pagan-Jewish-Christian relations in the Roman Empire. Her latest book, *When Christians Were Jews*, appeared as כשהנוצרים היו יהודים from Magnes Press in 2021.

Martin Goodman is Professor emeritus of Jewish Studies and Fellow of Wolfson College at the University of Oxford. He is a Fellow of the Oxford Centre for Hebrew and Jewish Studies, of which he served as President from 2014 to 2018, and he is a Fellow of the British Academy. His research focuses on Jews in the Roman world. He has published extensively on both Jewish and Roman history. His books include *Rome and Jerusalem: The Clash of Ancient Civilizations* (London: Allen Lane, 2007) and *A History of Judaism* (London: Allen Lane, 2017).

Aryeh Kofsky, PhD from the Hebrew University of Jerusalem in 1991, is Professor of Comparative Religion at the University of Haifa. He is the author of *Eusebius of Caesarea against Paganism* (Leiden: Brill, 2000), and co-author, inter alia, of *The Monastic School of Gaza* (Leiden: Brill, 2006), *Syriac Idiosyncrasies: Theology and Hermeneutics in Early Syriac Literature* (Leiden: Brill, 2010), and *Reshaping Identities in Late Antique Syria-Mesopotamia* (Piscataway: Gorgias, 2016).

Joshua Levinson is Professor of Rabbinic Literature in the Department of Hebrew Literature, at the Hebrew University of Jerusalem. He has published articles on the hermeneutics and cultural poetics of rabbinic narratives and the rewritten Bible in midrash, including *The Twice-Told Tale: A Poetics of the Exegetical Narrative in Rabbinic Midrash* (Jerusalem: Magnes, 2005). His current projects are the study of travel narratives in rabbinic literature and the literary anthropology and sense of self in the law and literature of the rabbis in Late Antiquity.

Ora Limor is Professor emerita in the Department of History, Philosophy and Judaic Studies at the Open University of Israel. She studies Medieval History, with a particular emphasis on pilgrimage, travel narratives, and sacred space in Christian and Jewish cultures, on the one hand, and Christian-Jewish encounters in Late Antiquity and the Middle Ages, on the other. She has published books and articles on both subjects. In her recent articles she has tried to connect these two fields of inquiry by turning her attention to shared holy places and parallel traditions.

Yonatan Livneh has a PhD from the Hebrew University of Jerusalem. His dissertation on ethnic identification and social grouping in Church historiography was supervised by Professor Oded Irshai.

Yonatan Moss, PhD from Yale University in 2013, is Leeds Senior Lecturer in Comparative Religion at the Hebrew University of Jerusalem. He works on the histories and comparative study of the three 'Abrahamic' religions, and on the relations between them. He is the author of *Incorruptible Bodies: Christology, Society and Authority in Late Antiquity* (Oakland: University of California Press, 2016), and a wide range of articles pertaining to issues of language, authority, and body in the Mediterranean basin during the first millennium.

Hillel I. Newman is Professor in the Department of Jewish History and Biblical Studies at the University of Haifa. His fields of interest include the history and literature of the Jews under Roman-Byzantine rule and relations between Jews and Christians in Late Antiquity. He is the author of *The Ma'asim of the People of the Land of Israel: Halakhah and History in Byzantine Palestine* (Jerusalem: Yad Ben-Zvi, 2011). He is also co-editor, together with Joseph Patrich and Ora Limor, of *Eretz Israel in Late Antiquity: Introductions and Studies* (Jerusalem: Yad Ben-Zvi, 2023).

Osnat Emily Rance is a PhD candidate in the Department of Jewish History and a member of the PhD honours programme at the Jack, Joseph and Morton Mandel School for Advanced Studies in the Humanities at the Hebrew University of Jerusalem. Her dissertation, 'The Devil Spoke from Scripture', written under the supervision of Professor Oded Irshai, deals with representations of religious violence in Late Antiquity. Her fields of interest include Jewish-Christian relations in Late Antiquity and contemporary literature and history. Her publications include '"The Impious Actions of the Greeks against the Jews": Riots of 491 in Antioch – between Reality and Fiction', *Zion: A Quarterly for Research in Jewish History* (2019) (in Hebrew). She is a co-author with Oded Irshai of an article on 'Holy Cartography Engraved with Blood: A Historical Appraisal of Eusebius of Caesarea's "Martyrs of Palestine"', to be published in a volume of collected studies edited by Tobias Nicklas and others, from Mohr Siebeck (STAC series), forthcoming.

Serge Ruzer, PhD from the Hebrew University of Jerusalem in 1996, is Professor of Comparative Religion at the Hebrew University of Jerusalem. He is the author of *Mapping the New Testament: Early Christian Writings as a Witness for Jewish Biblical Exegesis* (Leiden: Brill, 2007), and *Early Jewish Messianism in the New Testament* (Leiden: Brill, 2020), and co-author, inter alia, of *Syriac Idiosyncrasies: Theology and Hermeneutics in Early Syriac Literature* (Leiden: Brill, 2010), and *Reshaping Identities in Late Antique Syria-Mesopotamia* (Piscataway: Gorgias, 2016).

Daniel R. Schwartz is the Herbst Family Professor emeritus of Judaic Studies in the Department of Jewish History and Contemporary Jewry at the Hebrew University of Jerusalem. His fields of interest include the history, and the ancient and modern historiography, of the Jews in the Second Temple period. Among his books are commentaries on 1 and 2 Maccabees (2022, 2008), monographs on Agrippa I (1990) and Philipp Jaffe (2017), *Reading the First Century: On Reading Josephus and Studying Jewish History of the First Century* (Tübingen: Mohr Siebeck, 2013), and *Judeans and Jews: Four Faces of Dichotomy in Ancient Jewish History* (Toronto: University of Toronto Press 2014).

Zeev Weiss is the Eleazar L. Sukenik Professor of Archaeology at the Hebrew University of Jerusalem. Trained in Classical Archaeology, he specializes in Roman and late antique art and architecture in the provinces of Syria-Palestine. His interests lie in various aspects of town-planning, architectural design, mosaic art, synagogues, and Jewish art, as well as the evaluation of archaeological finds in the light of the socio-cultural behaviour of Jewish society and its dialogue with Greco-Roman culture and Christian cultures.

Israel Jacob Yuval is the Teddy Kollek Professor (Emeritus) for Cultural Studies of Vienna and Jerusalem in the Department of Jewish History at the Hebrew University in Jerusalem. He is the founder and Academic Head of the Mandel Scholion Research Center (since 2002) and of the Jack, Joseph, and Morton Mandel School for Advanced Studies in the Humanities (since 2012) at the Hebrew University of Jerusalem. His book *Scholars in Their Time: The Religious Leadership of German Jewry in the Late Middle Ages*, won in 1988 the Zalman Shazar Prize in Jewish history. His book *'Two Nations in Your Womb'. Perceptions of Jews and Christians*, published in Hebrew, English, German and French, won in 2002 the Bialik Prize and in 2013 Le prix des amis de P. A. Bernheim, awarded by the French Académie des Inscriptions et Belles-Lettres. He was recipient of Verdienstkreuz der Bundesrepublik Deutschland in 2016; the Österreichisches Ehrenkreuz für Wissenschaft und Kunst 1. Klasse in 2019; and the Mount Zion Award for 2021–2022.

Noa Yuval-Hacham, PhD from the Hebrew University of Jerusalem in 2011, is Dean of the Schechter Institute of Jewish Studies, where she is a lecturer in the Jerusalem and Land of Israel studies and Judaism and the Arts tracks. Her research interests are late antique art and the interrelationship between the visuality of the Jewish world and that of the cultures surrounding it. She also investigates the affinities between Jewish art of the Land of Israel and of the Diaspora, and the tension between visuality and halachic conceptions in Late Antiquity. Her book: *Figureless Art Anti-Figural Trends in Jewish Art during the Late Byzantine and Early Islamic Periods* was published by Magnes Press in 2021.

Index

Acacius of Caesarea: 105, 106, 111

Adomnán of Iona: 187, 188, 192, 193, 194, 195, 196, 197, 199, 202

Alexander of Jerusalem: 97, 105

Allegorizing: 166, 167, 168, 170, 176, 171

Antichrist: 12, 166, 168, 169, 170, 173, 176, 184, 254, 256, 257, 258, 259, 260, 261, 263, 265, 266, 269

Anti-messiah: 257, 258, 259, 262, 263, 264, 265, 267

Antioch: 96, 120–21, 124, 143, 144–45, 146, 147, 148, 149, 150, 151, 152, 153, 154, 174, 221, 222, 225, 255, 276, 286

Apocalypse: 171, 172, 189, 256, 258, 260, 267

Apostolic Succession: 97, 112

Ascension: 96, 107, 129, 184, 185, 188, 189, 190, 191, 192, 194, 195, 196, 197, 198, 199, 203

Augustine: 191, 197, 199, 275, 283, 284, 291

Barsauma: 131, 132, 173

Beda Venerabilis (The Venerable Bede): 194, 195, 196, 197, 199, 200, 202, 203

Bet Alpha: 21, 22, 45

Bethesda, the church of: 125, 130

Binding spells: 230, 231, 236, 238

Breviarius de Hierosolyma: 125, 135, 187, 191, 200

Brown, Peter: 50, 90, 145, 155, 225, 228, 229, 236

Capitoline Hill: 245–47

Casa Romuli: 245–47

Catechetical Lectures (Catecheses ad illuminandorum): 95, 99, 100, 102, 104, 107, 108, 109, 110, 112, 113, 169

Cave of Treasures: 175, 177

Christian art: 17, 43, 56, 65, 66, 67, 70, 71, 196

Christianization: 16, 39, 43, 44, 144, 163, 188

Christians: 11, 12, 13, 16, 17, 28, 30, 32, 38, 41, 45, 75, 88, 97, 98, 103, 110, 112, 132, 166, 166, 168, 174, 175, 176–77, 199, 229, 241, 255, 261, 267, 272, 276, 278, 279, 280, 283, 285, 289, 290

Church: 16, 23, 46, 68, 75, 76, 77, 79, 80, 82, 83, 84, 85, 86, 87–88, 95, 96, 97, 100, 103, 104, 107, 112, 119, 121, 122, 123, 124, 125, 126, 127, 128, 129, 130, 131, 133, 134, 143, 144, 145, 146, 147, 150, 151, 152, 153, 161, 170, 184, 187, 188, 189, 192, 194, 195, 196, 197, 206, 225, 229, 261, 279

Church, of Jerusalem: 96–99, 101, 103, 105, 106, 107, 108, 109, 110, 111, 113, 119, 128, 198

Church, of the Apostles: 40

Church Fathers: 9, 96, 276, 278, 289

Commodian: 17, 256, 259, 260, 261, 262, 263, 264, 265, 268

Constantine: 10, 13, 24, 28, 29, 30, 32, 33, 34, 35, 37, 39, 40, 41,

INDEX

42, 44, 46, 96, 100, 110, 112, 113,
173, 188, 277, 278
Constantinople: 16, 33, 38, 39, 82,
98, 106, 120, 121, 122, 126, 127, 128,
129, 130, 131, 133, 134, 279, 280
Corippus: 37, 47, 48
Cultural mimicry: 225, 230, 234
Cyril of Alexandria: 11, 121, 128, 129
Cyril of Antioch: 145, 147
Cyril of Jerusalem: 12, 15, 16, 95,
96, 98–99, 100–03, 104–05, 106,
107–10, 111–13, 114–17, 167, 169,
170, 176, 177, 179, 180
Cyril of Scythopolis: 122, 123, 126, 130

Daniel: 143, 149, 151, 153, 157,
165, 167, 169, 170, 171, 169, 255,
256, 257, 258, 268
David, king: 164, 171, 176
December: 130, 148, 150–54, 153,
154, 273
de-sacralization: 29, 38–39
Diaspora: 30, 31, 32, 43, 51, 73, 162,
173, 174, 221, 223, 224, 225, 226,
227, 232, 235, 237, 238, 239, 293
Diocaesarea: 78, 83, 87
Dura Europus: 7, 55–56, 58, 59, 60,
61, 62, 63, 65–67, 68, 69, 71

Edessa: 142, 145, 172
Egeria: 106, 189, 201
Eisler, Robert: 206, 208–10, 216–17
Elijah, Book of (*Sefer Eliyahu*): 17,
253, 254, 256, 269, 270
Encomium: 141–42, 143, 145, 147,
148, 149–50, 152, 153, 154
Epistle to Constantius II (*Epistula
ad Constantium*): 95, 99, 100,
103, 111
Eschatology: 10, 12, 100, 161, 165,
166, 167, 168, 169, 177
Estienne, Henri: 213–14, 217–18

Estienne, Robert: 214, 217
Eusebius of Caesarea: 9, 13, 24,
30, 32–36, 37, 38, 39, 40, 41, 42,
44, 45, 47, 50, 87, 89, 96–98, 103,
104–05, 112, 113, 114–17, 141, 142,
143, 144, 145–48, 154, 155–57, 167,
168, 173, 177, 181, 205, 206, 208,
210, 216, 218
Euthymius: 126, 128, 130, 132
Exodus: 7, 55, 56, 58, 59, 60, 63, 64,
65, 67–71, 208, 274, 282–84, 288,
289,

Fasting: 239, 272, 279, 280, 292, 293
Flood, biblical story of: 274
Foundation: 21, 77, 84, 123, 242,
243, 244, 245, 246

Gethsemane: 130, 188, 195, 197
Golgotha: 96, 99, 100, 109, 175, 188

Hammat Tiberias: 21, 22, 23, 24, 25,
27, 28, 32, 33, 38, 39, 43, 46
Hand of God: 7, 17, 55–56, 58, 59,
60, 61–63, 64, 65, 66, 67, 68–71
Havdala ceremony: 289, 290
Hegesippus: 97, 106
Holy Sepulchre, church of the: 112,
122, 124, 125, 129, 188, 192
Holy Zion, church of: 121, 124,
125, 131
Hybridity: 234

Identity: 10, 12, 26, 44, 45, 46,
58, 84, 90, 106, 115, 116, 146,
156, 163, 175, 179, 180, 203, 221,
222, 223, 224, 225, 226, 227, 228,
229, 232, 233, 234, 237, 239, 258,
266, 272, 290, 293
Idleness: 273, 275, 276, 278, 279,
287, 293
Ignatius of Loyola: 183, 184, 200, 201

Imperial cult: 25, 27, 28, 29, 31, 43, 48, 52, 72, 73

Irshai, Oded: 9, 10, 11, 12, 13, 14, 15, 17, 22, 23, 32, 39, 46, 50, 53, 89, 91, 95, 96, 97, 98, 100, 105, 111, 116, 141, 148, 156, 161, 169, 173, 179, 185, 222, 237, 271, 272

James the Just: 96, 97, 98, 100, 101, 102, 103, 104, 105, 106

Jeroboam: 172, 241–44, 246

Jerusalem: 10, 12, 13, 15, 16, 55, 58, 80, 82, 86, 95, 96, 97, 98–99, 100–05, 104–05, 106, 107–10, 111–13, 114–17, 118, 120–26, 128–34, 136–39, 141, 147, 151, 153, 159–63, 165, 166, 167–68, 169–70, 171–72, 173–75, 176, 183–85, 186, 188, 189, 191–92, 194–97, 198, 199, 202–03, 217, 224, 241, 242, 244, 254, 265, 269, 273

Jesus: 28, 35, 75, 83, 88, 100, 101, 106, 130, 163–64, 165, 166–68, 171, 176, 184, 185, 186–87, 188–89, 191, 193, 194, 195, 197–200, 205, 206, 207, 208, 210, 211, 212, 215, 229, 276, 283, 284, 285, 289, 290

Jewish life: 14, 43

Jewish liturgy: 17, 270, 281, 282, 283, 293

Jewish-Christian relations: 32, 46

Jews: 10, 11, 12, 13, 15, 16, 17, 25–29, 29–34, 35, 37–40, 42–46, 57, 59, 82, 87, 88, 98, 100, 104, 105, 109, 110, 112, 11, 131, 132, 149, 151, 161–64, 169, 170, 172–74, 176, 197, 199, 205, 207, 209, 213, 215, 221–26, 229, 233, 143, 154, 255, 256, 258, 259, 260–61, 262–65, 267, 272, 275, 276, 279–81, 287–90

Josephus: 30, 150, 205, 206, 207–11, 212–13, 214–17

Judaeo-Christian controversy: 82, 285

Juvenal of Jerusalem: 16, 95, 106, 119, 120, 121, 126, 128–30, 131, 132, 133, 134, 221

Kabbalat Shabbat: 277, 293

Lactantius: 169, 170, 258, 260, 263, 264, 265, 266, 268

Land of Israel: 159, 163, 165, 167, 171, 175, 176, 177, 186, 222, 224, 225, 226, 242, 259, 263, 265, 280

Leisure culture: 273, 278

Leo of Rome, pope: 128, 132

Life of Constantine (Vita Constantini): 40, 41, 42, 112, 113

Maccabees: 142, 148–52

Madaba Map: 125

Magic: 48, 212, 223, 224, 225, 227, 228, 229, 230, 231, 232, 233, 234, 235, 236, 237, 238, 271

Marcian: 118, 126, 128, 129, 133

Martyrdom: 103, 109, 142, 146, 148, 149, 150, 151, 152, 261

Martyrs: 13, 84, 87, 105, 109, 111, 121, 127, 141, 142–44, 145, 146, 147, 148, 149, 150, 151, 152, 153, 154, 187, 261

Martyrs of Palestine (De martyribus palestinae): 13, 111, 141, 142, 143, 145, 148, 154

Melania the Elder: 189, 199, 203

Melania the Younger: 121, 126, 129

Mesopotamian myths: 273

Michael (archangel): 171, 176, 184, 185, 242, 253, 254, 256

Midrash: 12, 16, 26, 61, 64, 65, 69, 82, 151, 173, 174, 222, 241, 242, 244, 254, 275, 284, 285, 286, 287

Monotheism: 29, 30, 35, 48, 53

302 INDEX

Mosaic: 15, 21–28, 30, 31, 35, 38, 39, 44, 46, 55, 66, 67, 71, 76, 80, 82–84, 86, 87, 125, 213, 225, 241

Moses: 55, 61, 62, 65, 66, 68, 69, 70, 71, 186, 208, 209, 213, 214, 215, 254, 275, 277, 281, 282, 283, 284, 289, 290, 291

Mount of Olives: 16, 99, 121, 129, 183, 184, 188, 189, 191, 199

Muhammad: 199

Narcissus of Jerusalem: 97, 105

Nero: 29, 255, 260, 261, 262, 263

New Testament: 13, 82, 112, 117, 163, 172, 179, 185, 188, 211, 217

Nicaea, Council of: 95, 110

Origen: 13, 149, 152, 167, 168, 170, 173, 176, 177

Pacatus Drepanius: 32, 36

Palatine hill: 245–47

Palmyra: 7, 57, 59, 60

Paradise: 167, 175

Paulinus of Nola: 189, 190, 197, 199, 201, 203

Persia: 146, 224, 236, 254, 255, 256, 257, 258, 259, 260, 261, 263, 264

Peter the Iberian: 124, 129

Philo: 70, 213, 214–15, 280

Phocas: 255, 257, 259

Piacenza Pilgrim: 83, 187, 191, 192

Pilgrimage: 12, 13, 83, 92, 96, 115, 116, 119, 122, 124, 126, 130, 131, 132, 133, 136, 137, 138, 153, 156, 159, 161, 168, 173, 178, 179, 183, 184, 186, 187, 189, 190, 191, 192, 193, 195, 199, 201, 202, 203

Proselytes: 162

Red Sea: 60, 61, 63, 64, 66, 67, 68

Reinach, Théodore: 206–08, 212, 213

Remus and Romulus: 16, 241–44, 246, 249

Resurrection: 96, 99, 101, 102, 103, 104, 107, 113, 165, 166, 167, 170, 171, 176, 188, 197, 254, 276, 279, 283, 284, 289

Rome: 10, 12, 16, 22, 36, 41, 67, 68, 69, 88, 106, 126, 128, 146–47, 187, 189, 221, 222–24, 226, 232, 234, 241–47, 254, 255, 256, 259, 260, 261, 262, 263, 264, 267, 273, 279, 280, 289

Sabbath: 11, 17, 188, 215, 222, 223, 239, 271, 272, 273, 274, 275, 276, 277, 278, 279, 280, 281, 282, 283, 284, 285, 286, 287, 288, 289, 290, 292–93

Santa Sabina, Rome: 68, 69

Sarcophagi: 67, 87

Schism of 1054 ('The Great Schism'): 279, 280, 293

Sepphoris: 17, 21, 75–85, 85–90

Simeon son of Clopas: 97, 98, 105

Sol Invictus: 22, 24, 25, 26, 27, 33, 37, 39, 40, 41, 43, 46, 49

Solomon: 169, 242

Sozomen: 105, 106, 127, 144

St. Stephen, the church of: 121, 122, 123, 124, 129

Stephanus: 153, 212–13

Sulpicius Severus: 189, 190, 191, 192, 193, 195, 196, 197, 199, 201, 189, 190, 191, 192, 193

Sun: 21, 22, 25, 26, 27, 28, 29, 30, 31, 32, 33, 34, 36, 37, 39, 40, 42, 45, 46, 49, 50, 277, 278, 289, 292

Sunday: 17, 42, 271, 272, 276, 277, 278, 279, 283, 284, 285, 286, 287, 289, 292

Synagogue: 21–28, 30, 38, 39, 42, 43, 45, 56, 55–64, 66, 69–71, 75, 79–83, 85, 149, 150, 152

Syria: 7, 55, 56, 58, 59, 60, 77, 141, 225, 229

Temple: 14, 30, 35, 57, 59, 63, 66, 70, 76–80, 82, 85–88, 113, 144, 145, 149, 151, 152, 159–61, 169, 172, 173, 174, 199, 222, 242, 243, 260, 265, 273, 277, 280, 287

Testimonium Flavianum: 204, 207, 208, 210, 215

Theodosius I: 31, 36, 144, 149, 150, 152

Theodosius II: 11, 119, 120, 121, 128, 129

Thesaurus linguae graecae: 213, 214

Travel narratives: 159, 191, 202, 223, 224

Turnèbe, Adrien: 214

Two huts: 241–45, 247

Tzrif: 243–45, 247

Zerubbabel, Book of (*Sefer Zerubavel*): 253, 254, 258, 267, 270, 269

Zodiac: 21, 22, 23, 24, 25, 26, 27, 30, 39, 40, 42, 43, 44, 45, 48, 49, 51, 53, 57, 58, 72, 80

Cultural Encounters in Late Antiquity and the Middle Ages

All volumes in this series are evaluated by an Editorial Board, strictly on academic grounds, based on reports prepared by referees who have been commissioned by virtue of their specialism in the appropriate field. The Board ensures that the screening is done independently and without conflicts of interest. The definitive texts supplied by authors are also subject to review by the Board before being approved for publication. Further, the volumes are copyedited to conform to the publisher's stylebook and to the best international academic standards in the field.

Titles in Series

De Sion exibit lex et verbum domini de Hierusalem: Essays on Medieval Law, Liturgy, and Literature in Honour of Amnon Linder, ed. by Yitzhak Hen (2001)

Amnon Linder, *Raising Arms: Liturgy in the Struggle to Liberate Jerusalem in the Late Middle Ages* (2003)

Thomas Deswarte, *De la destruction à la restauration: L'idéologie dans le royaume d'Oviedo-Léon (VIIIe-XIe siècles)* (2004)

The Jews of Europe in the Middle Ages (Tenth to Fifteenth Centuries): Proceedings of the Inter-national Symposium held at Speyer, 20–25 October 2002, ed. by Christoph Cluse (2004)

Christians and Christianity in the Holy Land: From the Origins to the Latin Kingdoms, ed. by Ora Limor and Guy G. Stroumsa (2006)

Carine van Rijn, *Shepherds of the Lord: Priests and Episcopal Statutes in the Carolingian Period* (2007)

Avicenna and his Legacy: A Golden Age of Science and Philosophy, ed. by Y. Tzvi Langer-mann (2010)

Writing 'True Stories': Historians and Hagiographers in the Late Antique and Medieval Near East, ed. by Arietta Papaconstantinou, Muriel Debié, and Hugh Kennedy (2010)

Carolingian Scholarship and Martianus Capella: Ninth-Century Commentary Traditions on 'De nuptiis' in Context, ed. by Mariken Teeuwen and Sinéad O'Sullivan (2011)

John-Henry Clay, *In the Shadow of Death: Saint Boniface and the Conversion of Hessia*, 721–54 (2011)

Ehud Krinis, *God's Chosen People: Judah Halevi's 'Kuzari' and the Shīʿī Imām Doctrine* (2013)

Strategies of Identification: Ethnicity and Religion in Early Medieval Europe, ed. by Walter Pohl and Gerda Heydemann (2013)

Post-Roman Transitions: Christian and Barbarian Identities in the Early Medieval West, ed. by Walter Pohl and Gerda Heydemann (2013)

Between Personal and Institutional Religion: Self, Doctrine, and Practice in Late Antique Eastern Christianity, ed. by Brouria Bitton-Ashkelony and Lorenzo Perrone (2013)

D'Orient en Occident: Les recueils de fables enchâssées avant les Mille et une Nuits de Galland (Barlaam et Josaphat, Calila et Dimna, Disciplina clericalis, Roman des Sept Sages), ed. by Marion Uhlig and Yasmina Foehr-Janssens (2014)

Conflict and Religious Conversation in Latin Christendom: Studies in Honour of Ora Limor, ed. by Israel Jacob Yuval and Ram Ben-Shalom (2014)

Visual Constructs of Jerusalem, ed. by Bianca kühnel, Galit Noga-Banai, and Hanna Vorholt (2014)

The Introduction of Christianity into the Early Medieval Insular World: Converting the Isles I, ed. by Roy Flechner and Máire Ní Mhaonaigh (2016)

Motions of Late Antiquity: Essays on Religion, Politics, and Society in Honour of Peter Brown, ed. by Jamie kreiner and Helmut Reimitz (2016)

The Prague Sacramentary: Culture, Religion, and Politics in Late Eighth-Century Bavaria, ed. by Maximilian Diesenberger, Rob Meens, and Els Rose (2016)

The Capetian Century, 1214–1314, ed. by William Chester Jordan and Jenna Rebecca Phillips (2017)

Transforming Landscapes of Belief in the Early Medieval Insular World and Beyond: Con-verting the Isles II, ed. by Nancy Edwards, Máire Ní Mhaonaigh, and Roy Flechner (2017)

Historiography and Identity I: Ancient and Early Christian Narratives of Community, ed. by Walter Pohl and Veronika Wieser (2019)

Inclusion and Exclusion in Mediterranean Christianities, 400–800, ed. by Yaniv Fox and Erica Buchberger (2019)

Leadership and Community in Late Antiquity: Essays in Honour of Raymond Van Dam, ed. by Young Richard Kim and A. E. T. McLaughlin (2020)

Pnina Arad, *Christian Maps of the Holy Land: Images and Meanings* (2020)

Historiography and Identity, II: Post-Roman Multiplicity and New Political Identities, ed. by Helmut Reimitz and Gerda Heydemann (2020)

Historiography and Identity, III: Carolingian Approaches, ed. by Helmut Reimitz, Rutger Kramer, and Graeme Ward (2021)

Minorities in Contact in the Medieval Mediterranean, ed. by Clara Almagro Vidal, Jessica Tearney-Pearce, and Luke Yarbrough (2021)

Historiography and Identity IV: Writing History Across Medieval Eurasia, edited by Walter Pohl and Daniel Mahoney (2021)

Historiography and Identity VI: Competing Narratives of the Past in Central and Eastern Europe, c. 1200–c. 1600, ed. by Pavlina Rychterová (2021)

Political Ritual and Practice in Capetian France: Essays in Honour of Elizabeth A. R. Brown, ed. by M. C. Gaposchkin and Jay Rubenstein (2021)

Yossi Maurey, *Liturgy and Sequences of the Sainte-Chapelle: Music, Relics, and Sacral Kingship in Thirteenth-Century France* (2022)

Les transferts culturels dans les mondes normands médiévaux (viiie–xiie siècle): objets, acteurs et passeurs, ed. by Pierre Bauduin, Simon Lebouteiller, and Luc Bourgeois (2022)

Civic Identity and Civic Participation in Late Antiquity and the Early Middle Ages, ed. by Cédric Brélaz and Els Rose (2022)

Zsuzsanna Papp Reed, *Matthew Paris on the Mongol Invasion in Europe* (2022)

From Sun-Day to the Lord's Day: The Cultural History of Sunday in Late Antiquity and the Early Middle Ages, ed. by Uta Heil (2023)

In Preparation

Historiography and Identity V: The Emergence of New Peoples and Polities in Europe, 1000–1300, ed. by Walter Pohl, Veronika Wieser, Francesco Borri